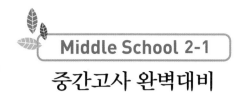

Middle School 2-1
중간고사 완벽대비

적중100
영어 기출 문제집

중2

금성 | 최인철

Best Collection

구성과 특징

교과서의 주요 학습 내용을 중심으로 학습 영역별 특성에 맞춰 단계별로 다양한 학습 기회를 제공하여 단원별 학습능력 평가는 물론 중간 및 기말고사 시험 등에 완벽하게 대비할 수 있도록 내용을 구성

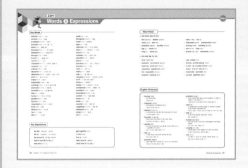

Words & Expressions

Step1 Key Words 단원별 핵심 단어 설명 및 풀이
Key Expression 단원별 핵심 숙어 및 관용어 설명
Word Power 반대 또는 비슷한 뜻 단어 배우기
English Dictionary 영어로 배우는 영어 단어

Step2 실력평가 단원별 수시평가 대비 주관식, 객관식 문제풀이

Step3 서술형 대비 학업성취도 및 수행능력평가 대비 서술형 문제풀이

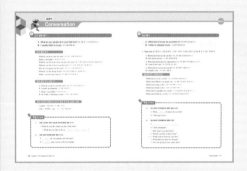

Conversation

Step1 핵심 의사소통 의사소통에 필요한 주요 표현 방법 요약
핵심 Check 기본적인 표현 방법 및 활용능력 확인

Step2 대화문 익히기 상황에 따른 대화문 활용 및 연습

Step3 기본평가 시험대비 기초 학습 능력 평가

Step4 실력평가 단원별 수시평가 대비 주관식, 객관식 문제풀이

Step5 서술형 대비 학업성취도 및 수행능력평가 대비 서술형 문제풀이

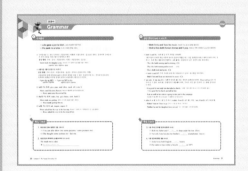

Grammar

Step1 주요 문법 단원별 주요 문법 사항과 예문을 알기 쉽게 설명

핵심 Check 기본 문법사항에 대한 이해 여부 확인

Step2 기본평가 시험대비 기초 학습 능력 평가

Step3 실력평가 단원별 수시평가 대비 주관식, 객관식 문제풀이

Step4 서술형 대비 학업성취도 및 수행능력평가 대비 서술형 문제풀이

Reading

Step1 구문 분석 단원별로 제시된 문장에 대한 구문별 분석과 내용 설명
확인문제 문장에 대한 기본적인 이해와 인지능력 확인

Step2 확인학습A 빈칸 채우기를 통한 문장 완성 능력 확인

Step3 확인학습B 제시된 우리말을 영어로 완성하여 작문 능력 키우기

Step4 실력평가 단원별 수시평가 대비 주관식, 객관식 문제풀이

Step5 서술형 대비 학업성취도 및 수행능력평가 대비 서술형 문제풀이
교과서 구석구석 교과서에 나오는 기타 문장까지 완벽 학습

Composition

|영역별 핵심문제|

단어 및 어휘, 대화문, 문법, 독해 등 각 영역별 기출문제의 출제 유형을 분석하여 실전에 대비하고 연습할 수 있도록 문제를 배열

|서술형 실전 및 창의사고력 문제|

학교 시험에서 점차 늘어나는 서술형 시험에 집중 대비하고 고득점을 취득하는데 만전을 기하기 위한 학습 코너

|단원별 예상문제|

기출문제를 분석한 후 새로운 시험 출제 경향을 더하여 새롭게 출제될 수 있는 문제를 포함하여 시험에 완벽하게 대비할 수 있도록 준비

|단원별 모의고사|

영역별, 단계별 학습을 모두 마친 후 실전 연습을 위한 모의고사

on the textbook

교과서 파헤치기

- **단어Test1~2** 영어 단어 우리말 쓰기와 우리말을 영어 단어로 쓰기
- **대화문Test1~2** 대화문 빈칸 완성 및 전체 대화문 쓰기
- **본문Test1~5** 빈칸 완성, 우리말 쓰기, 문장 배열연습, 영어 작문하기 복습 등 단계별 반복 학습을 통해 교과서 지문에 대한 완벽한 습득
- **구석구석지문Test1~2** 지문 빈칸 완성 및 전문 영어로 쓰기

Contents

Lesson 1

My Special Interests

🎙 의사소통 기능

- 좋아하는 것 묻기
  What's your favorite club?

- 관심 표현하기
  I'm interested in the photo club.

🎙 언어 형식

- 접속사 If
  If you are interested in saving the planet, please join us.

- 부가의문문
  Protecting our planet is important, **isn't it**?

Words & Expressions

Key Words

- **able**[éibl] 형 유능한, ~할 수 있는
- **abroad**[əbrɔ́ːd] 부 해외에(서), 해외로
- **actor**[ǽktər] 명 배우
- **application**[æpləkéiʃən] 명 지원[신청]서, 적용
- **cafeteria**[kæfətíəriə] 명 구내식당
- **classmate**[klǽsmeit] 명 급우, 반 친구
- **chart**[tʃɑːrt] 명 도표
- **club**[klʌb] 명 동아리
- **cooking**[kúkiŋ] 명 요리
- **costume**[kástjuːm] 명 의상, 복장
- **crew**[kruː] 명 선원, 승무원, (함께 일하는) 팀, 제작진
- **direction**[dirékʃən] 명 방향
- **drone**[droun] 명 드론, 무인 비행기
- **environmental**[invàiərənméntl] 형 환경의
- **favorite**[féivərit] 형 가장 좋아하는
- **helpful**[hélpfəl] 형 도움이 되는
- **hovering**[hʌ́vəriŋ] 명 공중 정지
- **interest**[intərəst] 명 관심, 흥미
- **leader**[líːdər] 명 지도자
- **leave**[liːv] 동 두다, 남기다
- **order**[ɔ́ːrdər] 동 주문하다

- **perform**[pərfɔ́ːrm] 동 수행하다, 공연하다
- **photographer**[fətágrəfər] 명 사진사
- **planet**[plǽnit] 명 행성
- **plate**[pleit] 명 그릇, 접시
- **pond**[pɑnd] 명 연못
- **prepare**[pripέər] 동 준비하다
- **prize**[praiz] 명 상, 상품
- **protect**[prətékt] 동 보호하다
- **quite**[kwait] 부 꽤, 많이
- **reduce**[ridjúːs] 동 줄이다
- **scenery**[síːnəri] 명 경치, 풍경
- **shall**[ʃəl] 조 ~할 것이다
- **skill**[skil] 명 기술, 솜씨
- **social**[sóuʃəl] 형 사회의
- **staff**[stæf] 명 직원
- **successful**[səksésfəl] 형 성공한, 성공적인
- **total**[tóutl] 명 합계, 총액
- **traditional**[trədíʃənl] 형 전통적인
- **volunteer**[vàləntíər] 명 자원 봉사자 동 자원하다
- **waste**[weist] 명 쓰레기, 폐기물
- **wrong**[rɔ́ːŋ] 형 틀린, 잘못된

Key Expressions

- **be good at** ~에 능숙하다
- **be good for** ~에 좋다
- **be interested in** ~에 관심이 있다
- **be ready to** ~할 준비가 되다
- **big fan** 열렬한 팬
- **by oneself** 혼자서
- **carry out** 수행하다

- **fall into** ~에 빠지다
- **have an interest in** ~에 관심이 있다
- **keep in shape** 건강을 유지하다
- **stay up late** 늦게까지 깨어 있다
- **take part in** ~에 참가하다
- **Why don't you[we]** ~하는 게 어때?
- **Why the long face?** 왜 우울하니?

Word Power

※ 서로 반대되는 뜻을 가진 단어

☐ **able** 할 수 있는 ↔ **unable** 할 수 없는

☐ **careful** 주의 깊은 ↔ **careless** 부주의한

☐ **prepared** 준비된 ↔ **unprepared** 준비되지 않은

☐ **known** 알려진 ↔ **unknown** 알려지지 않은

☐ **success** 성공 ↔ **failure** 실패

☐ **change** 바꾸다 ↔ **maintain** 유지하다

☐ **enter** 들어가다 ↔ **exit** 나가다

☐ **leave** 떠나다 ↔ **arrive** 도착하다

☐ **right** 맞는 ↔ **wrong** 틀린

☐ **ancient** 고대의 ↔ **modern** 현대의

※ 남성명사 : 여성명사

☐ **bull** 수소 : **cow** 암소

☐ **actor** 남배우 : **actress** 여배우

☐ **prince** 왕자 : **princess** 공주

☐ **hero** 영웅 : **heroine** 여걸

English Dictionary

☐ **abroad** 해외로
→ in or to a foreign country
외국에 또는 외국으로

☐ **actor** 배우
→ a person who performs on the stage, on television or in films/movies, especially as a profession
무대, 텔레비전 또는 영화에서 특히 직업으로 연기하는 사람

☐ **application** 지원서
→ a formal (often written) request for something, such as a job, permission to do something or a place at a college or university
직업, 무언가를 하기 위한 허가 또는 대학의 자리 같은 어떤 것에 대한 공식적인 (종종 서면으로 된) 요청

☐ **classmate** 급우, 반 친구
→ a person who is or was in the same class as you at school or college
학교나 대학에서 당신과 같은 교실에 있거나 있었던 사람

☐ **chart** 도표, 표
→ a page or sheet of information in the form of diagrams, lists of figures, etc.
표, 목록 등의 형태로 정보를 나타내는 페이지나 쪽

☐ **costume** 의상, 복장
→ the clothes worn by people from a particular place or during a particular historical period
특정한 장소나 특정한 역사적 기간 동안에 사람들이 입었던 옷

☐ **environmental** 환경의
→ connected with the natural conditions in which people, animals and plants live
사람, 동물, 식물이 사는 자연 상태와 관련된

☐ **favorite** 가장 좋아하는
→ liked more than others of the same kind
같은 종류의 다른 것들보다 더 좋아하는

☐ **leader** 지도자
→ a person who leads a group of people, especially the head of a country, an organization, etc.
사람들의 모임을 이끄는 사람. 특히 국가나 조직 등의 우두머리

☐ **photographer** 사진사
→ a person who takes photographs, especially as a job
특히 직업으로 사진을 찍는 사람

☐ **planet** 행성
→ a large round object in space that moves around a star (such as the sun) and receives light from it
태양과 같은 항성 주위를 돌며 그 항성으로부터 빛을 받는 우주에 있는 크고 둥근 물체

☐ **prepare** 준비하다
→ to make something or somebody ready to be used or to do something
무언가 또는 누군가를 사용되도록 또는 어떤 일을 하도록 준비되게 만들다

☐ **skill** 기술
→ the ability to do something well
무언가를 잘하는 능력

☐ **waste** 쓰레기, 폐기물
→ materials that are no longer needed and are thrown away
더 이상 필요하지 않아서 내다버린 물질

01 다음 영영풀이가 가리키는 것을 고르시오.

> a person who performs on the stage, on television or in films/movies, especially as a profession

① photographer　　② leader
③ actor　　④ staff
⑤ volunteer

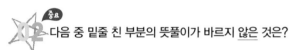

02 다음 중 밑줄 친 부분의 뜻풀이가 바르지 <u>않은</u> 것은?

① Practice <u>hovering</u> first before you change the directions. 공중에서 맴도는 것
② We should <u>protect</u> our planet by planning some campaigns. 준비하다
③ Why don't we try to reduce food <u>waste</u>? 쓰레기
④ The passengers and <u>crew</u> were injured. 승무원
⑤ I met famous <u>photographers</u> and learned their skills.　사진사

03 다음 문장에 공통으로 들어갈 말을 고르시오.

> • A computer can _____ many tasks at once.
> • Henry will _____ Hamlet in a play.
> • I'm going to _____ on the flute soon.

① perform　　② act
③ role　　④ lead
⑤ prepare

서답형
04 다음 짝지어진 단어의 관계가 같도록 빈칸에 알맞은 말을 쓰시오.

> enter : exit = arrive : _____

서답형
05 다음 문장의 빈칸에 들어갈 말을 〈보기〉에서 골라 쓰시오.

> ┤ 보기 ├
> order / shall / protect / abroad

(1) Minsu hopes to travel _____ next year.
(2) I will _____ some books from France.
(3) I think you should wear shoes to _____ your feet.
(4) _____ we meet again this Saturday?

06 다음 주어진 문장의 밑줄 친 waste와 같은 의미로 쓰인 것은?

> What can we do to reduce food <u>waste</u>?

① The problem is that people <u>waste</u> so much water.
② Have you heard of recycling the household <u>waste</u>?
③ Why did you <u>waste</u> your money on clothes you don't wear?
④ I don't want to <u>waste</u> my time.
⑤ We should not <u>waste</u> paper to keep a forest.

01 다음 짝지어진 단어의 관계가 같도록 빈칸에 알맞은 말을 쓰시오.

> right : wrong = able : _____

02 다음 문장의 빈칸에 들어갈 말을 〈보기〉에서 골라 쓰시오.

┌─ 보기 ├─
environmental / favorite / skill / scenery
└────────────────────────┘

(1) I'm sure that cooking is a useful _____.

(2) My _____ subject is the social studies.

(3) After enjoying the mountain _____, I felt better than before.

(4) We should do our best to solve the _____ problems.

03 다음 주어진 우리말과 일치하도록 주어진 단어를 배열하여 영작하시오.

(1) 게임을 너무 많이 하는 것은 네 건강에 좋지 않아.
(much / is / too / games / health / playing / your / not / good / for)
➡ _____

(2) 우리의 영어 동아리를 무엇이라고 부를까?
(shall / call / our / English / we / club / what)
➡ _____

(3) 너는 상을 탈 기회를 가질 수 있어.
(a prize / a chance / of / you / winning / can / have)
➡ _____

04 다음 우리말에 맞게 빈칸에 알맞은 말을 쓰시오.

(1) 너는 보통 건강을 유지하기 위해 무엇을 하니?
➡ What do you usually do to _____ _____ _____?

(2) 나는 늦게까지 깨어 있었기 때문에 피곤했다.
➡ I was tired because I _____ _____ _____.

(3) 나는 학교 댄스 경연에 참가할 것이다.
➡ I'm going to _____ _____ _____ the school dancing contest.

05 다음 우리말을 주어진 단어를 이용하여 영작하시오.

(1) 공이 연못에 빠졌다. (pond, fall)
➡ _____

(2) 학교 사진 경연 대회에 참가하는 게 어때? (why, take, photo)
➡ _____

(3) 나는 스포츠에 전혀 관심이 없어. (any, have)
➡ _____

06 다음 대화의 빈칸에 보기에 주어진 단어를 알맞게 채워 넣으시오.

┌──────────────────────────┐
A: Do you like sports?
B: No, I'm not. I'm (A)____ in speaking.
C: Me too. I want to be (B)____ to speak well.
D: Then, let's start a (C)____ club.
A: What (D)____ we call our club?
└──────────────────────────┘

┌─ 보기 ├─
shall / able / interested / speech
└────────────────────────┘

➡ (A) _____, (B) _____
   (C) _____, (D) _____

Conversation

1 좋아하는 것 묻기

What's your favorite club? 네가 가장 좋아하는 동아리는 무엇이니?

■ favorite은 '가장 좋아하는'을 뜻하며 좋아하는 것을 말할 때 쓰는 표현으로 love, like 등의 동사를 이용할 수 있다.

좋아하는 것 묻기

- What's your favorite animal? (네가 가장 좋아하는 동물은 무엇이니?)
- Which color do you like best(= most)? (어느 색을 가장 좋아하니?)
- Do you like listening to music? (음악 듣는 것을 좋아하니?)

좋아하는 것 표현하기

- My favorite activity is watching movies. (내가 가장 좋아하는 활동은 영화를 보는 것이야.)
- Listening to music is my favorite hobby. (음악 감상은 내가 가장 좋아하는 취미야.)
- I like to play soccer very much. (나는 축구하는 것을 매우 좋아해.)
- I love playing computer games. (나는 컴퓨터 게임하는 것을 매우 좋아해.)
- I'm fond of cooking. (나는 요리하는 것을 좋아해.)
- I prefer to bake bread. (나는 빵을 굽는 것을 선호해.)

핵심 Check

1. 다음 우리말과 일치하도록 빈칸에 알맞은 말을 쓰시오.

(1) A: _____ _____ _____ color? (네가 가장 좋아하는 색은 무엇이니?)

B: I love red. (나는 빨간색을 매우 좋아해.)

(2) A: _____ _____ do you like best? (어느 과목을 가장 좋아하니?)

B: I like English best. (나는 영어를 가장 좋아해.)

(3) A: _____ _____ _____ _____ soccer? (너는 축구하는 것을 좋아하니?)

B: Sure. It's my favorite sport. (물론이지. 그것은 내가 가장 좋아하는 스포츠야.)

2 관심 표현하기

I'm interested in the photo club. 나는 사진 동아리에 관심이 있다.

- 'be interested in ~'은 '~에 관심이 있다.'는 의미로 'have an interest in ~'으로 바꾸어 쓸 수 있다.

관심 표현하기

- I'm interested in sports. (나는 스포츠에 관심이 있다.)
- I have an interest in cooking. (나는 요리에 관심이 있다.)
- I'm thinking about joining the speech club. (나는 말하기 동아리에 가입할 생각이야.)

무관심 표현하기

- I have no interest in watching movies. (나는 영화를 보는 것에 관심이 없어.)
- I'm not (very) interested in singing. (나는 노래 부르기에 (별로) 관심이 없어.)
- I don't have any interest in dancing. (나는 춤추기에 아무 관심이 없어.)
- I don't have much interest in taking pictures. (나는 사진 찍는 것에 많은 관심이 없어.)

핵심 Check

2. 다음 우리말과 일치하도록 빈칸에 알맞은 말을 쓰시오.

(1) A: What are you interested in? (무엇에 관심이 있나요?)

B: _____ _____ _____ traveling. (나는 여행에 관심이 있어요.)

(2) A: Which club do you _____ _____ _____? (어느 동아리를 마음에 두고 있나요?)

B: I have _____ _____ _____ the cooking club. (나는 요리 동아리에 관심이 있어요.)

(3) A: Do you have an interest in taking pictures? (당신은 사진 찍기에 관심이 있나요?)

B: No, I _____ _____ _____ _____ _____ it. (아니요. 그것에 전혀 관심이 없어요.)

 A. Everyday English 2 – B Listening Activity

Brian: Look! This is a chart about our classmates' interests.

Sujin: Let's ❶look at it more closely. The chart shows that 30% of students ❷are interested in sports. The school's Sports Day will be so much fun.

Brian: Right. The chart also shows that 27% of students are interested in actors. I know you are also ❸a big fan of ❹them.

Sujin: Yes. I love them. How about you?

Brian: I'm not interested in actors. I'm interested in computer games. 20% of students are interested in them.

Sujin: Computer games are fun, but playing ❺them too much is not good for you.

Brian: I agree.

Brian: 봐! 이것은 우리 반 친구들의 관심에 대한 도표야.

Sujin: 더 자세히 보자. 학생들의 30%는 스포츠에 관심이 있구나. 운동회가 굉장히 재미있을 것 같아.

Brian: 맞아. 도표에 의하면 27%의 학생은 배우에 관심이 있어. 너도 배우들을 아주 좋아한다고 알고 있어.

Sujin: 응. 매우 좋아해. 너는 어때?

Brian: 난 배우에는 관심이 없어. 난 컴퓨터 게임에 관심이 있어. 20%의 학생이 컴퓨터 게임에 관심이 있어.

Sujin: 컴퓨터 게임은 재밌지. 그러나 너무 많이 하는 것은 안 좋아.

Brian: 나도 동의해.

❶ look at: ~을 보다
❷ be interested in: ~에 관심이 있다
❸ a big fan: 열렬한 팬
❹ them은 actors를 가리킨다.
❺ them은 computer games를 가리킨다.

Check(√) True or False

(1) Sujin is a big fan of actors. T ☐ F ☐

(2) Brian is interested in sports. T ☐ F ☐

 B. In Real Life

Junho: Adia, you know what? We have to choose our club next week.

Adia: I know. Which club do you ❶have in mind, Junho?

Junho: I'm interested in the photo club.

Adia: Sounds great. Look at this chart. 80% of the photo club's members said that ❷they liked its activities last year.

Junho: That's right. ❸How about you, Adia? What's your favorite club?

Adia: I want to join the board game club. But last year its members said that they didn't like ❹it much.

Junho: You're right. 60% of its members said they didn't like it.

Adia: Yes. I'm going to think about it more.

Junho: Adia, 그것 아니? 우리는 다음 주에 동아리를 선택해야 해.

Adia: 알고 있어. 준호야. 어느 동아리를 마음에 두고 있니?

Junho: 나는 사진 동아리에 관심이 있어.

Adia: 좋아. 이 도표를 봐. 80퍼센트의 사진 동아리 회원들이 작년 활동을 좋아했다고 말했어.

Junho: 맞아. 너는 어떠니, Adia? 네가 가장 좋아하는 동아리는 무엇이니?

Adia: 나는 보드게임 동아리에 가입하고 싶어. 하지만 작년에 동아리의 회원들이 동아리를 별로 좋아하지 않았다고 말했어.

Junho: 맞아. 60퍼센트의 회원들이 좋아하지 않았다고 말했어.

Adia: 그래. 나는 그것에 대해 더 생각해 볼 거야.

❶ have ~ in mind: ~을 마음에 두다
❷ they는 the photo club's members를 가리킨다.
❸ 'How about you?'는 '너는 어때?'라고 상대방의 의견을 묻는 표현으로 'What about you?'와 바꾸어 쓸 수 있다.
❹ it은 the board game club을 가리킨다.

Check(√) True or False

(3) Junho is interested in the photo club. T ☐ F ☐

(4) Adia is very satisfied with the board game club. T ☐ F ☐

Everyday English 1. A Function Practice 2

B: I'm hungry. Did you have lunch?

G: No. ❶Let's have lunch together. What's your favorite food?

B: ❷I love chicken. Why don't we ❸order ❹it?

G: That's a good idea.

❶ Let's ~: '~하자'라고 제안하는 표현으로 'Why don't we ~?' 또는 'How about ~?'으로 바꾸어 쓸 수 있다.

❷ My favorite food is chicken.으로 바꾸어 쓸 수 있다.

❸ order: 주문하다   ❹ it은 chicken을 가리킨다.

Everyday English 1 - B. Listening Activity

G: What's your favorite hobby? We asked the students at our school and all of them answered the question. ❶Most of the students said they liked watching movies. 20 boys and 42 girls loved ❷it. ❸This means a total of 62 students said watching movies was their favorite hobby. Many boys liked playing computer games. 32 boys and 13 girls liked doing ❹that. 25 boys and 20 girls liked sports. Their favorite sports were soccer, baseball, and basketball.

❶ most of: ~의 대부분   ❷ it은 watching movies를 가리킨다.

❸ This는 바로 앞 문장의 내용을 받는다.   ❹ that은 computer game을 나타낸다.

Everyday English 2. A Function Practice 2

G: You ❶look tired. What's the matter?

B: I ❷stayed up late to watch TV.

G: What did you watch?

B: I watched a traveling program. ❸I'm interested in traveling.

❶ look+형용사: ~하게 보이다   ❷ stay up late: 늦게까지 깨어 있다

❸ be interested in: ~에 관심이 있다

Everyday English 2. A Function Practice 2

G: What are you doing?

B: I'm reading a newspaper. ❶Look at this picture.

G: The food ❷in the picture looks delicious. What's the story about?

B: The story is about cooking. ❸I'm interested in cooking.

❶ look at: ~을 보다   ❷ in the picture는 The food을 수식하는 형용사구

❸ 'I have an interest in cooking.'으로 표현할 수 있다.

Check Your Progress 1

Inho: Hello, I'm Inho from the school newspaper club. Daily school life is our topic for the newspaper this month. Studying different subjects ❶is the biggest part of our school life. We asked all the second graders about their favorite subject. The most popular subject was ❷P.E. 35% of students said they liked P.E. best. ❸The second most popular subject was English. 25% of students said they were interested in English. Music and ❹social studies were the third most popular subjects. 15% of students liked music and ❺another 15% liked social studies. What is your favorite subject?

❶ 동명사 Studying이 주어이므로 단수동사 is가 적절하다.

❷ P.E. = physical education = 체육

❸ the 서수(second)+최상급: (두) 번째로 가장 인기 있는

❹ social studies: 사회   ❺ another: 또 다른, 다른 하나의

Check Your Progress 2

Mike: Jenny, ❶why the long face?

Jenny: I ❷have to buy my friend's birthday present, but I can't choose the present.

Mike: Look at this chart from the Internet. It is about popular birthday presents.

Jenny: What is the most popular present?

Mike: A soccer ball for boys and a diary for girls.

Jenny: My friend is not interested in sports. What is the second most popular present for a boy?

Mike: For ❸both boys and girls, the second most popular present is a cap.

Jenny: Okay. I'll buy a cap.

❶ '왜 우울하니?'라고 묻는 표현이다.   ❷ have to: ~해야 한다

❸ both A and B: A와 B 둘 다

● 다음 우리말과 일치하도록 빈칸에 알맞은 말을 쓰시오.

Everyday English 1. A Function Practice 2

B: I'm hungry. Did you have lunch?

G: No. Let's have lunch together. _____ _____ _____ _____?

B: I love chicken. _____ _____ _____ _____ _____?

G: That's a good idea.

B: 배가 고프네. 점심 먹었어?
G: 아니, 점심 같이 먹자. 좋아하는 음식이 뭐야?
B: 난 닭고기가 좋더라. 그것으로 주문하는 게 어때?
G: 좋은 생각이야.

Everyday English 1. B. Listening Activity

G: _____ _____ _____ _____? We asked the students at our school and all of them answered the question. Most of the students said _____ _____ _____ _____. 20 boys and 42 girls loved it. This means _____ _____ _____ 62 students said _____ _____ _____ _____ _____ _____. Many boys liked playing computer games. 32 boys and 13 girls _____ _____ that. 25 boys and 20 girls liked sports. Their _____ _____ were soccer, baseball, and basketball.

G: 네가 좋아하는 취미는 뭐니? 우리는 학교 학생들에게 물어보았고 그들 모두가 질문에 대답을 했어. 대부분의 학생들이 영화 보는 것을 좋아한다고 했어. 남학생 20명과 여학생 42명이 영화가 좋대. 이것은 총 62명의 학생들이 영화 보는 것이 좋아하는 취미라고 말했음을 의미해. 많은 남학생들은 컴퓨터 게임을 좋아했어. 남학생 32명과 여학생 13명이 컴퓨터 게임하는 것을 좋아한대. 남학생 25명과 여학생 20명은 스포츠가 좋다고 했어. 그들이 좋아하는 스포츠는 축구, 야구, 그리고 농구였어.

Everyday English 2. A Function Practice 2

G: You look tired. What's _____ _____?

B: I _____ _____ _____ _____ _____ _____.

G: What did you watch?

B: I watched a traveling program. _____ _____ _____.

G: 너 피곤해 보인다. 무슨 일 있니?
B: TV 보느라 늦게까지 깨어 있었어.
G: 뭘 봤는데?
B: 여행 프로그램을 봤어. 나는 여행에 관심이 있거든.

Everyday English 2. A Function Practice 2

G: _____ are you _____?

B: I'm reading a newspaper. _____ _____ this picture.

G: The food in the picture looks delicious. _____ _____ _____ _____?

B: The story is about cooking. _____ _____ _____ _____.

G: 뭐 하고 있니?
B: 신문 읽고 있어. 이 신문 좀 봐.
G: 사진 속의 음식이 맛있어 보이네. 무엇에 관한 이야기야?
B: 요리에 관한 이야기야. 난 요리에 관심이 있어.

해석

Everyday English 2. A Function Practice 2

G: _____ _____ we go to see a musical this Saturday? I have some free tickets.

B: Sure. _____ _____ _____ _____ _____. What's the musical's title?

G: It's *The Shower.* Hwang Sunwon wrote it.

B: Wow. _____ _____ _____ _____ _____ _____.

G: 이번 주 토요일에 뮤지컬 보러 가는 게 어때? 무료입장권이 몇 장 있거든.
B: 물론이지. 나는 뮤지컬에 관심이 있어. 뮤지컬 제목이 뭐야?
G: 소나기야. 황순원이 썼어.
B: 와. 그것을 빨리 보고 싶어.

Everyday English 2 – B Listening Activity

Brian: Look! This is a chart about our classmates' interests.

Sujin: Let's look at it more _____. The chart shows that _____ _____ _____ _____ _____ _____ _____ _____. The school's Sports Day will be so much fun.

Brian: Right. The chart also shows that 27% of students are interested in actors. I know _____ _____ _____ _____ _____ _____.

Sujin: Yes. I love them. How about you?

Brian: _____ _____ _____ _____ _____ _____. I'm interested in computer games. 20% of students are interested in them.

Sujin: Computer games are fun, but _____ _____ _____ _____ _____ _____ _____ _____.

Brian: I agree.

Brian: 봐! 이것은 우리 반 친구들의 관심에 대한 도표야.
Sujin: 자세히 보자. 학생들의 30%는 스포츠에 관심이 있구나. 운동회가 굉장히 재미있을 것 같아.
Brian: 맞아. 도표에 의하면 27%의 학생은 배우에 관심이 있어. 너도 배우들을 좋아한다고 알고 있어.
Sujin: 응. 배우를 좋아해. 너는?
Brian: 난 배우에는 관심이 없어. 난 컴퓨터 게임에 관심이 있어. 20%의 학생이 컴퓨터 게임에 관심이 있어.
Sujin: 컴퓨터 게임은 재밌지. 그러나 너무 많이 하는 것은 안 좋아.
Brian: 나도 동의해.

In Real Life

Junho: Adia, you _____ _____? We have to choose our club next week.

Adia: I know. _____ _____ _____ _____ _____ _____ _____ _____, Junho?

Junho: _____ _____ _____ _____ _____ _____ _____ _____.

Adia: _____ grcat. Look at _____ _____. 80% of the photo club's members said that they liked its activities last year.

Junho: That's right. How about you, Adia? _____ _____ _____ _____ _____?

Adia: _____ _____ _____ _____ _____ _____ _____. But _____ _____ its members said that they didn't like it much.

Junho: You're _____. 60% of its members said they didn't like it.

Adia: Yes. I'm going to _____ _____ it more.

Junho: Adia, 그것 아니? 우리는 다음 주에 동아리를 선택해야 해.
Adia: 알고 있어. 준호야, 어느 동아리를 마음에 두고 있니?
Junho: 나는 사진 동아리에 관심이 있어.
Adia: 좋아. 이 도표를 봐. 80퍼센트의 사진 동아리 회원들이 작년 활동을 좋아했다고 말했어.
Junho: 맞아, 너는 어떠니, Adia? 네가 가장 좋아하는 동아리는 무엇이니?
Adia: 나는 보드게임 동아리에 가입하고 싶어. 하지만 작년에 그 동아리의 회원들이 별로 좋아하지 않는다고 말했어.
Junho: 맞아. 60퍼센트의 회원들이 좋아하지 않는다고 말했어.
Adia: 그래. 나는 그것에 대해 좀 더 생각해 볼 거야.

01 다음 대화의 빈칸에 들어갈 말로 <u>어색한</u> 것은?

> A: What's your favorite sport?
> B: _____

① I love playing soccer.

② My favorite activity is basketball.

③ I like to play table tennis very much.

④ I can't wait to play soccer.

⑤ Volleyball is the best for me.

02 다음 대화가 자연스럽게 이어지도록 순서대로 배열하시오.

> (A) The food in the picture looks delicious. What's the story about?
> (B) I'm reading a newspaper. Look at this picture.
> (C) The story is about cooking. I'm interested in cooking.
> (D) What are you doing?

➡ _____

[03~04] 다음 대화를 읽고 물음에 답하시오.

> G: You look tired. (A)_____
> B: I stayed up late to watch TV.
> G: What did you watch?
> B: I watched a traveling program. (B)나는 여행에 관심이 있거든.

03 위 대화의 빈칸 (A)에 들어갈 말로 <u>어색한</u> 것은?

① What happened?

② What's wrong?

③ What's the matter with you?

④ What's up?

⑤ What do you do?

04 위 대화의 밑줄 친 (B)의 우리말을 영어로 쓰시오.

➡ _____

[01~02] 다음 대화를 읽고 물음에 답하시오.

> B: I'm hungry. Did you have lunch?
> G: No. Let's have lunch together. What's your favorite food?
> B: (A)_____ (B)Why don't we order it?
> G: That's a good idea.

01 위 대화의 빈칸 (A)에 들어갈 말로 어색한 것은?

① I love chicken.
② I like chicken best.
③ My favorite food is chicken.
④ I'm fond of chicken.
⑤ I hate chicken.

02 위 대화의 밑줄 친 (B)와 바꾸어 쓸 수 있는 것을 모두 고르시오.

① I don't want to order it.
② How about ordering it?
③ How did you order it?
④ Let's order it.
⑤ Are you interested in ordering it?

[03~04] 다음 설명을 읽고 물음에 답하시오.

> G: What's your favorite hobby? We asked the students at our school and all of them answered the question. Most of the students said they liked watching movies. 20 boys and 42 girls loved it. This means a total of 62 students said watching movies was their favorite hobby. Many boys liked playing computer games. 32 boys and 13 girls liked doing that. 25 boys and 20 girls liked sports. Their favorite sports were soccer, baseball, and basketball.

03 What is the topic of the speaker?

① kinds of sports   ② favorite hobbies
③ computer games   ④ watching movies
⑤ playing sports

04 위의 내용과 일치하도록 표를 완성하시오.

Hobbies	Boys	Girls
Movies	20	(A)
Computer Games	(B)	(C)
Sports	(D)	20

➡ (A) _____ (B) _____
   (C) _____ (D) _____

[05~07] 다음 대화를 읽고 물음에 답하시오.

> B: I'm looking for a baseball cap.
> G: That kind of cap comes in a few different colors. (A)What's your favorite color? (best, what)
> B: My favorite color is green. Do you have a green one?
> G: Here you go.

05 위 대화의 밑줄 친 (A)와 의미가 같도록 주어진 표현을 이용하여 다시 쓰시오.

➡ _____

06 What color of a baseball cap is the boy looking for?

➡ _____

07 위 대화의 남자와 여자의 관계로 적절한 것은?

① teacher – student
② customer – clerk
③ patient – doctor
④ tourist – guide
⑤ player – coach

[08~10] 다음 대화를 읽고 물음에 답하시오.

> G: Why don't we go to see a musical this Saturday? I have some ⓐfree tickets.
> B: Sure. I'm very interested in musicals. What's the musical's title?
> G: It's *The Shower*. Hwang Sunwon wrote it.
> B: Wow. (A)＿＿＿＿＿＿

서답형

08 위 대화의 빈칸 (A)에 들어갈 말을 〈보기〉에 주어진 단어를 배열하여 영작하시오.

┌─ 보기 ─┐
can't / I / it / see / wait / to
└──────┘

➡ ＿＿＿＿＿＿＿＿＿＿＿＿＿＿＿

중요

09 위 대화의 밑줄 친 ⓐfree와 같은 의미로 쓰인 것은?

① All the students are free to use the reading room.
② Jane felt free like a bird.
③ I usually listen to music in my free time.
④ Please feel free to contact me.
⑤ We don't have to pay for the drinks because they're all free.

10 위 대화의 내용과 일치하지 않는 것은?

① 소녀는 이번 주 토요일에 뮤지컬을 보러 갈 것을 제안하였다.
② 소녀는 무료 입장권을 갖고 있다.
③ 소년은 뮤지컬에 관심이 많다.
④ *The Shower*의 작가는 Hwang Sunwon이다.
⑤ 소년은 뮤지컬 *The Shower*에 지루함을 느꼈다.

[11~12] 다음 대화를 읽고 물음에 답하시오.

> Junho: Adia, you know what? We have to choose our club next week.
> Adia: I know. Which club do you have in mind, Junho?
> Junho: I'm interested in the photo club.
> Adia: Sounds great. Look at this chart. 80% of the photo club's members said that they liked its activities last year.
> Junho: That's right. How about you, Adia? What's your favorite club?
> Adia: I want to join the board game club. But last year its members said that they didn't like it much.
> Junho: You're right. 60% of its members said they didn't like it.
> Adia: Yes. I'm going to think about it more.

서답형

11 What percent of the photo club's members were satisfied with its activities last year?

➡ ＿＿＿＿＿＿＿＿＿＿＿＿＿＿＿

서답형

12 What percent of the board game club's members were not satisfied with its activities last year?

➡ ＿＿＿＿＿＿＿＿＿＿＿＿＿＿＿

중요

13 다음 중 짝지어진 대화가 어색한 것은?

① A: What fruit do you like?
  B: I like apples.
② A: What are you interested in?
  B: I'm interested in reading books.
③ A: What's your favorite food?
  B: My favorite food is pizza.
④ A: Are you interested in sports?
  B: Yes. I love sports.
⑤ A: Do you have an interest in baseball?
  B: I'm not good at playing soccer.

[01~02] 다음 대화를 읽고 물음에 답하시오.

G: You look tired. What's the matter?
B: I stayed up late to watch TV.
G: What did you watch?
B: I watched a traveling program. I'm interested in traveling.

01 Why did the boy look tired?

➡ _____

02 What does the boy have an interest in?

➡ _____

[03~04] 다음 대화를 읽고 물음에 답하시오.

Mike: Jenny, (A)<u>왜 이렇게 우울하니?</u> (face)
Jenny: I have to buy my friend's birthday present, but I can't choose the present.
Mike: Look at this chart from the internet. It is about popular birthday presents.
Jenny: What is the most popular present?
Mike: A soccer ball for boys and a diary for girls.
Jenny: My friend is not interested in sports. What is the second most popular present for a boy?
Mike: For both boys and girls, the second most popular present is a cap.
Jenny: Okay. I'll buy a cap.

03 위 대화의 밑줄 친 (A)의 우리말을 주어진 단어를 사용하여 4단어로 영작하시오.

➡ _____

04 위 대화의 내용과 일치하도록 대화를 완성하시오.

Q: What's the matter with Jenny?
A: She has much difficulty _____.

➡ _____

[05~07] 다음 대화를 읽고 물음에 답하시오.

Brian: Look! This is a chart about our classmates' interests.
Sujin: Let's look at it more closely. The chart shows that 30% of students are interested in sports. The school's Sports Day will be so much fun.
Brian: Right. The chart also shows that 27% of students are interested in actors. I know you are also a big fan of them.
Sujin: Yes. I love them. How about you?
Brian: (A)<u>나는 배우들에게 관심이 없어.</u> I'm interested in computer games. 20% of students are interested in them.
Sujin: Computer games are fun, but playing them too much is not good for you.
Brian: I agree.

05 위 대화의 밑줄 친 (A)의 우리말을 주어진 단어를 써서 영어로 옮기시오. (interested)

➡ _____

06 위 대화에서 다음 영영풀이가 나타내는 말을 찾아 쓰시오.

a page or sheet of information in the form of diagrams, lists of figures, etc.

➡ _____

07 위 대화의 내용과 일치하도록 다음 질문에 대한 대답을 완성하시오.

Q: There are 30 students in my class. Then, how many students are interested in sports?
A: _____

➡ _____

Grammar

1 접속사 If

- **If** you want to get some tips, I will tell you. 조언을 얻고 싶다면, 내가 말해 줄게.
- **If** she likes me, she will call me. 그녀가 날 좋아한다면, 내게 전화할 거야.

■ 접속사 if는 명사절, 조건의 부사절 등을 이끌 수 있다. 조건의 부사절에서는 '만약 ~라면'의 의미를 가지며, 현재시제를 사용하여 미래를 나타낸다.
- If you **tell** me a lie again, I **will** not **forgive** you. 네가 다시 거짓말하면, 나는 널 용서하지 않을 거야.
- If it **is** heavy, I **will help** you to move it. 그것이 무겁다면, 네가 그것을 옮기도록 내가 도와줄게.

■ if절이 명사 역할을 하는 경우도 있다. 명사절 접속사 if와 부사절 접속사 if의 쓰임을 구별하자. 명사절 접속사 if의 경우 '~인지 아닌지'로 해석하며 미래를 나타낼 때에는 미래시제를 써야 한다.
- Do you know **if** he **will** apply for the job or not? 〈명사절〉
  그가 그 일자리에 지원할지 하지 않을지 알고 있니?
- If you **break** the promise, people **will** not **trust** you. 〈부사절〉
  네가 그 약속을 어기면, 사람들은 너를 신뢰하지 않을 거야.

■ If ~ not은 '만약 ~하지 않으면'의 의미인 Unless로 쓸 수 있다. Unless 역시 조건의 부사절이므로 현재시제로 미래를 나타낸다.
- **If** you **don't** go out with me, I will be sad.
= **Unless** you go out with me, I will be sad.
  저와 데이트해 주지 않는다면, 저는 슬플 거예요.

핵심 Check

1. 다음 우리말과 같도록 빈칸에 알맞은 말을 쓰시오.

(1) 네가 아프다면, 내가 널 돌봐 줄 거야.
➡ If you _____ sick, I _____ _____ _____ _____ you.

(2) 그가 내 책을 빌릴지 궁금해.
➡ I wonder _____ he _____ _____ my book.

(3) 그가 오지 않으면, 너는 무엇을 할 거니?
➡ _____ he comes, what _____ you _____?

② 부가의문문

- He is your partner, **isn't he**? 그는 너의 파트너지, 그렇지 않니?
- The woman makes pizza, **doesn't she**? 그 여자는 피자를 만들지, 그렇지 않니?

■ 부가의문문은 문장 끝에 붙은 의문문으로, 상대방의 동의를 구하거나 정보를 확인할 때 사용한다.
- It **is** Thursday, **isn't it**? 오늘은 목요일이지, 그렇지 않니?
- You **don't** like being here, **do you**? 너 이곳에 있는 것을 좋아하지 않지, 그렇지?
- The man **is not** your father, **is he**? 그 남자는 너의 아버지가 아니지, 그렇지?
- Julia **made** you happy, **didn't** she? Julia는 널 행복하게 했어, 그렇지 않니?

■ 부가의문문을 만드는 법은 다음과 같다.

1. 앞 문장에 be동사나 조동사가 쓰이면 해당 be동사나 조동사를 그대로 사용한다. 일반동사가 사용된 경우라면 'do / does / did'를 사용한다.
2. 앞 문장이 긍정이면 부정, 부정이면 긍정으로 쓴다.
3. 주어는 반드시 인칭대명사를 쓴다.
4. 부정형의 경우 반드시 동사의 축약형을 쓴다.

- You **are** hungry, **aren't you**? 너 배가 고프지, 그렇지 않니?
- You **didn't** do your homework, **did you**? 너 숙제를 하지 않았지, 그렇지?
- Tom and Mary **are** married, **aren't they**? Tom과 Mary는 결혼했지, 그렇지 않니?
- He **is not** driving the car, **is he**? 그는 운전하는 중이 아니지, 그렇지?
- The children **didn't take** part in the game, **did they**? 그 아이들은 게임에 참가하지 않았지, 그렇지?

■ 명령문의 부가의문문은 will you?를 쓰고(긍정의 명령문에서는 won't you?도 가능함), 권유문(Let's ~)의 경우에는 shall we?를 쓴다.
- **Close** the door, **will[won't] you**? 문을 닫아, 그러지 않을래?
- **Let's** go out with me, **shall we**? 나와 함께 나가자, 그럴래?

핵심 Check

2. 다음 빈칸에 알맞은 부가의문문을 쓰시오.

(1) Ms. Jefferson is your teacher, _____ _____?

(2) You came from Canada, _____ _____?

(3) James is her boyfriend, _____ _____?

(4) You are telling me the truth, _____ _____?

(5) The dog and the cat are resting under the tree, _____ _____?

(6) They went to school, _____ _____?

(7) She doesn't like me, _____ _____?

01 다음 문장에서 어법상 <u>어색한</u> 부분을 바르게 고쳐 쓰시오.

(1) You missed the bus, did you?

_____ ➡ _____

(2) If you will take me home, I will be glad.

_____ ➡ _____

(3) Kevin doesn't like my project, is he?

_____ ➡ _____

(4) If you are hungry, I make you a pie.

_____ ➡ _____

02 다음 빈칸에 알맞은 부가의문문을 쓰시오.

(1) He will not do the laundry, _____ _____?

(2) You don't want to be friends with me, _____ _____?

(3) Mr. Brandon is one of our guests, _____ _____?

(4) It is your dictionary, _____ _____?

(5) She can't drive, _____ _____?

03 주어진 단어를 바르게 배열하여 다음 우리말을 영어로 쓰시오. 필요하다면 단어를 첨가하거나 변형하시오.

(1) 그녀는 지금 바빠, 그렇지 않니? (is / she / now / busy / is / she)

➡ _____

(2) 그 남자는 갈 준비가 되지 않았어, 그렇지? (he / go / is / is / the man / ready)

➡ _____

(3) 그녀가 편지를 쓴다면, 그들은 답장할 거야. (if / back / write / they / write / a letter / she)

➡ _____

(4) 나의 엄마가 내일 그 소식을 들으시면, 놀라실 거야. (surprised / my / mom / if / the news / hear / she / be / will / tomorrow)

➡ _____

01 다음 빈칸에 들어갈 말로 가장 적절한 것은?

> Tommy has trouble in speaking English,
> _____?

① does he
② isn't he
③ didn't he
④ doesn't he
⑤ is he

02 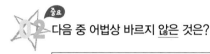 다음 중 어법상 바르지 <u>않은</u> 것은?

> ①Will you ②tell Jimmy ③to go home alone if I ④will have to stay here ⑤at night?

①　　②　　③　　④　　⑤

03 다음 중 빈칸에 공통으로 들어갈 말은?

> • Tom and Jerry do the same work, _____?
> • The children sleep well, _____?

① did they
② does she
③ don't they
④ doesn't he
⑤ do they

04 다음 중 if의 쓰임이 같은 것끼리 바르게 묶은 것은?

> ⓐ What will you do if she doesn't want to talk with you?
> ⓑ I wonder if he will answer the phone.
> ⓒ We couldn't tell if James told us the truth or not.
> ⓓ If you lend the I-pad to me, I will be very thankful.
> ⓔ Do you know if the actor will direct the movie?

① ⓐⓑ, ⓒⓓⓔ
② ⓐⓑⓒ, ⓓⓔ
③ ⓐⓓ, ⓑⓒⓔ
④ ⓐⓓⓔ, ⓑⓒ
⑤ ⓐⓔ, ⓑⓒⓓ

05 다음 중 어법상 <u>어색한</u> 것은?

① Your brothers entered the school, didn't they?
② If you want to know more about it, I will tell you.
③ She made you do the dishes, didn't she?
④ If I see her tomorrow morning, I will let you know.
⑤ The computers are broken, don't they?

06 서답형 다음 우리말을 영어로 쓰시오.

> 그 샌드위치는 맛있었어, 그렇지 않니?

➡ _____

07 다음 중 빈칸에 들어갈 말이 바르게 짝지어진 것은?

> • Picasso was a successful painter, _____?
> • Ms. Kim taught us Math, _____?
> • The man will keep the secret, _____?

① wasn't he – did she – will he
② wasn't he – didn't she – won't he
③ was he – did she – will he
④ was he – didn't she – won't he
⑤ wasn't he – didn't she – doesn't he

08 서답형 주어진 단어를 활용하여 다음 우리말을 영어로 쓰시오.

> 그 물을 마시면, 너는 더 작아질 거야.
> (drink / get)

➡ _____

09 다음 중 빈칸에 들어갈 말이 <u>다른</u> 하나는?

① Jimmy worked really hard, _____?
② Kevin wanted to go abroad, _____?
③ The man waited for her, _____?
④ A man is standing outside, _____?
⑤ A boy played the piano, _____?

10 다음 중 우리말을 영어로 바르게 옮기지 <u>않은</u> 것은?

① 네가 울면 그 아이도 울 거야.
→ If you cry, the child will cry too.
② 비가 그치면, 나는 밖으로 나갈 거야.
→ If the rain stops, I will go out.
③ 네가 이 잡지를 원한다면, 내가 내일 빌려줄게.
→ If you want this magazine, I lend it to you tomorrow.
④ 그가 필요하다면, 내가 그에게 전화할게.
→ If you need him, I will call him.
⑤ 그것이 고장 나면, 하나 살 거니?
→ If it is broken, will you buy one?

11 다음 빈칸에 들어갈 말로 가장 적절한 것은?

He _____ satisfied with the hotel service, is he?

① didn't   ② wasn't   ③ is
④ isn't   ⑤ was

12 주어진 어휘를 활용하여 다음 우리말을 영어로 쓰시오.

내일 눈이 오면, 그 산은 눈으로 덮일 거야.
(be covered with)

➡ _____

_____

13 다음 중 우리말을 영어로 바르게 옮긴 것은?

나는 파티에 초대되지 않았어, 그렇지?

① I wasn't invited to the party, wasn't I?
② I didn't invite to the party, did I?
③ I wasn't invited to the party, was I?
④ I was invited to the party, wasn't I?
⑤ I was invited to the party, was I?

14 다음 중 괄호 안에 들어갈 말이 바르게 짝지어진 것은?

• He can't swim, (does he / can he)?
• You made a mistake, (didn't you / did you)?
• She will not do it again, (will she / won't she)?

① does he – didn't you – will she
② does he – didn't you – won't she
③ can he – didn't you – will she
④ can he – did you – won't she
⑤ can he – did you – will she

15 다음 우리말을 영어로 옮길 때 빈칸에 알맞은 말을 쓰시오.

더우면, 나는 아이스크림을 먹을 거야.
If it ____ ____, ____
____ ice cream.

16 다음 빈칸에 알맞은 말은?

Mike had a meeting with you, _____?

① did he   ② did you   ③ didn't he
④ didn't you   ⑤ doesn't he

17 다음 중 밑줄 친 부분이 어법상 바르지 <u>않은</u> 것은?

① Minju and Minjae are twins, <u>aren't they</u>?

② You didn't do your best, <u>did you</u>?

③ Butter is made from milk, <u>doesn't it</u>?

④ Junto was born in Tokyo, <u>wasn't he</u>?

⑤ He built the house ten years ago, <u>didn't he</u>?

18 다음 빈칸에 알맞은 말이 바르게 짝지어진 것은?

> • Can you tell me if they _____ us this weekend?
> • _____ you hurry, you will miss the bus.

① visit – If

② will visit – If

③ will visit – Unless

④ visit – Unless

⑤ visited – If

19 주어진 단어를 바르게 배열하여 다음 우리말을 영어로 쓰시오. 필요하다면 단어를 추가하시오.

> 너는 하루에 세 번 이를 닦았어, 그렇지 않니?
> (you / you / brushed / a day / times / teeth / your / three)

➡ _____

20 다음 중 어법상 <u>어색한</u> 것은?

① Unless you tell her, she will forget about it.

② If you don't stay up late at night, you will feel better next morning.

③ Rachel often loses her keys, doesn't she?

④ We enjoyed our vacation, didn't we?

⑤ You are living in Seoul, don't you?

21 주어진 단어를 활용하여 다음 우리말을 영어로 쓰시오.

> 내가 약간의 돈을 가지고 있다면, 자전거 한 대를 살 거야. (have / some / buy)

➡ _____

22 다음 우리말을 영어로 바르게 옮긴 것을 <u>모두</u> 고르시오.

> 재킷을 입지 않는다면, 너는 감기에 걸릴 거야.

① If you don't wear a jacket, you will catch a cold.

② If you wear a jacket, you will catch a cold.

③ If you don't wear a jacket, you catch a cold.

④ Unless you wear a jacket, you will catch a cold.

⑤ Unless you wear a jacket, you catch a cold.

23 주어진 단어를 활용하여 다음 우리말을 영어로 쓰시오.

> 너는 세차를 하지 않았어, 그렇지?
> (your car)

➡ _____

 24 다음 빈칸에 공통으로 들어갈 말로 가장 적절한 것은?

> • I don't know _____ she will arrive on time.
> • What will happen _____ Kyle doesn't accept the apology?

① as

② because

③ whether

④ if

⑤ while

01 다음 빈칸에 알맞은 말을 쓰시오.

> A: _____ _____ _____ this morning,
> _____ _____?
> B: Yes, I was.
> A: Why were you late this morning?

02 주어진 동사를 어법에 맞게 쓰시오.

> A: I will go to the movies. Will you join me?
> B: If I (finish) my work, I (join) you.

➡ _____

03 다음 빈칸에 알맞은 말을 써서 부가의문문을 완성하시오.
(1) Kathy came late last night, _____
  _____?
(2) He couldn't find a new job, _____
  _____?
(3) You don't need my advice, _____
  _____?
(4) Emily can't call me right now, _____
  _____?
(5) Romeo and Juliet fell in love in the
  book, _____ _____?
(6) They were very surprised, _____
  _____?
(7) The woman remembered you, _____
  _____?

04 주어진 단어를 활용하여 다음 우리말을 영어로 쓰시오.

> 내가 내일 너를 보러 간다면, DVD 몇 개를 가
> 져갈게. (come to see, bring, some)

➡ _____

05 접속사 if로 두 개의 문장을 연결하여 자연스러운 하나의 문
장을 만드시오.

> • You don't reduce your speed.
> • You are smaller.
> • You join a club.

> • You will make many friends.
> • You will have an accident.
> • You can go through the door.

➡ _____
➡ _____
➡ _____

06 다음 우리말을 두 가지의 영어 문장으로 쓰시오.

> 빠르게 걷지 않으면, 너는 학교에 늦을 거야.

➡ _____
➡ _____

07 괄호 안의 단어를 어법에 맞게 쓰시오.

> A: How can I enter Wonderland?
> B: If you (follow) the white rabbit, you
> (enter) Wonderland.

➡ _____

08 다음 우리말을 영어로 쓰시오.

> 그것은 네 책이야, 그렇지 않니?

➡ _____

09 다음 우리말에 맞게 빈칸에 알맞은 말을 쓰시오.

(1) 그녀가 날 도와준다면, 나도 언젠가 그녀를 도울 거야.
➡ If she _____ me, I _____ _____ her someday.

(2) 너는 창문을 닫았어, 그렇지 않니?
➡ You _____ the window, _____ _____?

(3) 네가 친절하다면, 너는 많은 친구들을 사귈 거야.
➡ If you _____ kind, you _____ _____ many friends.

(4) 그녀는 꽃을 좋아하지 않아, 그렇지?
➡ She _____ _____ flowers, _____ _____?

(5) 규칙적으로 운동한다면, 너는 더 건강해 질 거야.
➡ If you _____ regularly, you _____ _____ healthier.

10 다음 주어진 문장과 같은 의미의 문장을 쓰시오.

If she doesn't want to talk with me, I will not talk with her.

➡ _____

11 다음 빈칸에 공통으로 들어갈 말을 쓰시오.

- You can catch the train _____ you go now.
- You will be sad _____ your parents are sick.

➡ _____

12 다음 우리말을 영어로 쓰시오.

그 꽃들은 정말 아름답다, 그렇지 않니?

➡ _____

13 주어진 어휘를 활용하여 다음 우리말을 영어로 쓰시오.

- 비누를 사용하지 않으면, 너의 옷은 깨끗해지지 않을 거야. (if / get clean)
- 그녀가 내일 일찍 일어난다면, 이곳에 올 거야. (wake up / come)
- 자동차를 사길 원한다면, 어떤 종류의 차를 살 거니? (want / what kind of)

➡ _____
➡ _____
➡ _____

14 다음 빈칸에 공통으로 들어갈 말을 쓰시오.

- Clara ran her own restaurant, _____?
- She did her best, _____?

➡ _____

15 다음 대화의 빈칸에 알맞은 말을 쓰시오.

A: You are going to be late tonight, _____?
B: Maybe. If I _____, don't wait for me.

➡ _____

16 주어진 단어를 활용하여 다음 우리말을 영어로 쓰시오.

(1) 늦지 마, 그럴거지? (be)
(2) 컴퓨터 게임을 그만해, 그럴래? (stop, play)
➡ (1) _____
   (2) _____

Reading

Join Our Club, Won't You?
_{긍정 명령문의 부가의문문}

Hello, everyone! I'm Suji and I'm the leader of the "Save the Earth"
_{lead+-er}

club. Our club is an environmental club.

We do volunteer work to protect our planet. Protecting our planet is
_{부사적 용법(목적: ~하기 위해서)}   _{동명사 주어}   _{동명사 주어에 일치시킨 단수 동사}

important, isn't it? Last year, we carried out a campaign to reduce
_{앞 문장이 긍정이므로 부정}   _{부사적 용법(목적)}

food waste in the school cafeteria. The campaign was successful. This
_{success+-ful}

year, we are preparing some special activities abroad. So, if you are

interested in saving the planet, please join us.
_{조건의 부사절 (만약 ~한다면)}   _{주절}

Hello, friends! I'm Diego of "Fly High." It is a drone club. We study
_{= "Fly High"}

every part of a drone and make some small drones by ourselves.
_{study와 병렬로 앞에 주어인 'we'가 생략됨}   _{by oneself: 스스로}

When you have your own drone, you need to practice hovering.
_{여러분 자신의}   _{practice의 목적어로 동명사}

"Hovering" means staying in the same place in the air. Once you are
_{means의 목적어로 동명사}   _{[접속사] 일단 ~하면, ~하자마자}

good at hovering, you will be ready to fly your drone in different
_{~에 능숙하다}   _{~할 준비가 되다}

directions. You're getting excited, aren't you?
_{부가의문문(be동사 긍정문 → be동사 부정형+주어?)}

---

leader: 지도자, 대표
environmental: (자연) 환경의
volunteer: 자원봉사, 자원봉사자
protect: 보호하다
planet: 행성
carry out: 수행하다
campaign: 캠페인
reduce: 줄이다
successful: 성공적인
aborad: 해외로, 해외에서
drone: 드론, 무인 비행기
by oneself: 혼자서, 스스로
hover: (허공을) 맴돌다

확인문제

● 다음 문장이 본문의 내용과 일치하면 T, 일치하지 않으면 F를 쓰시오.

1 Suji is interested in protecting the planet. ☐

2 Diego is the leader of the club "Fly High." ☐

3 The campaign of the "Save the Earth" club was about reducing food waste in their home. ☐

4 Diego studies every part of a drone with his club members. ☐

Hello, I'm Junho. What do you want to do when you see beautiful
scenery? You want to take a picture of it, don't you?
If you join our photo club, "Photo World," you can meet famous
photographers and learn their skills. Every December, you can take
part in the school photo contest. So, by joining "Photo World" you
can learn a new hobby and have a chance of winning a prize!
Welcome to my musical club, "Story Singers"! My name is Olivia. In
the musical club, there are two groups: actors and crew.
We first choose the subject of our musical and then write a story
together. Then, the actors practice singing and dancing, while the
crew make costumes. We perform our musical in the school
festival. You can get an application from me. You will join our
club, won't you?

photographer: 사진사
skill: 솜씨, 기술
scenery: 경치
take part in: ~에 참가하다
by Ving: V함으로써
a chance of Ving: V할 기회
win a prize: 상을 받다
crew: 제작진, 승무원, 선원
application: 지원[신청](서), 적용

확인문제

● 다음 문장이 본문의 내용과 일치하면 T, 일치하지 <u>않으면</u> F를 쓰시오.

1   Junho belongs to the photo club. ☐

2   Famous photographers teach their skills to the photo club members. ☐

3   Olivia is interested in taking pictures. ☐

4   Only actors choose the subject of their musical. ☐

5   Costumes are made by the crew. ☐

6   You need an application to join the "Story Singers" club. ☐

● 우리말을 참고하여 빈칸에 알맞은 말을 쓰시오.

Join Our Club, Won't You?

1 Hello, everyone! I'm Suji and I'm _____ _____ _____ the "Save the Earth" club.

2 Our club is _____ _____ _____.

3 We _____ _____ _____ to protect our planet.

4 _____ _____ _____ is important, _____ it?

5 Last year, we _____ _____ a campaign _____ _____ _____ _____ in the school cafeteria.

6 The campaign was _____.

7 This year, we are _____ _____ _____ _____ abroad.

8 So, if you _____ _____ _____ saving the planet, please join us.

9 Hello, friends! I'm Diego _____ "Fly High."

10 _____ _____ a drone club.

11 We study _____ _____ _____ a drone and make some small drones _____ _____.

12 When you have _____ _____ _____, you need to _____ _____.

13 "_____" means _____ _____ the same place in the air.

14 Once you _____ _____ _____ hovering, you will _____ _____ _____ _____ your drone in different directions.

15 You're _____ _____, _____ _____?

우리 동아리에 가입해, 그러지 않을래?

1 모두들 안녕. 나는 수지이고 "Save the Earth" 동아리의 대표야.

2 우리 동아리는 환경 동아리야.

3 우리는 우리 행성(지구)을 지키기 위해 자원봉사 활동을 해.

4 지구를 지키는 것은 중요해, 그렇지 않니?

5 작년에 우리는 학교 식당에서 음식물 쓰레기 줄이기 캠페인을 했어.

6 캠페인은 성공적이었어.

7 올해 우리는 몇몇 특별한 해외 활동을 준비 중이야.

8 그러니, 지구를 구하는 데 관심이 있다면 우리와 함께하자.

9 안녕, 친구들! 나는 "Fly High"의 Diego야.

10 그건 드론 동아리야.

11 우리는 드론의 모든 부분을 공부하고 우리 스스로 작은 드론을 만들어.

12 네 드론이 있으면, 너는 공중 정지를 연습해야 해.

13 "공중 정지"란 공중에서 한자리에 머무는 것을 의미해.

14 공중 정지를 잘한다면, 너는 너의 드론을 다른 방향으로 날릴 준비가 될 거야.

15 점점 흥미가 생기지, 그렇지 않니?

16 Hello, I'm Junho. What do you want _____ _____ when you _____ _____ _____ ?

17 You want _____ _____ _____ _____ of it, _____ _____?

18 If you _____ _____ _____ _____, "Photo World," you can meet famous photographers and _____ _____ _____ .

19 Every December, you can _____ _____ _____ the school photo contest.

20 So, _____ _____ "Photo World" you can _____ _____ _____ _____ a n d   h a v e _____ _____ _____ winning a prize!

21 _____ _____ my musical club, "Story Singers"!

22 My name is Olivia. In the musical club, _____ _____ _____ _____ : actors and crew.

23 We first _____ _____ _____ of our musical and then _____ _____ _____ together.

24 Then, the actors _____ _____ and _____ , while the crew _____ _____ .

25 We _____ our musical _____ _____ _____ _____ _____ .

26 You can _____ _____ from me.

27 You will _____ _____ _____ , _____ _____ ?

16 안녕, 난 준호야. 너는 아름다운 풍경을 볼 때 무엇을 하고 싶니?

17 사진을 찍고 싶을 거야. 그렇지 않니?

18 우리 사진 동아리 "Photo World"에 가입한다면 너는 유명한 사진작가들을 만나고, 그들의 기술을 배울 수 있어.

19 매년 **12**월에 너는 학교 사진 대회에 참가할 수 있어.

20 그렇게 "Photo World"에 가입하는 것으로 너는 새로운 취미를 배우고 상을 받는 기회를 가질 수 있어!

21 나의 뮤지컬 동아리, "Story Singers"에 온 걸 환영해!

22 내 이름은 Olivia야. 뮤지컬 동아리에는 배우와 제작진이라는 두 그룹이 있어.

23 우리는 우선 뮤지컬의 주제를 고르고 함께 이야기를 써.

24 그리고는 제작진이 의상을 만드는 동안 배우들은 노래와 춤을 연습하지.

25 우리는 학교 축제에서 뮤지컬 공연을 해.

26 가입신청서는 나한테서 받을 수 있어.

27 너는 우리 동아리에 가입할 거야, 그렇지?

● 우리말을 참고하여 본문을 영작하시오.

Join Our Club, Won't You?

1 모두들 안녕. 나는 수지이고 "Save the Earth" 동아리의 대표야.

➡ _____

2 우리 동아리는 환경 동아리야.

➡ _____

3 우리는 우리 행성(지구)을 지키기 위해 자원봉사 활동을 해.

➡ _____

4 지구를 지키는 것은 중요해, 그렇지 않니?

➡ _____

5 작년에 우리는 학교 식당에서 음식물 쓰레기 줄이기 캠페인을 했어.

➡ _____

6 캠페인은 성공적이었어.

➡ _____

7 올해 우리는 몇몇 특별한 해외 활동을 준비 중이야.

➡ _____

8 그러니, 지구를 구하는 데 관심이 있다면 우리와 함께하자.

➡ _____

9 안녕, 친구들! 나는 "Fly High"의 Diego야.

➡ _____

10 그건 드론 동아리야.

➡ _____

11 우리는 드론의 모든 부분을 공부하고 우리 스스로 작은 드론을 만들어.

➡ _____

12 네 드론이 있으면, 너는 공중 정지를 연습해야 해.

➡ _____

13 "공중 정지"란 공중에서 한자리에 머무는 것을 의미해.

➡ _____

14 공중 정지를 잘한다면, 너는 너의 드론을 다른 방향으로 날릴 준비가 될 거야.

➡ _____

15 점점 흥미가 생기지, 그렇지 않니?

➡ _____

16 안녕, 난 준호야. 너는 아름다운 풍경을 볼 때 무엇을 하고 싶니?

➡ _____

17 사진을 찍고 싶을 거야, 그렇지 않니?

➡ _____

18 우리 사진 동아리 "Photo World"에 가입한다면 너는 유명한 사진작가들을 만나고, 그들의 기술을 배울 수 있어.

➡ _____

19 매년 12월에 너는 학교 사진 대회에 참가할 수 있어.

➡ _____

20 그렇게 "Photo World"에 가입하는 것으로 너는 새로운 취미를 배우고 상을 받는 기회를 가질 수 있어!

➡ _____

21 나의 뮤지컬 동아리, "Story Singers"에 온 걸 환영해!

➡ _____

22 내 이름은 Olivia야. 뮤지컬 동아리에는 배우와 제작진이라는 두 그룹이 있어.

➡ _____

23 우리는 우선 뮤지컬의 주제를 고르고 함께 이야기를 써.

➡ _____

24 그리고는 제작진이 의상을 만드는 동안 배우들은 노래와 춤을 연습하지.

➡ _____

25 우리는 학교 축제에서 뮤지컬 공연을 해.

➡ _____

26 가입신청서는 나한테서 받을 수 있어.

➡ _____

27 너는 우리 동아리에 가입할 거야, 그렇지?

➡ _____

[01~04] 다음 글을 읽고 물음에 답하시오.

Hello, everyone! I'm Suji and I'm the leader of the "Save the Earth" club. Our club is an environmental club. We do volunteer work (A)_____ our planet. (B)_____ our planet is important, isn't it? Last year, we carried out a campaign to reduce food waste in the school cafeteria. The campaign was successful. This year, we are preparing some special activities abroad. So, (C)_____ you are interested in saving the planet, please join us.

서답형

01 동사 'protect'를 어법에 맞게 (A)와 (B)에 각각 쓰시오.

➡ (A)_____ (B)_____

중요

02 다음 중 빈칸 (C)에 들어갈 말로 가장 적절한 것은?

① because   ② for   ③ if
④ although   ⑤ as soon as

03 다음 중 위 글의 내용과 일치하지 <u>않는</u> 것은?

① Suji is the leader of the club.
② Suji's club is an environmental club.
③ Suji carried out many campaigns last year.
④ Suji is interested in saving the planet.
⑤ Suji tried to reduce food waste last year.

서답형

04 다음 빈칸에 들어갈 말을 위 글에서 찾아 쓰시오.

If you go _____, you go to a foreign country.

[05~08] 다음 글을 읽고 물음에 답하시오.

Hello, friends! I'm Diego of "Fly High." It is a drone club. We study every (A)[part / parts] of a drone and make some small drones by ourselves. When you have your own drone, you need to practice (B)[hovering / to hover]. "Hovering" means staying in the same place in the air. Once you are good at hovering, you will be ready (C)[fly / to fly] your drone in different directions. You're getting excited, aren't you?

05 다음 중 위 글에서 그 반의어를 찾을 수 <u>없는</u> 것은?

① same   ② different   ③ low
④ big   ⑤ little

중요

06 (A)~(C)에서 어법상 옳은 것끼리 바르게 짝지어진 것은?

① part – hovering – fly
② part – to hover – fly
③ part – hovering – to fly
④ parts – to hover – fly
⑤ parts – to hover – to fly

서답형

07 다음 물음에 완전한 문장의 영어로 답하시오.

What club is "Fly High"?

➡ _____

서답형

08 위 글의 내용에 맞게 다음 대화의 빈칸에 알맞은 말을 쓰시오.

A: What is hovering?
B: _____

➡ _____

[09~12] 다음 글을 읽고, 물음에 답하시오.

Hello, I'm Junho. What do you want to do when you see beautiful scenery? You want to take a picture ⓐ_____ it, don't you? If you join our photo club, "Photo World," you can meet famous photographers and learn their skills. Every December, you can take part in the school photo contest. So, ⓑ_____ joining "Photo World" you can learn a new hobby and have a chance of winning a prize!

09 빈칸 ⓐ와 ⓑ에 들어갈 말이 바르게 짝지어진 것은?

① at – on
② of – in
③ of – by
④ by – at
⑤ about – on

서답형

10 다음과 같이 풀이되는 단어를 위 글에서 찾아 쓰시오.

very well known

➡ _____

11 다음 중 위 글을 읽고 답할 수 없는 것은?

① What is the name of the club that Junho is in?
② Who can the club members meet?
③ What can the club members learn from photographers?
④ When is the school photo contest held?
⑤ Who won a prize in the school photo contest last December?

서답형

12 위 글의 내용에 맞게 빈칸에 알맞은 말을 쓰시오.

The school photo contest is held in _____ every year.

➡ _____

[13~16] 다음 글을 읽고 물음에 답하시오.

Welcome to my musical club, "Story Singers"! My name is Olivia. In the musical club, there are two groups: actors and ⓐcrew. We first choose the ⓑsubject of our musical and then write a story together. Then, the actors practice (A)_____, ⓒwhile the crew make costumes. We ⓓperform our musical in the school festival. You can get an ⓔapplication from me. (B)너는 우리 동아리에 가입할 거야, 그렇지?

서답형

13 주어진 어휘를 어법에 맞게 빈칸 (A)에 쓰시오.

sing and dance

➡ _____

서답형

14 밑줄 친 우리말 (B)를 영어로 쓰시오. (7 words)

➡ _____

15 ⓐ~ⓔ 중 낱말의 의미가 잘못 짝지어진 것은?

① ⓐ - 제작진
② ⓑ - 학과목
③ ⓒ - ~하는 동안에
④ ⓓ - 공연하다
⑤ ⓔ - 가입신청서

16 다음 중 위 글을 읽고 답할 수 있는 것의 개수는?

ⓐ What club does Olivia belong to?
ⓑ How many groups are there in the "Story Singers"?
ⓒ What subject do the club members like most?
ⓓ How many musical does the club members perform a year?
ⓔ Who writes a story for a musical?

① 1개   ② 2개   ③ 3개   ④ 4개   ⑤ 5개

[17~19] 다음 글을 읽고 물음에 답하시오.

Hello, everyone! I'm Suji and I'm the leader of the "Save the Earth" club. Our club is an environmental club. We do volunteer work ⓐto protect our planet. Protecting our planet is important, ⓑ_____? Last year, we carried out a campaign to reduce food waste in the school cafeteria. The campaign was successful. This year, we are preparing some special activities abroad. So, if you are interested in saving the planet, please join us.

17 다음 중 밑줄 친 ⓐ와 쓰임이 같은 것은?

① It is important to protect our planet.
② Do you want to protect your children?
③ I need to learn how to protect myself.
④ I'm trying to protect my life.
⑤ She told a lie to protect their family.

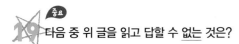

18 빈칸 ⓑ에 알맞은 말을 써서 부가의문문을 완성하시오.

➡ _____

19 다음 중 위 글을 읽고 답할 수 없는 것은?

① Who is the leader of the club?
② What did the club members do last year?
③ Why does the club members do volunteer work?
④ What did the club members want to reduce last year?
⑤ What are the special activities that the club members are going to do this year?

[20~23] 다음 글을 읽고 물음에 답하시오.

Hello, friends! I'm Diego of "Fly High." It is a drone club. We study every part of a drone and make some small drones ⓐby ourselves. When you have your own drone, you need to practice hovering. "Hovering" means staying in the same place in the air. Once you are good at hovering, you will be ready to fly your drone in different directions. You're getting ⓑ_____, aren't you?

20 다음 중 밑줄 친 ⓐ를 대신하여 쓰일 수 있는 것은?

① with help
② on our own
③ that way
④ in ourselves
⑤ on our way

21 주어진 단어를 어법에 맞게 빈칸 ⓑ에 쓰시오.

excite

➡ _____

22 다음 중 위 글의 내용과 일치하지 <u>않는</u> 것은?

① Diego is a member of the club called "Fly High."
② Diego studies all parts of a drone with his club members.
③ You need to stay in the same place when you fly a drone.
④ After practicing hovering, you can fly your drone in different directions.
⑤ "Fly High" is a drone club.

23 다음 물음에 완전한 문장의 영어로 쓰시오.

Q: What do the members of "Fly High" do?

➡ _____

[24~27] 다음 글을 읽고 물음에 답하시오.

Hello, I'm Junho. What do you want to do when you see beautiful scenery? You want to ⓐ_____ a picture of ⓑit, don't you? If you join our photo club, "Photo World," you can meet famous photographers and learn their skills. Every December, you can take part in the school photo contest. So, by joining "Photo World" you can learn ⓒa new hobby and have a chance of winning a prize!

24 다음 중 빈칸 ⓐ에 들어갈 말과 같은 것은?

① Milk _____s into cheese or yogurt.
② I may _____ into sleep early tonight.
③ Just come and _____ a good time.
④ Let's _____ a walk in the park.
⑤ Don't _____ off going to the dentist.

25 밑줄 친 ⓑ가 가리키는 것을 위 글에서 찾아 쓰시오.

➡ _____

26 다음 중 밑줄 친 ⓒ가 의미하는 것으로 가장 적절한 것은?

① to take part in the photo contest
② to meet famous photographers
③ to see beautiful scenery
④ to take a picture
⑤ to make many friends in the club

27 What can you learn from the famous photographers? Answer in English with a full sentence.

➡ _____

[28~30] 다음 글을 읽고 물음에 답하시오.

Welcome to my musical club, "Story Singers"! My name is Olivia. In the musical club, there are two groups: actors and crew. We first choose the subject of our musical and then write a story together. Then, the actors practice singing and dancing, (A)[during / while] the crew make costumes. We perform our musical in the school festival. You can get an application (B)[from / to] me. You will join our club, (C)[don't you / won't you]?

28 (A)~(C) 중 어법상 옳은 것끼리 바르게 짝지은 것은?

① during – from – don't you
② while – from – don't you
③ during – to – won't you
④ while – from – won't you
⑤ during – to – don't you

29 다음 중 위 글의 내용과 일치하지 <u>않는</u> 것은?

① Olivia is one of the members of the musical club.
② The members choose the subject of their musical together.
③ Only the crew write a story for the musical.
④ Olivia has applications for students who want to join the club.
⑤ The members make costumes by themselves.

30 What do the musical club members do first? Answer in English with a full sentence.

➡ _____

[01~03] 다음 글을 읽고 물음에 답하시오.

Hello, everyone! I'm Suji and I'm the leader of the "Save the Earth" club. Our club is an environmental club. We do volunteer work to protect our planet. Protecting our planet is important, isn't it? Last year, we carried out a campaign to reduce food waste in the school cafeteria. The campaign was successful. This year, we are preparing some special activities abroad. So, if you are interested in saving the planet, please join us.

01 위 글의 표현을 이용하여 다음 대화를 완성하시오.

> Suji: Jason, _____ _____ _____
>
> _____ _____ _____ _____,
>
> _____ _____?
>
> Jason: Yes, I am.
>
> Suji: Then, how about joining "Save the Earth" club?

02 In order to save the earth, what did the club members do last year? Answer in English with a full sentence.

➡ _____

_____

03 다음은 캠페인을 끝낸 후 수지가 한 말이다. 위 글의 내용에 맞게 빈칸에 알맞은 말을 쓰시오.

> Suji: Wow, the campaign was _____,
>
> _____ _____?

[04~07] 다음 글을 읽고 물음에 답하시오.

Hello, friends! I'm Diego of "Fly High." It is a drone club. We study every part of a drone and make some small drones by ourselves. When you have your own drone, you need to practice hovering. "Hovering" means staying in the same place in the air. Once you are good at hovering, you will be ready to fly your drone in different directions. (A)점점 흥미가 생기지, 그렇지 않니?

04 위 글의 내용에 맞게 다음 대화의 빈칸에 알맞은 말을 쓰시오.

> A: Wow, flying a drone is very exciting! When will I be ready to fly it in different directions?
>
> B: _____, you will be able to do it.

05 What do you need to do after making a small drone by yourself? Answer in English with a full sentence.

➡ _____

06 위 글의 내용에 맞게 빈칸에 알맞은 말을 쓰시오.

> Unless you _____ _____ _____
>
> _____, you _____ _____ _____
>
> to fly your drone in different directions.

07 주어진 단어를 활용하여 밑줄 친 우리말 (A)를 영어로 쓰시오.

> (get / excite / are)

➡ _____

[08~11] 다음 글을 읽고 물음에 답하시오.

Hello, I'm Junho. What do you want to do when you see beautiful scenery? You want to take a picture of it, don't you? If you join our photo club, "Photo World," you can meet famous photographers and learn their skills. Every December, you can take part in the school photo contest. So, by joining "Photo World" you can learn a new hobby and have (A)상을 받는 기회!

08 주어진 단어를 활용하여 밑줄 친 우리말 (A)를 영어로 쓰시오.

(chance / of / win)

➡ _____

09 What club does Junho belong to? Answer in English with a full sentence.

➡ _____

10 다음 대화의 빈칸을 알맞게 채우시오.

A: I want to learn how _____ _____
_____ _____.
B: Then, how about joining "Photo World?"

11 위 글의 내용에 맞게 다음 대화의 빈칸을 채우시오.

Kelly: Junho, you enjoy _____ _____,
_____ _____?
Junho: Yes, I do. That's why I am in the photo club.

[12~15] 다음 글을 읽고 물음에 답하시오.

Welcome to my musical club, "Story Singers"! My name is Olivia. In the musical club, there are two groups: actors and crew. We first choose the subject of our musical and then write a story together. Then, the actors practice singing and dancing, while the crew make costumes. We perform our musical in the school festival. You can get an application from me. You will join our club, won't you?

12 위 글을 참고하여 다음 대화의 빈칸에 알맞은 말을 쓰시오.

A: I want to join the "Story Singers" club. How can I join the club?
B: If you go to _____, she _____
_____ you _____ _____.

13 위 글의 내용에 맞게 다음 빈칸에 알맞은 말을 쓰시오.

In our musical club, we can be either an _____ or a _____ member.

14 다음은 동아리를 찾는 친구에게 해준 조언이다. 주어진 어구를 활용하여 영작하시오.

네가 많은 사람들 앞에서 춤추고 노래하는 것에 흥미가 있다면, 너는 뮤지컬 동아리를 좋아할 거야.
(be / interest / in front of)

➡ _____
_____

15 How many groups are there in the musical club? Answer in English with a full sentence.

➡ _____

Project Work – Make your own club

A: What shall we call our speaking club?
    OC ~할 것이다 V   O

B: How about "Raise Your Voice?"
    ~이 어때? = What about ~?

C: Good! Then, when and where should we meet?

D: Let's meet in the music room.

B: How about on Mondays after school?
              요일 앞에는 전치사 on

A: Sounds good.

해석

A: 우리의 말하기 동아리를 뭐라 부를까?

B: "Raise Your Voice" 어때?

C: 좋아! 그럼, 우리 언제 어디서 만날까?

D: 음악실에서 만나자.

B: 방과 후 월요일이 어때?

A: 좋아.

Express Yourself

True Reporters

Join "True Reporters"!

You want to share interesting news with your friends, don't you? If you join
                      흥미를 유발하는   부가의문문

our club, you will help make the school newspaper every month. We meet and
          = help to make: 만드는 것을 돕다

work in the library every Wednesday after school. So, if you are interested in
                    수요일마다   = have an interest in

joining our club, come for an interview on Wednesday. We can't wait to meet
동명사(전치사 in의 목적어)   요일 앞에 전치사 on   can't wait to V: 어서 V하고 싶다

you!

구문해설 • share A with B: A와 B를 공유하다 • join: ~에 가입하다 • library: 도서관
• after school: 방과 후에

True Reporters

"True Reporters"에 가입해!

너는 흥미로운 소식을 친구들과 함께 공유하길 원하지, 그렇지 않니? 만약 네가 우리 동아리에 가입한다면, 너는 매달 학교 신문을 만드는 것을 도울 거야. 우리는 방과 후 매주 수요일마다 도서관에서 만나서 일해. 그러니 만약 네가 우리 동아리에 가입하는 것에 관심이 있다면, 수요일에 면접을 보러 오렴. 우리는 어서 너를 만나고 싶어!

Project Work

You want to speak well, don't you? If you are interested in speaking well, you
to부정사를 목적어로 취하는 동사   부가의문문   동명사(전치사 in의 목적어)

should join the club, "Raise Your Voice"! We practice speaking in the music
                                    동명사(practice의 목적어)

room every Monday after school. If you learn to speak well, you may
                                      추측을 나타내는 조동사

be able to change people's minds!

구문해설 • be interested in: ~에 흥미가[관심이] 있다 • raise: ~을 올리다 • practice: ~을 연습하다
• be able to V: V할 수 있다 • mind: 사고방식

너는 말을 잘하고 싶지, 그렇지 않니? 만약 네가 말을 잘하는 것에 관심이 있다면, 너는 "Raise Your Voice" 동아리에 가입해야 해! 우리는 매주 월요일 방과 후에 음악실에서 말하는 것을 연습해. 만약 네가 말을 잘하는 것을 배운다면, 너는 사람들의 사고방식을 바꿀 수 있을 거야.

01 다음 짝지어진 단어의 관계가 같도록 빈칸에 알맞은 말을 쓰시오.

> thin : thick = careful : _____

02 다음 영영풀이가 가리키는 것을 고르시오.

> to make something or somebody ready to be used or to do something

① perform   ② prepare

③ protect   ④ order

⑤ reduce

03 다음 중 밑줄 친 부분의 뜻풀이가 바르지 않은 것은?

① This is a traditional Chinese <u>costume</u>. 의상

② I became the <u>leader</u> of our team. 지도자

③ Jeju island is famous for its beautiful <u>scenery</u>. 풍경

④ We are going to the wrong way. We have to change <u>direction</u>. 방향

⑤ The school dance team will <u>perform</u> in the school festival. 보호하다

04 다음 문장에 공통으로 들어갈 말을 고르시오.

> • I don't have any interests _____ actors.
> • I'll take part _____ the English speech contest.
> • It is not easy for us to keep ____ shape.

① on   ② for   ③ in

④ to   ⑤ by

05 다음 문장의 빈칸에 들어갈 말을 〈보기〉에서 골라 쓰시오.

> ┤ 보기 ├
> keep in shape / stay up late / take part in / be good at

(1) I used to _____ _____ _____ and watch movies.

(2) Sue goes to the gym every day to _____ _____ _____.

(3) I want to _____ _____ _____ drawing pictures.

(4) I decided to _____ _____ _____ a marathon race.

06 다음 우리말에 맞게 주어진 단어를 사용하여 영작하시오.

(1) 나는 요리에 관심이 있어. (interested)

➡ _____

(2) 나는 쿠키를 구을 준비가 되어 있어. (bake)

➡ _____

(3) 나는 Queen의 열렬한 팬이야. (big)

➡ _____

[07~08] 다음 대화를 읽고 물음에 답하시오.

B: I'm (A)[looking after / looking for] a baseball cap.

G: That kind of cap comes in (B)[a few / few] different colors. What's your favorite color?

B: My favorite color is green. Do you have a green (C)<u>one</u>?

G: Here you go.

07 위 대화의 (A)와 (B)에 들어갈 말로 적절한 것을 고르시오.

➡ (A) _____ (B) _____

08 위 대화의 밑줄 친 (C)가 가리키는 것을 찾아 쓰시오.

➡ _____

[09~10] 다음 설명을 읽고 물음에 답하시오.

> Inho: Hello, I'm Inho from the school newspaper club. Daily school life is our topic for the newspaper this month. Studying different subjects ⓐare the biggest part of our school life. We asked all the second graders about their favorite subject. The most popular subject ⓑwas P.E. 35% of students said they ⓒliked P.E. best. The second most popular subject was English. 25% of students said they were ⓓinterested in English. Music and social studies were the third most popular subjects. 15% of students liked music and ⓔanother 15% liked social studies. What is your favorite subject?

09 위 글의 밑줄 친 ⓐ~ⓔ 중 어법상 어색한 것은?

① ⓐ　　② ⓑ　　③ ⓒ　　④ ⓓ　　⑤ ⓔ

10 위 글의 내용과 일치하지 <u>않는</u> 것은?

① The topic for the school newspaper this month is the daily school life.
② P.E is the most popular subject for students.
③ A fourth of students like studying English.
④ 15% of students like music.
⑤ A third of students are interested in studying social studies.

[11~12] 다음 대화를 읽고 물음에 답하시오.

> G: (A)<u>이번 주 토요일에 우리 뮤지컬을 보러 가는 게 어때</u>? I have some free tickets.
> B: Sure. I'm very interested in musicals. What's the musical's title?
> G: It's *The Shower*. Hwang Sunwon wrote it.
> B: Wow. (B)<u>I can't wait to see it.</u>

11 위 대화의 밑줄 친 (A)의 우리말을 주어진 단어를 사용하여 영작하시오. (we, why)

➡ _____

12 위 대화의 밑줄 친 (B)와 바꾸어 쓸 수 있는 것은?

① I'm worried about seeing it.
② I'm interested in seeing it.
③ I don't want to see it.
④ It's too boring to see it.
⑤ I'm looking forward to seeing it.

[13~15] 다음 대화를 읽고 물음에 답하시오.

> Brian: Look! This is a chart about our classmates' interests.
> Sujin: Let's look at it more closely. The chart shows that 30% of students are interested in sports. The school's Sports Day will be so much fun.
> Brian: Right. The chart also shows that 27% of students are interested in actors. I know you are also a big fan of ⓐthem.
> Sujin: Yes. I love them. (A)<u>너는 어떠니?</u>
> Brian: I'm not interested in actors. I'm interested in computer games. 20% of students are interested in them.
> Sujin: Computer games are fun, but playing ⓑthem too much is not good for you.
> Brian: I agree.

13 위 대화의 밑줄 친 ⓐ와 ⓑ가 가리키는 것을 각각 쓰시오.

➡ ⓐ _____, ⓑ _____

14 위 대화의 밑줄 친 (A)의 우리말을 3 단어를 사용하여 영작하시오.

➡ _____

15 위 대화의 내용과 일치하지 <u>않는</u> 것은?

① 30% of students are interested in sports.

② Sujin is a big fan of actors.

③ Brian has an interest in computer games.

④ A fifth of students like playing computer games.

⑤ More than a third of students are interested in actors.

16 다음 대화가 자연스럽게 이어지도록 순서대로 배열하시오.

(A) What did you watch?

(B) I stayed up late to watch TV.

(C) You look tired. What's the matter?

(D) I watched a traveling program. I'm interested in traveling.

➡ _____

Grammar

17 다음 빈칸에 들어갈 말로 적절한 것을 바르게 짝지은 것은?

• Thomas Edison invented the electric light bulb, _____?

• The electric light bulb was invented by Thomas Edison, _____?

① didn't he – wasn't he

② does he – was he

③ didn't it – wasn't it

④ didn't he – wasn't it

⑤ didn't he – was he

18 다음 우리말을 영어로 바르게 옮긴 것은?

내일 그를 만난다면, 무엇을 할 거니?

① If you meet him tomorrow, what do you do?

② If he meets you tomorrow, what will he do?

③ If you meet him tomorrow, what will you do?

④ If you meet him, what do you usually do?

⑤ Unless you meet him, what will you do?

19 주어진 어구를 활용하여 다음 우리말을 영어로 쓰시오.

일기를 매일 쓰는 것은 쉽지 않아, 그렇지?
(keep a diary)

➡ _____

20 다음 중 어법상 바르지 <u>않은</u> 것은?

① If I fail the driving test, I will take it again.

② Carlos didn't like my best friend, did he?

③ You are fond of singing songs, aren't you?

④ If you pass the exam, mom is very happy.

⑤ You sleep too much, don't you?

21 주어진 단어를 이용하여 다음 우리말을 영어로 쓰시오.

그 고양이는 벤치 위에 앉아 있어, 그렇지 않니? (sit)

➡ _____

22 다음 중 밑줄 친 부분의 쓰임이 어법상 바르지 <u>않은</u> 것은?

① He made you the cake, <u>didn't he</u>?

② The frog will help the princess, <u>won't it</u>?

③ They kept calling him, <u>didn't they</u>?

④ You didn't wait for me, <u>did you</u>?

⑤ She was not proud of herself, <u>wasn't she</u>?

23 다음 빈칸에 알맞은 말을 쓰시오.

> A: Your brothers _____ _____
> _____, _____ _____?
> B: That's not true. My brothers can ride bikes well.

24 다음 중 밑줄 친 부분의 쓰임이 다른 하나는?

① I will make some food if you are hungry.
② Mary wants to know if he will like her story.
③ If Tim likes you, he will understand you.
④ What will you do if they raise the price?
⑤ If we win this game, we will throw a party.

25 다음 중 빈칸에 들어갈 말이 다른 하나는?

① Minho did his homework yesterday, _____?
② Jihun got the ticket, _____?
③ He graduated from college, _____?
④ Mr. Tod wanted to see you, _____?
⑤ The man did not look after you, _____?

26 다음 빈칸에 들어갈 말이 바르게 짝지어진 것은?

> A: Your sister will join the club, _____?
> B: I don't know. Let me figure it out.
> If she _____, I will let you know.

① will she – will join the club
② won't she – joins the club
③ will you – will join the club
④ won't you – joins the club
⑤ won't she – joined the club

27 다음 주어진 문장과 같은 의미의 문장을 쓰시오.

> Unless you turn down the radio, I will be annoyed.

➡ _____

Reading

[28~29] 다음 글을 읽고 물음에 답하시오.

Hello, everyone! I'm Suji and I'm the leader of the "Save the Earth" club. Our club is an environmental club. We do volunteer work (A) [protecting / to protect] our planet. Protecting our planet is important, (B)[isn't it / doesn't it]? Last year, we carried out a campaign to reduce food waste in the school cafeteria. The campaign was successful. This year, we are preparing some special activities abroad. So, if you are interested in saving the planet, please (C)[join / join with] us.

28 (A)~(C)에서 어법상 옳은 것끼리 바르게 짝지어진 것은?

① protecting – isn't it – join
② to protect – isn't it – join
③ protecting – isn't it – join with
④ to protect – doesn't it – join with
⑤ protecting – doesn't it – join

29 다음 중 위 글의 내용과 일치하는 것은?

① Suji wants to join the "Save the Earth" club.
② Someone pays some money to the club members.
③ Suji thinks that it is important to protect our planet.
④ The purpose of the campaign was wasting food.
⑤ The club members don't have any plans for this year.

[30~32] 다음 글을 읽고 물음에 답하시오.

Hello, friends! I'm Diego ①of "Fly High." It is a drone club. We study every part of a drone and ②make some small drones by ourselves. When you have your own drone, you need ③ to practice hovering. "Hovering" means ④ staying in the same place in the air. Once you are good ⓐ_____ hovering, you will be ready to fly your drone in different directions. You're getting excited, ⑤don't you?

30 다음 중 빈칸 ⓐ에 들어갈 말과 같은 것은?

① I feel proud _____ myself.
② Are you interested _____ knitting?
③ Do you mind turning _____ the light?
④ The plane took _____ at 8 o'clock.
⑤ I will stay _____ my friend's home.

31 밑줄 친 ①~⑤ 중 어법상 바르지 <u>않은</u> 것을 골라 바르게 고쳐 쓰시오.

➡ _____

32 다음 중 위 글을 읽고 답할 수 <u>없는</u> 것은?

① What club is Diego in?
② What is the name of the drone club?
③ What do the club members study?
④ How many drones did the club members make?
⑤ What should you be good at in order to fly your drone in different directions?

[33~36] 다음 글을 읽고 물음에 답하시오.

Welcome to my musical club, "Story Singers"! My name is Olivia. In the musical club, there are two groups: actors and crew. We first choose the subject of our musical and then write a story together. Then, the actors practice singing and dancing, while the crew make costumes. We perform our musical in the school festival. You can get an application from me. You will join our club, won't you?

33 다음 중 위 글의 내용과 일치하는 것은?

① Olivia belongs to actors group.
② Olivia doesn't choose the subject of the musical.
③ The members don't dance in the musical.
④ You need an application to join the club.
⑤ Teachers help the members make costumes.

34 Where do they perform their musical? Answer in English with a full sentence.

➡ _____

35 다음은 동아리의 제작진과 배우의 대화이다. 빈칸에 알맞은 말을 쓰시오.

A: What do you do _____ _____ _____ _____?
B: I practice dancing and singing while you do it.

36 다음과 같이 풀이되는 단어를 위 글에서 찾아 쓰시오.

the set of clothes that actors wear while they are performing

➡ _____

단원별 예상문제

[01~02] 다음 글을 읽고 물음에 답하시오.

Inho: Hello, I'm Inho from the school newspaper club. Daily school life is our topic for the newspaper this month. Studying different subjects is the biggest part of our school life. ⓐ The most popular subject was P.E. ⓑ 35% of students said they liked P.E. best. The second most popular subject was English. ⓒ 25% of students said they were interested in English. Music and social studies were the third most popular subjects. ⓓ 15% of students liked music and another 15% liked social studies. ⓔ What is your favorite subject?

출제율 95%

01 위 글의 ⓐ~ⓔ 중 주어진 문장이 들어가기에 가장 적절한 곳은?

We asked all the second graders about their favorite subject.

① ⓐ ② ⓑ ③ ⓒ ④ ⓓ ⑤ ⓔ

출제율 85%

02 위 글을 읽고 대답할 수 없는 것은?

① What was the topic for the school newspaper this month?
② What club is Inho in?
③ What percent of students were interested in English?
④ What was the most popular subject among the students?
⑤ What was the least popular subject among the students?

[03~04] 다음 글을 읽고 물음에 답하시오.

G: What's your favorite hobby? We asked the students at our school and all of them (A) [answering / answered] the question. Most of the students said they liked watching movies. 20 boys and 42 girls loved it. This means a total of 62 students said watching movies (B) [was / were] their favorite hobby. Many boys liked playing computer games. 32 boys and 13 girls liked doing that. 25 boys and 20 girls liked sports. Their favorite sports (C)[was / were] soccer, baseball, and basketball.

출제율 100%

03 위 글의 (A)~(C)에 들어갈 말로 적절한 것을 쓰시오.

➡ (A) _____, (B) _____, (C) _____

출제율 90%

04 위 글의 내용과 일치하지 않는 것은?

① Most of the students enjoy watching movies.
② 42 female students love watching movies.
③ The most popular hobby of male students is playing computer games.
④ The number of the students who like sports is 45.
⑤ The least popular hobby among girls is playing sports.

[05~06] 다음 대화를 읽고 물음에 답하시오.

B: I'm hungry. Did you have lunch?
G: No. Let's have lunch together. (A)좋아하는 음식이 뭐야?
B: I love chicken. Why don't we order it?
G: That's a good idea.

05 위 대화의 밑줄 친 (A)의 우리말을 영어로 쓰시오.

➡ _____

출제율 95%

06 What are they going to do next?

➡ _____

[07~09] 다음 대화를 읽고 물음에 답하시오.

Junho: Adia, you know what? We have to choose our club next week.

Adia: I know. (A)_____

Junho: I'm interested in the photo club.

Adia: Sounds great. Look at this chart. 80% of the photo club's members said that they liked ⓐits activities last year.

Junho: That's right. How ____(B)____ you, Adia? What's your favorite club?

Adia: I want to join the board game club. ____(C)____ last year ⓑits members said that they didn't like ⓒit much.

Junho: You're right. 60% of its members said they didn't like ⓓit.

Adia: Yes. I'm going to think about ⓔit more.

출제율 100%

07 위 대화의 밑줄 친 ⓐ~ⓔ 중 가리키는 대상이 나머지 넷과 다른 것은?

① ⓐ ② ⓑ ③ ⓒ ④ ⓓ ⑤ ⓔ

출제율 95%

08 위 대화의 빈칸 (A)에 들어갈 말을 주어진 단어를 배열하여 영작하시오.

┌─ 보기 ┤

in / do / mind / which / you / club / have

➡ _____

출제율 90%

09 위 대화의 (B)와 (C)에 알맞은 것으로 짝지어진 것은?

① of – But ② about – But
③ of – And ④ about – And
⑤ with – For

출제율 90%

10 다음 대화의 내용과 일치하지 않는 것은?

Mike: Jenny, why the long face?

Jenny: I have to buy my friend's birthday present, but I can't choose the present.

Mike: Look at this chart from the Internet. It is about popular birthday presents.

Jenny: What is the most popular present?

Mike: A soccer ball for boys and a diary for girls.

Jenny: My friend is not interested in sports. What is the second most popular present for a boy?

Mike: For both boys and girls, the second most popular present is a cap.

Jenny: Okay. I'll buy a cap.

① Mike와 Jenny는 인터넷에서 인기 있는 생일 선물에 관한 도표를 보고 있다.
② 남학생들에게 가장 인기 있는 선물은 축구공이다.
③ 일기장은 여학생들에게 가장 인기 있는 선물이다.
④ Jenny의 친구는 스포츠에 관심이 많다.
⑤ Jenny는 친구의 생일 선물로 모자를 살 것이다.

출제율 95%

11 다음 문장의 빈칸에 들어갈 말로 가장 적절한 것은?

_____ your bag again, I will not buy you one again.

① Because you lost ② If you lose
③ If you will lose ④ As you lost
⑤ Though you lose

출제율 90%

12 다음 우리말을 영어로 바르게 옮긴 것은?

> 내일 그를 만나면, 이 파일을 전해줄게.

① If I will meet him tomorrow, I will give him this file.
② If I met him tomorrow, I will give him this file.
③ If I meet him tomorrow, I will give him this file.
④ If you meet him tomorrow, I will give him this file.
⑤ If you meet him tomorrow, you will give this file to him.

출제율 95%

13 다음 빈칸에 알맞은 말을 쓰시오.

> **A:** What _____ _____ _____ if you _____ _____ _____?
> **B:** If I have time tomorrow, I will play a computer game.

출제율 100%

14 다음 중 어법상 바르지 <u>않은</u> 것은?

① If he leaves here, where will he go?
② Let me know if you will go to church on foot.
③ The car and the bike are yours, aren't you?
④ She didn't feel tired, did she?
⑤ I did the right thing, didn't I?

출제율 90%

15 주어진 단어를 바르게 배열하여 다음 우리말을 영어로 쓰시오. 필요하다면 단어를 첨가하시오.

> 그는 항상 일을 열심히 해, 그렇지 않니?
> (he / he / always / hard / works)

➡ _____

출제율 95%

16 주어진 단어를 활용하여 다음 우리말을 영어로 쓰시오.

> 내일 아침에 널 보지 못하면, 내일 오후에 너에게 전화할게. (see / call / tomorrow afternoon)

➡ _____
_____

출제율 95%

17 다음 빈칸에 들어갈 말이 바르게 짝지어진 것은?

> • The news about the accident was surprising, _____?
> • If she _____ my pan, I will be glad.

① isn't it – will use ② wan't it – uses
③ aren't they – will use ④ was it – uses
⑤ is it – will use

출제율 85%

18 다음 주어진 문장과 자연스럽게 이어지도록 (A)~(C)를 바르게 나열한 것은?

> Hello, friends! I'm Diego of "Fly High."

(A) When you have your own drone, you need to practice hovering. "Hovering" means staying in the same place in the air.
(B) It is a drone club. We study every part of a drone and make some small drones by ourselves.
(C) Once you are good at hovering, you will be ready to fly your drone in different directions. You're getting excited, aren't you?

① (A)-(C)-(B) ② (B)-(A)-(C)
③ (B)-(C)-(A) ④ (C)-(A)-(B)
⑤ (C)-(B)-(A)

[19~22] 다음 글을 읽고 물음에 답하시오.

Hello, I'm Junho. What do you want ⓐ _____ when you see beautiful scenery? You want to take a picture of it, don't you? If you join our photo club, "Photo World," you can meet famous photographers and learn their skills. Every December, you can take part in the school photo contest. So, by joining "Photo World" you can learn a new hobby and have a chance of winning a prize!

출제율 90%

19 다음 중 빈칸 ⓐ에 들어갈 동사 do의 형태와 같은 것은?

① I enjoy _____ the dishes.
② What do you _____ for a living?
③ Would you _____ me a favor?
④ What can I _____ for you?
⑤ What are you going _____ this weekend?

출제율 95%

20 다음 중 위 글의 내용과 일치하지 <u>않는</u> 것은?

① Junho is a member of "Photo World."
② You can learn to take pictures in the club.
③ There is a school photo contest every year.
④ The school photo contest is held in the summer.
⑤ The club members can participate in the photo contest.

출제율 100%

21 위 글의 내용에 맞게 다음 빈칸에 알맞은 말을 쓰시오.

If you _____ _____ _____
_____, famous photographers _____
_____ you their skills.

출제율 85%

22 다음 빈칸에 들어갈 말을 위 글에서 찾아 쓰시오.

The _____ in a country area is the land, water, or plants that you can see around you.

[23~25] 다음 글을 읽고 물음에 답하시오.

Welcome to my musical club, "Story Singers"! My name is Olivia. In the musical club, there ①are two groups: actors and ②crew. We first choose the subject of our musical and then write a story together. Then, the actors practice ③ singing and dancing, ④while the crew make costumes. We perform our musical in the school festival. You can get an application from me. You ⑤join our club, won't you?

출제율 90%

23 다음 중 위 글을 읽고 답할 수 있는 것은?

① How many members are there in the musical club?
② How many actors are there in the musical club?
③ What kind of subject are they going to choose?
④ Who wants to join the club?
⑤ What do the crew do while the actors doing their things?

출제율 95%

24 밑줄 친 ①~⑤ 중 어법상 바르지 <u>않은</u> 것은?

①   ②   ③   ④   ⑤

출제율 90%

25 위 글의 내용에 맞게 다음 물음에 영어로 답하시오.

Q: Who has applications?

➡ _____

[01~03] 다음 대화를 읽고 물음에 영어로 답하시오.

Brian: Look! This is a chart about our classmates' interests.

Sujin: Let's look at it more closely. The chart shows that 30% of students are interested in sports. The school's Sports Day will be so much fun.

Brian: Right. The chart also shows that 27% of students are interested in actors. I know you are also a big fan of them.

Sujin: Yes. I love them. How about you?

Brian: I'm not interested in actors. I'm interested in computer games. 20% of students are interested in them.

Sujin: Computer games are fun, but playing them too much is not good for you.

Brian: I agree.

01 Why does Sujin think that the school's Sports Day will be so much fun?

➡ _____

02 What are a fifth of students interested in?

➡ _____

03 What does Sujin think of playing computer games too much?

➡ _____

04 주어진 단어를 바르게 배열하여 다음 우리말을 영어로 쓰시오. 필요하다면 단어를 추가하거나 변형하시오.

우리 엄마가 내게 영어를 가르쳐 주신다면, 나는 공부를 더 열심히 할 거야.
(harder / if / study / my mom / me / I / English / teach)

➡ _____

05 다음 대화의 빈칸에 알맞은 말을 쓰시오.

A: _____ _____ _____ _____,
_____ _____?
B: Yes. I was sick yesterday, but I'm fine now.

06 주어진 단어를 활용하여 다음 우리말을 영어로 쓰시오.

그 소년들은 축구를 하길 원해, 그렇지 않니?
(play, soccer)

➡ _____

07 다음 빈칸에 알맞은 말을 쓰시오.

A: You lost the brush, _____ _____?
B: Yes. If you go to the market, _____ _____ buy me one?

08 다음 주어진 단어를 활용하여 빈칸에 알맞은 말을 쓰시오.

_____, will you go out with us? (busy)

= _____, will you go out with us?

[09~10] 다음 글을 읽고 물음에 답하시오.

Hello, friends! I'm Diego of "Fly High." It is a drone club. We study every part of a drone and make some small drones by ⓐus. When you have your own drone, you need to practice hovering. "Hovering" means staying in the same place in the air. Once you are good at hovering, you will be ready to fly your drone in different directions. You're getting excited, aren't you?

09 밑줄 친 ⓐ를 어법에 맞게 고치시오.

➡ _____

10 글의 내용에 맞게 다음 빈칸에 알맞은 말을 쓰시오.

A: Is the drone hovering in the air? It is so cool.
B: Thanks. Actually I _____ _____ _____ by myself.

[11~13] 다음 글을 읽고, 물음에 답하시오.

Hello, everyone! I'm Suji and I'm the leader of the "Save the Earth" club. Our club is an environmental club. We do volunteer work to protect our planet. Protecting our planet is important, isn't it? Last year, we carried out a campaign to reduce food waste in the school cafeteria. The campaign was successful. This year, we are preparing some special activities abroad. So, ⓐ지구를 구하는 데 관심이 있다면, please join us.

11 위 글을 읽고, 다음 대화의 내용을 알맞게 채우시오.

A: Suji, you are planning to do _____ _____ _____, _____ _____?
B: Yes, I am. We are going to go abroad to do them.

12 위 글의 표현을 이용하여 다음 우리말을 영어로 쓰시오.

학교 식당에서 음식물 쓰레기를 줄이는 것은 너희 캠페인이었어, 그렇지 않니?

➡ _____
_____

13 주어진 단어를 어법에 맞게 활용하여 밑줄 친 우리말 ⓐ를 영어로 쓰시오.

interested / the planet

➡ _____

01 그래프와 대화의 내용이 일치하도록 다음 빈칸을 완성하시오.

> Our Classmates' Interests
>
> ■ Sports ■ Computer Games
> ■ Actors ■ Cooking
>
> 30 27 20 15
>
> **Brian:** Look! This is a chart about our classmates' interests.
>
> **Sujin:** Let's look at it more closely. The chart shows that 30% of students are interested in (A)_____. The school's Sports Day will be so much fun.
>
> **Brian:** Right. The chart also shows that (B)_____ of students are interested in actors. I know you are also a big fan of them.
>
> **Sujin:** Yes. I love them. How about you?
>
> **Brian:** I'm not interested in actors. 20% of students are interested in (C)_____.
>
> **Sujin:** Computer games are fun, but playing them too much is not good for you.
>
> **Brian:** I agree.

➡ (A) _____, (B) _____, (C) _____

02 주어진 어구와 if를 이용하여 문장을 만드시오.

> drink milk   my favorite movie star   make many friends   become a writer

(1) _____
(2) _____
(3) _____
(4) _____

03 주어진 동사를 활용하여 여러 가지 부가의문문 문장을 쓰시오.

> like hate want break spill be

(1) _____
(2) _____
(3) _____
(4) _____
(5) _____
(6) _____

단원별 모의고사

01 다음 영영풀이가 가리키는 것을 고르시오.

> materials that are no longer needed and are thrown away

① waste   ② ingredient
③ object   ④ element
⑤ equipment

02 다음 주어진 문장의 밑줄 친 application과 다른 의미로 쓰인 것은?

> You can get an application from me.

① His application to the company was refused.
② Many scientists are studying the application of new technology to biology.
③ I sent an application for admission to Harvard University.
④ Would you fill out this application now?
⑤ I'll look over your application and then call you soon.

03 다음 우리말에 맞게 빈칸에 알맞은 말을 쓰시오.

(1) 너는 숙제를 혼자서 끝내야 한다.
➡ You should finish your homework _____ _____.

(2) 나는 많은 실험을 수행할 계획이다.
➡ I'm planning to _____ _____ lots of experiments.

(3) 연못에 빠지지 않게 조심해.
➡ Be careful not to _____ _____ the pond.

[04~06] 다음 글을 읽고 물음에 답하시오.

G: What's your favorite hobby? We asked the students at our school and all of them answered the question. Most of the students said they liked watching movies. 20 boys and 42 girls loved it. This means a total of 62 students said watching movies was their favorite hobby. Many boys liked playing computer games. 32 boys and 13 girls liked doing that. 25 boys and 20 girls liked sports. Their favorite sports were soccer, baseball, and basketball.

04 Which hobby is the most popular among the students?

➡ _____
_____

05 How many boy students like playing computer games?

➡ _____

06 Which hobby is the least popular among boy students?

➡ _____

[07~08] 다음 대화를 읽고 물음에 답하시오.

G: You look ⓐtiring. What's the matter?
B: (A)_____
G: What did you watch?
B: I watched a traveling program. I'm ⓑ interesting in traveling.

07 위 대화의 밑줄 친 ⓐ와 ⓑ를 문맥에 맞게 고치시오.

➡ ⓐ: _____ ⓑ: _____

08 위 대화의 빈칸 (A)에 들어갈 말을 〈보기〉에 주어진 단어를 모두 배열하여 영작하시오.

> ┌── 보기 ├──
> TV / stayed / late / I / to / watch / up

➡ _____

09 다음 우리말을 주어진 단어를 이용하여 영작하시오.

(1) 동아리에 가입함으로써, 너는 건강을 유지하고 스트레스를 줄일 수 있다. (shape, joining)

➡ _____

_____

(2) 나는 네가 비틀즈의 열렬한 팬이라는 것을 알아. (*The Beatles*, big)

➡ _____

(3) 너는 어느 활동을 마음에 두고 있니? (which, have)

➡ _____

10 다음 우리말에 맞게 빈칸에 알맞은 말을 쓰시오.

(1) 왜 우울하니?

➡ Why the _____ _____ ?

(2) 지금 당장 계획을 수행하자.

➡ Let's _____ _____ the plan right now.

(3) 나는 혼자 이것을 할 수 없기 때문에 네 도움이 필요해.

➡ I need your help because I can't do it _____ _____ .

[11~12] 다음 대화를 읽고 물음에 답하시오.

Mike: Jenny, why the long face?

Jenny I have to buy my friend's birthday present, but I can't choose the present.

Mike: Look at this chart from the internet. It is about popular birthday presents.

Jenny What is the most popular present?

Mike: A soccer ball for boys and a diary for girls.

Jenny My friend is not interested in sports. What is the second most popular present for a boy?

Mike: For both boys and girls, the second most popular present is a cap.

Jenny Okay. I'll buy a cap.

11 What is the second most popular present for girls?

➡ _____

12 What is Jenny going to buy as her friend's birthday present?

➡ _____

13 다음 빈칸에 들어갈 말로 가장 적절한 것은?

> The nurses took care of me very well, _____ ?

① don't you   ② didn't you

③ didn't they   ④ aren't you

⑤ did they

14 다음 중 어법상 바르지 않은 것은?

> You are ①looking for a place to live, ② aren't you? ③Unless you can't ④find a right place for you, where ⑤will you go?

①   ②   ③   ④   ⑤

15 다음 우리말을 영어로 쓰시오.

> 그는 지금 바쁘지 않아, 그렇지?

➡ _____

16 다음 중 어법상 어색한 것은?

① If you leave me, I will be very sad.
② Frank drank lots of water, didn't he?
③ The kids kicked the ball, didn't they?
④ If you take a taxi, you will be here soon.
⑤ He never called you back, didn't he?

17 주어진 단어를 활용하여 다음 우리말을 영어로 쓰시오.

> 네가 아프면, 내가 널 병원으로 데려갈게.
> (take / to)

➡ _____

[18~21] 다음 글을 읽고 물음에 답하시오.

> Hello, everyone! I'm Suji and I'm the leader of the "Save the Earth" club. Our club is an ①environmental club. We do volunteer work ②to protect our planet. Protecting our planet is ③important, isn't it? Last year, we carried out a campaign ④to produce food waste in the school cafeteria. The campaign was successful. This year, we are preparing some special activities abroad. So, if you are ⑤ interested in saving the planet, please join us.

18 ①~⑤ 중 글의 흐름상 어색한 것은?

①   ②   ③   ④   ⑤

19 According to the passage, what are they planning this year? Answer in English with a full sentence.

➡ _____
_____

20 다음 중 위 글을 읽고 답할 수 <u>없는</u> 것은?

① What club is Suji in?
② Why did the club members carry out the campaign last year?
③ Why do the club members volunteer work?
④ What are the club members preparing this year?
⑤ How much food waste did the club members reduce?

21 다음 중 위 글에서 유의어를 찾을 수 <u>없는</u> 것은?

① unique   ② preserve   ③ overseas
④ garbage   ⑤ attack

[22~23] 다음 글을 읽고 물음에 답하시오.

Hello, friends! I'm Diego of "Fly High." It is a drone club. We study every part of a drone and make some small drones by ourselves. When you have your own drone, you need to practice hovering. "Hovering" means staying in the same place in the air. ⓐ_____ you are good at hovering, you will be ready to fly your drone in different directions. You're getting excited, aren't you?

22 다음 중 빈칸 ⓐ에 들어갈 말로 가장 적절한 것은?

① Because   ② Although
③ Once   ④ Until
⑤ Unless

23 다음 중 위 글의 내용과 일치하는 것은?

① Diego is not interested in flying a drone.
② The club members don't have an interest in studying drones.
③ The club members can make small drones on their own.
④ Practicing hovering is not important.
⑤ Hovering means flying drones high.

[24~25] 다음 글을 읽고, 물음에 답하시오.

Hello, friends! Nice to meet you. I'm Susan from "Cool Ride." It is a bike club. We ride bikes every Wednesday after school. We ride them in the park next to our school. By joining our club, you can keep in shape and reduce stress at the same time. If you are riding a bike, you can go faster than anyone. But be careful! Always remember that safety is the most important thing. Are you a beginner? If so, you don't have to worry about your bike riding skills because we have special lessons for beginners. (A)재미있게 들리지, 그렇지 않니?

24 밑줄 친 우리말 (A)를 영어로 옮기시오. (4 words)

➡ _____

25 다음 중 위 글의 내용과 일치하지 <u>않는</u> 것은?

① Susan rides a bike every Wednesday with her club members.
② Riding a bike helps you keep in shape.
③ Riding a bike is helpful to reduce stress.
④ Although you are a beginner, there is nothing to worry about.
⑤ Beginners have to learn bike riding skills by themselves.

Lesson 2

Planting Seeds of Hope

 의사소통 기능

- 보고하기
  The weather report said that yellow dust would be terrible today.

- 기대 표현하기
  We are looking forward to stopping the yellow dust.

 언어 형식

- 의문사+to부정사
  Most people did not know **how to stop** the yellow dust problem.

- 목적을 나타내는 부사절 so that
  People began to cut down trees **so that** they **could** build cities.

Words & Expressions

Key Words

- **advice** [ædváis] 명 조언
- **brush** [brʌʃ] 동 이를 닦다, 머리를 빗다
- **cause** [kɔːz] 명 원인
- **crybaby** [kráibeibi] 명 울보
- **desert** [dézərt] 명 사막
- **dust** [dʌst] 명 먼지
- **engineer** [èndʒiníər] 명 기술자, 기관사
- **environment** [inváirənmnt] 명 환경
- **festival** [féstəvəl] 명 축제
- **fight** [fait] 동 싸우다
- **forest** [fɔ́ːrist] 명 숲
- **future** [fjúːtʃər] 명 미래
- **global** [glóubəl] 형 세계적인, 지구의
- **guest** [gest] 명 손님
- **hero** [híərou] 명 영웅
- **homework** [hóumwərk] 명 숙제
- **kick** [kik] 동 차다
- **map** [mæp] 명 지도
- **match** [mætʃ] 명 경기
- **mistake** [mistéik] 명 실수

- **past** [pæst] 명 과거, 형 지나간
- **performance** [pərfɔ́ːrməns] 명 공연
- **plant** [plænt] 동 심다, 명 식물, 공장
- **prepare** [prípeər] 동 준비하다
- **protect** [prətékt] 동 보호하다
- **seed** [siːd] 명 씨앗
- **share** [ʃɛər] 동 나누다
- **sneeze** [sniːz] 동 재채기하다
- **solution** [səlúːʃən] 명 해결책
- **terrible** [térəbl] 형 끔찍한
- **throat** [θrout] 명 목(구멍)
- **togetherness** [təgéðərnis] 명 친목, 연대감
- **trash** [træʃ] 명 쓰레기
- **trip** [trip] 명 여행
- **unwelcome** [ənwélkəm] 형 환영 받지 못하는
- **upset** [ʌ́pset] 형 화난
- **volunteer** [váləntiər] 동 자원봉사하다
- **wash** [waʃ] 동 씻다
- **wear** [wɛər] 동 입다
- **widespread** [wáidspred] 형 널리 퍼진

Key Expressions

- **a long time ago** 옛날에
- **can't wait to** 빨리 ~하고 싶어하다
- **catch a cold** 감기에 걸리다
- **come about** 발생하다
- **find out** 알아내다, 알아차리다
- **get rid of** ~을 없애다
- **look forward to -ing** ~을 고대하다, 기대하다

- **keep away from** ~을 피하다
- **keep on** 계속하다
- **not only A but also B** A뿐만 아니라 B도
- **take a look at** ~을 살펴보다
- **throw away** 버리다
- **turn off** ~을 끄다
- **yellow dust** 황사

Word Power

※ 서로 반대되는 뜻을 가진 단어

☐ **cause** 원인 ↔ **result** 결과

☐ **turn on** ~을 켜다 ↔ **turn off** ~을 끄다

☐ **sick** 아픈 ↔ **healthy** 건강한

☐ **send** 보내다 ↔ **receive** 받다

☐ **hero** 영웅 ↔ **villain** 악당

☐ **expensive** 비싼 ↔ **cheap** 값이 싼

☐ **upset** 화난 ↔ **calm** 침착한

☐ **pick** 뽑다 ↔ **plant** 심다

☐ **future** 미래 ↔ **past** 과거

☐ **global** 세계적인 ↔ **local** 지역의

☐ **guest** 손님 ↔ **host** 주인, 사회자

☐ **waste** 낭비하다 ↔ **save** 절약하다

English Dictionary

☐ **desert** 사막
→ a large area of land that has very little water and very few plants growing on it
이곳에 자라는 식물이 거의 없거나 물이 거의 없는 넓은 지역의 땅

☐ **cause** 원인
→ the person or thing that makes something happen
무언가 일어나게 만드는 사람 또는 일

☐ **environment** 환경
→ the natural world in which people, animals and plants live
사람, 동물, 그리고 식물들이 사는 자연 세상

☐ **forest** 숲
→ a large area of land that is thickly covered with trees
나무로 무성하게 덮여 있는 넓은 지역의 땅

☐ **hero** 영웅
→ a person, especially a man, who is admired by many people for doing something brave or good
용감하게나 좋은 일을 한 일에 대해 많은 사람들에 의해 칭찬받는 사람, 특히 남자

☐ **match** 경기
→ a sports event where people or teams compete against each other
사람들이나 팀들이 서로에 대항하여 경쟁하는 스포츠 행사

☐ **mistake** 실수
→ an action or an opinion that is not correct, or that produces a result that you did not want
맞지 않거나 당신이 원하지 않았던 결과를 만들어내는 행동 또는 의견

☐ **performance** 공연
→ the act of performing a play, concert or some other form of entertainment
연극, 콘서트 또는 다른 연예 형식을 수행하는 활동

☐ **plant** 심다
→ to put plants, seeds, etc. in the ground to grow
식물, 씨앗 등을 땅에 자라나도록 놓다

☐ **seed** 씨앗
→ the small hard part produced by a plant, from which a new plant can grow
그 부분에서 새로운 식물이 자랄 수 있는 식물에 의해 만들어지는 작고 단단한 부분

☐ **solution** 해결책
→ a way of solving a problem or dealing with a difficult situation
문제를 해결하거나 어려운 상황을 다루는 방식

☐ **togetherness** 친목, 연대감
→ the happy feeling you have when you are with people you like, especially family and friends
특히 가족, 친구들처럼 당신이 좋아하는 사람들과 함께 있을 때 갖는 행복한 감정

☐ **volunteer** 자원봉사하다
→ to offer to do something without being forced to do it or without getting paid for it
강요받거나 그것에 대해 돈을 받지 않고 무언가를 하기 위해 자청하다

☐ **widespread** 널리 퍼진
→ existing or happening over a large area or among many people
넓은 지역에 걸쳐서 또는 많은 사람들 사이에서 존재하거나 일어나는

01 다음 짝지어진 단어의 관계가 같도록 빈칸에 알맞은 말을 쓰시오.

> future : past = _____ : result

02 주어진 문장의 밑줄 친 brush의 의미와 같은 의미로 쓰인 것은?

> When you brush your teeth, you should use cups.

① What do you need to brush your shoes?
② This brush has been worn out.
③ The artist used various kinds of brush to work.
④ You'd better remove soil with a stiff brush.
⑤ My teacher told me to bring my brush and paint.

03 다음 중 밑줄 친 부분의 뜻풀이가 바르지 않은 것은?

① What was the cause of the fire? 원인
② We need to get rid of all this trash. 쓰레기
③ Share this cake with your friends. 나누다
④ She talked so loud that her throat hurt. 목
⑤ The band showed family togetherness.
　　　　　　　　　　　　　　　　　함께

04 다음 문장의 빈칸에 들어갈 말을 〈보기〉에서 골라 쓰시오.

> ┤ 보기 ├
> unwelcome / widespread / throat / share

(1) Two families can _____ this big house.
(2) Football players received _____ support.
(3) The yellow dust is called a(n) _____ guest.
(4) I have a runny nose and a sore _____ .

05 다음 영영풀이가 가리키는 것을 고르시오.

> the small hard part produced by a plant, from which a new plant can grow

① seed　　　　　② forest
③ match　　　　④ root
⑤ leaf

06 다음 문장에 공통으로 들어갈 말을 고르시오.

> • You should _____ away from the wild dogs.
> • You have to _____ on reading the book and find out the secret of popularity.
> • It is helpful to _____ you from making mistake.

① catch　　　　② keep
③ take　　　　　④ trip
⑤ fight

01 다음 짝지어진 단어의 관계가 같도록 빈칸에 알맞은 말을 쓰시오.

expensive : cheap = _____ : healthy

02 다음 문장의 빈칸에 들어갈 말을 〈보기〉에서 골라 쓰시오.

┌─ 보기 ┤
desert / seed / map / hero / trip
└─

(1) It's not easy to find water in the _____.
(2) I planted a tulip _____ in the garden in May.
(3) He marked his town on the _____.
(4) My father left for a business _____ to China.

03 다음 주어진 우리말과 일치하도록 주어진 단어를 모두 배열하여 완성하시오.

(1) 나의 영어 선생님은 친절할 뿐만 아니라 인기 있다.
(teacher / my / but / only / also / not / popular / kind / is / English)
➡ _____

(2) 어린이들이 선물을 받기를 기대하고 있다.
(forward / are / presents / children / looking / receiving / to)
➡ _____

(3) 내가 어떻게 비밀을 알아낼 수 있을까요?
(the / can / how / secret / out / I / find)
➡ _____

04 다음 우리말에 맞게 빈칸에 알맞은 말을 쓰시오.

(1) 나는 내 오랜 친구들을 빨리 만나고 싶어.
➡ I can't _____ _____ _____ my old friends.
(2) 어떻게 차 사고가 일어났니?
➡ How did the car accident_____ _____?
(3) 명단을 살펴보는 게 어때?
➡ How about _____ _____ _____ _____ the list?

05 다음 문장의 괄호 안에 알맞은 낱말을 고르시오.

(1) Let's wear our (masks / boots) because there is yellow dust.
(2) We should (plant / push) some trees to protect the environment.
(3) The rumor about the ghost (caught / spread) around the village.
(4) If some people help others for free, we call them (engineers / volunteers).
(5) I love animals, so I want to become a (vet / vat) in the future.

06 다음 우리말에 맞게 주어진 단어를 사용하여 영작하시오.

(1) 나는 제주도를 방문하길 기대하고 있어. (looking, Jejudo)
➡ _____

(2) 지도를 살펴보자. (look, take)
➡ _____

(3) 엄마는 나쁜 친구들을 피해야 한다고 말씀하셨다. (keep, should, away)
➡ _____

교과서

Conversation

1 보고하기

The weather report said that yellow dust would be terrible today.

일기 예보는 황사가 오늘 심할 것이라고 예보했다.

My homeroom teacher said that we should come to school early tomorrow.

담임 선생님은 우리가 내일 학교에 일찍 와야 한다고 말씀하셨다.

■ 'The news(weather report) said ~'처럼 뉴스나 일기 예보 등에서 들은 말을 전달할 때나 다른 사람에게 들은 말을 전달할 때 'He(She) said ~'와 같은 형식으로 나타낸다.

다른 사람의 말을 보고하는 표현

- He told me that she moved to New York. (그는 나에게 그녀가 뉴욕으로 이사 갔다고 말했다.)
- She explained to me that it wasn't a true story. (그녀는 나에게 이것은 실화가 아니라고 설명했다.)
- The news reported that the diamonds are genuine. (뉴스는 다이아몬드가 진품이라고 보도했다.)
- Emily spoke about the history of Korea. (Emily는 한국의 역사에 대해 이야기했다.)
- Jack mentioned that he would go fishing. (Jack은 그가 낚시를 갈 것이라고 언급했다.)

핵심 Check

1. 다음 우리말과 일치하도록 빈칸에 알맞은 말을 쓰시오.

(1) **A:** Why do you have an umbrella? (왜 우산을 갖고 있니?)

    B: _____ _____ _____ _____ it would rain this afternoon.

    (일기 예보에서 오늘 오후에 비가 온대.)

(2) **A:** What did he tell you? (그가 너에게 무엇을 이야기했니?)

    B: _____ _____ _____ _____ he didn't want to go to the school

    festival. (그는 학교 축제에 가고 싶지 않다고 내게 이야기했어.)

(3) **A:** Did the teacher give us any homework? (선생님이 숙제를 내주셨니?)

    B: Yes. _____ _____ _____ _____ _____ lesson 3 in our English

    book. (응. 그는 우리가 영어책에서 3과를 읽어야 한다고 말씀하셨어.)

② 기대 표현하기

We are looking forward to stopping the yellow dust. 우리는 황사가 멈추기를 기대하고 있다.

I can't wait to volunteer at a library this year. 나는 올해 빨리 도서관에서 봉사하고 싶어.

■ 'look forward to ~ing'는 '~을 기대하다, 고대하다'는 의미로 기대감을 나타내는 표현으로 'can't wait to ~' 등을 사용하여 기대감을 표현할 수도 있다.

기대감 표현하기

- I can't wait to see you soon. (너를 빨리 만나고 싶어.)
- I'm excited to go on a picnic. (나는 소풍가게 되어 신나.)
- I'm expecting to hear from Mr. Brown. (나는 Brown씨로부터 소식을 기다리고 있어요.)
- I anticipate happy holiday in Taiwan this summer. (나는 이번 여름 대만에서 행복한 휴가를 기대한다.)

핵심 Check

2. 다음 우리말과 일치하도록 빈칸에 알맞은 말을 쓰시오.

(1) **A:** What will you do this weekend? (이번 주말에 무엇을 할 거니?)

   B: I will go to the zoo. _____ _____ _____ _____ _____ _____.

   (나는 동물원에 갈 거야. 나는 동물들을 보길 기대하고 있어.)

(2) **A:** _____ _____ _____ _____ _____ _____. How about you? (나는 캠핑 가는 것이 너무 신나. 너는 어때?)

   B: Me too. I'm looking forward to the camping trip.

   (나도 그래. 나는 캠핑 가는 것을 기대하고 있어.)

(3) **A:** Someone said that the school band practiced a lot this time.

   (누군가 그러는데 학교 밴드가 이번에 연습을 아주 많이 했대.)

   B: _____ _____ _____ _____ hear them! (나는 그들을 빨리 듣고 싶어!)

Everyday English 1- B. Listening Activity

Sujin: John, what happened to your foot?

John: Last week, there was a soccer match. I kicked a rock ❶by mistake.

Sujin: Oh, your foot ❷must hurt very much! Did you go to the hospital?

John: Yes, the doctor ❸said I shouldn't play soccer for a month.

Sujin: Oh, no. What will you do for the next game?

John: I'll need to find another soccer player.

Sujin: ❹Why don't you ask Kevin? ❺He's good at playing soccer.

John: That's a good idea. I'll go ask him now.

Sujin: John, 발이 어떻게 된 거야?

John: 지난주에, 축구 시합이 있었어. 난 실수로 돌을 찼어.

Sujin: 오, 발이 진짜 아팠겠다! 병원에는 갔었어?

John: 응. 의사가 난 한 달 동안 축구하면 안 된다고 했어.

Sujin: 아, 안됐다. 다음 시합은 어떻게 할 거니?

John: 난 다른 축구 선수를 찾아야 해.

Sujin: Kevin에게 물어보는 게 어때? 그는 축구를 잘해.

John: 좋은 생각이야. 지금 그에게 물어봐야겠다.

❶ by mistake: 실수로   ❷ must: ~임에 틀림 없다
❸ 다른 사람에게 들은 말을 전달할 때 '주어+said ~'와 같은 형식으로 나타낸다.
❹ Why don't you ~?: '~하는 게 어때?'라고 제안하는 표현이다.   ❺ be good at: ~를 잘하다

Check(√) True or False

(1) John hurt his foot during the soccer match last week.　　　　　　　　　　T ☐ F ☐

(2) Sujin asked Kevin if he could take part in the next soccer game.　　　　　T ☐ F ☐

B. In Real Life

Diego: Achoo! Achoo!

Suji: Did you ❶catch a cold, Diego?

Diego: No, I don't feel sick, but I can't ❷stop sneezing. Achoo!

Suji: Then, it must be ❸because of the yellow dust. The weather report said the yellow dust would be terrible today.

Diego: Oh, I guess I'm sneezing because of ❹that. Can't we stop the yellow dust?

Suji: Yes, we can. My club members are preparing to do some special activities abroad.

Diego: What are they?

Suji: We're planning to plant trees in China because a lot of the yellow dust comes from China.

Diego: That sounds good.

Suji: Yes. We are ❺looking forward to stopping the yellow dust.

Diego: 에취! 에취!

Suji: 감기 걸렸니, Diego?

Diego: 아니, 아프진 않아. 하지만 재채기를 멈출 수가 없어. 에취!

Suji: 그럼 황사 때문일 거야. 일기 예보에서는 오늘 황사가 심각할 거라고 했어.

Diego: 아, 그것 때문에 재채기하나봐. 황사를 멈출 수 없을까?

Suji: 응, 우린 할 수 있어. 우리 동아리 회원들은 외국에서 특별한 활동을 할 준비를 하고 있어.

Diego: 그게 뭔데?

Suji: 우린 중국에 나무를 심을 계획을 하고 있어. 왜냐하면 황사의 대부분은 중국에서 오거든.

Diego: 멋지다.

Suji: 응. 우린 황사를 멈추길 기대하고 있어.

❶ catch a cold: 감기에 걸리다   ❷ stop ~ing: ~하던 것을 멈추다
❸ 'because of+명사(구)', 'because+주어+동사'   ❹ The yellow dust would be terrible today.를 가리킨다.
❺ look forward to ~ing: ~를 고대하다, 기대하다

Check(√) True or False

(3) Diego caught a cold, so he could not stop sneezing.　　　　　　　　　　T ☐ F ☐

(4) Suji's club members made a plan to plant trees in China.　　　　　　　　T ☐ F ☐

Everyday English 1 A. Function Practice 2-(1)

Lisa: Hey, Tom. Why didn't you come to school today?

Tom: I ❶had a bad cold. Did the teacher give us any homework?

Lisa: Yes. ❷He said ❸we should read lesson 3 in our English book.

Tom: Okay. Thank you, Lisa.

❶ have a cold: 감기에 걸리다
❷ the teacher에게 들은 말을 전달하고 있다.
❸ 숙제 내용을 가리킨다.

Everyday English 1 A. Function Practice 2-(2)

B: The weather is so nice today. Why do you have an umbrella?

G: ❶The weather report said it would rain this afternoon.

B: Oh, no. I didn't know ❷that! I don't have an umbrella.

G: Don't worry. You can ❸share my umbrella.

❶ 일기 예보에서 들은 말을 전달하고 있다.
❷ It would rain this afternoon.을 가리킨다.
❸ share: 나누다

Everyday English 1 A. Function Practice 2-(3)

Jane: Do you want to watch the movie, *The Big Zoo*?

Alex: No, I don't. My brother watched the movie last week. He said ❶it was ❷terrible.

Jane: Then, what shall we do?

Alex: We can ❸take a walk in the park ❹instead.

❶ The Big Zoo를 가리킨다.　　❷ terrible: 끔찍한
❸ take a walk: 산책하다　　❹ instead: ～대신에

Everyday English 2 A Function practice 2-(1)

Brain: Susan, do you want to watch a movie this Saturday?

Susan: Sure. What movie do you want to watch?

Brain: The new superhero movie just ❶came out. ❷I'm looking forward to seeing ❸it.

Susan: Wow! I love superhero movies. See you then!

❶ come out: 나오다　　❷ look forward to ~ing: ～를 고대하다, 기대하다
❸ it은 the new superhero movie를 가리킨다.

Everyday English 2 A Function practice 2-(2)

B: You ❶look happy. What's up?

G: ❷I'm looking forward to the school festival this weekend.

B: ❸Me too! Someone said that the school band practiced a lot this time.

G: I ❹can't wait to hear them!

❶ look + 형용사: ～해 보이다
❷ look forward to ~ing: ～를 고대하다, 기대하다
❸ Me too. = So am I. = 나도 그래.
❹ can't wait to: 빨리 ～하고 싶어하다

Everyday English 2 B. Listening Activity

Chris: Do you have any plans for this coming Friday?

Emily: I do. I ❶volunteer at a lost pet center every Friday.

Chris: What do you do at the lost pet center?

Emily: Well, I take the dogs out for a walk. Also, I help to wash ❷them.

Chris: That sounds wonderful. Why do you go ❸there every week?

Emily: It's because I love animals. I want to become ❹an animal doctor in the future.

Chris: I love animals too. Can I join you this Friday?

Emily: Sure. I look forward to seeing you at the center.

❶ volunteer: 자원 봉사하다　　　　❷ them은 dogs를 가리킨다.
❸ there는 the lost pet center을 가리킨다.
❹ an animal doctor = a vet(veterinarian) = 수의사

● 다음 우리말과 일치하도록 빈칸에 알맞은 말을 쓰시오.

Everyday English 1 A. Function Practice 2-(1)

Lisa: Hey, Tom. Why didn't you come to school today?

Tom: _____ _____ _____ _____ _____. Did the teacher give us any homework?

Lisa: Yes. _____ _____ we should read lesson 3 in our English book.

Tom: Okay. Thank you, Lisa.

Everyday English 1 A. Function Practice 2-(2)

B: The weather is so nice today. Why do you have an umbrella?

G: _____ _____ _____ _____ _____ _____ _____ _____ _____ _____.

B: Oh, no. I didn't know that! I don't have an umbrella.

G: Don't worry. _____ _____ _____ _____ _____.

Everyday English 1 A. Function Practice 2-(3)

Jane: Do you want to watch the movie, *The Big Zoo*?

Alex: No, I don't. My brother watched the movie last week. _____ _____ _____ _____ _____.

Jane: Then, what shall we do?

Alex: We can _____ _____ _____ _____ _____ _____ instead.

Everyday English 1 B. Listening Activity

Sujin: John, what happened to your foot?

John: Last week, there was a soccer match. I kicked a rock _____ _____.

Sujin: Oh, _____ _____ _____ _____ _____ _____! Did you go to the hospital?

John: Yes, _____ _____ _____ I shouldn't play soccer for a month.

Sujin: Oh, no. What will you do for the next game?

John: I'll need to find another soccer player.

Sujin: _____ _____ _____ _____ _____? He's _____ _____ _____ _____.

John: That's a good idea. I'll go ask him now.

해석

Lisa: 안녕, Tom. 오늘 왜 학교에 오지 않았니?
Tom: 감기가 심했어. 선생님이 숙제를 내주셨니?
Lisa: 응. 그는 우리가 영어책에서 3과를 읽어야 한다고 말씀하셨어.
Tom: 알았어. 고마워, Lisa.

B: 오늘 날씨가 정말 좋다. 너는 왜 우산을 가져왔니?
G: 일기 예보에서 오늘 오후에 비가 온대.
B: 오, 이런. 나는 몰랐단 말야! 나는 우산이 없어.
G: 걱정 마. 나랑 우산 같이 쓰자.

Jane: 넌 Big Zoo라는 영화 보고 싶니?
Alex: 아니. 내 남동생이 지난주에 그 영화를 봤어. 끔찍하다고 말했어.
Jane: 그럼, 우리 뭐 할까?
Alex: 대신에 공원에서 산책을 할 수 있지.

Sujin: John, 발이 어떻게 된 거야?
John: 지난주에, 축구 시합이 있었어. 난 실수로 돌을 찼어.
Sujin: 오, 발이 진짜 아팠겠다! 병원에는 갔었어?
John: 응, 의사가 난 한 달 동안 축구하면 안 된다고 했어.
Sujin: 아, 안됐다. 다음 시합은 어떻게 할 거니?
John: 난 다른 축구 선수를 찾아야 해.
Sujin: Kevin에게 물어보는 게 어때? 그는 축구를 잘해.
John: 좋은 생각이야. 지금 그에게 물어봐야겠다.

Everyday English 2 A Function practice 2-(1)

Brain: Susan, do you want to watch a movie this Saturday?
Susan: Sure. _____ _____ _____ _____
_____?
Brain: The new superhero movie just came out. _____ _____
_____ _____ _____ _____.

Susan: Wow! I love superhero movies. See you then!

Everyday English 2 B. Listening Activity

Chris: Do you have any plans for this coming Friday?
Emily: I do. _____ _____ _____ _____ _____
_____ _____ _____.

Chris: What do you do at the lost pet center?
Emily: Well, _____ _____ _____ _____ _____
_____ _____. Also, I help to wash them.
Chris: That sounds wonderful. Why do you go there every week?
Emily: It's because I love animals. _____ _____ _____
_____ _____ _____ _____ _____ _____.

Chris: I love animals too. Can I join you this Friday?
Emily: Sure. _____ _____ _____ _____ _____
_____ _____ _____.

In Real Life

Diego: Achoo! Achoo!
Suji: Did you catch a cold, Diego?
Diego: No, I don't feel sick, but _____ _____ _____ _____.
Achoo!
Suji: Then, it must be _____ _____ _____ _____ _____.
_____ _____ _____ the yellow dust would be
_____ today.
Diego: Oh, I guess _____ _____ _____ _____ _____.
Can't we stop the yellow dust?
Suji: Yes, we can. My club members are preparing to do some special
activities abroad.
Diego: What are they?
Suji: _____ _____ _____ _____ _____ _____
_____ because a lot of the yellow dust comes from China.
Diego: That sounds good.
Suji: Yes. _____ _____ _____ _____ _____
_____ _____ _____.

해석

Brian: Susan, 이번 주 토요일에 영화
볼래?
Susan: 좋아. 넌 무슨 영화 보고 싶니?
Brian: 새로운 슈퍼 영웅 영화가 막 나왔
어. 난 그 영화를 정말 보고 싶어.
Susan: 와! 나는 슈퍼 영웅 영화를 정말
좋아해. 그때 보자!

Chris: 다가오는 금요일에 계획 있니?
Emily: 있어. 난 금요일마다 유기동물 센
터에서 자원봉사를 해.
Chris: 유기동물 센터에서 뭐해?
Emily: 음, 난 개를 산책시켜. 또한 씻기
는 것도 도와.
Chris: 멋지구나. 왜 매주 거기에 가니?
Emily: 난 동물이 좋아. 장래에 수의사가
되고 싶어.
Chris: 나도 동물이 좋아. 이번 금요일에
같이 가도 될까?
Emily: 그래. 센터에서 보기를 기대해.

Diego: 에취! 에취!
Suji: 감기 걸렸니, Diego?
Diego: 아니, 아프진 않아. 하지만 재채
기를 멈출 수가 없어. 에취!
Suji: 그럼 황사 때문일 거야. 일기 예보
에서는 오늘 황사가 심각할 거라고
했어.
Diego: 아, 그것 때문에 재채기하나봐.
황사를 멈출 수 없을까?
Suji: 응, 우린 할 수 있어. 우리 동아리
회원들은 외국에서 특별한 활동을
할 준비를 하고 있어.
Diego: 그게 뭔데?
Suji: 우린 중국에 나무를 심을 계획을
하고 있어. 왜냐하면 황사의 대부분
은 중국에서 오거든.
Diego: 멋지다.
Suji: 응. 우린 황사를 멈추길 기대하고
있어.

Conversation 시험대비 기본평가

01 다음 대화의 빈칸에 들어갈 말로 적절한 것은?

> A: What did your math teacher say?
> B: _____

① She said I should study harder.
② Because there was so much trash in the park.
③ I was angry last weekend.
④ Someone said Sujin won the dance contest last month.
⑤ It's because there will be a class meeting tomorrow.

02 다음 대화가 자연스럽게 이어지도록 순서대로 배열하시오.

> (A) Okay. Thank you, Lisa.
> (B) Hey, Tom. Why didn't you come to school today?
> (C) Yes. He said we should read lesson 3 in our English book.
> (D) I had a bad cold. Did the teacher give us any homework?

➡ _____

[03~04] 다음 대화를 읽고 물음에 답하시오.

> B: The weather is so nice today. Why do you have an umbrella?
> G: The weather report said it would rain this afternoon.
> B: Oh, no. I didn't know ⓐthat! I don't have an umbrella.
> G: Don't worry. You can ⓑ_____ my umbrella.

03 위 대화의 밑줄 친 ⓐ가 의미하는 것을 우리말 15자 내외로 쓰시오.

➡ _____

04 위 대화의 빈칸 ⓑ에 들어갈 말로 적절한 것은?

① collect   ② gather
③ share   ④ divide
⑤ split

01 다음 대화의 빈칸에 들어갈 말로 적절한 것은?

> A: I'm so excited to be going camping. How about you?
> B: Me too. _____

① I don't like a camping trip.
② I'm looking forward to the camping trip.
③ I'm scared of camping.
④ I'm afraid of a camping trip.
⑤ I used to go camping.

[02~03] 다음 대화를 읽고 물음에 답하시오.

> Brain: Susan, do you want to watch a movie this Saturday?
> Susan: Sure. What movie do you want to watch?
> Brain: The new superhero movie just came out. (A)_____
> Susan: Wow! I love superhero movies. See you then!

서답형

02 What kind of movie are Brian and Susan going to see?

➡ _____

03 위 대화의 빈칸 (A)에 들어가기에 어색한 것은?

① I'm looking forward to seeing it.
② I'm not able to see it.
③ I'm excited to see it.
④ I can't wait to see it.
⑤ I really want to see it.

[04~05] 다음 대화를 읽고 물음에 답하시오.

> Chris: Do you have any plans for this coming Friday?
> Emily: I do. I volunteer at a lost pet center every Friday.
> Chris: What do you do at the lost pet center?
> Emily: (A) Also, I help to wash them.
> Chris: (B) That sounds wonderful. Why do you go there every week?
> Emily: (C) It's because I love animals. I want to become an animal doctor in the future.
> Chris: (D) I love animals too. Can I join you this Friday?
> Emily: (E) Sure. I look forward to seeing you at the center.

04 위 대화의 (A)~(E) 중 주어진 문장이 들어가기에 적절한 곳은?

> Well, I take the dogs out for a walk.

① (A) ② (B) ③ (C) ④ (D) ⑤ (E)

05 위 대화를 읽고 대답할 수 없는 것은?

① What is Emily going to do this Friday?
② What does Emily do at the lost pet center?
③ What is Emily's dream in the future?
④ What does Chris want to do this Friday?
⑤ Why does Chris go to the lost pet center every week?

[06~07] 다음 대화를 읽고 물음에 답하시오.

> Minji: I was so angry yesterday.
>
> Eric: (A) Why, what happened?
>
> Minji: (B) Yesterday, I went to the park. Many people were there.
>
> Eric: (C) Were you angry about that?
>
> Minji: (D) I was angry because I saw those people picking the flowers and kicking the trees.
>
> Eric: (E) Oh, that is not good.
>
> Minji: Yes, I told them to stop, but they said they didn't care about the flowers or the trees.

06 위 대화의 (A)~(E) 중 다음 주어진 문장이 들어가기에 적절한 곳은?

> Of course not.

① (A) ② (B) ③ (C) ④ (D) ⑤ (E)

07 위 대화의 내용과 일치하지 않는 것은?

① Minji went to the park yesterday.
② Minji was upset because of many people at the park.
③ Minji saw many people picking the flowers and kicked the trees.
④ Many people didn't care about the flowers and trees at the park.
⑤ Minji tried to keep people from picking flowers, but it didn't work.

[08~09] 다음 대화를 읽고 물음에 답하시오.

> Jane: Do you want to watch the movie, *The Big Zoo*?
>
> Alex: No, I don't. My brother watched the movie last week. He said it was (A)[terrible / terrific].

> Jane: Then, what (B)[shell / shall] we do?
>
> Alex: We can (C)[take / get] a walk in the park instead.

08 ^{서답형} 위 대화의 (A)~(C)에 들어갈 알맞은 말을 쓰시오.

➡ (A) _____, (B) _____, (C) _____

09 위 대화의 내용과 일치하지 않는 것은?

① Alex didn't want to see *The Big Zoo*.
② Alex's brother saw the *The Big Zoo* last week.
③ Alex's brother said *The Big Zoo* was terrible.
④ Alex suggested taking a walk in the park to Jane.
⑤ Jane and Alex made a plan to go to the movies.

[10~11] 다음 대화를 읽고 물음에 답하시오.

> Brain: Susan, do you want to watch a movie this Saturday?
>
> Susan: Sure. What movie do you want to watch?
>
> Brain: The new superhero movie just came out. (A)난 그 영화를 정말 보고 싶어. (forward)
>
> Susan: Wow! I love superhero movies. See you then!

10 ^{서답형} When are Brian and Susan going to see a movie?

➡ _____

11 ^{서답형} 위 대화의 밑줄 친 (A)의 우리말을 주어진 단어를 사용하여 영작하시오.

➡ _____

[01~02] 다음 대화를 읽고 물음에 답하시오.

B: You look (A)[sad / happy]. What's up?
G: I'm looking forward to the school festival this weekend.
B: Me too! Someone said (B)[that / which] the school band practiced a lot this time.
G: I (C)[can / can't] wait to hear them!

01 위 대화의 (A)~(C)에 들어갈 말로 적절한 것을 고르시오.

➡ (A) _____, (B) _____, (C) _____

02 What are the boy and the girl going to hear this weekend?

➡ _____

[03~04] 다음 대화를 읽고 물음에 답하시오.

Minji: I was so angry yesterday.
Eric: Why, what happened?
Minji: Yesterday, I went to the park. Many people were there.
Eric: Were you angry about that?
Minji: Of course ⓐnot. I was angry ⓑbecause I saw those people picking the flowers and ⓒkicked the trees.
Eric: Oh, that is not good.
Minji: Yes, I told them ⓓto stop, but they said they didn't care ⓔabout the flowers or the trees.

03 위 대화의 밑줄 친 ⓐ~ⓔ 중 어법상 바르지 않은 것을 찾아 바르게 고치시오.

➡ _____

04 위 대화에서 Minji가 어제 공원에서 화가 난 이유를 우리말 20자 이내로 간략히 설명하시오.

➡ _____

[05~07] 다음 대화를 읽고 물음에 답하시오.

Diego: Achoo! Achoo!
Suji: Did you catch a cold, Diego?
Diego: No, I don't feel sick, but I can't stop (A)[to sneeze / sneezing]. Achoo!
Suji: Then, it must be (B)[because / because of] the yellow dust. The weather report said the yellow dust would be terrible today.
Diego: Oh, I guess I'm sneezing because of that. Can't we stop the yellow dust?
Suji: Yes, we can. My club members are preparing to do some special activities abroad.
Diego: What are they?
Suji: We're planning to plant trees in China because a lot of the yellow dust (C)[come / comes] from China.
Diego: That sounds good.
Suji: Yes. We are looking forward to stopping the yellow dust.

05 위 대화의 (A)~(C)에 들어갈 말로 적절한 것을 쓰시오.

➡ (A) _____, (B) _____, (C) _____

06 How's the weather today?

➡ _____

07 What are Suji's club members going to do to stop the yellow dust?

➡ _____

Grammar

1 의문사+to부정사

> • I don't know **where to go**. 어디로 가야 할지 모르겠어.
> • He asked me **how to get there**. 그는 그곳으로 가는 방법을 내게 물었다.

■ '의문사+to부정사'는 문장 속에서 명사구로 주어, 목적어, 보어 역할을 한다. 해당하는 의문사는 what, when, where, how, which, who, whom이 있으며, 'where to go'는 '어디로 가야 할지'와 같이 의문사와 동사의 의미를 넣어 해석해 준다.

　• Can you tell me **where to stay**? (어디에서 머무를지 나에게 말해 줄래?)

　• I need to know **how to do it**. (나는 그것을 하는 방법을 알 필요가 있어.)

　• She didn't know **whom to ask**. (그녀는 누구에게 물어봐야 할지 몰랐다.)

　• I didn't tell you **when to go home**. (네가 언제 집으로 가야 할지 나는 말하지 않았어.)

■ '의문사+to부정사'는 '의문사+주어+조동사+동사원형'으로 바꾸어 쓸 수 있다.

　• They didn't ask me **what to do**. (그들은 내게 무엇을 해야 할지 묻지 않았다.)
　　= They didn't ask me **what they should do**.

　• I don't know **how to use** the copy machine. (나는 그 복사기를 사용하는 방법을 모른다.)
　　= I don't know **how I should use** the copy machine.

　• Let's think **what to eat** for dinner. (저녁으로 무엇을 먹을지 생각하자.)
　　= Let's think **what we should eat** for dinner.

핵심 Check

1. 다음 우리말과 같도록 빈칸에 알맞은 말을 쓰시오.

(1) 운전하는 법을 배우는 것은 쉬워.

➡ Learning ＿＿＿＿＿ ＿＿＿＿＿ ＿＿＿＿＿ is easy.

= Learning ＿＿＿＿＿ ＿＿＿＿＿ ＿＿＿＿＿ drive is easy.

(2) 언제 소금을 넣을지 알려줘.

➡ Let me know ＿＿＿＿＿ ＿＿＿＿＿ ＿＿＿＿＿ salt.

= Let me know ＿＿＿＿＿ ＿＿＿＿＿ ＿＿＿＿＿ ＿＿＿＿＿ salt.

(3) 나는 누구에게 그 돈을 줘야 할지 모르겠어.

➡ I don't know ＿＿＿＿＿ ＿＿＿＿＿ ＿＿＿＿＿ the money.

= I don't know ＿＿＿＿＿ ＿＿＿＿＿ ＿＿＿＿＿ ＿＿＿＿＿ the money.

② so that

> • Jason did his best **so that** he could meet the deadline.
> Jason은 마감시한을 맞추기 위해서 최선을 다했다.
>
> • We turned off our cell phones **so that** we could focus.
> 우리는 집중할 수 있도록 휴대전화를 껐다.

■ 'so that+주어+조동사'는 목적을 나타내는 부사절로 '~하기 위해서' 혹은 '~하도록'이라는 의미로 쓰인다.
  • Tom studies hard **so that** he can make his mother happy. (Tom은 엄마를 행복하게 해드리려고 공부를 열심히 한다.)
  • Come close **so that** I can see you. (내가 널 볼 수 있도록 가까이 오렴.)

■ 같은 의미로 'in order that+주어+조동사'가 있으며, to부정사의 부사적 용법 중 목적도 같은 의미로 쓰일 수 있다.
  • Emily practiced hard **in order that** she might win the medal.
    = Emily practiced hard **to** win the medal. (Emily는 메달을 딸 수 있도록 열심히 연습했다.)

■ 원인과 결과를 나타내어 '너무 ~해서 …하다'라고 해석되는 'so ~ that …'과 혼동하지 않도록 유의한다.
  • He was **so** scared **that** he couldn't fall into sleep. (그는 너무 무서워서 잠들 수 없었다.)
  • Jenny is **so** brave **that** she laughed off the threat. (Jenny는 너무 용감해서 그 위협을 웃어 넘겼다.)

핵심 Check

2. 다음 우리말과 같도록 빈칸에 알맞은 말을 쓰시오.

(1) 그 아이스크림이 녹지 않도록 냉동실에 넣어라.
➡ Put the ice cream in the freezer _____ _____ it will not melt.
➡ Put the ice cream in the freezer _____ _____ _____ it will not melt.

(2) 동생에게 방해되지 않도록 조용히 해라.
➡ Be quiet _____ _____ your sister will not be disturbed.
➡ Be quiet _____ _____ _____ your sister will not be disturbed.

(3) 그는 손님들에게 대접할 수 있도록 샌드위치를 만들었다.
➡ He made some sandwiches _____ _____ he could serve his guests.
➡ He made some sandwiches _____ _____ his guests.

01 다음 문장에서 어법상 <u>어색한</u> 부분을 바르게 고쳐 쓰시오.

(1) Can you teach me how cook the meal?

_____ ➡ _____

(2) I am not certain what I to do next.

_____ ➡ _____

(3) Can you clear a space in that I can sit down?

_____ ➡ _____

(4) I keep a diary in order to I can remember my life.

_____ ➡ _____

02 다음 괄호 안에 주어진 단어를 어법에 맞게 빈칸에 쓰시오.

(1) I think he doesn't know how he _____ politely. (talk)

(2) He kept the door open so that anyone _____ in. (come)

(3) I would like to know whom _____. (thank)

(4) Go early _____ you may get a good seat. (order)

(5) I can't decide where _____ this chair. (put)

03 주어진 단어를 바르게 배열하여 다음 우리말을 영어로 쓰시오. 필요하면 단어를 추가하시오.

(1) 어디에 제 이름을 써야 할지 말해 주시겠어요? (my name / you / tell / write / can / me / where)

➡ _____

(2) 이 종이를 언제 사용해야 할지 모르겠어. (this / I / don't / use / paper / know / when)

➡ _____

(3) 우리가 알아들을 수 있도록 분명하게 말해. (you / speak / understand / clearly / that / we / can / so)

➡ _____

(4) 너의 눈을 보호할 수 있도록 그 안경을 써라. (eyes / wear / your / the glasses / can / that / you / protect / so)

➡ _____

 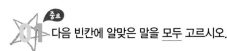

01 다음 빈칸에 알맞은 말을 <u>모두</u> 고르시오.

> He always says nice things _____ everyone around him feels happy.

① unless   ② in order that
③ so that   ④ because
⑤ as well as

02 다음 우리말을 영어로 바르게 옮긴 것을 <u>모두</u> 고르면?

> 연어는 알을 낳기 위해 강으로 회귀한다.

① The salmon return to the river in order breed.
② The salmon return to the river in order to breed.
③ The salmon return to the river so fast that they can breed.
④ The salmon return to the river so that they can breed.
⑤ The salmon return to the river in order not to breed.

03 다음 중 빈칸에 공통으로 들어갈 말로 가장 적절한 것은?

> • I can't decide what _____ wear for the graduation party.
> • He called his friends for help _____ move heavy furniture.

① that   ② in   ③ to
④ about   ⑤ will

서답형
04 다음 우리말을 두 가지의 영어로 쓰시오.

> 나는 언제 가야 할지 모르겠어.

➡ _____
➡ _____

05 다음 중 어법상 바르지 <u>않은</u> 것은?

① Do you know what to ride to go to the place?
② Daisy works hard so that her child can live a comfortable life.
③ I don't know what should say to her.
④ He knows how to amuse people.
⑤ Lora saved some money so that she could buy a new bag.

06 다음 주어진 문장과 같은 의미의 문장은?

> Po practices hard so that he can be good at kung fu.

① Po practices hard for that he can be good at kung fu.
② Po practices so hard that he can be good at kung fu.
③ Po practices hard in order to he can be good at kung fu.
④ Po practices hard to be good at kung fu.
⑤ Po practices hard for he can be good at kung fu.

07 다음 중 어법상 옳은 문장의 개수는?

> ⓐ Harry had to learn how to cook.
> ⓑ Mindy always tells me what do.
> ⓒ Wear a helmet in order to you can ride the bike safely.
> ⓓ Jerry ran fast to winning the race.
> ⓔ I studied hard so that my parents could feel proud of me.

① 1개   ② 2개   ③ 3개
④ 4개   ⑤ 5개

08 다음 대화의 빈칸에 알맞은 말을 쓰시오.

> **A:** I don't know _____ _____ _____
> for the party.
> **B:** How about the black suit you bought
> last year?

09 다음 중 어법상 바르지 <u>않은</u> 것은?

> Kelvin wanted ①to know ②how to make a
> cake ③so that he could give ④it ⑤for his
> girlfriend as a birthday present.

10 다음 빈칸에 들어갈 말로 가장 적절한 것은?

> Go to bed early _____ you can get up early
> tomorrow.

① and   ② if   ③ unless
④ so that   ⑤ after

11 다음 중 빈칸에 들어갈 말이 <u>다른</u> 하나는?

① My cell phone doesn't work _____ the
battery is dead.
② Karen doesn't want to talk to me _____
she is mad at me.
③ Tom couldn't do the project _____ he
hadn't enough time.
④ I will call you _____ you don't have to
worry about me.
⑤ We postponed our trip _____ the
weather was bad.

12 다음 빈칸에 적절한 말을 쓰시오.

> **A:** Did you decide _____ _____
> _____?
> **B:** No, not yet.
> **A:** How about coffee?

13 다음 주어진 문장과 같은 의미의 문장은?

> I still don't know whom to be afraid of.

① I still don't know who is afraid of me.
② I still don't know who I am afraid of.
③ I still don't know who I should be afraid
of.
④ I still don't know who should be afraid
of me.
⑤ I still don't know who you are afraid of.

14 다음 빈칸에 들어갈 말이 바르게 짝지어진 것은?

> Mowgli was hungry, but he didn't know
> _____. His bear friend, Baloo, taught
> him _____ fish.

① when to go – how to eat
② what to do – how to catch
③ how to do – who to cook
④ what to do – when to find
⑤ where to go – where to find

15 다음 (A)~(C)에서 어법상 옳은 것끼리 바르게 짝지은 것은?

> • I think Jane forgot (A)[where / when] to
> go to church.
> • Julia told me (B)[how / where] to get to
> the bank.
> • I was (C)[so embarrassed that /
> embarrassed so that] I couldn't say a word.

① where – how – so embarrassed that
② when – how – embarrassed so that
③ where – where – so embarrassed that
④ when – how – so embarrassed that
⑤ where – where – embarrassed so that

서답형

16 주어진 단어를 바르게 배열하여 다음 우리말을 영어로 쓰시오. 필요하다면 단어를 추가하시오.

> 네가 길을 잃지 않도록 그곳으로 가는 방법을 알려줄게.
> (show / lost / you / you / how / let / get / so / won't / get / that / there / me)

➡ _____

_____

17 다음 우리말을 영어로 바르게 옮긴 것은?

> 그 코코아가 너무 뜨거워서 마실 수 없었어.

① The hot chocolate was hot so that I could drink it.
② The hot chocolate was hot so that I couldn't drink it.
③ The hot chocolate was so hot that I could not drink it.
④ The hot chocolate was hot enough that I could drink it.
⑤ The hot chocolate was hot, so I could not drink.

18 다음 빈칸에 가장 적절한 것은?

> Can you tell me _____ this math problem? I am not good at math.

① who to solve ② when to solve
③ what to solve ④ how to solve
⑤ where to solve

19 다음 빈칸에 들어갈 말로 가장 적절한 것은?

> 어느 것을 선택할지 알려줘.
> Let me know _____ to pick.

① when ② how ③ who
④ which ⑤ whom

서답형

20 주어진 단어를 활용하여 다음 우리말을 12 단어로 이루어진 문장으로 쓰시오.

> 나는 너무 피곤해서 다음에 무엇을 해야 할지 생각할 수 없었어. (so / that / think / to)

➡ _____

21 다음 중 어법상 바르지 않은 것은?

① He did his best so that he might succeed.
② I was happy so that I jumped up and down.
③ Jimmy didn't want to tell me what to do.
④ The doctor told me how I should wash my hands.
⑤ Mom didn't tell me when I should leave.

서답형

22 다음 우리말에 맞게 빈칸에 알맞은 말을 쓰시오.

> 그는 나에게 어느 펜을 사야 할지 말해 주었다.
> He told me _____.

➡ _____

서답형

23 다음 문장을 읽고 빈칸에 알맞은 말을 쓰시오.

> Be sure to put the meat in the oven at 5:00. Then it will be ready to eat by 6:30.

➡ Be sure to put the meat in the oven at 5:00

_____

서답형

24 다음 빈칸에 적절한 말을 쓰시오.

> I am not a good talker. I don't know _____ to start a conversation.

01 주어진 단어를 활용하여 다음을 영어로 쓰시오.

> • Tom은 시험에 통과하기 위해서 열심히 공부했다.
> • Tom은 열심히 공부해서 시험에 통과할 수 있었다.
> (so / that)

➡ _____

➡ _____

02 to부정사를 이용하여 다음 대화의 빈칸에 알맞은 말을 쓰시오.

> A: Do you know _____ _____
> _____ this item?
> B: Yes, I do. You can buy it on the second
> floor.

03 다음 문장을 두 가지의 영어 문장으로 쓰시오.

> 테니스를 잘 치는 방법을 말해줄 수 있니?

➡ _____

➡ _____

04 주어진 단어를 어법에 맞게 빈칸에 쓰시오.

> I will take my umbrella so that _____
> _____ .
> (I / get wet)

05 다음과 같이 두 문장을 한 문장으로 바꿔 쓰시오.

> • Mary practiced the violin every day.
> • She won the contest.
> → Mary practiced the violin every day so
> that she could win the contest.

(1) • Please turn down the TV.
 • I want to be able to get to sleep.
 ➡ _____

(2) • Can you give me a ride to the hospital?
 • I want to see a doctor.
 ➡ _____
 _____

(3) • The little girl pretended to be sick.
 • She wanted to stay home from school.
 ➡ _____
 _____

06 주어진 단어를 활용하여 다음 우리말을 영어로 쓰시오.

> 내가 수영을 잘 할 수 있도록 수영하는 방법을 가
> 르쳐 주시겠어요?
> (can / how / so that)

➡ _____

07 다음 대화를 읽고 빈칸에 알맞은 말을 쓰시오.

> Jason: Excuse me, can you tell me where
> I should find a restroom?
> Waiter: Follow me. I will show you.

➡ A waiter showed Jason _____ _____
 _____ _____ _____ .

08 다음 대화의 빈칸에 알맞은 말을 쓰시오.

> Po: Shifu, can you teach me _____
>
> _____ _____ _____ _____?
>
> Shifu: Okay. I will teach you how you
>
> should do kung fu _____ _____
>
> you can be good at it.

09 주어진 단어를 바르게 배열하여 다음 우리말을 영어로 쓰시오. 필요하다면 하나의 단어를 추가하시오.

> 너는 나에게 너무 친절해서 나는 너에게 어떻게 고마워해야 할지 모르겠어.
> (so / you / you / kind / how / I / thank / that / been / know / have / don't)

➡ _____

_____

10 다음 글의 문맥에 맞게 빈칸에 알맞은 말을 쓰시오.

> June knew how to _____ food waste.
> She didn't take too much food and ate it
> all. She told her friends how to do it so
> that they _____ _____ _____
> _____.

11 다음 상황을 읽고 적절한 접속사를 이용하여 빈칸에 알맞은 낱말 쓰시오.

> Tom and Jane have a five-year-old child.
> Tonight they're going to hire a baby
> sitter. They want to be able to go out
> with some friends.

➡ Tom and Jane are going to hire a baby sitter
for their five-year-old child _____

_____

12 주어진 단어를 활용하여 각 조건에 맞게 다음 우리말을 영어로 쓰시오.

> Amelia는 여행 가이드가 되기 위해서 영어 공부를 열심히 했다.
> (a tour guide / become)

(1) so를 활용하여

➡ _____

_____

(2) order를 활용하여

➡ _____

(3) to부정사를 활용하여

➡ _____

_____

13 다음 문장이 서로 같은 의미가 되도록 빈칸에 알맞은 말을 쓰시오.

(1) Jason asked me where he should hand
in the report.
= Jason asked me _____.
(2) It's up to her to decide what she should
do after graduating from college.
= It's up to her to decide _____

_____.
(3) I haven't decided which dress I should
buy.
= I haven't decided _____.

14 주어진 단어를 활용하여 다음 우리말을 영어로 쓰시오.

> 늦지 않도록 나는 택시를 탈 거야.
> (take / so)

➡ _____

Reading

교과서

The Green News

Many people are wearing masks <u>so that</u> they can keep away from
<small>so that ~ can에서 can 대신에 may 등 다른 조동사 사용 가능</small>

an unwelcome guest in the spring: yellow dust. Every year, there is

widespread yellow dust in Korea. Many people <u>become sick</u> <u>because</u>
<small>2형식 동사 ~하게 되다   ~이기 때문에 (이유를 나타내는 접속사)</small>

the yellow dust hurts their eyes and throats. Why does the yellow dust

come about? Is there any way <u>to stop</u> the yellow dust? Yes, there is!
<small>to부정사의 형용사적 용법</small>

Let's take a look at the causes of and the solutions to <u>the problem of</u>
<small>전치사 of와 to의 공통 목적어</small>

<u>yellow dust</u> through the work of some volunteers in Gansu Sheng,

China.

Li Na(16, a middle school student)

A long time ago, this place was a big forest. But people began to cut

down trees so that they could build cities. <u>As</u> time passed, the forest
<small>~함에 따라서</small>

lost many trees. Finally, the forest became a desert and the desert

became <u>bigger and bigger</u>. Now, when the spring brings strong winds
<small>비교급+비교급: 점점 더 ~한</small>

from the west, the yellow dust spreads. In the past, most people did

not know <u>how to stop</u> the yellow dust problem. Now, many volunteers
<small>의문사+to부정사: 어떻게 ~할지, ~하는 방법</small>

plant trees <u>to solve</u> this problem.
<small>to부정사의 부사적 용법 중 목적(~하기 위해서)</small>

keep away from: ~을 가까이 하지 않다
unwelcome: 반갑지 않은
widespread: 널리 퍼진
throat: 목(구멍)
come about: 발생하다
take a look at: 살펴보다
cause: 원인
solution: 해법, 해결책
a long time ago: 오래 전에
desert: 사막
past: 과거

 확인문제

● 다음 문장이 본문의 내용과 일치하면 T, 일치하지 <u>않으면</u> F를 쓰시오.

1 The reason why people wear masks is to avoid yellow dust. ☐

2 There is yellow dust in Korea every spring. ☐

3 There is no clear reason why the yellow dust comes about. ☐

4 Li Na does volunteer work in China. ☐

Minsu(18, a high school student)

Planting trees in the desert is hard and expensive. However, many
상반되는 뜻을 나타내는 역접의 연결 부사
Chinese people know that they cannot live if they don't plant trees.
조건 부사절 접속사: 만약 ~하면
They always thank us, Korean volunteers, because we plant trees with
us = Korean volunteers 동격
them. However, we plant trees to help not only China but also Korea.
중국뿐만 아니라 한국도

Suji(15, a middle school student)

At first, I didn't know what to do to get rid of the yellow dust.
의문사+to부정사: 무엇을 해야 할지   to부정사의 부사적 용법 중 목적
Then, Minsu, my group leader, told me that planting trees can help to

solve the problem. I also found out that planting trees and protecting
help의 목적어로 쓰인 to부정사   명사절 접속사: find out의 목적절   planting trees와 연결
the environment help my family and me. In China, many people are

planting trees in deserts so that they can stop the spread of the yellow

dust. The work is not easy, but they are working hard to protect the
to부정사의 부사적 용법 중 목적
world. With this kind of global togetherness, the seeds of hope will

keep on growing.
동명사(전치사 on의 목적어)

not only A but also B: A 뿐만 아
니라 B도
get rid of: ~을 처리하다, 없애다
find out: 알아내다[알게 되다]
global: 세계적인, 지구의
togetherness: 친목, 연대감
seed: 씨앗
keep on: ~를 계속하다

 **확인문제**

● 다음 문장이 본문의 내용과 일치하면 T, 일치하지 <u>않으면</u> F를 쓰시오.

1 It is cheap to plant trees in the desert. ☐

2 Not only Chinese people but also Korean people plant trees. ☐

3 At first, Suji had no idea about how to get rid of the yellow dust. ☐

4 Suji is the leader of the volunteer work team. ☐

5 Only Chinese people are worried about the spread of the yellow dust. ☐

6 Many people in China work hard in order that they could protect the world. ☐

● 우리말을 참고하여 빈칸에 알맞은 말을 쓰시오.

The Green News

1 Many people _____ _____ masks _____ _____ they _____ _____ _____ _____ an unwelcome guest in the spring: yellow dust.

2 Every year, _____ _____ _____ yellow dust in Korea.

3 Many people _____ _____ because the yellow dust _____ _____ _____ and _____.

4 Why does the yellow dust _____ _____?

5 Is there any way _____ _____ the yellow dust? Yes, there is!

6 Let's _____ _____ _____ _____ the causes _____ and the solutions _____ the problem of yellow dust _____ the work of some volunteers in Gansu Sheng, China.

Li Na(16, a middle school student)

7 A long time ago, this place _____ _____ _____ _____.

8 But people began _____ _____ _____ _____ so that they _____ _____ cities.

9 As time _____, the forest _____ many trees.

10 Finally, the forest _____ a desert and the desert _____ _____ _____ _____.

11 Now, when the spring _____ strong winds _____ the west, the yellow dust _____.

12 In the past, most people did not know _____ _____ _____ the yellow dust problem.

녹색 뉴스

1 많은 사람이 봄에 찾아오는 반갑지 않은 손님인 황사 때문에 마스크를 끼고 있습니다.

2 매년 한국에는 황사가 널리 퍼집니다.

3 황사가 많은 사람들의 눈과 목을 아프게 해서 많은 사람들이 병에 걸립니다.

4 황사는 왜 일어나는 것일까요?

5 황사를 막을 수 있는 방법이 있을까요? 네, 있습니다!

6 중국의 간쑤성에 있는 자원봉사자들의 작업을 통해 황사의 원인과 해결책을 살펴봅시다.

리나(16, 중학생)

7 예전에 이곳은 큰 숲이었습니다.

8 그러나 사람들이 도시를 세우기 위해 나무를 베기 시작했습니다.

9 시간이 지나면서 숲은 많은 나무를 잃었습니다.

10 마침내, 숲은 사막이 되었고 사막은 점점 더 커졌습니다.

11 이제, 봄에 서쪽에서 세찬 바람이 불 때, 황사가 퍼집니다.

12 이전에는 대부분의 사람들이 황사 문제를 어떻게 막을 수 있는지 알지 못했습니다.

13 Now, many volunteers _____ trees _____ _____ _____ _____.

Minsu(18, a high school student)

14 _____ _____ in the desert _____ hard and expensive.

15 _____, many Chinese people know _____ they cannot _____ _____ _____ _____ _____ trees.

16 They always _____ us, Korean volunteers, _____ we plant trees _____ _____.

17 _____, we plant trees _____ _____ not only China _____ _____ Korea.

Suji(15, a middle school student)

18 At first, I didn't know _____ _____ to _____ _____ _____ the yellow dust.

19 Then, Minsu, my group leader, told me that _____ _____ can help _____ _____ _____ _____.

20 I also found out that _____ trees and _____ the environment _____ my family and me.

21 In China, many people _____ _____ trees in deserts _____ _____ they _____ _____ the spread of the yellow dust.

22 The work is not easy, but they are working _____ _____ _____ the world.

23 With this kind of global _____, the seeds of hope will _____ _____ _____.

13 이제는 많은 자원봉사자들이 이 문제를 해결하기 위해 나무를 심고 있습니다.

민수(18. 고등학생)

14 사막에 나무를 심는 것은 힘들고 비용이 많이 듭니다.

15 하지만 많은 중국인들은 자신들이 나무를 심지 않으면 살 수 없다는 것을 알고 있습니다.

16 그들은 우리가 그들과 나무를 심기 때문에 우리 한국인 봉사자들에게 늘 감사해 하고 있습니다.

17 그러나 우리가 나무를 심는 이유는 단지 중국만이 아니라 한국도 돕기 위해서입니다.

수지(15. 중학생)

18 처음에 저는 황사를 없애기 위해서 무엇을 해야 할지 몰랐습니다.

19 그 때, 우리 조장인 민수가 나무를 심는 것이 문제를 해결하는 데 도움이 된다고 얘기해 줬습니다.

20 저는 나무를 심고 환경을 보호하는 것이 우리 가족과 제 자신도 돕는 일이라는 것임을 알게 되었습니다.

21 중국에서는 많은 사람들이 황사가 퍼지는 것을 막기 위해서 사막에 나무를 심고 있습니다.

22 이 작업은 쉽지 않지만 그들은 세계를 보호하기 위해서 열심히 일하고 있습니다.

23 이러한 세계적인 협업으로 희망의 씨앗은 계속해서 자랄 것입니다.

● 우리말을 참고하여 본문을 영작하시오.

The Green News

1 많은 사람이 봄에 찾아오는 반갑지 않은 손님인 황사 때문에 마스크를 끼고 있습니다.

➡ _____

2 매년 한국에는 황사가 널리 퍼집니다.

➡ _____

3 황사가 많은 사람들의 눈과 목을 아프게 해서 많은 사람들이 병에 걸립니다.

➡ _____

4 황사는 왜 일어나는 것일까요?

➡ _____

5 황사를 막을 수 있는 방법이 있을까요? 네, 있습니다!

➡ _____

6 중국의 간쑤성에 있는 자원봉사자들의 작업을 통해 황사의 원인과 해결책을 살펴봅시다.

➡ _____

_____

Li Na(16, a middle school student)

7 예전에 이곳은 큰 숲이었습니다.

➡ _____

8 그러나 사람들이 도시를 세우기 위해 나무를 베기 시작했습니다..

➡ _____

9 시간이 지나면서 숲은 많은 나무를 잃었습니다.

➡ _____

10 마침내, 숲은 사막이 되었고 사막은 점점 더 커졌습니다.

➡ _____

11 이제, 봄에 서쪽에서 세찬 바람이 불 때, 황사가 퍼집니다.

➡ _____

12 이전에는 대부분의 사람들이 황사 문제를 어떻게 막을 수 있는지 알지 못했습니다.

➡ _____

13 이제는 많은 자원봉사자들이 이 문제를 해결하기 위해 나무를 심고 있습니다.

➡ _____

Minsu(18, a high school student)

14 사막에 나무를 심는 것은 힘들고 비용이 많이 듭니다.

➡ _____

15 하지만 많은 중국인들은 자신들이 나무를 심지 않으면 살 수 없다는 것을 알고 있습니다.

➡ _____

16 그들은 우리가 그들과 나무를 심기 때문에 우리 한국인 봉사자들에게 늘 감사해 하고 있습니다.

➡ _____

17 그러나 우리가 나무를 심는 이유는 단지 중국만이 아니라 한국도 돕기 위해서입니다.

➡ _____

Suji(15, a middle school student)

18 처음에 저는 황사를 없애기 위해서 무엇을 해야 할지 몰랐습니다.

➡ _____

19 그 때, 우리 조장인 민수가 나무를 심는 것이 문제를 해결하는 데 도움이 된다고 얘기해 줬습니다.

➡ _____

20 저는 나무를 심고 환경을 보호하는 것이 우리 가족과 제 자신도 돕는 일이라는 것임을 알게 되었습니다.

➡ _____

21 중국에서는 많은 사람들이 황사가 퍼지는 것을 막기 위해서 사막에 나무를 심고 있습니다.

➡ _____

22 이 작업은 쉽지 않지만 그들은 세계를 보호하기 위해서 열심히 일하고 있습니다.

➡ _____

23 이러한 세계적인 협업으로 희망의 씨앗은 계속해서 자랄 것입니다.

➡ _____

[01~03] 다음 글을 읽고 물음에 답하시오.

Many people are wearing masks ⓐ_____ they can keep away from an unwelcome guest in the spring: yellow dust. Every year, (A) [there is / there are] widespread yellow dust in Korea. Many people become sick (B)[because / because of] the yellow dust hurts their eyes and throats. Why does the yellow dust come about? Is there (C)[some / any] way to stop the yellow dust? Yes, there is! Let's take a look at the causes of and the solutions to the problem of yellow dust through the work of some volunteers in Gansu Sheng, China.

01 다음 중 빈칸 ⓐ에 들어갈 말로 가장 적절한 것은?

① until ② when

③ if ④ in order that

⑤ or

02 위 글에 이어질 내용으로 가장 적절한 것은?

① the masks that are good for us

② the work of some volunteers

③ how we can protect our eyes

④ how to get to Gansu Sheng

⑤ the benefit of wearing masks

중요

03 (A)~(C)에서 어법상 옳은 것끼리 바르게 짝지은 것은?

① there is – because – some

② there are – because of – some

③ there is – because – any

④ there are – because – some

⑤ there is – because of – any

[04~06] 다음 글을 읽고 물음에 답하시오.

Li Na(16, a middle school student)
A long time ago, ⓐthis place was a big forest. But people began to cut down trees so that they could build cities. As time passed, the forest lost many trees. Finally, the forest became a desert and the desert became bigger and bigger. Now, when the spring brings strong winds from the west, the yellow dust spreads. In the past, most people did not know how to stop the yellow dust problem. Now, many volunteers plant tress to solve this problem.

서답형

04 다음은 밑줄 친 ⓐ에 관한 설명이다. 빈칸에 알맞은 말을 쓰시오.

The place used to be _____, but it is _____ now.

05 다음 중 위 글을 읽고 답할 수 없는 것은?

① How old is Li Na?

② What made the forest lose many trees?

③ What did the forest become after people cut down so many trees?

④ What does the spring bring from the west?

⑤ How far does the yellow dust spread?

서답형

06 Write the reason why people started to cut down trees. Use the phrase "It was because."

➡ _____

_____

[07~09] 다음 글을 읽고 물음에 답하시오.

Minsu(18, a high school student)
Planting trees in the desert is hard and expensive. However, many Chinese people know ⓐthat they cannot live if they don't plant trees. They always thank us, Korean volunteers, because we plant trees with them. However, we plant trees to help not only China but also Korea.

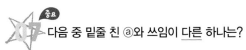

07 다음 중 밑줄 친 ⓐ와 쓰임이 다른 하나는?

① Did you hear that David won the election?
② Amelia said that Tom likes me.
③ Do you know the man that is talking with your sister?
④ There is a rumor that you cheated on the test.
⑤ The fact that you made me embarrassed doesn't change.

08 다음 중 글의 내용과 일치하는 것은?

① To plant in the desert is easy.
② Many Chinese people don't want to plant trees.
③ Chinese people don't know the value of planting trees.
④ Korean volunteers plant trees by themselves.
⑤ Chinese people feel thankful to Korean volunteers.

서답형
09 다음 빈칸에 알맞은 말을 쓰시오.

> Korean volunteers plant trees in China to help _____ as well as_____.

[10~13] 다음 글을 읽고 물음에 답하시오.

Suji(15, a middle school student)
At first, I didn't know ①what to do to get rid of the yellow dust. Then, Minsu, my group leader, told me ②that planting trees can help to solve the problem. I also found out that planting trees and protecting the environment ③help my family and me.
In China, many people are planting trees ④in deserts ⓐ_____ they can stop the spread of the yellow dust. ⓑThe work is not easy, but they are working ⑤hardly to protect the world. With this kind of global togetherness, ⓒ희망의 씨앗들 will keep on growing.

10 다음 중 빈칸 ⓐ에 들어갈 말과 같은 말이 들어가는 것은?

① Call me _____ you arrive safely.
② _____ the sun was shining, it wasn't that warm.
③ I will give you a map _____ you won't get lost.
④ Molly had a headache, _____ she went to see a doctor.
⑤ He is quite strong _____ he is old.

서답형
11 다음 중 밑줄 친 ⓑ가 의미하는 것을 4 단어의 영어로 쓰시오.

➡ _____

서답형
12 밑줄 친 우리말 ⓒ를 영어로 쓰시오.

➡ _____

13 밑줄 친 ①~⑤ 중 어법상 바르지 않은 것은?

① ② ③ ④ ⑤

[14~16] 다음 글을 읽고 물음에 답하시오.

Many people are wearing masks so that they can keep away from an unwelcome guest in the spring: yellow dust. Every year, there is widespread yellow dust in Korea. Many people become sick because the yellow dust hurts their eyes and throats. Why does the yellow dust ⓐcome about? Is there any way to stop the yellow dust? Yes, there is! Let's take a look at the causes of and the solutions to the problem of yellow dust through the work of some volunteers in Gansu Sheng, China.

14 다음 중 밑줄 친 ⓐ를 대신하여 쓰일 수 있는 것은?

① come through   ② take place
③ come in   ④ wander around
⑤ look up to

15 다음 중 위 글의 내용과 일치하지 <u>않는</u> 것은?

① Yellow dust is an unwelcome guest in Korea.
② There are many people wearing masks in the spring.
③ There is widespread yellow dust in Korea once in two years.
④ Many people become sick because of the yellow dust.
⑤ Yellow dust makes people's throat sore.

서답형
16 According to the passage, when does the yellow dust show up? Answer in English with a full sentence.

➡ _____

[17~20] 다음 글을 읽고 물음에 답하시오.

Li Na(16, a middle school student)
A long time ago, this place was a big forest. But people began to cut down trees so that they could build cities. As time passed, the forest (A)[gained / lost] many trees. ⓐ_____, the forest became a desert and the desert became bigger and bigger. Now, when the spring (B)[brings / blocks] strong winds from the west, the yellow dust spreads. In the past, most people did not know ⓑhow to stop the yellow dust problem. Now, many volunteers (C)[plant / cut] trees to solve this problem.

17 다음 중 빈칸 ⓐ에 들어갈 말로 적절한 것을 <u>모두</u> 고르면?

① Finally   ② However
③ Besides   ④ For example
⑤ In the end

서답형
18 적절한 주어와 동사를 이용하여 밑줄 친 ⓑ와 같은 의미의 문장을 쓰시오.

➡ _____

19 (A)~(C)에서 글의 흐름상 적절한 것끼리 바르게 짝지은 것은?

① gained – brings – plant
② lost – blocks – plant
③ gained – blocks – cut
④ lost – brings – plant
⑤ gained – brings – cut

서답형
20 다음 빈칸에 들어갈 말을 위 글에서 찾아 쓰시오.

A _____ is a large area of land, where there is almost no water, rain, trees, or plants.

➡ _____

[21~25] 다음 글을 읽고 물음에 답하시오.

Minsu(18, a high school student)
Planting trees in the desert is hard and expensive. However, many Chinese people know that they cannot live if they don't plant trees. They always thank us, Korean volunteers, because we plant trees with them. However, ⓐwe plant trees to help not only China but also Korea.

Suji(15, a middle school student)
At first, I didn't know what to do ⓑto get rid of the yellow dust. Then, Minsu, my group leader, told me that planting trees can help to solve the problem. ⓒ_____, I found out that planting trees and protecting the environment help my family and me.

서답형

21 주어진 단어를 이용하여 밑줄 친 ⓐ와 같은 의미의 문장을 쓰시오.

in order that

➡ _____

_____

22 다음 중 밑줄 친 ⓑ와 쓰임이 같은 것은?

① She entered the room to find her car key.
② The children were looking for a toy to play with.
③ Jack decided to learn a musical instrument.
④ I am so glad to see you again.
⑤ Danny wanted me to accept Jenny's apology.

중요

23 빈칸 ⓒ에 들어갈 말로 가장 적절한 것은?

① For example   ② In addition
③ However   ④ Instead
⑤ Thus

서답형

24 다음은 수지와 민수의 대화이다. 빈칸에 알맞은 말을 쓰시오.

Minsu: Do you know _____ causes many problems in Korea?
Suji: Really? I didn't know that. Can you tell me how _____ the problem?

25 다음 중 위 글의 내용과 일치하지 <u>않는</u> 것은?

① Planting trees in the desert is costly.
② It is hard to plant trees in the desert.
③ Both Chinese and Korean plant trees in the desert.
④ Suji belongs to Minsu's group.
⑤ Suji plants trees in order to protect only her family.

중요
26 주어진 문장과 자연스럽게 이어지도록 (A)~(C)를 바르게 나열한 것은?

Planting trees in the desert is hard and expensive.

(A) They always thank us, Korean volunteers, because we plant trees with them.
(B) However, we plant trees to help not only China but also Korea.
(C) However, many Chinese people know that they cannot live if they don't plant trees.

① (B)-(A)-(C)   ② (B)-(C)-(A)
③ (C)-(A)-(B)   ④ (C)-(B)-(A)
⑤ (A)-(C)-(B)

[01~03] 다음 글을 읽고 물음에 답하시오.

Many people are wearing masks so that they can keep away from an unwelcome guest in the spring: yellow dust. Every year, there is widespread yellow dust in Korea. Many people become sick because the yellow dust hurts their eyes and throats. Why does the yellow dust come about? Is there any way to stop the yellow dust? Yes, there is! Let's take a look at the causes of and the solutions to the problem of yellow dust through the work of some volunteers in Gansu Sheng, China.

01 위 글의 내용에 맞게 빈칸에 알맞은 말을 쓰시오.

> A: Why did you wear a mask in this picture?
> B: I wore it to _____.
> A: Unwelcome guest? What was it?
> B: _____.
> A: Oh, it must have been annoying.

➡ _____

02 According to the passage, what makes people sick in Korea? Answer in English with a full sentence.

➡ _____

03 위 글의 표현을 이용하여 다음 우리말을 8 단어로 이루어진 영어 문장으로 쓰시오.

> 너는 황사를 멈추는 방법을 아니?

➡ _____

[04~07] 다음 글을 읽고 물음에 답하시오.

Li Na(16, a middle school student)
A long time ago, this place was a big forest. But people began to cut down trees so that they could build cities. As time passed, the forest lost many trees. Finally, the forest became a desert and the desert became bigger and bigger. Now, when the spring brings strong winds from the west, the yellow dust spreads. In the past, most people did not know ⓐ_____ the yellow dust problem. Now, many volunteers plant trees to solve this problem.

04 주어진 단어를 활용하여 빈칸 ⓐ에 알맞은 말을 세 단어로 쓰시오. (stop)

➡ _____

05 다음 물음에 완전한 문장의 영어로 답하시오.

> Q: Where does the yellow dust come from?

➡ _____

06 위 글의 내용에 맞게 빈칸에 알맞은 말을 쓰시오.

> People who loved in a big forest began to cut down trees in order to _____.

07 주어진 표현을 이용하여 다음 물음에 답하시오.

> Q: Why do many volunteers plant trees?
> A: (in order that)

➡ _____

[08~11] 다음 글을 읽고 물음에 답하시오.

Minsu(18, a high school student)
Planting trees in the desert is hard and expensive. However, many Chinese people know that they cannot live if they don't plant trees. They always thank ⓐus, Korean volunteers, because we plant trees with ⓑ them. However, we plant trees to help not only China but also Korea.

Suji(15, a middle school student)
__ⓒ__ first, I didn't know what to do to get rid of the yellow dust. Then, Minsu, my group leader, told me that planting trees can help to solve the problem. I also found out that planting trees and protecting the environment help my family and me.

08 밑줄 친 ⓐ와 ⓑ가 가리키는 것을 각각 쓰시오.

➡ ⓐ ______________ ⓑ ______________

09 위 글의 빈칸 ⓒ에 알맞은 전치사를 쓰시오.

➡ ______________________

10 What did Suji find out from the volunteer activity?

➡ ________________________________

____

11 (중요) 다음 대화의 빈칸을 알맞게 채우시오.

A: Suji, did you know ________ ________ ________ ________ in order to get rid of the yellow dust?
B: At first I didn't, but now I do.

[12~15] 다음 글을 읽고 물음에 답하시오.

Jimin's father grew plants in a small garden at their house. He ⓐdid this so that he could help to protect the environment. When many students became sick because of bad air, Jimin decided that he wanted to do something about it. His father said that growing plants could help solve this problem. At first, however, Jimin didn't know ⓑwhere to grow the plants. He asked his club members for some advice. One member had a good idea. They could grow plants at their school! All of the club members were very happy because, by growing plants, they could also plant some seeds of hope.

12 밑줄 친 ⓐ가 의미하는 것을 영어로 쓰시오.

➡ ______________________

13 위 글의 내용에 맞게 다음 빈칸에 알맞은 말을 4 단어로 쓰시오.

Bad air made ______________________.

14 (중요) 적절한 주어와 동사를 이용하여 밑줄 친 ⓑ와 같은 의미의 문장을 쓰시오.

➡ ________________________________

15 위 글의 내용에 맞게 다음 빈칸에 알맞은 말을 쓰시오.

By planting trees, they can not only help ______________________ but also plant ______________________.

Check Your Progress 1

G: I was so angry yesterday.
= upset. mad

B: Why, what happened?
무슨 일이야? = what's the matter? =what's the problem?

G: Yesterday, I went to the park. Many people were there.
= at the park

B: Were you angry about that?

G: Of course not. I was angry because I saw those people picking the flowers
현재분사(목적보어)

and kicking the trees.

B: Oh, that is not good.

G: Yes, I told them to stop, but they said they didn't care about the flowers or
꽃을 뽑고 나무를 차던 사람들을 가리킨다.

the trees.

구문해설 • angry: 화난 • pick: 뽑다 • kick: 차다 • care about: ~에 마음을 쓰다. ~에 관심을 가지다

G: 나 어제 무척 화가 났었
어.

B: 왜, 무슨 일 있었어?

G: 어제. 나는 공원에 갔어.
많은 사람들이 그곳에 있
었어.

B: 그것 때문에 화가 났어?

G: 당연히 아니지. 나는 그
사람들이 꽃을 뽑고 나무
를 차는 것을 보고 화가 났
어.

B: 오, 그건 좋지 않아.

G: 응. 나는 그들에게 멈추라
고 말했지만, 그들은 꽃과
나무에 신경을 쓰지 않는
다고 말했어.

After You Read

Diego: Yellow dust causes many problems in Korea.

Suji: Yes. Many people become sick because of the yellow dust.
~ 때문에

For example, their throats hurt because of it.

Diego: That's right. Do you know how to solve such problems?
의문사+to부정사(= how we should solve)

Suji: In the past, many people cut down trees to build cities. This made the
사역동사+목적어+동사원형: 목적어가 ~하게 하다

forests turn into deserts of yellow dust. Now, we must plant trees together

to stop the yellow dust.
멈추기 위해서(= so that we can stop ~)

Diego: That's a good idea. By planting trees, we can help the world.
~해서(수단)

Suji: Yes, with global togetherness, the world will become green again!

구문해설 • yellow dust: 황사 • cause: 유발하다, 야기하다 • cut down: 베다 • global: 세계적인

Diego: 한국에서 황사는 많
은 문제를 유발해.

Suji: 응. 많은 사람들이 황사
때문에 아파. 예를 들어,
황사 때문에 사람들 목
이 아프지.

Diego: 맞아. 그러한 문제를
어떻게 해결해야 할
지 아니?

Suji: 과거에는, 많은 사람들
이 도시를 세우기 위해
나무를 베었어. 이것이 숲
을 황사의 사막으로 변하
게 했지. 이제, 우리는 황
사를 멈추기 위해서 함께
나무를 심어야 해.

Diego: 그거 좋은 생각이네.
나무를 심음으로써,
우리는 세상을 도울
수 있어.

Suji: 응. 세계적 협업으로,
세상은 다시 푸르러 질
거야.

Project Work

We should use cups when we brush our teeth so that we can save water. We
~해야 한다 (충고할 때 쓰이는 조동사)   목적의 부사절(= to save water)

look forward to saving water by using cups!
look forward to Ving: V하는 것을 기대하다

구문해설 • brush one's teeth: 양치질하다 • save: 절약하다 • by+ -ing: ~함으로써

우리는 물을 절약할 수 있도
록 이를 닦을 때 컵을 사용해
야 합니다. 우리는 컵을 사용
함으로써 물을 아끼는 것을
기대합니다.

01 다음 짝지어진 단어의 관계가 같도록 빈칸에 알맞은 말을 쓰시오.

> send : receive = _____ : result

02 다음 중 밑줄 친 부분의 뜻풀이가 바르지 않은 것은?

① He was an unwelcome guest at the party.
환영 받지 못하는
② I had a terrible headache at night. 끔찍한
③ No one can go back to the past. 지난
④ He was the hero of the war. 영웅
⑤ The trees are standing in the forest. 숲

03 다음 주어진 우리말과 일치하도록 주어진 단어를 모두 배열하여 영작하시오.

(1) 나는 집을 떠날 때 스위치를 끄는 것을 잊어버렸다.
(home / when / switch / I / to / leaving / forgot / off / turn / the)
➡ _____

(2) 황사가 어디에서 오나요?
(does / from / come / the / dust / yellow / where)
➡ _____

(3) 너는 애완동물과 산책하는 것을 즐기니?
(with / do / taking / enjoy / you / your / a / pet / walk)
➡ _____

04 다음 우리말에 맞게 빈칸에 알맞은 말을 쓰시오.

(1) 나는 가격이 계속 오르기 때문에 이 차를 살 수 없다.
➡ I can't buy this car because the price _____ _____ increasing.

(2) 오래 전에 공룡은 사라졌다.
➡ Dinosaurs disappeared _____ _____ _____ _____.

(3) 나쁜 습관을 없애기는 쉽지 않다.
➡ It's not easy to _____ _____ _____ a bad habit.

05 다음 영영풀이가 가리키는 것을 고르시오.

> a large area of land that has very little water and very few plants growing on it.

① cause
② solution
③ throat
④ desert
⑤ forest

06 다음 문장의 빈칸에 들어갈 말을 보기에서 골라 알맞은 형태로 쓰시오.

> ┤ 보기 ├
> catch a cold / look forward to / get rid of / keep away from

(1) _____ your bag _____ _____ the fireplace.
(2) The boy was _____ _____ _____ watching the parade.
(3) He didn't come to school. Did he _____ _____ _____?
(4) What can I do to _____ _____ _____ my stress?

Conversation

[07~09] 다음 대화를 읽고 물음에 답하시오.

Sujin: John, (A) _____

John: Last week, there was a soccer match. I kicked a rock by mistake.

Sujin: Oh, your foot must hurt very much! Did you go to the hospital?

John: ⓐ Yes, the doctor (B)_____ I shouldn't play soccer for a month.

Sujin: ⓑ Oh, no. What will you do for the next game?

John: ⓒ I'll need to find another soccer player.

Sujin: ⓓ He's good at playing soccer.

John: ⓔ That's a good idea. I'll go ask him now.

07 위 대화의 빈칸 (A)에 들어갈 말로 어색한 것은?

① what's the problem with your foot?
② what's the matter with your foot?
③ what happened to your foot?
④ what's wrong with your foot?
⑤ what do you do?

08 위 대화의 빈칸 (B)에 들어갈 수 있는 것을 모두 고르시오.

① said
② told
③ spoke
④ explained
⑤ asked

09 위 대화의 ⓐ~ⓔ 중 주어진 문장이 들어가기에 가장 적절한 곳을 고르시오.

Why don't you ask Kevin?

① ⓐ ② ⓑ ③ ⓒ ④ ⓓ ⑤ ⓔ

[10~11] 다음 대화를 읽고 물음에 답하시오.

B: The weather is so nice today. Why do you have an umbrella?

G: _____

B: Oh, no. I didn't know that! I don't have an umbrella.

G: Don't worry. You can share my umbrella.

10 위 대화의 빈칸에 들어갈 말을 보기에 주어진 단어를 배열하여 완성하시오.

보기
said / rain / this / the weather / it / afternoon / report / would

➡ _____

11 What will the girl do for the boy when it rains?

➡ _____

[12~14] 다음 대화를 읽고 물음에 답하시오.

Diego: Achoo! Achoo!

Suji: Did you catch a cold, Diego?

Diego: No, I don't feel sick, but I can't stop sneezing. Achoo!

Suji: Then, it must be because of the yellow dust. The weather report said the yellow dust would be terrible today.

Diego: Oh, I guess I'm sneezing because of (A)that. Can't we stop the yellow dust?

Suji: Yes, we can. My club members are preparing to do some special activities abroad.

Diego: What are (B)they?

Suji: We're planning to plant trees in China because a lot of the yellow dust comes from China.

Diego: That sounds good.

Suji: Yes. (C)_____

12 위 대화의 밑줄 친 (A)와 (B)가 각각 가리키는 것을 찾아 쓰시오.

➡ (A) _____ (B) _____

13 위 대화의 빈칸 (C)에 들어갈 말을 <보기>에 주어진 어휘를 이용하여 영작하시오.

> ┌─── 보기 ───
> we / looking / stop / the yellow
> dust

➡ _____

14 위 대화의 내용과 일치하지 <u>않는</u> 것은?

① Diego couldn't stop sneezing due to the yellow dust.

② According to the weather report, the yellow dust would be terrible today.

③ There was nothing to do to stop the yellow dust.

④ Suji's club members made a plan to plant trees in China.

⑤ A lot of the yellow dust comes from China.

Grammar

15 다음 주어진 두 문장을 하나의 문장으로 쓸 때 빈칸에 들어갈 말로 가장 적절한 것은?

> • I put the milk in the refrigerator.
> • I wanted to make sure it didn't spoil.
> = I put the milk in the refrigerator _____
> _____.

① so that I don't have to spoil it

② so spoiled that I had to put it in there

③ so that I can spoil it

④ so that it wouldn't spoil

⑤ so spoiled that you couldn't drink it

16 so ~ that이나 so that을 이용하여 두 문장을 자연스럽게 연결하시오.

> • The wind was strong.
> • Clara got a new job.

> • She could be closer to her house.
> • It blew my hat off my head.

➡ _____

➡ _____

17 다음 빈칸에 들어갈 말로 적절한 것을 고르시오.

> Do you know _____ to the mart?

① why to go   ② where to go

③ how to do   ④ when to go

⑤ which to go

18 다음 중 어법상 올바른 문장의 개수는?

> ⓐ Can you tell me how I to behave in front of the elderly?
> ⓑ Susan exercises regularly so that she can be in good shape.
> ⓒ Mike was so nervous that he couldn't even drink water.
> ⓓ Tell her when she should enter the room for an interview.
> ⓔ I spoke slowly so that she will understand me.

① 1개   ② 2개   ③ 3개   ④ 4개   ⑤ 5개

19 다음 빈칸에 알맞은 말을 쓰시오.

> A: I don't know _____ _____ _____ _____ to her.
> B: Saying it with flowers is one of good ways to say sorry.

20 다음 중 우리말을 영어로 바르게 옮기지 않은 것은?

① 나는 너무 피곤해서 어제 일찍 잤어.

  I was so tired that I went to sleep early yesterday.

② 안녕이라고 말하는 방식은 문화마다 다르다.

  How to say hello varies in different cultures.

③ 함께 외출할 수 있도록 집에 일찍 와.

  Come home early so that we can go out together.

④ 무엇을 찾아야 할지 알려줄게.

  I will tell you what you should find.

⑤ 내 심장이 너무 빠르게 뛰어서 거의 말을 할 수 없어.

  My heart beat fast so that I can hardly speak.

21 다음 빈칸에 들어갈 말이 바르게 짝지어진 것은?

Tell them _____ clearly _____ they can do the work perfectly.

① when to go – because
② what to do – so that
③ how to do – or
④ where to do – so that
⑤ whom to ask – unless

22 알맞은 접속사를 이용하여 다음 두 문장을 하나의 문장으로 쓰시오.

Be quiet. I want to be able to hear what Sharon is saying.

➡ _____

23 다음 빈칸에 가장 적절한 것은?

A: Would you tell me _____ to the museum?
B: Just go straight. Then you can see it on your left side.

① when I should go   ② where to go
③ how you should go   ④ how to go
⑤ who I should go with

24 다음 중 빈칸에 들어갈 말로 가장 적절한 것은?

Dad gave me some money _____ I could buy the book.

① because   ② so that   ③ but
④ while   ⑤ until

25 주어진 단어를 활용하여 다음 우리말을 영어로 쓰시오.

영화 보는 것을 즐길 수 있도록 나는 내 휴대전화기를 껐다. (turn off / enjoy / watch)

➡ _____

  _____

Reading

[26~28] 다음 글을 읽고 물음에 답하시오.

Minsu(18, a high school student)
Planting trees in the desert (A)[is / are] hard and expensive. However, many Chinese people know that they cannot live (B)[if / unless] they don't plant trees. They always thank us, Korean volunteers, because we plant trees with them. However, we plant trees (C)[to help / helping] not only China but also Korea.

26 다음 중 위 글을 읽고 답할 수 <u>없는</u> 것은?

① How old is Minsu?

② Who plants trees in China?

③ Where do they plant trees?

④ Why do they plant trees?

⑤ How much does it cost to plant trees?

27 (A)~(C)에서 어법상 옳은 것을 바르게 짝지은 것은?

① is – if – to help

② are – if – to help

③ is – if - helping

④ are – unless – to help

⑤ is – unless – to help

28 Why do the Chinese people thank the Korean volunteers? Answer in English with a full sentence.

➡ _____

[29~33] 다음 글을 읽고 물음에 답하시오.

Jimin's father grew plants in a small garden at their house. He did this ①so that he could help to protect the environment. When many students became sick because of bad air, Jimin decided that he wanted to do something about it. His father said ②that ⓐ_____ could help ③solve this problem. At first, however, Jimin didn't know ⓑ_____ the plants. He asked his club members for ④some advices. One member had a good idea. They could grow plants at their school! All of the club members ⑤were very happy because, by growing plants, they could also plant some seeds of hope.

29 빈칸 ⓐ에 들어갈 말을 위 글에서 찾아 쓰시오.

➡ _____

30 다음 중 빈칸 ⓑ에 들어갈 말로 가장 적절한 것은?

① when to do   ② what to do with

③ where to grow   ④ how to grow

⑤ why he should grow

31 위 글의 내용에 맞게 다음 대화의 빈칸에 알맞은 말을 쓰시오.

> **Jimin:** Dad, why do you grow plants in the garden?
>
> **Dad:** I do this _____ _____ _____ _____.

32 ①~⑤ 중 어법상 <u>틀린</u> 것은?

① ② ③ ④ ⑤

33 다음 중 위 글의 내용과 일치하지 <u>않는</u> 것은?

① There was a small garden at Jimin's house.

② Jimin's father wanted to protect the environment.

③ Jimin decided to grow plants at his school by himself.

④ One of Jimin's club members gave Jimin a good idea.

⑤ All of the club members felt happy about growing plants.

[01~03] 다음 대화를 읽고 물음에 답하시오.

Sujin: John, what happened ⓐto your foot?

John: Last week, there was a soccer match. I kicked a rock ⓑon mistake.

Sujin: Oh, your foot (A)must hurt very much! Did you go to the hospital?

John: Yes, the doctor said I shouldn't play soccer ⓒfor a month.

Sujin: Oh, no. What will you do ⓓfor the next game?

John: I'll need to find another soccer player.

Sujin: Why don't you ask Kevin? He's good ⓔ at playing soccer.

John: That's a good idea. I'll go ask him now.

출제율 90%

01 위 대화의 ⓐ~ⓔ 중 어색한 것을 골라 바르게 고치시오.

➡ _____

출제율 100%

02 위 대화의 밑줄 친 (A)와 같은 의미로 쓰인 것은?

① You must keep quiet in the library.

② He must be hungry after working all day.

③ The visitors must not walk on the grass.

④ The students must hand in their assignment on time.

⑤ The doctor said that I must stay in the hospital for a month.

출제율 90%

03 위 대화의 내용과 일치하지 않는 것은?

① John은 지난주 축구 경기 중에 발을 다쳤다.

② 의사 선생님은 John에게 한 달 동안 축구하지 말아야 한다고 했다.

③ John은 다음 경기를 위해 다른 축구 선수가 필요하다.

④ John은 지금 Kevin에게 갈 것이다.

⑤ John은 다음 축구 경기에 Kevin과 함께 출전할 것이다.

[04~05] 다음 설명을 읽고 물음에 답하시오.

Jane: Do you want to watch the movie, *The Big Zoo*?

Alex: No, I don't. My brother watched the movie last week. He said it was terrible.

Jane: Then, what shall we do?

Alex: _____

출제율 95%

04 위 대화의 빈칸에 들어갈 말로 어색한 것은?

① We can take a walk in the park instead.

② Why don't we take a walk in the park?

③ How about taking a walk in the park?

④ Let's take a walk in the park.

⑤ We don't have to walk in the park.

출제율 90%

05 Why didn't Alex want to see *The Big Zoo*?

➡ _____

[06~07] 다음 대화를 읽고 물음에 답하시오.

Diego: Achoo! Achoo!

Suji: Did you catch a cold, Diego?

Diego: No, I don't feel sick, but I can't stop sneezing. Achoo!

Suji: Then, it must be because of the yellow dust. The weather report said the yellow dust would be terrible today.

Diego: Oh, I guess I'm sneezing because of that. Can't we stop the yellow dust?

Suji: Yes, we can. My club members are preparing to do some special activities abroad.

Diego: What are they?

Suji: We're planning to (A)<u>plant</u> trees in China because a lot of the yellow dust comes from China.

Diego: That sounds good.

Suji: Yes. We are looking forward to stopping the yellow dust.

06 위 대화의 밑줄 친 (A)와 같은 의미로 쓰인 것은?

① The scientists investigated the animal and <u>plant</u> life of the area.

② A huge chemical <u>plant</u> is being built.

③ We are going to <u>plant</u> flowers in the garden.

④ Sunlight and water are needed for <u>plant</u> growth.

⑤ My father always waters the <u>plant</u> in the morning.

07 위 대화를 읽고 대답할 수 <u>없는</u> 것은?

① Why can't Diego stop sneezing?

② How is the weather today?

③ What did Suji's club members make a plan to do in China?

④ What are Suji's club members looking forward to?

⑤ What do Suji's club members prepare to plant trees?

[08~10] 다음 대화를 읽고 물음에 답하시오.

Sujin: John, what happened to your foot?

John: Last week, there was a soccer match. I kicked a rock by mistake.

Sujin: Oh, your foot must hurt very much! Did you go to the hospital?

John: Yes, the doctor said I shouldn't play soccer for a month.

Sujin: Oh, no. What will you do for the next game?

John: I'll need to find another soccer player.

Sujin: Why don't you ask Kevin? He's good at playing soccer.

John: That's a good idea. I'll go ask him now.

08 When did John hurt his foot?

➡ _____

09 Why did Sujin recommend Kevin to John?

➡ _____

10 How long shouldn't John play soccer?

➡ _____

11 다음 빈칸에 들어갈 말로 가장 적절한 것은?

| A: Let's decide _____. |
| B: I think we should start on April 1st. |

① where to go   ② what to eat

③ when to begin   ④ who to tell

⑤ how to do it

출제율 90%

12 다음 우리말을 영어로 바르게 옮긴 것은?

> 이 차를 어디에 주차해야 하는지 말해주세요.

① I wonder how I should park this car.
② Tell me where to park this car.
③ I wonder who to park this car.
④ Tell me when I should park this car.
⑤ I wonder how to park this car.

출제율 95%

13 다음 중 어법상 바르지 <u>않은</u> 것은?

① He allowed me to use the computer so that I could find the file.
② The noise was so loud that I was really annoyed.
③ I don't know when to send the message.
④ Ron went to Chicago in order that he could visit his grandparents.
⑤ He wanted to know where should learn Chinese.

출제율 90%

14 다음 우리말을 영어로 옮길 때 빈칸에 알맞은 말을 쓰시오.

> 그들은 우리에게 무엇을 먹을지 그리고 언제 그 것을 먹을지 말해준다.

➡ They tell us _____

출제율 90%

15 다음 문장과 의미가 같은 것을 <u>모두</u> 고르시오.

> Rita has to work at two jobs to support her three children.

① Rita has to work at two jobs in order that she could support her three children.
② Rita has to work at two jobs so hard that she could support her three children.
③ Rita has to work at two jobs so that she could support her three children.
④ Rita has to work at two jobs unless she had to support her three children.
⑤ Rita has to work at two jobs that could support her and her three children.

출제율 95%

16 다음 글을 읽고 알맞은 접속사를 이용하여 화자의 상황을 한 문장으로 쓰시오.

> Helen wants to get an A. So she studies English very hard.

➡ _____

출제율 100%

17 다음 대화의 빈칸에 알맞은 말을 쓰시오.

> A: I don't know _____ this picture.
> B: I think you should hang it in the livingroom.

[18~21] 다음 글을 읽고 물음에 답하시오.

> Li Na(16, a middle school student)
> A long time ago, this place was a big forest. ① But people began to cut down trees so that they could build cities. ② As time passed, the forest lost many trees. ③ Now, when the spring brings strong winds from the west, the yellow dust spreads. ④ In the past, most people did not know how to stop the yellow dust problem. ⑤ Now, many volunteers plant trees ⓐto solve this problem.

출제율 90%

18 ①~⑤ 중 주어진 문장이 들어가기에 가장 적절한 곳은?

> Finally, the forest became a desert and the desert became bigger and bigger.

①   ②   ③   ④   ⑤

19 다음 중 밑줄 친 ⓐ와 쓰임이 같은 것은?

① Is there anyone to talk with you?

② She went out to buy something.

③ All I need is to be alone.

④ It is nice to see you again.

⑤ Thomas wanted to be the greatest son in the world.

20 다음 중 위 글의 내용과 일치하지 <u>않는</u> 것은?

① There were many trees in the place.

② People cut down trees to build cities.

③ The forest turned into a desert.

④ The desert became a forest by the effort of the volunteers.

⑤ The yellow dust is spread by the spring winds.

21 위 글의 내용에 맞게 빈칸에 알맞은 말을 쓰시오.

> The solution to the problem of the yellow dust is _____ .

➡ _____

[22~25] 다음 글을 읽고 물음에 답하시오.

Jimin's father grew plants in a small garden at their house. He did this so that he could help to protect the environment. When many students became sick because of bad air, Jimin decided that he wanted to do something about it. His father said that growing plants could help solve this problem. At first, ⓐ_____, Jimin didn't know where to grow the plants. He asked his club members for some advice. One member had a good idea. They could grow plants at their school! All of the club members were very happy ⓑ_____, by growing plants, they could also plant some seeds of hope.

22 빈칸 ⓐ와 ⓑ에 들어갈 말이 바르게 짝지어진 것은?

① for example – on the other hand

② however – because

③ in addition – on the contrary

④ because – thus

⑤ in fact – that is to say

23 다음 중 위 글을 읽고 답할 수 <u>없는</u> 것은?

① Who grew plants at Jimin's house?

② What made many students become sick?

③ How many members were there in Jimin's club?

④ Why were all the club members happy?

⑤ What made Jimin want to do something about bad air?

24 위 글의 내용에 맞게 다음 빈칸에 알맞은 말을 쓰시오.

> Jimin: I don't know _____ _____ _____ _____ the plants.
>
> Friend: How _____ _____ them _____ _____ _____ ?
>
> Jimin: That's a great idea!

25 다음 빈칸에 알맞은 말을 위 글에서 찾아 쓰시오.

> A _____ is the small, hard part of a plant from which a new plant grows.

[01~03] 다음 대화를 읽고 물음에 답하시오.

> Chris: Do you have any plans for this coming Friday?
>
> Emily: I do. I volunteer at a lost pet center every Friday.
>
> Chris: What do you do at the lost pet center?
>
> Emily: Well, I take the dogs out for a walk. Also, I help to wash them.
>
> Chris: That sounds wonderful. Why do you go there every week?
>
> Emily: It's because I love animals. I want to become an animal doctor in the future.
>
> Chris: I love animals too. Can I join you this Friday?
>
> Emily: Sure. (A)I look forward to seeing you at the center. (wait, to)

01 위 대화의 밑줄 친 (A)와 의미가 같도록 주어진 단어를 사용하여 다시 쓰시오.

➡ _____

02 What are Chris and Emily going to do this Friday?

➡ _____
_____

03 Why does Chris want to join Emily this Friday?

➡ _____

04 주어진 어구를 활용하여 다음 우리말을 영어로 쓰시오.

> 엄마, 내가 똑똑해지기 위해서 무엇을 해야 할지 말해주시겠어요?
> (can / to / so that / smart)

➡ Mom, _____
_____

05 주어진 접속사를 이용하여 다음 문장과 같은 의미의 문장을 쓰시오.

> Dave, can you borrow me some money? I have to pay my rent. (so that)

➡ Dave, _____
_____

06 다음 빈칸에 알맞은 말을 쓰시오.

> This book taught me _____ _____ think.
> = This book taught me how _____ _____ _____.

07 주어진 어구를 활용하여 다음 우리말을 영어로 쓰시오.

> 돈을 더 벌기 위해서 나는 새로운 직장을 얻었다.
> (get a new job / earn / so that)

➡ _____

08 주어진 어구를 바르게 배열하여 다음 우리말을 영어로 쓰시오.

> 내가 나의 이메일을 확인할 수 있도록 그 남자는 내게 약간의 시간을 주었다.
> (my e-mail / the man / could / that / order / check / in / me / some time / gave / I)

➡ _____

_____

[09~10] 다음 글을 읽고 물음에 답하시오.

> Many people are wearing masks ⓐ<u>so that they can keep away from an unwelcome guest in the spring: yellow dust.</u> Every year, there is widespread yellow dust in Korea. Many people become sick because the yellow dust hurts their eyes and throats. Why does the yellow dust come about? Is there any way to stop the yellow dust? Yes, there is!

09 to부정사를 이용하여 밑줄 친 ⓐ와 같은 의미의 문장을 쓰시오.

➡ _____

_____

10 위 글의 빈칸 ⓐ, ⓑ에 알맞은 말을 각각 세 단어로 쓰시오.

> A: My eyes and throat are sore because of yellow dust. I don't know ⓐ _____
> _____ _____.
> B: Here's what you should do. ⓑ _____
> _____ _____ whenever you go out.

[11~13] 다음 글을 읽고 물음에 답하시오.

> Minsu(18, a high school student)
> Planting trees in the desert is hard and expensive. However, many Chinese people know that they cannot live if they don't plant trees. They always thank us, Korean volunteers, because we plant trees with them. However, we plant trees to help not only China but also Korea.

11 위 글의 내용에 맞게 빈칸에 알맞은 말을 쓰시오.

> Many Chinese people know that they cannot live unless _____.

12 According to the passage, to whom do the Chinese feel thankful?

➡ _____

13 Write the reason why Korean volunteers plant trees. Use the given phrase.

> so that

➡ _____

_____

01 다음 대화의 내용과 일치하도록 Sujin의 일기를 완성하시오.

> Sujin: John, what happened to your foot?
> John: Last week, there was a soccer match. I kicked a rock by mistake.
> Sujin: Oh, your foot must hurt very much! Did you go to the hospital?
> John: Yes, the doctor said I shouldn't play soccer for a month.
> Sujin: Oh, no. What will you do for the next game?
> John: I'll need to find another soccer player.
> Sujin: Why don't you ask Kevin? He's good at playing soccer.
> John: That's a good idea. I'll go ask him now.

> Mon, April 29th, 2020
> I was surprised when I saw John's foot. He said that he hurt his foot during (A)_____. I thought his foot must hurt very much. He told me that he should not (B)_____. He was worried about the next game. So, I recommended Kevin to him because (C)_____. John looked happy and went to ask him if he could take part in the next game. I was pleased to help him.

02 주어진 어구와 '의문사+to부정사'를 활용하여 다양한 문장을 써보시오.

> find my key / go for the club meeting / for my homework / bake cookies / ask the questions

(1) _____
(2) _____
(3) _____
(4) _____
(5) _____

03 목적의 부사절을 적절히 이용하여 자연스러운 문장을 만드시오.

> Kevin went to England _____
> I bought the picture _____
> We need to exercise _____
> I study hard _____

(1) _____
(2) _____
(3) _____
(4) _____

단원별 모의고사

01 다음 영영풀이가 가리키는 것을 고르시오.

> existing or happening over a large area or among many people

① terrible   ② widespread
③ welcome   ④ limited
⑤ unknown

02 다음 우리말에 맞게 빈칸에 알맞은 말을 쓰시오.

(1) 세계에서 가장 큰 사막은 사하라이다.
  ➡ The world's biggest _____ is the Sahara.

(2) 나는 자원봉사 활동에서 그녀를 만났다.
  ➡ I met her during the _____ _____.

03 다음 주어진 문장의 밑줄 친 match와 같은 의미로 쓰인 것은?

> He hurt his knee at the soccer <u>match</u>.

① This scarf doesn't <u>match</u> your dress.
② I need a <u>match</u> to light up this room.
③ The doors were painted white to <u>match</u> the wallpaper.
④ The <u>match</u> was tied three to tree yesterday.
⑤ The dark clouds <u>match</u> her mood.

04 다음 우리말을 주어진 단어를 이용하여 영작하시오.

(1) Mike는 영어뿐만 아니라 불어도 한다. (not only, French)
  ➡ _____

(2) 우리는 이 모든 쓰레기를 없앨 필요가 있다. (rid, trash)
  ➡ _____

(3) 에어컨을 꺼주시겠어요? (would, turn)
  ➡ _____

[05~06] 다음 대화를 읽고 물음에 답하시오.

Jane: Do you want to watch the movie, *The Big Zoo*?
Alex: No, I don't. My brother watched the movie last week. (A)<u>He said it was terrible.</u> (told)
Jane: Then, what shall we do?
Alex: We can take a walk in the park instead.
Jane: Sounds great.

05 위 대화의 밑줄 친 (A)를 주어진 단어를 사용하여 의미가 같도록 쓰시오.

➡ _____

06 What are Alex and Jane going to do together?

➡ _____

07 다음 대화가 자연스럽게 이어지도록 순서대로 배열하시오.

> John, what happened to your foot?

> (A) Oh, no. What will you do for the next game?
> (B) I'll need to find another soccer player.
> (C) Yes, the doctor said I shouldn't play soccer for a month.
> (D) Oh, your foot must hurt very much! Did you go to the hospital?
> (E) Last week, there was a soccer match. I kicked a rock by mistake.

➡ _____

[08~10] 다음 대화를 읽고 물음에 답하시오.

Chris: Do you have any plans for this coming Friday?

Emily: I do. I volunteer at a lost pet center every Friday.

Chris: What do you do at the lost pet center?

Emily: Well, I take the dogs out ⓐfor a walk. Also, I help ⓑto wash them.

Chris: That sounds ⓒwonderful. Why do you go there every week?

Emily: It's ⓓbecause I love animals. I want to become an animal doctor in the future.

Chris: I love animals too. Can I join you this Friday?

Emily: Sure. I look forward to ⓔsee you at the center.

08 위 대화의 밑줄 친 ⓐ~ⓔ 중 어법상 어색한 것을 찾아 바르게 고치시오.

➡ _____

09 위 대화에서 다음 영영풀이가 나타내는 말을 찾아 쓰시오.

to offer to do something without being forced to do it or without getting paid for it

➡ _____

10 위 대화의 내용과 일치하지 <u>않는</u> 것은?

① Emily는 매달 유기 동물 센터에서 봉사활동을 한다.

② Emily는 유기 동물 센터에서 개들을 산책시키고 그들을 씻기는 것을 도와준다.

③ Emily는 미래에 수의사가 되고 싶어 한다.

④ Chris는 동물을 좋아해서 Emily와 함께 자원봉사에 참여하길 원한다.

⑤ Emily는 이번 주 Chris를 유기 동물 센터에서 만나길 기대한다.

[11~12] 다음 대화를 읽고 물음에 답하시오.

B: You look happy. What's up?

G: (A)_____

B: (B)Me too! Someone said that the school band practiced a lot this time.

G: I can't wait to hear them!

11 위 대화의 빈칸 (A)에 들어갈 말을 주어진 단어를 모두 배열하여 완성하시오.

┌─── 보기 ───┐
forward / the / school / weekend / this / I'm / to / looking / festival
└──────────┘

➡ _____

_____

12 위 대화의 밑줄 친 (B)와 바꾸어 쓸 수 있는 것은?

① So am I.　　　　② So do I.

③ Neither am I.　　④ Neither do I.

⑤ Neither did I.

13 다음 중 어법상 바르지 <u>않은</u> 것은?

① He didn't tell me where to hang my clothes.

② I went to Seoul so that I could meet my friends.

③ Most people have no idea how to dictate.

④ Jenny went to the library in order to she could study hard.

⑤ I don't know how to make a kite.

14 적절한 접속사를 활용하여 다음 두 문장을 하나의 문장으로 쓰시오.

> • Harry cleans his classroom.
> • It becomes very clean.

➡ _____

_____

15 다음 빈칸에 들어갈 말로 적절한 것을 <u>모두</u> 고르면?

> Molly writes a lot of short stories _____ she may become a writer.

① so that
② in order to
③ in order that
④ although
⑤ but

16 다음 문장의 밑줄 친 부분과 같은 의미의 문장을 고르시오.

> Today is my mom's birthday, but I don't know <u>what to buy for her</u>.

① what she should buy for her
② what I buy for her
③ what I should buy for her
④ what she should buy herself
⑤ what we should buy her

17 주어진 어구를 활용하여 다음 우리말을 영어로 쓰시오.

> 그는 화가가 되기 위해서 매일 그림을 그린다.
> (draw / every day / order / can / painter)

➡ _____

_____

[18~21] 다음 글을 읽고 물음에 답하시오.

Minsu(18, a high school student)
Planting trees in the desert is hard and expensive. ⓐ_____, many Chinese people know that they cannot live if they don't plant trees. They always thank us, Korean volunteers, because we plant trees with them. ⓑ_____, we plant trees to help not only China but also Korea.

Suji(15, a middle school student)
At first, I didn't know what to do to get rid of the yellow dust. Then, Minsu, my group leader, told me that planting trees can help ⓒto solve the problem. I also found out that planting trees and protecting the environment help my family and me.

18 빈칸 ⓐ와 ⓑ에 공통으로 들어갈 말로 가장 적절한 것은?

① Instead
② For example
③ However
④ Nevertheless
⑤ On the other hand

19 다음 중 위 글의 내용과 일치하지 <u>않는</u> 것은?

① Minsu is Suji's group leader.
② It is hard to say that planting trees in the desert is expensive.
③ Chinese people plant trees with Korean volunteers.
④ Suji talked with Minsu about the yellow dust.
⑤ Chinese people know the need to plant trees.

20 밑줄 친 ⓒ가 의미하는 것을 위 글에서 찾아 쓰시오.

➡ _____

21 위 글의 내용에 맞게 빈칸에 알맞은 말을 쓰시오.

By _____, we can help the world.

➡ _____

22 주어진 문장과 자연스럽게 연결되도록 (A)~(D)를 바르게 나열하시오.

Jimin's father grew plants in a small garden at their house.

(A) His father said that growing plants could help solve this problem. At first, however, Jimin didn't know where to grow the plants.

(B) All of the club members were very happy because, by growing plants, they could also plant some seeds of hope.

(C) He did this so that he could help to protect the environment. When many students became sick because of bad air, Jimin decided that he wanted to do something about it.

(D) He asked his club members for some advice. One member had a good idea. They could grow plants at their school!

➡ _____

[23~25] 다음 글을 읽고 물음에 답하시오.

Jimin's father grew plants in a small garden at their house. (A)He did this so that he could help to protect the environment. When many students became sick (B)because of bad air, Jimin decided that he wanted to do something about it. His father said that growing plants could help solve (C)this problem. At first, however, Jimin didn't know where to grow the plants. He asked his club members for some advice. One member had a good idea. They could grow plants at their school! All of the club members were very happy because, by growing plants, they could also plant some seeds of hope.

23 다음 중 밑줄 친 (A)와 의미가 다른 것은?

① He did this in order that he could help to protect the environment.

② He did this to help to protect the environment.

③ He did this in order to help to protect the environment.

④ He did this so as he could help to protect the environment.

⑤ He did this so as to help to protect the environment.

24 다음 중 밑줄 친 (B)를 대신하여 쓰일 수 있는 것은?

① despite of ② because

③ due to ④ according to

⑤ although

25 밑줄 친 (C)가 의미하는 것을 두 단어의 영어로 쓰시오.

➡ _____

Lesson 3

I'll Always Be There for You.

🔍 의사소통 기능

- 의견 표현하기
  In my opinion, she is too famous.

- 알고 있는지 묻기
  You know about Helen Keller, don't you?

🔍 언어 형식

- to부정사의 형용사적 용법
  The poor girl needed **somebody to take** care of her.

- 동사의 강조
  She **did become** a totally different person.

Words & Expressions

Key Words

- **accident** [ǽksidənt] 명 사고
- **active** [ǽktiv] 형 활발한
- **appreciate** [əprí:ʃièit] 동 고마워하다
- **attack** [ətǽk] 동 공격하다
- **bitter** [bítər] 형 맛이 쓴, 씁쓸한
- **blind** [blaind] 형 눈이 먼, 맹인인
- **boring** [bɔ́:riŋ] 형 지루한, 재미없는
- **chance** [tʃæns] 명 기회
- **choose** [tʃu:z] 동 선택하다
- **composer** [kəmpóuzər] 명 작곡가
- **contest** [kántest] 명 경연
- **decide** [disáid] 동 결정하다
- **difficult** [dífikʌlt] 형 어려운, 힘든
- **drummer** [drʌ́mər] 명 드럼 연주자
- **experience** [ikspíəiəns] 명 경험
- **famous** [féiməs] 형 유명한
- **librarian** [laibrɛ́əriən] 명 사서
- **interview** [íntərvjù:] 동 인터뷰하다
- **invite** [inváit] 동 초대하다
- **math** [mæθ] 명 수학
- **miracle** [mírəkl] 명 기적
- **nurse** [nə:rs] 명 간호사
- **opinion** [əpínjən] 명 의견
- **overcome** [ouvərkʌ́m] 동 극복하다
- **pond** [pɑnd] 명 연못
- **prepare** [pripɛ́ər] 동 준비하다
- **realize** [rí:əlàiz] 동 실현하다, 깨닫다
- **scary** [skɛ́əri] 형 무서운, 두려운
- **score** [skɔ:r] 명 점수
- **scream** [skri:m] 동 비명을 지르다
- **sheep** [ʃi:p] 명 양
- **social studies** 사회
- **taste** [teist] 명 기호, 취향
- **terrible** [térəbl] 형 끔찍한
- **thirsty** [θə́:rsti] 형 목마른
- **throw** [θrou] 동 던지다
- **totally** [tóutəli] 부 완전히, 전적으로
- **touching** [tʌ́tʃiŋ] 형 감동적인
- **trouble** [trʌ́bl] 명 곤경, 곤란
- **volunteer** [vɑ́ləntíər] 동 자원봉사하다

Key Expressions

- **at last** 마침내
- **be able to** ~할 수 있다
- **be afraid of** ~을 두려워하다
- **be proud of** ~을 자랑스러워하다
- **give up** 포기하다
- **little by little** 조금씩, 천천히
- **make a choice** 선택하다
- **pass away** 죽다
- **put someone to bed** 누군가를 재우다
- **take care of** ~을 돌보다

Word Power

※ 서로 반대되는 뜻을 가진 단어

□ **famous** 유명한 ↔ **unknown** 알려지지 않은

□ **active** 활발한 ↔ **inactive** 활발하지 않은

□ **attack** 공격하다 ↔ **defend** 방어하다

□ **forget** 잊다 ↔ **remember** 기억하다

□ **send** 보내다 ↔ **receive** 받다

□ **difficult** 어려운 ↔ **easy** 쉬운

□ **boring** 지루한 ↔ **interesting** 흥미로운

□ **worried** 걱정스러운 ↔ **relieved** 안도한

□ **special** 특별한 ↔ **general** 일반적인

□ **interviewer** 면접관 ↔ **interviewee** 면접자

English Dictionary

□ **appreciate** 고마워하다
  → to be grateful for something that somebody has done
  누군가가 한 무언가에 대해 감사해하다

□ **attack** 공격
  → an act of using violence to try to hurt or kill somebody
  누군가를 다치게 하거나 죽이려고 폭력을 사용하는 행위

□ **blind** 눈이 먼
  → not able to see
  볼 수 없는

□ **choose** 선택하다
  → to decide which thing or person you want out of the ones that are available
  이용 가능한 것들 가운데 당신이 원하는 것이나 사람을 결정하다

□ **composer** 작곡가
  → a person who writes music, especially classical music
  음악, 특히 클래식 음악을 쓰는 사람

□ **contest** 경연
  → a competition in which people try to win something
  사람들이 무언가를 쟁취하려고 노력하는 경쟁

□ **drummer** 드럼 연주자
  → a person who plays a drum or drums
  드럼을 연주하는 사람

□ **librarian** 사서
  → a person who is in charge of or works in a library
  도서관을 담당하거나 도서관에서 일하는 사람

□ **miracle** 기적
  → an act or event that does not follow the laws of nature and is believed to be caused by God
  자연 법칙을 따르지 않거나 신에 의해 야기되었다고 믿어지는 행동이나 사건

□ **overcome** 극복하다
  → to succeed in dealing with or controlling a problem that has been preventing you from achieving something
  당신이 무언가를 성취하는 것을 막고 있는 문제를 다루거나 조절하는데 성공하다

□ **pond** 연못
  → a small area of still water, especially one that is artificial
  흐르지 않는 물이 있는 작은 지역으로, 특히 인공인 곳

□ **opinion** 의견
  → your feelings or thoughts about somebody/something, rather than a fact
  사실보다는 누군가 또는 무언가에 대한 당신의 생각이나 느낌

□ **thirsty** 목마른
  → needing or wanting to drink
  물을 마실 필요가 있거나 마시기를 원하는

□ **touching** 감동적인
  → causing feelings of pity or sympathy; making you feel emotional
  유감이나 동정심을 야기하는, 당신을 감정적으로 느끼게 만드는

01 다음 짝지어진 단어의 관계가 같도록 빈칸에 알맞은 말을 쓰시오.

> forget : remember = _____ : defend

02 다음 문장의 빈칸에 공통으로 들어갈 말을 고르시오.

> • My teacher was proud _____ herself because of her students.
> • I always take care _____ my babies.
> • Don't be afraid _____ wild animals.

① on   ② by   ③ for
④ to   ⑤ of

03 다음 대화의 빈칸에 들어갈 말로 가장 적절한 것을 고르시오.

> My sister is a _____. She helps sick people in the hospital.

① nurse   ② reporter
③ librarian   ④ teacher
⑤ photographer

04 서답형 다음 우리말을 주어진 단어를 이용하여 영작하시오.

(1) 그의 어머니는 그가 어릴 때 돌아가셨다. (passed)

➡ _____

(2) 나는 조금씩 나아지고 있다. (little)

➡ _____

(3) 나는 내 여동생을 돌보아야 한다. (have, care, younger)

➡ _____

05 다음 영영풀이가 의미하는 것을 고르시오.

> to succeed in dealing with or controlling a problem that has been preventing you from achieving something

① compete   ② overcome
③ fail   ④ attack
⑤ choose

06 다음 중 밑줄 친 부분의 뜻풀이가 바르지 않은 것은?

① I would <u>appreciate</u> it if you could give me a ride. 감상하다
② I fell asleep because the movie was too <u>boring</u>. 지루한
③ A <u>composer</u> is a person who writes music. 작곡가
④ It was a <u>miracle</u> that she was able to see again. 기적
⑤ You can <u>realize</u> your dream when you do your best. 실현하다

07 서답형 다음 문장의 빈칸에 들어갈 말을 보기에서 골라 쓰시오.

> ┌ 보기 ┐
> thirsty / taste / touching / miracle

(1) It is a _____ that he's still alive.
(2) My mother and I have the same _____ in clothes.
(3) I cried a lot, reading the _____ story.
(4) I'm _____. I want something to drink.

01 다음 짝지어진 단어의 관계가 같도록 빈칸에 알맞은 말을 쓰시오.

famous : unknown = send : _____

02 다음 우리말에 맞게 주어진 단어를 사용하여 영작하시오.

(1) 내 생각에, 그것은 감동적인 영화야.
(touching, opinion)

➡ _____

(2) 이 그림에 대해 어떻게 생각해? (what, of)

➡ _____

(3) 너는 베토벤에 대해 알고 있지, 그렇지 않니?
(Beethoven, about)

➡ _____

03 다음 우리말에 맞게 빈칸에 알맞은 말을 쓰시오.

(1) 간호사는 맹인이 길을 건너는 것을 돕고 있다.
➡ The _____ is helping the _____
man cross the street.

(2) 너는 어둠을 두려워할 필요가 없어.
➡ You don't have to _____ _____
_____ the dark.

(3) 당신은 이 문제를 어떻게 극복하셨나요?
➡ How did you _____ this trouble?

(4) 우리 힐머니는 작년에 돌아가셨다.
➡ My grandmother _____ _____
last year.

(5) 나의 영어는 조금씩 향상되고 있다.
➡ My English is improving _____
_____ _____.

(6) 나는 지금 당장 선택해야 한다.
➡ I have to _____ _____
right now.

04 다음 영영풀이가 가리키는 것을 쓰시오.

not able to see

➡ _____

05 다음 주어진 우리말과 일치하도록 주어진 단어를 모두 배열하여 영작하시오.

(1) 내 생각에, 우리가 그녀를 방문한다면 그녀는
매우 행복할 거야.
(opinion / she / be / very / in / if / we /
visit / will / her / my / happy)

➡ _____

(2) Annie가 물건을 던지기 시작했을 때, 간호사
는 그녀를 두려워하지 않았다.
(started / wasn't / Annie / things / the
nurse / when / throwing / of / afraid / her)

➡ _____
_____

(3) 나는 쌍둥이를 재울게.
(to / put / I'll / bed / twins / the)

➡ _____

06 다음 우리말에 맞게 영작하시오.

(1) 내 생각에, 우리 영어 선생님은 학교에서 가장
친절하신 선생님이시다.

➡ _____

(2) 너는 모차르트에 대해 알고 있니?

➡ _____

(3) 포기하지 마. 너도 그것을 할 수 있어!

➡ _____

Conversation

1 의견 표현하기

In my opinion, she is too famous. 내 생각에, 그녀는 너무 유명해.
I think it's beautiful. 나는 이것이 아름답다고 생각해.

■ 의견 표현하기
자신의 의견을 표현할 때, 'In my opinion' 또는 'I think ~' 등의 표현을 사용하여 나타낼 수 있다.

의견 표현하기

• In my opinion, she would love some letters from her students. (내 생각에, 그녀는 학생들로부터 받은 편지를 매우 좋아할 거야.)

• (Well,) I think we need to talk about it. ((음.) 나는 우리가 그것에 대해 이야기를 할 필요가 있다고 생각해.)

• I believe you can make it. (나는 네가 해낼 수 있을 것이라 믿어.)

• I feel you can win the contest. (나는 네가 그 경연에서 우승할 수 있을 것 같아.)

의견 묻기

• What do you think about this picture? (이 그림에 대해 어떻게 생각해?)

• How do you feel about my new hair style? (내 새 헤어스타일이 어떠니?)

• What is your opinion? (네 의견은 어때?)

핵심 Check

1. 다음 우리말과 일치하도록 빈칸에 알맞은 말을 쓰시오.

(1) **A:** You know about Helen Keller, don't you? I chose to write about her.

(너는 Hellen Keller에 대해 알고 있지, 그렇지 않니? 나는 그녀에 대해 쓰기로 선택했어.)

B: _____ _____ _____, she is great. (내 생각에, 그녀는 훌륭해.)

(2) **A:** _____ _____ _____ _____ _____ this movie?

(이 영화에 대해 어떻게 생각해?)

B: I think it is so touching. (나는 매우 감동적이라고 생각해.)

(3) **A:** I'm so nervous because of my English contest. (나는 영어 경연대회 때문에 매우 긴장돼.)

B: _____ _____ _____ _____ _____ _____.

(나는 네가 해낼 수 있을 것이라고 믿어.)

2 알고 있는지 묻기

You know about Helen Keller, don't you? 너는 Helen Keller에 대해 알고 있지, 그렇지?

Do you know about Lee Hee Ah? 너는 이희아에 관해서 알지?

■ 알고 있는지 묻기
상대방이 어떠한 사실이나 일에 대해 알고 있는지 물을 때 Do you know (about) ~? 또는 'You know ~, don't you?' 등의 표현을 이용하여 물을 수 있다.

알고 있는지 묻기

- Do you know (about) Dr. Schweitzer? (너는 Schweitzer 박사에 대해 알고 있니?)
- Have you heard (about) the new teacher? (너는 새 선생님에 관해 들어 들어봤니?)
- You know Mr. Song, don't you? (너는 Mr. Song을 알고 있지. 그렇지 않니?)
- Are you aware of the time? (시간은 알고 있나요?)

알고 있음을 표현하기

- I know (about) Helen Keller. (나는 Helen Keller를(에 대해) 알고 있어.)
- I heard (about) Mozart. (나는 모차르트에 대해 들어봤어.)
- I have heard (about) Beethoven. (나는 베토벤에 대해 들어봤어.)
- I've been told (about) my new English teacher. (나는 새로운 영어 선생님에 대해 들었어.)
- I'm aware of the rules. (나는 규칙에 대해 알고 있어.)

모르고 있음을 표현하기

- I don't know. (저는 모르겠어요.)
- I have no idea. (저는 모르겠어요.)
- I haven't got a clue. (짐작이 안 되네요.)

핵심 Check

2. 다음 우리말과 일치하도록 빈칸에 알맞은 말을 쓰시오.

(1) **A:** You know the class singing contest is next Friday, _____ _____?
(당신은 학급 노래 경연이 다음 주 금요일이라는 것을 알고 있죠, 그렇지 않나요?)

B: _____ _____ _____. (네, 알고 있어요.)

(2) **A:** Do you know the history project? (너는 역사 프로젝트를 알고 있니?)

B: No. _____ _____ _____ _____. (아니요. 저는 모르겠어요.)

(3) **A:** _____ _____ _____ Rick Allen, don't you? (너는 Rick Allen에 대해 알고 있지, 그렇지?)

B: Of course I do. Isn't he the drummer with one arm? (물론 알지. 그는 한쪽 팔만 있는 드러머 아냐?)

A. Everyday English1 B. Listening Activity

Brian: What's the matter? You ❶look worried.

Amy: ❷I'm worried about my history test. My history score is lower than my math score.

Brian: ❸Why don't you take Mr. Choi's afterschool class?

Amy: Well, I took his social studies class last month, but ❹it was a little boring for me.

Brian: ❺In my opinion, his history class is more interesting than his social studies class.

Amy: Really?

Brian: Yes. I also got a high score on my history test after taking his class.

Amy: Maybe I should take his class too. Thanks.

Brian: 무슨 일이야? 걱정하는 듯 보여.

Amy: 역사 시험이 걱정이야. 역사 성적이 수학 성적보다 낮거든.

Brian: 최 선생님의 방과 후 수업을 듣는 건 어때?

Amy: 글쎄. 지난달에 사회 수업을 들었는데 약간 지루하더라고.

Brian: 내 생각에는, 그의 역사 수업은 사회 수업보다는 더 재미있어.

Amy: 진짜?

Brian: 응. 난 그 선생님 수업 듣고 나서 역사 성적도 올랐어.

Amy: 아마 나도 그 수업 들어야 할 것 같다. 고마워.

❶ look+형용사: ~해 보이다　　　　❷ be worried about ~: ~을 걱정하다
❸ Why don't you ~?: ~하는 게 어때? = How about ~?
❹ it은 Mr. Choi's social studies를 가리킨다.　　❺ 의견을 나타내는 표현이다.

Check(√) True or False

(1) Amy was worried about her history exam.　　　　T ☐ F ☐

(2) Brian liked Mr. Choi's social studies class more than his history class.　　　　T ☐ F ☐

B. In Real Life

Olivia: What are you doing, Junho?

Junho: I'm working on my history project. I need to write about a famous person. That person should have a story of ❶overcoming difficulties in their life.

Olivia: Hmm. Who did you choose?

Junho: You know about Helen Keller, ❷don't you? I chose to write about ❸her.

Olivia: In my opinion, she is too famous. It may not be interesting.

Junho: Then, who should I choose?

Olivia: Do you know the story about Little Annie?

Junho: Who is that?

Olivia: I will show you a video about her life. ❹She'll be a great topic for your project.

Olivia: 준호야, 뭐 하고 있니?

Junho: 역사 과제를 하고 있어. 유명한 사람에 관해 써야 해. 인생에 있어 어려움을 극복한 이야기가 있는 사람이어야 해.

Olivia: 음, 넌 누구를 골랐니?

Junho: Helen Keller에 관해 알지, 그렇지? 그녀에 관해 쓸 거야.

Olivia: 내 생각에는, 그녀는 너무 유명해. 재미없을지도 몰라.

Junho: 그럼, 누구를 골라야 할까?

Olivia: Little Annie에 관한 이야기를 아니?

Junho: 그게 누군데?

Olivia: 그녀의 삶에 관한 비디오를 보여줄게. 네 과제를 위한 좋은 주제가 될 거야.

❶ overcome: 극복하다　　　　❷ 부가의문문으로 대답은 'Yes, I do.' 또는 'No, I don't.'로 한다.
❸ her는 Helen Keller를 가리킨다.　　❹ She는 Little Annie를 가리킨다.

Check(√) True or False

(3) Junho and Olivia were talking about the topic of his history project.　　　　T ☐ F ☐

(4) Olivia thought that Helen Keller is a great topic for Junho's history project.　　　　T ☐ F ☐

📌 Everyday English 1 A. Function Practice 2-(1)

G: We ❶have to choose a story for our school play.

B: ❷Why don't we choose one of Shakespeare's plays?

G: How about *Hamlet*? It's very ❸famous.

B: ❹In my opinion, it's too sad for our school play. Let's find another story.

❶ have to는 조동사로 '～해야 한다'라는 의무를 나타낸다.
❷ Why don't we ～?: '～하는 게 어때?'라며 제안하는 표현이다.
❸ famous: 유명한
❹ 의견을 나타내는 표현이다.

📌 Everyday English 2 A. Function Practice 2-(2)

Amy: I really love the drums, but ❶I'm not good at playing. Maybe I should ❷give up.

Bob: Hey, don't say ❸that. You know about Rick Allen, don't you?

Amy: Of course I do. Isn't ❹he the drummer with one arm?

Bob: Yes, he is. Don't give up! You can do it too!

❶ be good at ～: ～을 잘하다
❷ give up: 포기하다
❸ that은 Amy가 이야기한 'Maybe I should give up.'을 가리킨다.
❹ he는 Rick Allen을 가리킨다.

📌 Everyday English 1 A. Function Practice 2-(2)

G: What is your favorite book?

B: My favorite book is *The Old Man and the Sea*.

G: Really? In my opinion, it's ❶a little ❷boring.

B: Everyone ❸has different ❹tastes.

❶ a little: 약간, 조금
❷ boring: 지루한
❸ Everyone은 단수 취급하므로 단수 동사가 이어진다.
❹ taste는 '취향'을 뜻한다.

📌 Everyday English 2 A. Function Practice 2-(1)

G: ❶You know about Lee Hee Ah, don't you?

B: No, I don't. Who is ❷she?

G: She plays the piano very well, ❸even though she only has two fingers on each hand.

B: ❹That's amazing.

❶ 상대방에게 알고 있음을 확인하는 표현이다.
❷ she는 Lee Hee Ah를 가리킨다.
❸ even though = though = 비록 ～일지라도
❹ 감탄을 나타내는 표현이다.

📌 Everyday English 2 B. Listening Activity

M: Hello. You all know me, don't you? As you can see, I don't have any arms or legs. When I was young, I was sad and angry about ❶myself. Then ❷one day, I read a story about a man ❸like me. He said that I had a choice in my life. I could be happy or angry about myself. So, I decided to love my life. Now, I am a happy man. I give speeches around the world, and give people hope. Here is my message for you. In life, you have a choice: better or bitter? Choose better, forget bitter.

❶ 주어와 목적어가 같을 때 재귀대명사를 쓴다.
❷ one day: 어느 날
❸ like는 전치사로 '～처럼, ～같은'을 의미한다.

● 다음 우리말과 일치하도록 빈칸에 알맞은 말을 쓰시오.

Everyday English 1 A. Function Practice 2-(1)

G: We have to choose a story for our school play.

B: _____ _____ _____ _____ one of Shakespeare's plays?

G: How about *Hamlet*? It's very _____.

B: _____ _____ _____, it's too sad for our school play. Let's find another story.

Everyday English 1 A. Function Practice 2-(2)

G: What is your favorite book?

B: My favorite book is *The Old Man and the Sea.*

G: Really? _____ _____ _____, it's a little _____.

B: _____ _____ _____ _____.

Everyday English 1 B. Listening Activity

Brian: What's the matter? You look _____.

Amy: _____ _____ _____ my history test. My history score is lower than my math score.

Brian: Why don't you take Mr. Choi's afterschool class?

Amy: Well, I took his _____ _____ _____ last month, but it was a little boring for me.

Brian: _____ _____ _____, his history class is _____ _____ _____ his social studies class.

Amy: Really?

Brian: Yes. I also got a high score on my history test after taking his class.

Amy: Maybe_____ _____ _____ _____ _____ _____ _____.
　　　Thanks.

Everyday English2 A. Function Practice 2-(1)

G: _____ _____ _____ Lee Hee Ah, don't you?

B: _____ _____ _____. Who is she?

G: She plays the piano very well, _____ _____ she only has two fingers on each hand.

B: That's amazing.

해석

G: 우리는 학교 연극을 위해 이야기를 골라야 해.
B: 셰익스피어 희곡 중 하나를 고르는 것은 어때?
G: 햄릿은 어때? 그건 아주 유명하잖아.
B: 내 생각에는, 그건 학교 연극으로는 너무 슬픈 것 같아. 다른 이야기를 찾아보자.

G: 가장 좋아하는 책이 뭐야?
B: 내가 가장 좋아하는 책은 '노인과 바다(The Old Man and the Sea,)'야.
G: 정말? 내 생각엔, 좀 지루하던데.
B: 모두가 다른 취향을 갖고 있지.

Brian: 무슨 일이야? 걱정하는 듯 보여.
Amy: 역사 시험이 걱정이야. 역사 성적이 수학 성적보다 낮거든.
Brian: 최 선생님의 방과 후 수업을 듣는 건 어때?
Amy: 글쎄. 지난달에 사회 수업을 들었는데 약간 지루하더라고.
Brian: 내 생각에는, 그의 역사 수업은 사회 수업보다는 더 재미있어.
Amy: 진짜?
Brian: 응. 난 그 선생님 수업 듣고 나서 역사 성적도 올랐어.
Amy: 아마 나도 그 수업 들어야 할 것 같다. 고마워.

G: 너 이희아에 관해서 알지, 그렇지?
B: 아니, 몰라. 누구니?
G: 그녀는 각 손에 오직 두 개의 손가락만 가졌음에도 피아노를 굉장히 잘 쳐.
B: 정말 놀랍다.

Everyday English 2 A. Function Practice 2-(2)

Amy: I really love the drums, but I'm _____ _____ _____ playing. Maybe I should _____ _____.

Bob: Hey, don't say that. You know about Rick Allen, don't you?

Amy: _____ _____ _____ _____. Isn't he the drummer with one arm?

Bob: Yes, he is. Don't give up! _____ _____ _____ _____ _____!

Everyday English 2 B. Listening Activity

M: Hello. You all know me, don't you? As you can see, I don't have any arms or legs. When I was young, I was _____ and _____ about _____. Then one day, I read a story about a man _____ me. He said that _____ _____ _____ _____ in my life. I could be happy or angry about myself. So, _____ _____ _____ _____ _____ _____. Now, I am a happy man. I give speeches around the world, and give people hope. Here is my message for you. In life, you have a choice: _____ or _____ ? _____ _____, _____ _____.

In Real Life

Olivia: What are you doing, Junho?

Junho: I'm working on my _____ _____. I need to write about a famous person. That person should have a story of _____ _____ in their life.

Olivia: Hmm. Who did you choose?

Junho: You know about Helen Keller, _____ _____? I chose to write about her.

Olivia: In my opinion, she is _____ _____. It may not be _____.

Junho: Then, who should I choose?

Olivia: _____ _____ _____ the story about Little Annie?

Junho: Who is that?

Olivia: I will show you a video about her life. She'll be a great topic for your project.

해석

Amy: 난 진짜 드럼이 좋아. 그러나 난 연주를 잘하지 못해. 아마도 난 포기해야 하나봐.
Bob: 이봐, 그렇게 말하지 마. Rick Allen 알지, 그렇지?
Amy: 물론 알지. 그는 한쪽 팔만 있는 드러머 아냐?
Bob: 그래. 그 사람이야. 포기하지 마! 너 또한 할 수 있어.

M: 안녕하세요, 모두 저 아시죠, 그렇죠? 여러분이 보다시피, 저는 팔과 다리가 없습니다. 제가 어렸을 때 저 자신에 대해 슬프고 화가 났습니다. 그런데 어느 날, 저와 같은 어떤 사람에 관한 이야기를 읽었습니다. 그는 내가 내 삶에 있어서 선택권이 있다고 말했습니다. 나는 나 자신에 대해 행복할 수도 화가 날 수도 있습니다. 그래서 난 내 삶을 사랑하기로 했습니다. 지금 저는 행복한 사람입니다. 저는 전 세계를 돌아다니며 강연을 하고 사람들에게 희망을 줍니다. 여기 제가 하고 싶은 말이 있습니다. 삶에 있어서, 당신은 선택권이 있습니다. 더 나아질 것이냐, 더 쓰라릴 것이냐? 나아지길 선택하세요. 쓰라린 것은 잊고요.

Olivia: 준호야, 뭐 하고 있니?
Junho: 역사 과제를 하고 있어. 유명한 사람에 관해 써야 해. 인생에 있어 어려움을 극복한 이야기가 있는 사람이어야 해.
Olivia: 음, 넌 누구를 골랐니?
Junho: Helen Keller에 관해 알지, 그렇지? 그녀에 관해 쓸 거야.
Olivia: 내 생각에는, 그녀는 너무 유명해. 재미없을지도 몰라.
Junho: 그럼, 누구를 골라야 할까?
Olivia: Little Annie에 관한 이야기를 아니?
Junho: 그게 누군데?
Olivia: 그녀의 삶에 관한 비디오를 보여줄게. 네 과제를 위한 좋은 주제가 될 거야.

01 다음 대화의 빈칸에 들어갈 말로 적절한 것을 <u>모두</u> 고르시오.

> A: What do you think of this picture?
>
> B: _____

① I'm thinking it's beautiful.　　② I'm glad you like it.

③ I'm afraid but I can't.　　④ I'm sorry to hear that.

⑤ In my opinion, it's not so great.

02 다음 대화의 빈칸 (A)에 들어갈 수 있는 말을 <u>모두</u> 고르시오.

> G: (A)_____
>
> B: No, I don't. Who is she?
>
> G: She plays the piano very well, even though she only has two fingers on each hand.
>
> B: That's amazing.

① Have you heard about Lee Hee Ah?

② You know about Lee Hee Ah, don't you?

③ Are you aware of Lee Hee Ah?

④ Do you know about Lee Hee Ah?

⑤ Does Lee Hee Ah know about you?

[03~04] 다음 대화를 읽고 물음에 답하시오.

> Amy: I really love the drums, but I'm not good at playing. Maybe I should give up.
>
> Bob: Hey, don't say that. You know about Rick Allen, don't you?
>
> Amy: (A)_____ Isn't he the drummer with one arm?
>
> Bob: Yes, he is. Don't give _____(B)_____! You can do it too!

03 위 대화의 빈칸 (A)에 들어갈 말로 적절한 것은?

① Yes, I am.　　② Of course I do.

③ No, I didn't.　　④ No, I do.

⑤ Of course I'm not.

04 위 대화의 빈칸 (B)에 알맞은 말을 쓰시오.

➡ _____

[01~02] 다음 대화를 읽고 물음에 답하시오.

G: We have to choose a story for our school play.

B: ___(A)___ don't we choose one of Shakespeare's plays?

G: How about *Hamlet*? It's very famous.

B: In my opinion, it's too sad for our school play. Let's find another story.

서답형

01 위 대화의 빈칸 (A)에 알맞은 말을 쓰시오.

➡ _____

02 위 대화의 내용과 일치하지 <u>않는</u> 것은?

① They had to choose a story for their school play.

② The boy suggested choosing one of Shakespeare's plays.

③ The girl recommended *Hamlet* for their school play.

④ The boy thought *Hamlet* was sad for their school play.

⑤ They are going to choose *Hamlet* as their school play.

[03~04] 다음 대화를 읽고 물음에 답하시오.

Brian: What's the matter? You look ⓐworried.

Amy: I'm worried about my history test. My history score is lower than my math score.

Brian: Why don't you ⓑtake Mr. Choi's afterschool class?

Amy: Well, I took his social studies class last month, but it was a little ⓒboring for me.

Brian: In my opinion, his history class is more

ⓓinterested than his social studies class.

Amy: Really?

Brian: Yes. I also got a high score on my history test after ⓔtaking his class.

Amy: Maybe I should take his class too. Thanks.

서답형

03 위 대화의 밑줄 친 ⓐ~ⓔ 중 어법상 <u>어색한</u> 것을 찾아 바르게 고치시오.

➡ _____

04 위 대화의 내용과 일치하지 <u>않는</u> 것은?

① Amy는 역사 시험을 걱정하고 있다.

② Amy의 역사 점수는 수학 점수보다 낮다.

③ Brian은 최 선생님의 방과 후 수업을 Amy에게 추천하였다.

④ Brian은 최 선생님의 사회 수업을 역사 수업보다 선호한다.

⑤ Brian은 최 선생님의 수업을 들은 후 역사 시험에서 높은 점수를 받았다.

[05~06] 다음 대화를 읽고 물음에 답하시오.

Amy: I really love the drums, but I'm not good at playing. Maybe I should give up.

Bob: Hey, don't say that. You know about Rick Allen, don't you?

Amy: Of course I do. Isn't he the drummer with one arm?

Bob: Yes, he is. Don't give up! You can do it too!

서답형

05 What's the matter with Amy?

➡ _____

서답형

06 Why is Rick Allen special?

➡ _____

[07~08] 다음 설명을 읽고 물음에 답하시오.

M: Hello. You all know me, don't you? As you can see, I don't have any arms or legs. When I was young, I was sad and angry about myself. Then one day, I read a story about a man like me. He said that I had a choice in my life. I could be happy or angry about myself. So, I decided to (A)[love / hate] my life. Now, I am a happy man. I give speeches around the world, and give people (B)[despair / hope]. Here is my message for you. In life, you have a choice: better or bitter? Choose better, (C)[remember / forget] bitter.

07 위 설명의 문맥상 (A)~(C)에 들어갈 말로 적절한 것끼리 짝지어진 것은?

	(A)	(B)	(C)
①	love	despair	remember
②	love	hope	forget
③	love	hope	remember
④	hate	hope	forget
⑤	hate	despair	remember

08 What is the speaker's message?

① Read a story about a person like you.
② Be happy with your life.
③ Choose bitter, forget better.
④ Help your friends in need.
⑤ Compare yourself with others.

[09~10] 다음 대화를 읽고 물음에 답하시오.

Olivia: What are you doing, Junho?
Junho: I'm working on my history project. I need to write about a famous person. (A) That person should have a story of overcoming difficulties in their life.
Olivia: (B) Hmm. Who did you choose?
Junho: (C) I chose to write about her.
Olivia: (D) In my opinion, she is too famous. It may not be interesting.

Junho: (E) Then, who should I choose?
Olivia: Do you know the story about Little Annie?
Junho: Who is that?
Olivia: I will show you a video about her life. She'll be a great topic for your project.

09 위 대화의 (A)~(E) 중 주어진 문장이 들어가기에 적절한 곳은?

> You know about Helen Keller, don't you?

① (A) ② (B) ③ (C) ④ (D) ⑤ (E)

10 위 대화를 읽고 대답할 수 없는 것은?

① What project is Junho working on?
② Who is Junho considering for the topic of the project?
③ What does Olivia think about Helen Keller as the topic?
④ Who does Olivia recommend to Junho?
⑤ Why can Little Annie be a good topic for Junho's project?

11 다음 짝지어진 대화가 어색한 것은?

① A: Did you watch *Spiderman*?
   B: Yes, I did. In my opinion, it's a funny movie.
② A: What do you think about our music teacher?
   B: I think he has a great voice and his class is a lot of fun.
③ A: Math is too hard for me.
   B: Buy Mr. Min's math book. In my opinion, it's good for beginners.
④ A: He was a famous composer. You know about him, don't you?
   B: Well, he wasn't. He was Beethoven.
⑤ A: You know about Stephen Hawking, don't you?
   B: I have no idea. Who is he?

[01~05] 다음 대화를 읽고 물음에 답하시오.

Brian: What's the matter? You look worried.

Amy: I'm worried about my history test. (A) My history score is lower than my math.

Brian: Why don't you take Mr. Choi's afterschool class?

Amy: Well, I took his social studies class last month, but it was a little boring for me.

Brian: In my opinion, his history class is more interesting than his social studies class.

Amy: Really?

Brian: Yes. I also got a high score on my history test after taking his class.

Amy: Maybe I should take his class too. Thanks.

01 What subject is Amy worried about?

➡ _____

02 What did Amy think about Mr. Choi's social studies class last month?

➡ _____

03 What is Brian's advice for Amy?

➡ _____

04 Why does Brian recommend Mr. Choi's afterschool class?

➡ _____

_____

05 위 대화의 밑줄 친 (A)에서 어법상 어색한 것을 찾아 바르게 고치시오.

➡ _____

06 다음 대화의 내용과 일치하도록 Junho의 일기의 빈칸을 완성하시오.

Olivia: What are you doing, Junho?

Junho: I'm working on my history project. I need to write about a famous person. That person should have a story of overcoming difficulties in their life.

Olivia: Hmm. Who did you choose?

Junho: You know about Helen Keller, don't you? I chose to write about her.

Olivia: In my opinion, she is too famous. It may not be interesting.

Junho: Then, who should I choose?

Olivia: Do you know the story about Little Annie?

Junho: Who is that?

Olivia: I will show you a video about her life. She'll be a great topic for your project.

⬇

Mon, June 19th, 2019

Today, I was working on my history project when I met Olivia. My project was to write about a famous person who (A) _____ .

I was thinking about Helen Keller. But Olivia said that she was too famous, so it might not be interesting. I asked her (B)_____ for the project. She recommended (C)_____ and showed me (D)_____ . I appreciated her about helping me to choose my topic.

Grammar

교과서

1 to부정사의 형용사적 용법

I have a friend to meet. 나는 만날 친구가 있다.
Jenny has much homework to do. Jenny에게는 해야 할 많은 숙제가 있다.

- to부정사는 'to+동사원형'의 형태로 명사, 형용사, 부사로 사용될 수 있다.
  - **To take** pictures is my hobby. 사진을 찍는 것은 나의 취미야.
  - Is there anything **to buy**? 살 만한 것이 있니?

- to부정사가 형용사로 사용될 때는 바로 앞에 위치한 명사를 꾸며준다.
  - I have a letter **to give** you. 나는 너에게 줄 편지를 가지고 있어.
  - There is nothing **to say** about it. 그것에 관해서 말할 것이 없어.

- to부정사가 형용사로 사용될 때 전치사로 끝나는 경우를 주의하자.
  수식받는 명사가 본래 전치사의 목적어로 사용되었기 때문에, 수식받는 명사를 to부정사 뒤에 넣어
  보아 전치사가 필요한지 여부를 확인하는 것이 좋다.
  - Do you have a dog **to look** after? (look after a dog (○))
    Do you have a dog to look? (look a dog (×))

- 형용사와 to부정사가 -thing, -body, -one으로 끝나는 부정대명사를 동시에 수식할 때는 '대명사+
  형용사+to부정사'의 어순을 따른다.
  - I want something cold **to drink**. 나는 차가운 마실 것을 원해요.

핵심 Check

1. 다음 우리말과 일치하도록 빈칸에 알맞은 말을 쓰시오.
   (1) 나는 만날 친구가 있다.
   ➡ I have a friend ＿＿＿＿＿ ＿＿＿＿＿.
   (2) 그녀는 내게 진실을 말해준 유일한 사람이다.
   ➡ She is the only person ＿＿＿＿＿ ＿＿＿＿＿ ＿＿＿＿＿ the truth.
   (3) 쓸 종이가 좀 필요해요.
   ➡ I need some paper ＿＿＿＿＿ ＿＿＿＿＿ ＿＿＿＿＿.
   (4) 걱정할 무언가가 있니?
   ➡ Do you have anything ＿＿＿＿＿ ＿＿＿＿＿ ＿＿＿＿＿?

2 동사의 강조

I **do** hate doing it. 나는 그것을 하는 것이 정말로 싫어.

John **did** accept the job. John이 그 일을 정말로 수락했어.

■ 동사를 강조하는 경우 주어의 인칭, 수, 그리고 동사의 시제에 따라서 동사원형 앞에 do, does, did를 써서 동사를 강조한다.

• Your mom **did** see your performance. 너희 어머니는 너의 공연을 정말로 보셨어.

• Betty **does** look good today. Betty는 오늘 정말로 좋아 보여.

• They **do** work together. 그들은 일을 정말로 같이 해.

• My friend **does** like you. 내 친구는 너를 정말로 좋아해.

• I **do** hate to learn English. 나는 영어를 배우기가 정말로 싫어.

• You **did** need my help at that time. 너는 그 당시에 내 도움이 정말로 필요했어.

• She **does** ride a bike on her own. 그녀가 정말로 혼자서 자전거를 타.

• Thomson **did** make the food without any help. Thompson은 정말로 아무 도움 없이 그 음식을 만들었다.

핵심 Check

2. 다음 문장을 동사를 강조하여 다시 쓰시오.

(1) The puppy really looks cute.

➡ _____

(2) I really made the pizza by myself.

➡ _____

(3) Kelly really wants to buy the car.

➡ _____

(4) The boy certainly understood what you said.

➡ _____

(5) We really had dinner together.

➡ _____

01 다음 문장에서 어법상 <u>어색한</u> 부분을 찾아 바르게 고쳐 쓰시오.

(1) Jenny did believed what you said.

_____ ➡ _____

(2) My brother needed something eat.

_____ ➡ _____

(3) The men does like the cake.

_____ ➡ _____

(4) There is no chance to winning the game.

_____ ➡ _____

02 주어진 동사를 어법에 맞게 빈칸에 쓰시오.

(1) I want to have the ability _____ well in front of people.
(speak)

(2) Yesterday, Julia _____ read the book from cover to cover. (do)

(3) I have no desire _____ math. (study)

(4) Is there another way _____ the situation? (solve)

(5) Amelia _____ keep a diary every day. (do)

> from cover to cover: 처음부터 끝까지

03 주어진 단어를 바르게 배열하여 다음 우리말을 영어로 쓰시오. 필요하다면 단어를 추가하거나 변형하시오.

(1) 읽을 메시지의 제목을 누르세요. (read / click / of / the title / the message)

➡ _____

(2) 선택할 많은 선택지가 있어. (choose / options / many / are / there)

➡ _____

(3) 나는 정말로 1등 상을 탔어요. (win / I / prize / the first)

➡ _____

(4) 너는 정말로 재능이 있어. (talent / you / have)

➡ _____

01 다음 중 빈칸에 들어갈 말이 다른 하나는?

① The boy _____ take an interest in your friend.
② A dog _____ follow me every morning.
③ My sister _____ go to school on foot.
④ Your feet _____ look cute.
⑤ The lion _____ look hungry.

02 다음 중 용법이 다른 하나는?

① There are many problems to solve.
② Katherine wanted to buy a house to live in.
③ He went to a department store to buy a new suit.
④ Do you have milk to use instead of cream?
⑤ I have a question to ask.

03 다음 중 'to say'가 들어갈 곳으로 적절한 곳은?

> I have ① something ② important ③ to ④ you ⑤ right now.

①   ②   ③   ④   ⑤

서답형
04 동사를 강조하여 다음 문장을 다시 쓰시오.

> Molly wanted to meet him soon.

➡ _____

05 다음 중 밑줄 친 부분의 쓰임이 틀린 것은?

① The doctor <u>did</u> warn me not to overeat.
② Many children <u>do</u> play computer games too much.
③ Your pants <u>does</u> look nice.
④ I <u>did</u> get this book for free.
⑤ One of my friends <u>does</u> hate oranges.

06 다음 중 우리말을 영어로 바르게 옮기지 않은 것은?

① 나는 모든 것을 잘 기억하는 능력이 있다.
→ I have the ability to remember everything well.
② 우리는 새로운 사무실을 열 계획을 가지고 있어.
→ We have a plan to open a new office.
③ Jason은 콘서트에서 BTS를 정말로 보았어.
→ Jason did see BTS at their concert.
④ 여행하면서 읽을 책 한 권을 빌릴 수 있을까요?
→ Can I borrow a book to read on my journey?
⑤ 그 소식은 날 정말로 실망스럽게 한다.
→ The news does makes me disappointed.

서답형
07 동사를 강조하는 문장을 써서 다음 우리말을 영어로 쓰시오.

> 그 가위는 정말로 위험해 보여.

➡ _____

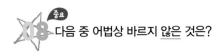

08 다음 중 어법상 바르지 <u>않은</u> 것은?

> In the animation movie, the princess ①
> does ②have the ability ③hold up a person
> ④with ⑤her hair.

①　　　②　　　③　　　④　　　⑤

09 다음 중 어법상 옳은 문장의 개수는?

> ⓐ Kevin did kept his promise.
> ⓑ Is there anything to see in this place?
> ⓒ The interview does make me nervous.
> ⓓ My attempt to fixing the radio failed.
> ⓔ She did stole my wallet.

① 1개　　　② 2개　　　③ 3개
④ 4개　　　⑤ 5개

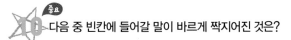

10 다음 중 빈칸에 들어갈 말이 바르게 짝지어진 것은?

> A: I have an important decision _____.
> B: Oh, that _____ sound serious. What is
> it?

① making – do　　② making – does
③ to make – does　④ to make – did
⑤ make – do

11 다음 주어진 문장에서 쓰인 to부정사와 그 용법이 같은 것은?

> Jina has many friends to talk to.

① I want you to be honest with me.
② Jane decided to go there by herself.
③ It was not easy to exercise every day.
④ Dad was sad to see them fighting again.
⑤ She had the kindness to invite me to
　 dinner.

서답형
12 주어진 단어를 바르게 배열하여 다음 우리말을 영어로 쓰시오.

> 엄마께 드릴 어떤 것을 찾고 있어요.
> (something / my mom / am / I / to / give /
> for / to / looking)

➡ _____

13 다음 빈칸에 들어갈 말로 가장 적절한 것은?

> King Sejong _____ Hangeul.

① does invent　　　② do invented
③ did invent　　　④ did invented
⑤ does invents

서답형
14 다음 중 어법상 바르지 <u>않은</u> 것을 <u>두 개</u> 찾아 바르게 고쳐
쓰시오.

> Stress is harmful to the body's ability
> fighting off illness. So we does need to
> manage stress well.

➡ _____
　 _____

15 다음 중 밑줄 친 부분의 쓰임이 바르지 <u>않은</u> 것은?

① The boys <u>did</u> run fast on the street.
② The pants you bought at the store <u>does</u>
　 look expensive.
③ It <u>did</u> turn into cheese.
④ Mike <u>did</u> break the vase with his bat
　 yesterday.
⑤ June <u>does</u> know well what happens in
　 the world.

서답형

16 주어진 문장의 밑줄 친 부분을 강조하는 문장을 쓰시오.

> Junho <u>wants</u> to be a historian.

➡ _____

17 다음 빈칸에 들어갈 말이 바르게 짝지어진 것은?

> • People _____ make mistakes sometimes.
> • The mice in the cage _____ look cute.
> • Sheep _____ sleep well on the hill.

① do – does – do
② did – does – did
③ did – does – do
④ does – did – do
⑤ do – do – do

18 다음 빈칸에 들어갈 말로 가장 적절한 것은?

> **A:** Does Porter really play the piano well?
> **B:** Yes. He _____ the piano well. I was really surprised.

① did play　　② do play
③ does play　　④ does plays
⑤ did played

19 나음 빈칸에 들어갈 말로 가장 적절한 것은?

> I need _____. Do you know a person like that?

① someone to work with diligent
② someone diligent to work with
③ someone diligent to work
④ diligent someone to work with
⑤ to work with diligent someone

20 다음 중 어법상 바르지 <u>않은</u> 것은?

① Is there anyone to help us?
② The character in the movie did make me scared.
③ Jason made a promise to be more careful.
④ The Roberts does love each other very much.
⑤ J. K. Rowling does write stories well.

21 다음 중 밑줄 친 부분의 쓰임이 <u>다른</u> 하나는?

① Preston went abroad <u>to study</u> medicine.
② We did our work hard <u>to finish</u> it on time.
③ You don't have a right <u>to do</u> this.
④ Thomas left early <u>to catch</u> the train for Busan.
⑤ Peter went to the library <u>to return</u> some books.

서답형

22 주어진 단어를 바르게 배열하여 다음 우리말을 영어로 쓰시오. 필요하다면 단어를 추가하시오.

> 나는 자동차를 살 돈이 정말로 필요해.
> (need / a car / I / money / do / buy)

➡ _____

서답형

23 다음 우리말에 맞게 빈칸에 알맞은 말을 쓰시오.

> 그곳으로 가는 가장 좋은 방법이 뭐죠?
> What is the best way _____?

➡ _____

01 주어진 단어를 활용하여 다음 우리말을 영어로 쓰시오.

> 그녀의 사과를 받아들일 이유가 없어.
> (there / reason / accept)

➡ _____

02 주어진 문장의 밑줄 친 부분을 강조하는 문장을 쓰시오.

> Body language <u>varies</u> from culture to culture.

➡ _____

3 다음 대화의 빈칸에 알맞은 말을 쓰시오.

> **A:** You _____.
> 너 정말로 바빠 보인다.
> **B:** I have _____.
> 나는 할 일을 많이 가지고 있어.

➡ A: _____
　 B: _____

04 다음 밑줄 친 부분을 강조하는 말로 문장을 다시 쓰시오.

(1) Parker <u>likes</u> to study math.

➡ _____

(2) Emily <u>went</u> on winter vacation.

➡ _____

(3) Your mom <u>worried</u> about you.

➡ _____

(4) They <u>know</u> what to do next.

➡ _____

05 주어진 단어를 바르게 배열하여 다음 우리말을 영어로 쓰시오. 필요하다면 단어를 추가하시오.

> 나는 나의 아이들을 보호할 권리가 있다.
> (the right / I / my / have / children / protect)

➡ _____

6 다음 빈칸에 알맞은 말을 쓰시오.

> I _____ _____ many things _____ _____ to you.
> 나는 너에게 할 말이 정말로 많아.

07 다음 대화의 빈칸에 알맞은 말을 쓰시오.

> **A:** Did you really see a man standing over there?
> **B:** I don't understand why you don't believe me. I _____ _____ _____ _____ _____ _____ _____.

08 주어진 단어를 바르게 배열하여 다음 우리말을 영어로 쓰시오. 필요하다면 단어를 추가하거나 변형하시오.

> 그녀는 그것에 관하여 생각할 시간이 정말로 필요해.
> (need / think / it / she / some time / about / do)

➡ _____

09 다음 빈칸에 알맞은 말을 쓰시오.

> Susan _____ _____ this doll. I saw her making it.

[10~12] 다음 글을 읽고 물음에 답하시오.

> In 1994, Heather Whitestone became Miss America. She was beautiful, but she couldn't dance to music. (A)하지만, 그녀는 대회에서 음악에 맞추어 정말로 춤을 추었습니다. After she won, (B)그녀는 그녀의 삶에 관하여 말할 기회를 가졌습니다. (C)Her story moved many people.

10 주어진 어구를 이용하여 밑줄 친 우리말 (A)를 동사를 강조하는 문장으로 쓰시오.

> dance to music

➡ _____

11 주어진 어구를 이용하여 밑줄 친 우리말 (B)를 영어로 쓰시오.

> have chances

➡ _____

12 동사를 강조하여 밑줄 친 문장 (C)를 다시 쓰시오.

➡ _____

13 주어진 단어를 활용하여 다음 우리말을 영어로 쓰시오.

> 나는 달콤한 어떤 것을 정말로 먹고 싶어. (want / something)

➡ _____

[14~15] 다음 대화를 읽고 물음에 답하시오.

> A: Rose, you look sad. What's up?
> B: As I am a new student here, I have no friends ⓐ(play / with / or / study / to).
> A: How about throwing a party and inviting some students?
> B: Oh, that's a great idea. ⓑI appreciate your advice.

14 ⓐ의 괄호 안의 단어를 바르게 배열하여 대화를 완성하시오.

➡ _____

15 밑줄 친 ⓑ를 appreciate을 강조하는 문장으로 바꿔 쓰시오.

➡ _____

16 다음 중 어법상 바르지 않은 곳을 찾아 바르게 고쳐 쓰시오.

(1) I don't like the acting class because it does makes me nervous.

➡ _____

(2) Amelia do need to buy a bed to sleep.

➡ _____

(3) Ian does have something to say to Molly yesterday, but she didn't have time talk with him.

➡ _____

The Story of Little Annie's Life

There was a little blind girl in a hospital. She was always angry.

When people tried to help her, she screamed and attacked them.

People called her "Crazy Little Annie," and didn't try to help her

anymore. The poor girl needed somebody to take care of her.

One day, an old nurse came to the hospital. She volunteered to help

Annie. When Annie met her, she started throwing things again.

However, the nurse wasn't afraid of her.

The nurse said to Annie, "Hi, Annie. I'm Nurse Laura. I'm here to be

your friend. I'll always be there for you."

Every night, Laura went to Annie's room and put her to bed. She said

to Annie, "Annie, I do love you. I'll always be there for you."

Laura knew that Annie needed love and understanding. With Laura's

help, Annie got better little by little.

blind: 눈이 먼, 맹인인
scream: 비명을 지르다
attack: 공격하다
take care of: ~을 돌보다
be afraid of: ~을 두려워하다
put somebody to bed: 누군가를 재우다
little by little: 조금씩, 천천히
totally: 완전히, 전적으로

확인문제

● 다음 문장이 본문의 내용과 일치하면 T, 일치하지 <u>않으면</u> F를 쓰시오.

1 Annie was angry from time to time. ☐

2 Nurse Laura was an old woman. ☐

3 Annie said to Laura she always loved her. ☐

4 Annie never threw anything at Laura. ☐

5 Laura helped Annie voluntarily. ☐

Two years later, Annie didn't scream or throw things. She did become a totally different person. People didn't call her "Crazy Little Annie" anymore.

2년 후에 　　　　　　　She became a totally different person.'에서 became을 강조하는 조동사

Laura decided to leave the hospital with Annie. She took Annie to a school for blind children. Annie loved her new school and studied hard. She wanted to become a teacher and help others like Nurse Laura did.

to부정사를 목적어로 취하는 동사

to부정사의 명사적 용법. wanted의 목적어로 to become과 병렬 관계

However, a few years later, Laura passed away. Annie was very sad, but she did not give up on her dream.

셀 수 있는 명사를 수식　　　후에

Then one day, Annie met a nice doctor. He helped Annie to see well. It was a miracle for Annie. At last, Annie realized her dream and became a teacher. This gave her a chance to meet a special student. The student wasn't able to hear or see. Instead, she screamed and threw things. She was just like Crazy Little Annie. Annie said to her, "Hi, Helen Keller. I'm your teacher, Anne Sullivan. I'll always be there for you."

help+목적어+(to) V

to부정사의 형용사적 용법: a chance 수식

= couldn't

your teacher = Anne Sullivan 동격

totally: 완전히, 전적으로
pass away: 사망하다, 돌아가시다
miracle: 기적
at last: 마침내
realize: 실현시키다, 깨닫다

📎 확인문제

● 다음 문장이 본문의 내용과 일치하면 T, 일치하지 않으면 F를 쓰시오.

1 Both Laura and Annie left the hospital. ☐

2 Annie liked her school very much. ☐

3 Annie studied hard to become a nurse like Laura. ☐

4 Laura was happy that Annie became a teacher. ☐

5 Annie was able to see later. ☐

● 다음 우리말을 참고하여 빈칸에 알맞은 말을 쓰시오.

The Story of Little Annie's Life

1 There _____ a little _____ _____ in a hospital.

2 She was _____ _____.

3 When people _____ _____ _____ her, she _____ and _____ them.

4 People _____ _____ "Crazy Little Annie," and didn't _____ _____ _____ her anymore.

5 The poor girl needed _____ _____ _____ _____ _____ her.

6 One day, an old nurse _____ _____ the hospital.

7 She _____ _____ _____ Annie.

8 When Annie met her, she _____ _____ again.

9 _____, the nurse wasn't _____ _____ her.

10 The nurse said to Annie, "Hi, Annie. I'm Nurse Laura. I'm here _____ _____ _____ _____. I'll _____ _____ _____ for you."

11 Every night, Laura _____ _____ Annie's room and _____ _____ _____ _____.

12 She said to Annie, "Annie, I _____ _____ _____. I'll _____ _____ _____ for you."

13 Laura knew _____ Annie _____ love and understanding.

14 _____ Laura's help, Annie got better _____ _____ _____.

15 Two years later, Annie didn't _____ _____ things.

16 She _____ _____ a totally _____ person.

꼬마 Annie의 인생 이야기

1 한 병원에 어린 눈먼 소녀가 있었습니다.

2 그녀는 항상 화가 나 있었습니다.

3 사람들이 그녀를 도우려고 할 때, 그녀는 소리 지르고 공격했습니다.

4 사람들은 그녀를 "Crazy Little Annie"라고 불렀고 더 이상 그녀를 도우려 하지 않았습니다.

5 병원은 Annie를 돌봐줄 사람이 필요했습니다.

6 어느 날, 나이 든 간호사가 병원에 왔습니다.

7 그녀는 Annie를 도울 것을 자원했습니다.

8 Annie가 그녀를 만났을 때, 그녀는 다시 물건을 던지기 시작했습니다.

9 그러나 간호사는 그녀를 두려워하지 않았습니다.

10 간호사가 Annie에게 말했습니다. "안녕, 난 간호사 Laura야. 나는 너의 친구가 될 거야. 내가 항상 너의 곁에 있을게."

11 매일 밤, Laura는 Annie의 방으로 가서 그녀를 재웠습니다.

12 그녀는 Annie에게 말했습니다. "Annie, 나는 널 정말 사랑한단다. 나는 항상 너의 곁에 있을 거야."

13 Laura는 Annie에게 사랑과 이해가 필요하다는 것을 알았습니다.

14 Laura의 도움으로 Annie는 조금씩 좋아졌습니다.

15 2년 후, Annie는 비명을 지르거나 물건을 던지지 않았습니다.

16 그녀는 전혀 다른 사람이 되었습니다.

17 People didn't _____ _____ "Crazy Little Annie" _____.

18 Laura decided _____ _____ the hospital _____ Annie.

19 She _____ Annie _____ a school _____ blind children.

20 Annie _____ her new school and _____ hard.

21 She wanted _____ _____ a teacher and _____ _____ like Nurse Laura _____.

22 However, _____ _____ _____ _____, Laura _____ _____.

23 Annie was very sad, but she _____ _____ _____ _____ on her dream.

24 Then _____ _____, Annie _____ a nice doctor.

25 He helped Annie _____ _____ _____.

26 It was _____ _____ _____ Annie.

27 At last, Annie _____ her dream and _____ a teacher.

28 This gave her a chance _____ _____ _____ _____.

29 The student _____ _____ _____ hear or see.

30 _____, she _____ and _____ things.

31 She was _____ _____ Crazy Little Annie.

32 Annie _____ _____ her, "Hi, Helen Keller. I'm your teacher, Anne Sullivan. I'll _____ _____ _____ for you."

17 사람들은 더 이상 그녀를 "Crazy Little Annie"라고 부르지 않았습니다.

18 Laura는 Annie와 병원을 떠나기로 결정했습니다.

19 그녀는 Annie를 시각장애인 학교에 데려갔습니다.

20 Annie는 새로운 학교를 좋아했으며 열심히 공부했습니다.

21 그녀는 선생님이 되어 간호사 Laura가 그랬듯 다른 사람들을 돕고 싶었습니다.

22 그러나 몇 년 후, Laura는 세상을 떠났습니다.

23 Annie는 매우 슬펐지만 그녀는 꿈을 포기하지 않았습니다.

24 그러던 어느 날, Annie는 좋은 의사를 만났습니다.

25 그는 Annie를 잘 볼 수 있게 도와주었습니다.

26 그것은 Annie에게 기적이었습니다.

27 마침내 Annie는 꿈을 실현하고자 교사가 되었습니다.

28 이것은 그녀에게 특별한 학생을 만날 기회를 주었습니다.

29 그 학생은 듣거나 볼 수 없었습니다.

30 대신에 그녀는 소리 지르고 물건을 던졌습니다.

31 그녀는 마치 "Crazy Little Annie" 같았습니다.

32 Annie는 그녀에게 말했습니다. "안녕, Helen Keller, 나는 너의 선생님 Anne Sullivan이야. 내가 항상 너의 곁에 있을게."

● 우리말을 참고하여 본문을 영작하시오.

The Story of Little Annie's Life

1 한 병원에 어린 눈먼 소녀가 있었습니다.
➡ _____

2 그녀는 항상 화가 나 있었습니다.
➡ _____

3 사람들이 그녀를 도우려고 할 때, 그녀는 소리 지르고 공격했습니다.
➡ _____

4 사람들은 그녀를 "Crazy Little Annie"라고 불렀고 더 이상 그녀를 도우려 하지 않았습니다.
➡ _____

5 병원은 Annie를 돌봐줄 사람이 필요했습니다.
➡ _____

6 어느 날, 나이 든 간호사가 병원에 왔습니다.
➡ _____

7 그녀는 Annie를 도울 것을 자원했습니다.
➡ _____

8 Annie가 그녀를 만났을 때, 그녀는 다시 물건을 던지기 시작했습니다.
➡ _____

9 그러나 간호사는 그녀를 두려워하지 않았습니다.
➡ _____

10 간호사가 Annie에게 말했습니다. "안녕, 난 간호사 Laura야. 나는 너의 친구가 될 거야. 내가 항상 너의 곁에 있을게."
➡ _____

11 매일 밤, Laura는 Annie의 방으로 가서 그녀를 재웠습니다.
➡ _____

12 그녀는 Annie에게 말했습니다. "Annie, 나는 널 정말 사랑한단다. 나는 항상 너의 곁에 있을 거야."
➡ _____

13 Laura는 Annie에게 사랑과 이해가 필요하다는 것을 알았습니다.
➡ _____

14 Laura의 도움으로 Annie는 조금씩 좋아졌습니다.
➡ _____

15 2년 후, Annie는 비명을 지르거나 물건을 던지지 않았습니다.
➡ _____

16 그녀는 전혀 다른 사람이 되었습니다.
➡ _____

17 사람들은 더 이상 그녀를 "Crazy Little Annie"라고 부르지 않았습니다.

➡ _____

18 Laura는 Annie와 병원을 떠나기로 결정했습니다.

➡ _____

19 그녀는 Annie를 시각장애인 학교에 데려갔습니다.

➡ _____

20 Annie는 새로운 학교를 좋아했으며 열심히 공부했습니다.

➡ _____

21 그녀는 선생님이 되어 간호사 Laura가 그랬듯 다른 사람들을 돕고 싶었습니다.

➡ _____

22 그러나 몇 년 후, Laura는 세상을 떠났습니다.

➡ _____

23 Annie는 매우 슬펐지만 그녀는 꿈을 포기하지 않았습니다..

➡ _____

24 그러던 어느 날, Annie는 좋은 의사를 만났습니다.

➡ _____

25 그는 Annie를 잘 볼 수 있게 도와주었습니다.

➡ _____

26 그것은 Annie에게 기적이었습니다.

➡ _____

27 마침내 Annie는 꿈을 실현하고자 교사가 되었습니다.

➡ _____

28 이것은 그녀에게 특별한 학생을 만날 기회를 주었습니다.

➡ _____

29 그 학생은 듣거나 볼 수 없었습니다.

➡ _____

30 대신에 그녀는 소리 지르고 물건을 던졌습니다.

➡ _____

31 그녀는 마치 "Crazy Little Annie" 같았습니다.

➡ _____

32 Annie는 그녀에게 말했습니다. "안녕, Helen Keller, 나는 너의 선생님 Anne Sullivan이야. 내가 항상 너의 곁에 있을게."

➡ _____

[01~04] 다음 글을 읽고 물음에 답하시오.

There was a little blind girl in a hospital. She was always angry. When people tried to help her, she screamed and attacked them. People called her "Crazy Little Annie," and didn't try to help her anymore. The poor girl needed somebody to take care of ①her.

One day, an old nurse came to the hospital. ②She volunteered to help Annie. When Annie met her, ③she started throwing things again. However, the nurse wasn't afraid of ④her. The nurse said to Annie, "Hi, Annie. I'm Nurse Laura. I'm here to be your friend. I'll always be there for ⑤you."

01 ①~⑤ 중 지칭하는 것이 다른 하나는?

①   ②   ③   ④   ⑤

02 다음 중 위 글의 내용과 일치하지 않는 것은?

① Annie was blind.
② Annie was called "Crazy Little Annie."
③ Laura was an old nurse.
④ Laura gave up helping Annie.
⑤ Annie threw things at Laura.

03 What did Laura volunteer to do? Answer in English with a full sentence.

➡ _____

서답형
04 다음과 같이 풀이되는 단어를 위 글에서 찾아 쓰시오.

unable to see

➡ _____

[05~09] 다음 글을 읽고 물음에 답하시오.

Every night, Laura went to Annie's room and ①put her to bed. She said to Annie, "Annie, I ⓐ_____ love you. I'll always be there for you."

Laura knew that Annie needed love and understanding. ②With Laura's help, Annie ③got better ④little by little.

Two years later, Annie didn't scream or throw things. ⓑShe became a totally different person. People didn't call her "Crazy Little Annie" anymore.

Laura decided to leave the hospital with Annie. She took Annie to a school for blind children. Annie loved her new school and ⑤studied hard. She wanted to become a teacher and help others like Nurse Laura did.

05 다음 빈칸 ⓐ에 들어갈 말과 다른 하나는?

① We _____ want to buy the flowers.
② They _____ think about it seriously.
③ The brothers _____ like my bike.
④ The cars _____ run fast last night.
⑤ Teachers _____ care about students.

06 다음 중 밑줄 친 ①~⑤의 풀이로 올바르지 않은 것은?

① 그녀를 재웠습니다
② Laura의 도움으로
③ 성적이 올랐습니다
④ 조금씩
⑤ 열심히 공부했습니다

서답형
07 밑줄 친 ⓑ를 동사를 강조하는 문장으로 다시 쓰시오.

➡ _____

08 다음 중 위 글의 내용과 일치하지 <u>않는</u> 것은?

① Laura put Annie to bed every night.

② Laura knew that what Annie needed was love and understanding.

③ Annie became a different person.

④ Annie screamed from time to time.

⑤ Annie was fond of her new school.

서답형

09 Where did Nurse Laura take Annie after they left the hospital? Answer the question with a full sentence.

➡ _____

[10~15] 다음 글을 읽고 물음에 답하시오.

Laura decided ⓐ_____ the hospital with Annie. She took Annie to a school for blind children. Annie loved her new school and studied hard. She wanted ⓑ_____ a teacher ⓒto help others.

However, a few years later, Laura passed away. Annie was very sad, but she did not give up on her dream.

Then one day, Annie met a nice doctor. He helped Annie to see well. It was a miracle for Annie. ⓓ At last, Annie realized her dream and became a teacher. ⓔThis gave her a chance to meet ⓕa special student. The student wasn't able to hear or see. Instead, she screamed and threw things. She was just like Crazy Little Annie. Annie said to her, "Hi, Helen Keller. I'm your teacher, Anne Sullivan. I'll always be there for you."

서답형

10 주어진 단어를 문맥과 어법에 맞게 빈칸 ⓐ, ⓑ에 쓰시오.

leave / become

➡ ⓐ_____ ⓑ_____

11 다음 중 밑줄 친 ⓒ와 쓰임이 같은 것은?

① I didn't mean <u>to make</u> you angry.

② They waited there <u>to attack</u> the enemy.

③ Joy was sad <u>to see</u> her crying.

④ It is good <u>to hear</u> from him again.

⑤ <u>To make</u> pizza is not difficult.

12 밑줄 친 ⓓ를 대신하여 쓸 수 있는 것은?

① In addition   ② Finally

③ Lastly   ④ On the contrary

⑤ On the other hand

서답형

13 밑줄 친 ⓔ가 의미하는 것을 우리말로 쓰시오.

➡ _____

14 다음 중 위 글의 내용과 일치하지 <u>않는</u> 것은?

① Annie left the hospital with Laura.

② Annie went to a school for blind children.

③ Annie studied hard to be a teacher.

④ Annie failed to make her dream real.

⑤ Annie's student couldn't see as well as hear.

15 다음 중 밑줄 친 ⓕ에 대한 설명으로 바르지 <u>않은</u> 것은?

① She was blind.

② She couldn't hear.

③ She threw things.

④ Her name is Anne Sullivan.

⑤ She shouted in a loud voice.

[16~18] 다음 글을 읽고 물음에 답하시오.

There was a little blind girl in a hospital.
[A] However, the nurse ①wasn't afraid of her. The nurse ②said to Annie, "Hi, Annie. I'm Nurse Laura. I'm here to be your friend. ③I'll always be there for you."
[B] People called her "Crazy Little Annie," and ④didn't try to help her anymore. The poor girl needed somebody to take care of her.
[C] One day, an old nurse came to the hospital. She volunteered @to help Annie. When Annie met her, she ⑤started throwing things again.
[D] She was always angry. When people tried to help her, she screamed and attacked them.

16 자연스러운 내용이 되도록 [A]~[D]를 바르게 나열한 것은?

① [B]-[A]-[C]-[D] ② [B]-[D]-[C]-[A]
③ [C]-[D]-[A]-[B] ④ [D]-[B]-[C]-[A]
⑤ [D]-[A]-[C]-[B]

17 다음 중 ①~⑤를 대신하여 쓸 수 없는 것은?

① wasn't scared of
② told Annie
③ I'll be there for you all the time
④ tried to help her one more time
⑤ started to throw things

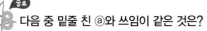
18 다음 중 밑줄 친 @와 쓰임이 같은 것은?

① Do you need something to sit on?
② Jenny went out to see her sister.
③ We didn't plan to do it at all.
④ There is much food to eat.
⑤ It is nice to hear your voice.

[19~23] 다음 글을 읽고 물음에 답하시오.

Every night, Laura went to Annie's room and put her to bed. She said to Annie, "Annie, I do love you. I'll (A)[be always / always be] there for you."
Laura knew that Annie needed love and understanding. ① With Laura's help, Annie got better little @_____ little.
Two years later, Annie didn't scream or throw things. ② She (B)[does / did] become a totally different person. People didn't call her "Crazy Little Annie" anymore. ③
Laura decided to leave the hospital with Annie. ④ Annie loved her new school and studied hard. ⑤ She wanted to become a teacher and help others like Nurse Laura (C) [was / did].

19 다음 중 빈칸 @에 들어갈 말로 가장 적절한 것은?

① in ② at ③ by ④ on ⑤ to

20 ①~⑤ 중 주어진 문장이 들어가기에 가장 적절한 곳은?

> She took Annie to a school for blind children.

①   ②   ③   ④   ⑤

21 (A)~(C)에서 어법상 옳은 것끼리 바르게 짝지어진 것은?

① be always – does – was
② be always – did – was
③ be always – does – did
④ always be – did – did
⑤ always be – did – was

서답형
22 What did Laura do for Annie every night?

➡ _____

23 다음 중 위 글을 읽고 답할 수 <u>없는</u> 것은?

① Where did Laura go every night?

② What did Laura do in Annie's room?

③ Why did Annie use to throw things and scream?

④ What did Laura decide to do?

⑤ What did Annie want to become?

[24~30] 다음 글을 읽고 물음에 답하시오.

When Helen Keller was 19 months old, she was very sick. After ⓐ<u>that</u>, she couldn't see or hear anymore.

Helen's parents thought that she needed somebody to take care of her, ⓑ_____ they asked Anne Sullivan (A)[teaching / to teach] her. Anne knew that Helen could not see or hear, but she also knew that Helen could feel things.

Anne began to write words into Helen's hand (B)[so that / in order to] Helen could learn letters. For a long time, Helen didn't understand Anne's teaching. However, Anne did not give up.

ⓒ<u>One day, Anne made Helen feel water.</u> Then she wrote w-a-t-e-r on Helen's (C) [other / the other] hand. At this point, Helen understood the lesson and wrote w-a-t-e-r on Anne's hand.

24 밑줄 친 ⓐ가 의미하는 것을 우리말로 쓰시오.

➡ _____

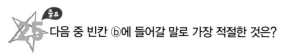

다음 중 빈칸 ⓑ에 들어갈 말로 가장 적절한 것은?

① because   ② so   ③ until

④ but   ⑤ or

26 밑줄 친 ⓒ를 동사를 강조하는 문장으로 다시 쓰시오.

➡ _____

27 (A)~(C)에서 어법상 옳은 것끼리 바르게 짝지은 것은?

① teaching – so that – other

② teaching – in order to – other

③ teaching – so that – another

④ to teach – so that – other

⑤ to teach – in order to – another

28 글의 내용에 맞게 빈칸에 알맞은 말을 쓰시오.

> Though Helen was not able to _____, she was able to _____.

29 다음 중 글의 내용과 일치하는 것의 개수는?

> ⓐ Helen couldn't see or hear after she was sick.
>
> ⓑ Helen's parents wanted someone to take care of her daughter.
>
> ⓒ Anne Sullivan taught Helen to understand letters.
>
> ⓓ It was easy for Helen to understand Anne's teaching.
>
> ⓔ Anne taught Helen letters by using hand.

① 1개   ② 2개   ③ 3개   ④ 4개   ⑤ 5개

30 What was the first thing that Helen felt? Answer in English with a full sentence.

➡ _____

[01~04] 다음 글을 읽고 물음에 답하시오.

There was a little blind girl in a hospital. She was always angry. When people tried to help her, she screamed and attacked them. People called her "Crazy Little Annie," and didn't try to help her anymore. The poor girl needed somebody to take care of her.

One day, an old nurse came to the hospital. She volunteered to help Annie. When Annie met her, she started throwing things again. However, the nurse wasn't afraid of her.

The nurse said to Annie, "Hi, Annie. I'm Nurse Laura. I'm here to be your friend. ⓐ내가 항상 너의 곁에 있을게."

01 밑줄 친 우리말 ⓐ를 영어로 쓰시오.

➡ _____

02 동사를 강조하는 문장으로 다음 대화의 빈칸을 채우시오.

> A: Is it true that people in the hospital called Annie "Crazy Little Annie?"
> B: Yes. _____ .

➡ _____

03 What did Annie do when she met Nurse Laura? Answer in English with a full sentence.

➡ _____

04 다음 Annie가 한 말을 영어로 쓰시오.

> 나는 날 도와줄 누군가를 필요로 하지 않아!

➡ _____

[05~08] 다음 글을 읽고 물음에 답하시오.

Every night, Laura went to Annie's room and put her to bed. She said to Annie, "Annie, I do love you. I'll always be there for you." Laura knew that Annie ⓐneeded love and understanding. With Laura's help, Annie got better little by little.

Two years later, Annie didn't scream or throw things. She did become a totally different person. People didn't call her "Crazy Little Annie" anymore.

Laura decided to leave the hospital with Annie. She took Annie to a school for blind children. Annie loved her new school and studied hard. She wanted to become a teacher and help others like Nurse Laura ⓑdid.

05 밑줄 친 ⓐ를 강조하는 문장으로 다시 쓰시오.

➡ _____

06 밑줄 친 ⓑ가 의미하는 것을 위 글에서 찾아 어법에 맞게 쓰시오.

➡ _____

07 According to the passage, what did people use to call Annie?

➡ _____

08 다음은 새로운 학교를 다녀온 Annie의 말이다. 빈칸에 알맞은 말을 쓰시오.

> Nurse Laura, I _____ _____ my new school!

[09~11] 다음 글을 읽고 물음에 답하시오.

However, a few years later, Laura ⓐ_____ away. Annie was very sad, but she did not give up on her dream.

Then one day, Annie met a nice doctor. He helped Annie (A)_____ well. It was a miracle for Annie. At last, Annie did ⓑ _____ her dream and became a teacher. This gave her a chance ⓒ_____ a special student. The student wasn't able to hear or see. Instead, she screamed and threw things. She was just like Crazy Little Annie. Annie said to her, "Hi, Helen Keller. I'm your teacher, Anne Sullivan. I'll always be there for you."

09 주어진 단어를 내용과 어법에 맞게 빈칸 ⓐ~ⓒ에 쓰시오.

realize / pass / meet

➡ ⓐ_____ ⓑ_____ ⓒ_____

10 주어진 단어를 어법에 맞게 빈칸 (A)에 쓰시오.

see

➡ _____

11 다음 물음에 완전한 문장의 영어로 답하시오.

Q: What was the miracle for Annie?

➡ _____

[12~15] 다음 글을 읽고 물음에 답하시오.

When Helen Keller was 19 months old, she was very sick. After that, she couldn't see or hear anymore.

Helen's parents thought that she needed somebody to take care of her, so they asked Anne Sullivan to teach her. Anne knew that Helen could not see or hear, but she also knew that Helen could feel things.

Anne began to write words into Helen's hand so that Helen could learn letters. For a long time, Helen didn't understand Anne's teaching. However, Anne did not give up.

One day, ⓐAnne은 Helen이 물을 느끼게 했다. Then she wrote w-a-t-e-r on Helen's other hand. At this point, Helen ⓑunderstood the lesson and wrote w-a-t-e-r on Anne's hand.

12 동사 'make'를 이용하여 밑줄 친 우리말 ⓐ를 영어로 쓰시오.

➡ _____

13 다음은 Helen Keller의 부모가 Anne Sullivan을 처음 만났을 때 한 말이다. 빈칸에 알맞은 말을 쓰시오.

We want to ask you _____ _____ _____ _____, Helen.

14 What did Anne do to teach Helen letters? Answer in English with a full sentence.

➡ _____

15 밑줄 친 ⓑ를 강조하여 문장을 다시 쓰시오.

➡ _____

교과서

구석구석

해석

Check Your Progress

W: Hello, students. I'm your music teacher, Ms. Song. You know the class singing

contest is next Friday, don't you?
　　　　　　　　　　　　　　부가의문문

Each class will prepare a song and perform it. You can choose any kind of
each+단수 명사　　　　　　　　　　　　　song을 가리킨다.

song. Please let me know the names of your songs by the end of this week.
　　　　　　　　　　　　　　　　　　　　　　　　이번 주말까지

You can also invite your homeroom teachers to join your performance. I

hope you enjoy preparing for the singing contest. Thank you.
　　　　　　　enjoy는 동명사를 목적어로 취한다.

구문해설 · invite: 초대하다 · prepare: 준비하다

W: 안녕하세요, 학생 여러분. 저는 여러분의 음악 선생님인, 송 선생님이에요. 여러분은 학급 노래 경연이 다음 주 금요일이란 걸 알죠, 그렇죠? 각 학급은 노래를 준비해서 공연할 거예요. 여러분은 어떠한 종류의 노래든 선택할 수 있어요. 이번 주말까지 여러분의 곡의 제목을 알려주세요. 여러분은 또한 여러분의 담임선생님과 공연을 함께 하도록 초대할 수도 있어요. 저는 여러분이 노래 경연을 위한 준비를 즐기기를 희망해요. 감사합니다.

After You Read

Dear Annie,

When I first met you, you were screaming and throwing things.
　　　　　　　　　　　　　　　과거진행형

However, I wasn't afraid of you. You weren't able to see, so I knew that I
　　　　　　　　　　　　　　　couldn't

needed to take care of you. Every night, when I put you to bed, I could see that
　　　　　　　　　　　　　　　　　　　　　명사절 접속사 (see의 목적절을 이끎)

you were getting better little by little. At last, you became a totally different

person. I am so proud of you. I hope you do well in your new school.
　　　　　　　　　　　　　hope (that) 명사절 접속사 that 생략 (hope의 목적절을 이끎)

Yours truly,

Laura

구문해설 · scream: 소리 지르다 · throw: ~을 던지다 · be afraid of: ~을 두려워하다 · take care of: ~을 돌보다 · put ~ to bed: ~을 재우다 · get better: 나아지다 · at last: 마침내 · totally: 완전히

Annie에게,

내가 너를 처음 만났을 때, 너는 소리를 지르고 물건을 던지고 있었단다. 하지만, 나는 네가 두렵지 않았어. 너는 볼 수 없었고, 그래서 나는 내가 너를 돌볼 필요가 있다는 것을 알았지. 매일 밤, 제가 너를 재울 때, 나는 네가 조금씩 나아지고 있다는 것을 알 수 있었단다. 마침내, 너는 완전히 다른 사람이 되었지. 나는 네가 매우 자랑스럽단다. 너의 새 학교에서 잘하기를 바란다.

그럼 이만,

Laura

Express Yourself

Dear Ms. Kim,

I wanted to take some time to thank you for your help. At first, English wasn't
　　　　　　　　　　　to부정사의 형용사적 용법 (some time 수식)

my favorite subject. Then you lent me some English books read and gave me
　　　　　　　　　　　　　　　　　　　　　　　　　　　　　to부정사의 형용사적 용법 (books 수식)

some English videos to watch.

Thanks to your help, English did become one of my favorite subjects. I do
　　　　　　English became one of my favorite subjects에서 동사 became을 강조한 문장

appreciate your help.

구문해설 · take some time: 시간을 할애하다 · subject: 과목 · lend: 빌려주다 · appreciate: 고마워하다

Ms. Kim에게,

저는 당신의 도움에 대하여 당신께 감사드리는 시간을 갖고 싶었습니다. 처음에, 영어는 제가 좋아하는 과목이 아니었습니다. 그때 당신은 저에게 읽을 영어 책을 빌려주셨고 볼 영어 비디오를 주셨습니다. 당신의 도움 덕분에, 영어는 정말로 제가 좋아하는 과목 중 하나가 되었습니다. 저는 당신의 도움에 정말로 감사드립니다.

144 Lesson 3. I'll Always Be There for You

영역별 핵심문제

01 다음 영영풀이가 가리키는 것을 고르시오.

> your feelings or thoughts about somebody or something, rather than a fact

① opinion
② experience
③ matter
④ principle
⑤ law

02 다음 대화의 빈칸에 들어갈 말로 가장 적절한 것을 고르시오.

> A: My brother is a _____
> B: That's wonderful! What song did he write?

① scientist
② composer
③ pianist
④ writer
⑤ painter

03 다음 문장에 공통으로 들어갈 말을 고르시오.

> • Her speech can _____ people hope and joy.
> • If you don't _____ up, you can succeed.

① take
② come
③ help
④ give
⑤ care

04 다음 중 밑줄 친 부분의 뜻풀이가 바르지 <u>않은</u> 것은?

① I fell asleep because the movie was too <u>boring</u>. 지루한
② I can't <u>decide</u> what to eat. 결정하다
③ We have different <u>tastes</u> in music. 취향
④ <u>Throw</u> the ball as far as you can. 받다
⑤ The boy was in big <u>trouble</u> because he broke the window. 곤경, 곤란

05 다음 문장의 빈칸에 들어갈 말을 <보기>에서 골라 쓰시오.

> ┤ 보기 ├
> at last / difficulties / decide / throw

(1) _____, we won the final match.
(2) Don't _____ stones into the pond.
(3) Which one do you want? Let's _____ now.
(4) I believe that she will overcome the _____ and give people hope.

06 다음 주어진 문장의 밑줄 친 appreciate와 같은 의미로 쓰인 것은?

> I do <u>appreciate</u> your help.

① This machine will help you <u>appreciate</u> each work better.
② Let's <u>appreciate</u> the beauty of a work of art.
③ I can't tell you how much I <u>appreciate</u> what you've done for me.
④ I can <u>appreciate</u> how sad you are now.
⑤ I don't think you <u>appreciate</u> how expensive it is.

[07~08] 다음 대화를 읽고 물음에 답하시오.

> G: We have to choose a story for our school play.
> B: (A)_____
> G: How about *Hamlet*? It's very famous.
> B: In my opinion, it's too sad for our school play. Let's find another story.

07 위 대화의 빈칸 (A)에 들어갈 말로 나머지와 의도가 다른 것은?

① I think we can choose one of Shakespeare's plays.
② Why don't we choose one of Shakespeare's plays?
③ What about choosing one of Shakespeare's plays.
④ Let's choose one of Shakespeare's plays.
⑤ What do you think about one of Shakespeare's plays?

08 What are they going to do instead of choosing *Hamlet*?

➡ _____

[09~10] 다음 대화를 읽고 물음에 답하시오.

G: You know about Lee Hee Ah, (A)그렇지?
B: No, I don't. Who is she?
G: She plays the piano very well, even though she only has two fingers on each hand.
B: That's amazing.

09 위 대화의 밑줄 친 우리말 (A)를 영어로 쓰시오.

➡ _____

10 다음 대화의 내용과 일치하도록 빈칸을 완성하시오.

Lee Hee Ah is the amazing pianist because she plays the piano very well with only _____ _____ on each hand.

[11~13] 다음 글을 읽고 물음에 답하시오.

W: Hello, students. I'm your music teacher, Ms. Song. You know the class singing contest is next Friday, ⓐdon't you? Each class will prepare a song and ⓑperform it. You can choose any kind of song. Please let me know the names of your songs ⓒby the end of this week. You can also invite your homeroom teachers ⓓto join your performance. I hope you enjoy ⓔto prepare for the singing contest. Thank you.

11 위 글의 밑줄 친 ⓐ~ⓔ 중 어법상 어색한 것을 찾아 바르게 고치시오.

➡ _____

12 위 글에서 다음 영영풀이가 나타내는 말을 찾아 쓰시오.

a competition in which people try to win something

➡ _____

13 위 글의 내용과 일치하지 않는 것은?

① The class singing contest is going to be held next Friday.
② Each class can choose any kind of song and perform it.
③ The students should let their music teacher know the names of their songs.
④ The students can invite their homeroom teachers to judge their performance.
⑤ Ms. Song wants the students to enjoy preparing for the singing contest.

[14~15] 다음 대화를 읽고 물음에 답하시오.

Olivia: What are you doing, Junho?

Junho: I'm working on my history project. I need to write about a famous person. That person should have a story of overcoming (A)difficulties in their life.

Olivia: Hmm. Who did you choose?

Junho: You know about Helen Keller, don't you? I chose to write about her.

Olivia: In my opinion, she is too famous. It may not be interesting.

Junho: Then, who should I choose?

Olivia: Do you know the story about Little Annie?

Junho: Who is that?

Olivia: I will show you a video about her life. She'll be a great topic for your project.

14 위 대화의 밑줄 친 (A)와 바꾸어 쓸 수 있는 것을 <u>모두</u> 고르시오.

① adversities　　② blessing

③ hardship　　④ happiness

⑤ success

15 위 대화의 내용과 일치하지 <u>않는</u> 것은?

① Junho는 역사 과제로 역경을 극복한 유명한 사람에 대한 이야기를 써야 한다.

② Junho는 Helen Keller에 대해 쓰려고 한다.

③ Olivia는 Helen Keller가 너무 유명해서 흥미롭지 않을지도 모른다고 생각한다.

④ Olivia는 Junho에게 Little Annie를 추천한다.

⑤ Junho는 Little Annie에 대해 잘 알고 있다.

16 다음 중 밑줄 친 부분의 형태가 어법상 <u>틀린</u> 것은?

① Jenny <u>does</u> like surfing the Internet.

② I <u>do</u> exercise regularly every morning.

③ Polly <u>does</u> write the letter last month.

④ Kate <u>does</u> have a free pass to Blue Aquarium.

⑤ Jin <u>did</u> take care of all the babies.

17 다음 중 빈칸에 들어갈 말로 가장 적절한 것은?

> I want to meet _____.
> 나는 대화하기에 흥미로운 사람을 만나고 싶어.

① anyone interesting to talk

② anyone interested to talk to

③ someone interested to talk

④ someone interested to talk to

⑤ someone interesting to talk to

18 다음 밑줄 친 부분을 강조하여 문장을 다시 쓰시오.

> Porter <u>enjoys</u> watching movies on Saturday nights.

➡ _____

_____

19 다음 중 쓰임이 <u>다른</u> 하나는?

① It is really fun <u>to fly</u> a drone.

② He forced me <u>to clean</u> his room.

③ Please lend me a book <u>to read</u>.

④ Jacob wanted <u>to become</u> a farmer.

⑤ The nurse advised me <u>to wash</u> hands.

20 다음 대화의 빈칸에 들어갈 말이 바르게 짝지어진 것은?

> A: You look really thirsty.
> B: I _____ need something _____ .

① am – to cold drink
② am – cold to drink
③ do – to drink cold
④ do – cold to drink
⑤ did – to drink cold

21 동사를 강조하여 다음 우리말을 영어로 쓰시오. 주어진 단어를 활용하시오.

> 비틀즈는 정말로 유명한 밴드가 되었다.
> (The Beatles / become)

➡ _____

22 다음 중 어법상 바르지 않은 것은?

① Mark Zuckerberg did found Facebook in 2004.
② Do you need anything to write about?
③ Melinda does appreciate your help.
④ I do want to be a teacher in the future.
⑤ I think you need someone to talk.

23 다음 중 어법상 바르지 않은 것은?

> William Hoy was a famous baseball player ①from 1888 to 1902. People ②called him "Dummy Hoy" ③because he couldn't hear or speak. But he did not hate his nickname. Actually, he ④does ask people ⑤to call him by his nickname.

① ② ③ ④ ⑤

24 다음 조건에 맞도록 우리말을 영어로 쓰시오.

> 나는 앉을 의자가 정말로 필요해.
> <동사를 강조할 것>

➡ _____

25 주어진 문장에서 쓰인 to부정사와 그 쓰임이 같은 것은?

> These days, teenagers have no time to rest.

① They decided to get rid of so much trash on the street.
② I do have many toys to play with.
③ Mark encourages me to do my best all the time.
④ Christine went to the museum to do her vacation homework.
⑤ He allowed me to wake up late next morning.

26 동사를 강조하여 다음 우리말을 영어로 쓰시오.

> Tom은 정말로 너에게 뭔가 보여줄 것이 있어.

➡ _____

Reading

[27~30] 다음 글을 읽고 물음에 답하시오.

> There was a little blind girl in a hospital. She was always angry. When people tried to help her, she screamed and attacked them. People called her "Crazy Little Annie," and didn't try to help her anymore. The poor girl needed somebody to ⓐ_____ care of her. One day, an old nurse came to the hospital. She volunteered to help Annie. When Annie

met her, she started throwing things again. ⓑ
_____, the nurse wasn't afraid of her.
The nurse said to Annie, "Hi, Annie. I'm Nurse
Laura. I'm here to be your friend. I'll always
be there for you."

27 다음 중 빈칸 ⓐ에 들어갈 말과 같은 말이 들어가는 것은?

① Sarah did _____ after your plants.
② The plane will _____ off at 3 o'clock.
③ I really _____ forward to seeing you.
④ Karen does _____ up with great ideas
all the time.
⑤ Did you _____ up your mind?

28 빈칸 ⓑ에 들어갈 말로 가장 적절한 것은?

① Thus   ② In addition
③ Instead   ④ However
⑤ For example

29 다음 중 위 글의 내용과 일치하지 않는 것은?

① Annie's nickname was "Crazy Little
Annie."
② Annie was unable to see.
③ Annie screamed and attacked people to
help her later.
④ Nurse Laura wanted to be Annie's friend.
⑤ Nurse Laura felt threatened by Annie.

30 What did Annie do when people tried to help her? Answer in English with a full sentence.

➡ _____

[31~34] 다음 글을 읽고 물음에 답하시오.

However, a few years later, Laura passed
away. Annie was very sad, but ⓐ그녀는 꿈을 포
기하지 않았습니다.
Then one day, Annie met a nice doctor.
[A] At last, Annie realized her dream and
became a teacher.
[B] The student ⓑwasn't able to hear or see.
[C] This gave her a chance to meet a special
student.
[D] He helped Annie to see well. It was a
miracle for Annie.
Instead, she screamed and threw things. She
was just like Crazy Little Annie. Annie said to
her, "Hi, Helen Keller. I'm your teacher, Anne
Sullivan. I'll always be there for you."

31 밑줄 친 우리말 ⓐ를 영어로 쓰시오.

➡ _____

32 밑줄 친 ⓑ를 대신할 수 있는 말을 4단어로 쓰시오.

➡ _____

33 자연스러운 글이 되도록 [A]~[D]를 바르게 나열한 것은?

① [B]-[D]-[A]-[C]   ② [B]-[C]-[D]-[A]
③ [C]-[B]-[A]-[D]   ④ [D]-[B]-[C]-[A]
⑤ [D]-[A]-[C]-[B]

34 다음 중 위 글의 내용과 일치하지 않는 것은?

① Laura died before Annie became a
teacher.
② Annie made her dream come true.
③ Annie was sad because Laura walked
away from her.
④ Helen threw things and screamed.
⑤ Annie became Helen Keller's teacher.

[01~02] 다음 대화를 읽고 물음에 답하시오.

> G: We have to choose a story for our school play.
> B: Why don't we choose one of Shakespeare's plays?
> G: How about *Hamlet*? It's very famous.
> B: In my opinion, it's too sad for our school play. Let's find another story.

출제율 90%

01 What does the girl recommend for their school play?

➡ _____

출제율 95%

02 Why doesn't the boy choose *Hamlet* for their school play?

➡ _____

[03~05] 다음 대화를 읽고 물음에 답하시오.

> Brian What's the matter? You look worried.
> Amy: I'm (A)worried about my history test. My history score is lower than my math score.
> Brian Why don't you take Mr. Choi's afterschool class?
> Amy: Well, I took his social studies class last month, but it was a little boring for me.
> Brian In my opinion, his history class is more interesting than his social studies class.
> Amy: Really?
> Brian Yes. I also got a high score on my history test after taking his class.
> Amy: Maybe I should take his class too. Thanks.

출제율 100%

03 위 대화의 밑줄 친 (A)와 바꾸어 쓸 수 있는 것을 모두 고르시오.

① anxious   ② pleased
③ concerned   ④ confident
⑤ satisfied

출제율 90%

04 위 대화를 읽고 대답할 수 없는 것은?

① What's the problem with Amy?
② When did Amy take Mr. Choi's class?
③ What subject did Brian study with Mr. Choi?
④ What does Brian advise to improve Amy's history score?
⑤ What score did Amy get on the social studies test?

출제율 90%

05 다음 대화가 자연스럽게 이어지도록 순서대로 배열하시오.

> (A) Yes, he is. Don't give up! You can do it too!
> (B) Hey, don't say that. You know about Rick Allen, don't you?
> (C) Of course I do. Isn't he the drummer with one arm?
> (D) I really love the drums, but I'm not good at playing. Maybe I should give up.

➡ _____

[06~08] 다음 대화를 읽고 물음에 답하시오.

> G: What is your favorite book?
> B: My favorite book is *The Old Man and the Sea*.
> G: Really? In my opinion, it's a little (A)bored.
> B: Everyone (B)have different (C)tastes.

06 위 대화의 밑줄 친 (A)와 (B)를 어법에 맞게 고치시오.

➡ (A) _____ , (B) _____

07 위 대화의 밑줄 친 (C)tastes와 같은 의미로 쓰인 것은?

① I love the fresh taste of seafood.
② The amount of sugar is a matter of personal taste.
③ Fast food may taste good but it's not good for your health.
④ The soup tastes a bit sour.
⑤ My students tasted coffee to see whether it had sugar or not.

08 What does the girl think about *The Old Man and the Sea*?

➡ _____

[09~10] 다음 설명을 읽고 물음에 답하시오.

M: Hello. You all know me, don't you? (A) As you can see, I don't have any arms or legs. When I was young, I was sad and angry about myself. (B) Then one day, I read a story about a man like me. (C) He said that I had a choice in my life. I could be happy or angry about myself. (D) Now, I am a happy man. I give speeches around the world, and give people hope. (E) Here is my message for you. In life, you have a choice: better or bitter? Choose better, forget bitter.

09 위 설명의 (A)~(E) 중 주어진 문장이 들어가기에 적절한 곳은?

So, I decided to love my life.

① (A) ② (B) ③ (C) ④ (D) ⑤ (E)

10 위 설명의 내용과 일치하지 않는 것은?

① The speaker doesn't have any arms or legs.
② The speaker used to be sad and angry when he was young.
③ The speaker made a decision to be a happy man.
④ The speaker gives speeches around the world these days.
⑤ The speaker delivers the message to choose bitter.

11 다음 중 어법상 옳은 문장의 개수는?

ⓐ She does joins our club. How exciting!
ⓑ Do you have anything to talk about?
ⓒ I don't need something to see boring.
ⓓ The team did win the game yesterday.
ⓔ I do want to meet you next time.

① 1개 ② 2개 ③ 3개
④ 4개 ⑤ 5개

12 다음 중 to부정사의 용법이 다른 하나는?

① Maggie wanted me to say to her everything.
② Everyone has the right to express their opinions.
③ Nick planned to leave the company on Friday.
④ What do you expect me to do?
⑤ It was good to get to know him well.

출제율 90%

13 동사를 강조하여 다음 우리말을 영어로 쓰시오. 주어진 단어를 활용하시오.

> 그녀는 너와 함께 논의할 무언가를 정말로 가지고 있어. (discuss)

➡ _____

출제율 100%

14 다음 빈칸에 들어갈 말이 바르게 짝지어진 것은?

> • The mice _____ eat everything.
> • Water _____ boil at 100℃.

① do – does
② do – do
③ does – does
④ does – do
⑤ does – did

출제율 90%

15 다음 우리말을 영어로 옮길 때 8개의 단어가 필요하다. 다섯 번째로 오는 단어는?

> 나는 그가 나의 도움을 정말로 필요로 한다는 것을 알아.

① that
② he
③ does
④ need
⑤ help

출제율 90%

16 다음 중 어법상 바르지 않은 것은?

> A: I need someone ①kind ②to look after my cat.
> B: Oh, I know someone ③like that. Also, she ④does ⑤likes cats.

① 　② 　③ 　④ 　⑤

출제율 95%

17 주어진 단어를 활용하여 다음 우리말을 영어로 쓰시오.

> 나는 영어를 잘 말할 수 있는 능력을 갖고 싶어.
> (want / the ability)

➡ _____

[18~21] 다음 글을 읽고 물음에 답하시오.

> Every night, Laura went to Annie's room and put her to bed. She said to Annie, "Annie, I do love you. I'll always be there for you."
> Laura knew ⓐthat Annie needed love and understanding. With Laura's help, Annie got better little by little.
> Two years later, Annie didn't scream or throw things. She did become a totally different person. People didn't call her "Crazy Little Annie" anymore.
> Laura decided to leave the hospital with Annie. She took Annie to a school for blind children. Annie loved her new school and studied hard. She wanted to become a teacher and help others like Nurse Laura did.

출제율 95%

18 다음 중 밑줄 친 ⓐ와 쓰임이 다른 것은?

① Did you hear that Paul was in prison?
② Amelia said that she didn't want it anymore.
③ The man that is standing there is Monica's brother.
④ The fact that I don't like your painting is beside the point.
⑤ James thought that I had to leave.

19 다음 중 위 글을 읽고 답할 수 <u>없는</u> 것은? *출제율 90%*

① What did Laura say to Annie every night?
② Who put Annie to bed every night?
③ Who helped Annie get better?
④ What did Annie study in her new school?
⑤ What did people call Annie?

20 What did Annie want to do in the future? Answer in English with a full sentence. *출제율 95%*

➡ _____

_____

21 다음과 같이 풀이되는 단어를 위 글에서 찾아 쓰시오. *출제율 95%*

to shout in a loud voice

➡ _____

[22~25] 다음 글을 읽고 물음에 답하시오.

Nurse Laura decided to leave the hospital ⓐ<u>with</u> Annie. She took Annie to a school for blind children. Annie loved her new school and studied ⓑ<u>hardly</u>. She wanted to become a teacher and help others like Nurse Laura did. However, a few years later, Laura passed away. Annie was very ⓒ<u>sad</u>, but she did not give up on her dream.
Then one day. Annie met a nice doctor. ① He helped Annie to see well. It was ⓓ<u>a miracle</u> for Annie. ② At last, Annie ⓔ<u>realized</u> her dream and became a teacher. ③ This gave her a chance to meet a special student. ④ Instead, she screamed and threw things. She was just

like Crazy Little Annie. ⑤ Annie said to her, "Hi, Helen Keller. I'm your teacher, Anne Sullivan. I'll always be there for you."

22 다음 중 주어진 문장이 들어가기에 가장 적절한 곳은? *출제율 95%*

The student wasn't able to hear or see.

①   ②   ③   ④   ⑤

23 ⓐ~ⓔ 중 글의 흐름상 어색한 것은? *출제율 95%*

① ⓐ   ② ⓑ   ③ ⓒ   ④ ⓓ   ⑤ ⓔ

24 다음 중 위 글의 내용과 일치하지 <u>않는</u> 것은? *출제율 90%*

① Laura and Annie left the hospital together.
② Annie was taken to a school for blind children.
③ Annie wanted to become a teacher like Laura.
④ Annie was able to see thanks to a nice doctor.
⑤ Annie met Helen when she could see well.

25 다음 빈칸에 알맞은 말을 쓰시오. *출제율 95%*

A: Is it true that a nice doctor helped Annie to see well?   B: Yes. He _____ _____ _____ see well.

[01~03] 다음 대화를 읽고 물음에 답하시오.

> Olivia: What are you doing, Junho?
>
> Junho: I'm working on my history project. I need to write about a famous person. That person should have a story of overcoming difficulties in their life.
>
> Olivia: Hmm. Who did you choose?
>
> Junho: You know about Helen Keller, don't you? I chose to write about her.
>
> Olivia: In my opinion, she is too famous. It may not be interesting.
>
> Junho: Then, who should I choose?
>
> Olivia: Do you know the story about Little Annie?
>
> Junho: Who is that?
>
> Olivia: I will show you a video about her life. She'll be a great topic for your project.

01 What are Olivia and Junho talking about?

➡ _____

02 Why doesn't Olivia like choosing Helen Keller as Junho's project topic?

➡ _____

_____

03 What are Olivia and Junho going to do next?

➡ _____

 04 다음 대화가 자연스럽게 이어지도록 순서대로 배열하시오.

> (A) That's amazing.
> (B) No, I don't. Who is she?
> (C) You know about Lee Hee Ah, don't you?
> (D) She plays the piano very well, even though she only has two fingers on each hand.

➡ _____

05 주어진 단어를 바르게 배열하여 다음 우리말을 영어로 쓰시오.

> 그들은 고향을 다시 보고 싶다는 열망으로 가득 차 있었다.
> (again / they / the desire / homeland / to / their / see / with / filled / were)

➡ _____

_____

06 동사를 강조하여 다음 우리말을 영어로 쓰시오.

(1) 그녀는 날 정말로 행복하게 해.

➡ _____

(2) 나는 너를 도와줄 약간의 시간이 정말로 있어.

➡ _____

07 다음 우리말에 맞게 빈칸에 알맞은 말을 쓰시오.

> I have _____ _____ _____ _____ to you.
> 너에게 말해 줄 중요한 것이 있어.

★08 다음 밑줄 친 부분을 강조하여 문장을 다시 쓰시오.

> Mr. Jefferson <u>visits</u> us very often.

➡ _____

09 다음 문장에서 어법상 바르지 <u>않은</u> 것을 찾아 바르게 고쳐 쓰시오.

> She did know that Allan didn't have anything interesting to talk.

➡ _____

10 주어진 어구를 활용하여 다음 우리말을 9 단어로 이루어진 한 문장의 영어로 쓰시오.

> 카멜레온(cameleon)은 그것의 색깔을 바꿀 수 있는 능력으로 유명해요.
> (is famous for)

➡ _____

[11~13] 다음 글을 읽고 물음에 답하시오.

> Every night, Laura went to Annie's room and put her to bed. She said to Annie, "Annie, I do love you. I'll always be there for you."
> Laura knew that Annie needed love and understanding. ⓐWith Laura's help, Annie got better little by little.
> Two years later, Annie didn't scream or throw things. She did become a totally different person. People didn't call her "Crazy Little Annie" anymore.
> Laura decided to leave the hospital with Annie. She took Annie to a school for blind children. Annie loved her new school and studied hard. She wanted to become a teacher and help others like Nurse Laura did.

11 동사를 강조하여 밑줄 친 문장 ⓐ를 다시 쓰시오.

➡ _____

★12 다음은 병원 사람들의 대화이다. 빈칸에 알맞은 말을 쓰시오.

> A: Is it true that Nurse Laura goes to Annie's room every night?
> B: Yes. She _____ _____ _____ Annie's room every night.

13 According to the passage, what did Laura decide to do when Annie became a totally different person?

➡ _____

[14~15] 다음 글을 읽고 물음에 답하시오.

> Dear Ms. Kim,
> I wanted to take some time to thank you for your help. At first, English wasn't my favorite subject. Then you lent me some ⓐ읽을 영어 책 and gave me some ⓑ볼 영어 비디오. Thanks to your help, ⓒEnglish became one of my favorite subject. ⓓI do appreciate your help.
>
> Best regards,
> Jiwon

★14 밑줄 친 우리말 ⓐ와 ⓑ를 영어로 쓰시오.

➡ ⓐ _____
   ⓑ _____

15 문장 ⓒ를 문장 ⓓ와 같이 쓰시오.

➡ _____

창의사고력 서술형 문제

01 다음 대화의 내용과 일치하도록 Amy의 담화를 완성하시오.

> Brian: What's the matter? You look worried.
> Amy: I'm worried about my history test. My history score is lower than my math score.
> Brian: Why don't you take Mr. Choi's afterschool class?
> Amy: Well, I took his social studies class last month, but it was a little boring for me.
> Brian: In my opinion, his history class is more interesting than his social studies class.
> Amy: Really?
> Brian: Yes. I also got a high score on my history test after taking his class.
> Amy: Maybe I should take his class too. Thanks.

⬇

> Brian gave me an advice when I was worried about my history score. I was shocked when my history score was lower than my math score. Then, Brian recommended (A)_____. At first, I didn't want to take his class again because (B)_____ when I took his social studies class last month. However, he said that his history class was more interesting than his social studies class. In addition, he told me that (C)_____. I decided to (D)_____ to improve my history score.

02 to부정사로 주어진 명사를 수식하여 여러 가지 문장을 써 보시오.

> sign   plan   decision   ability   opportunity   way

(1) _____
(2) _____
(3) _____
(4) _____
(5) _____

03 주어진 동사를 강조한 여러 가지 문장을 써 보시오.

> love   ask   make   learn   call

(1) _____
(2) _____
(3) _____
(4) _____
(5) _____

단원별 모의고사

01 다음 대화의 빈칸에 들어갈 말로 적절한 것을 <u>모두</u> 고르시오.

> A: _____
>
> B: Yes, I know him. He is my history teacher.

① Do you know Mr. Nam?
② Does Mr. Nam know you?
③ You know Mr. Nam, don't you?
④ Have you heard about Mr. Nam?
⑤ What do you think of Mr. Nam?

02 다음 주어진 문장의 밑줄 친 touching과 같은 의미로 쓰인 것은?

> In my opinion, it is a very <u>touching</u> movie.

① The boy is <u>touching</u> his nose.
② <u>Touching</u> the computer screen, he explained today's topic.
③ We can sense the world by <u>touching</u> things.
④ She's <u>touching</u> the buttons on her coat.
⑤ Her <u>touching</u> story made me cry and shed tears.

[03~05] 다음 설명을 읽고 물음에 답하시오.

> M: Hello. You all know me, don't you? As you can see, I don't have any arms or legs. When I was young, I was sad and angry about myself. Then one day, I read a story about a man like me. He said that I had a choice in my life. I could be happy or angry about myself. So, I decided to love my life. Now, I am a happy man. I give speeches around the world, and give people hope. Here is my message for you. In life, you have a choice: better or bitter? Choose better, forget bitter.

03 위 설명에서 다음 영영풀이가 나타내는 말을 찾아 쓰시오.

> a belief that something you want will happen

➡ _____

04 What did the speaker decide to do?

➡ _____

05 What does the speaker do for people around the world?

➡ _____

_____

[06~07] 다음 대화를 읽고 물음에 답하시오.

> G: You know Teacher's Day is next Monday, don't you? What should I do for my homeroom teacher?
> B: Hmm.... In my opinion, she would love some letters from her students.
> G: I think so too, but I want to make it special.
> B: Why don't you take part in our school radio's project?
> G: A project? What is (A)<u>it</u> about?
> B: Write a letter and send (B)<u>it</u> to the school radio. They will read your letter on Teacher's Day.
> G: That's wonderful!

06 위 대화에서 밑줄 친 (A), (B)가 가리키는 대상을 찾아 쓰시오.

➡ (A) _____,
(B) _____

07 위 대화의 내용과 일치하지 <u>않는</u> 것은?

① 다음 주 월요일은 스승의 날이다.

② 소년과 소녀는 담임선생님을 위한 이벤트를 계획하고 있다.

③ 소년은 담임선생님이 학생들의 편지를 매우 좋아할 것이라고 생각한다.

④ 소년은 학교 라디오 프로젝트에 참여할 것을 제안하였다.

⑤ 학교 라디오 프로젝트는 편지를 써서 보내면 선생님께 편지를 배달해 준다.

[08~10] 다음 설명을 읽고 물음에 답하시오.

W: Hello, students. I'm your music teacher, Ms. Song. You know the class singing contest is next Friday, don't you? Each class will prepare a song and perform it. You can choose any kind of song. Please let me know the names of your songs by the end of this week. You can also invite your homeroom teachers to join your performance. I hope you enjoy preparing for the singing contest. Thank you.

08 What event is supposed to be held next Friday?

➡ _____

09 By when should the students hand in the title of their songs to the music teacher?

➡ _____

_____

10 What can the students do with their homeroom teachers?

➡ _____

_____

11 다음 대화의 내용과 일치하도록 Amy의 담화를 완성하시오.

Amy: I really love the drums, but I'm not good at playing. Maybe I should give up.

Bob: Hey, don't say that. You know about Rick Allen, don't you?

Amy: Of course I do. Isn't he the drummer with one arm?

Bob: Yes, he is. Don't give up! You can do it too!

⬇

I was depressed because I was not good at (A)_____ even though I loved it. When I talked about it to Bob, he encouraged me a lot not to (B)_____. He told me about Rick Allen who is (C)_____. I really appreciated Bob because he said that I can make it like Rick Allen.

12 다음 우리말을 주어진 단어를 사용하여 영작하시오.

(1) 나는 사람들에게 그들의 꿈을 포기해서는 안 된다고 이야기할 거야. (tell, give)

➡ _____

(2) 우리 엄마는 나를 자랑스러워하신다. (proud)

➡ _____

(3) Mike는 그의 아기를 재우고 있다. (putting)

➡ _____

13 주어진 문장을 영어로 쓸 때 마지막에 오는 단어를 쓰시오.

> 그들에겐 앉을 의자가 정말로 필요해요.

➡ _____

14 다음 중 빈칸에 들어갈 말이 바르게 짝지어진 것은?

> • Every person has the right _____ .
> • My teeth _____ hurt badly these days.

① voting – does   ② voting – do
③ to vote – does   ④ to vote – do
⑤ vote – does

15 다음 중 어법상 바르지 않은 것은?

① Angela did come to like the city life.
② I want someone to support me.
③ Henry does drive the motorbike well.
④ We had a chance to hearing her music once.
⑤ There is no need to explain everything to me.

16 다음 우리말을 영어로 바르게 옮긴 것은?

> 나를 도와줄 사람이 아무도 없었다.

① There wasn't someone to help.
② There wasn't anyone to help.
③ There was no one to help.
④ There was no one to help me.
⑤ There was someone to help me.

17 다음 밑줄 친 단어를 강조하여 문장을 다시 쓰시오.

> Ross did his homework.

➡ _____

[18~21] 다음 글을 읽고 물음에 답하시오.

Every night, Laura went to Annie's room and put her to bed. She said to Annie, "Annie, I ⓐdo love you. I'll always be there for you."
Laura knew ⓑthat Annie needed love and understanding. With Laura's help, Annie got better little by little.
Two years later, Annie didn't scream or throw things. ⓒShe did become a totally different person. People didn't call her "Crazy Little Annie" anymore.
Laura decided to leave the hospital (A)[with / without] Annie. She took Annie to a school for blind children. Annie did (B)[love / loved] ⓓher new school and studied ⓔhard. She wanted to become a teacher and (C)[help / helped] others like Nurse Laura did.

18 (A)~(C)에서 어법상 또는 문맥상 옳은 것끼리 바르게 짝지은 것은?

① with – love – help
② with – love – helped
③ with – loved – help
④ without – love – helped
⑤ without – loved – help

19 다음 중 위 글의 내용과 일치하는 것을 모두 고르시오.

① Annie wanted to become a nurse like Laura.
② Laura put Annie to bed every night.
③ Annie always told Laura that she loved her.
④ Annie got better thanks to Laura.
⑤ People still called Annie "Crazy Little Annie."

20 사건이 발생한 순서대로 (A)~(D)를 바르게 나열하시오.

> (A) Annie went to a school for blind children.
> (B) Annie did not attack people anymore.
> (C) Annie studied hard to become a teacher.
> (D) Annie became better and better.

➡ _____

21 다음 중 ⓐ~ⓔ에 대한 설명으로 바르지 않은 것은?

① ⓐ - 일반동사 love를 강조하는 조동사이다.
② ⓑ - 명사절을 이끄는 접속사로 생략이 가능하다.
③ ⓒ - 'She became a totally different person.'에서 동사를 강조한 문장이다.
④ ⓓ - Laura를 가리키는 소유격 대명사이다.
⑤ ⓔ - '열심히'라는 의미의 부사이다.

[22~25] 다음 글을 읽고 물음에 답하시오.

When Helen Keller was 19 months old, she was very sick. After that, she couldn't see or hear anymore.
Helen's parents thought that she ①needed somebody to take care of her, so they asked Anne Sullivan ②to teach her. Anne knew that Helen could not see or hear, but she also knew that Helen could feel things.
Anne began ③to write words into Helen's hand ④so that Helen could learn letters. For a long time, Helen didn't understand Anne's teaching. However, Anne did not give up.
One day, Anne made Helen ⑤to feel water. Then she wrote w-a-t-e-r on Helen's other hand. At this point, Helen understood the lesson and wrote w-a-t-e-r on Anne's hand.

22 ①~⑤ 중 어법상 틀린 것은?

①　　②　　③　　④　　⑤

23 다음 중 위 글을 읽고 답할 수 없는 것은?

① What caused Helen to be blind?
② What did Helen's parents ask Anne to do for her daughter?
③ What did Anne know about Helen?
④ How did Anne to teach Helen letters?
⑤ When did Helen's parents meet Anne Sullivan?

24 When did Helen Keller lose her sight? Answer in English with a full sentence.

➡ _____
_____

25 다음은 Helen이 수업을 이해한 첫 날 Anne Sullivan이 Helen의 부모님에게 한 말이다. 밑줄 친 말을 강조하여 다시 쓰시오.

> Anne: I think Helen understands the lesson.

➡ _____

INSIGHT
on the textbook

교과서 파헤치기

※ 다음 영어를 우리말로 쓰시오.

01 cafeteria	22 successful
02 interest	23 staff
03 environmental	24 scenery
04 helpful	25 total
05 favorite	26 wrong
06 hovering	27 prepare
07 cooking	28 perform
08 protect	29 social
09 application	30 prize
10 order	31 plate
11 costume	32 volunteer
12 able	33 skill
13 crew	34 leader
14 abroad	35 be ready to
15 waste	36 carry out
16 club	37 keep in shape
17 reduce	38 be interested in
18 classmate	39 by oneself
19 actor	40 take part in
20 traditional	41 stay up late
21 photographer	42 fall into
	43 be good at

※ 다음 우리말을 영어로 쓰시오.

01 도표	_____
02 방향	_____
03 직원	_____
04 그릇, 접시	_____
05 기술, 솜씨	_____
06 틀린, 잘못된	_____
07 상, 상품	_____
08 지도자	_____
09 사회의	_____
10 수행하다, 공연하다	_____
11 행성	_____
12 두다, 남기다	_____
13 경치, 풍경	_____
14 준비하다	_____
15 드론, 무인 비행기	_____
16 꽤, 많이	_____
17 주문하다	_____
18 연못	_____
19 성공한, 성공적인	_____
20 자원 봉사자; 자원하다	_____
21 합계, 총액	_____

22 구내식당	_____
23 환경의	_____
24 공중 정지	_____
25 사진사	_____
26 의상, 복장	_____
27 전통적인	_____
28 해외에(서), 해외로	_____
29 쓰레기, 폐기물	_____
30 보호하다	_____
31 지원(신청)서, 적용	_____
32 관심, 흥미	_____
33 도움이 되는	_____
34 줄이다	_____
35 ~에 관심이 있다	_____
36 늦게까지 깨어 있다	_____
37 ~할 준비가 되다	_____
38 ~에 참가하다	_____
39 수행하다	_____
40 혼자서	_____
41 ~에 빠지다	_____
42 건강을 유지하다	_____
43 ~에 능숙하다	_____

※ 다음 영영풀이에 알맞은 단어를 <보기>에서 골라 쓴 후, 우리말 뜻을 쓰시오.

1 _____ : the ability to do something well: _____

2 _____ : in or to a foreign country: _____

3 _____ : a person who takes photographs, especially as a job: _____

4 _____ : materials that are no longer needed and are thrown away: _____

5 _____ : liked more than others of the same kind: _____

6 _____ : a page or sheet of information in the form of diagrams, lists of figures, etc.: _____

7 _____ : to make something or somebody ready to be used or to do something: _____

8 _____ : to make sure that somebody/something is not harmed, injured, damaged, etc.: _____

9 _____ : a person who performs on the stage, on television or in films/movies, especially as a profession: _____

10 _____ : connected with the natural conditions in which people, animals and plants live: _____

11 _____ : an area of water that is surrounded by land and that is smaller than a lake: _____

12 _____ : a person who is or was in the same class as you at school or college: _____

13 _____ : a formal (often written) request for something, such as a job, permission to do something or a place at a college or university: _____

14 _____ : a person who leads a group of people, especially the head of a country, an organization, etc.: _____

15 _____ : the clothes worn by people from a particular place or during a particular historical period: _____

16 _____ : a large round object in space that moves around a star (such as the sun) and receives light from it: _____

보기			
planet	prepare	chart	pond
environmental	leader	skill	favorite
actor	application	protect	classmate
waste	costume	photographer	abroad

※ 다음 우리말과 일치하도록 빈칸에 알맞은 말을 쓰시오.

Everyday English 1. A Function Practice 2-(1)

B: I'm _____. Did you _____ _____?

G: No. _____ have lunch together. What's your _____ _____?

B: I love chicken. _____ _____ _____ order it?

G: That's a _____ _____.

B: 배가 고프네. 점심 먹었어?

G: 아니, 점심 같이 먹자. 좋아하는 음식이 뭐야?

B: 난 닭고기가 좋더라. 그것으로 주문하는 게 어때?

G: 좋은 생각이야.

Everyday English 1. B. Listening Activity

G: What's your _____ _____? We _____ the students at our school and _____ _____ _____ answered the question. _____ of the students _____ they liked _____ _____. 20 boys and 42 girls loved it. This means _____ _____ _____ 62 students said _____ _____ was their _____ _____. Many boys liked _____ _____ _____. 32 boys and 13 girls _____ _____ that. 25 boys and 20 girls liked sports. _____ _____ _____ were soccer, baseball, and basketball.

G: 네가 좋아하는 취미는 뭐니? 우리는 학교 학생들에게 물어보았고 그들 모두가 질문에 대답을 했어. 대부분의 학생들이 영화 보는 것을 좋아한다고 했어. 남학생 20명과 여학생 42명이 영화가 좋대. 이것은 총 62명의 학생들이 영화 보는 것이 좋아하는 취미라고 말했음을 의미해. 많은 남학생들은 컴퓨터 게임을 좋아했어. 남학생 32명과 여학생 13명이 컴퓨터 게임하는 것을 좋아한데. 남학생 25명과 여학생 20명은 스포츠가 좋다고 했어. 그들이 좋아하는 스포츠는 축구, 야구, 그리고 농구였어.

Everyday English 2. A Function Practice 2-(1)

G: You _____ _____. What's _____ _____?

B: I _____ _____ _____ to watch TV.

G: What _____ you _____?

B: I _____ a traveling program. _____ _____ _____ traveling.

G: 너 피곤해 보인다. 무슨 일 있니?

B: TV 보느라 늦게까지 깨어 있었어.

G: 뭘 봤는데?

B: 여행 프로그램을 봤어. 나는 여행에 관심이 있거든.

Everyday English 2. A Function Practice 2-(2)

G: What _____ you _____?

B: I'm _____ a newspaper. _____ _____ this picture.

G: The food in the picture _____ _____. _____ the story _____?

B: The story _____ _____ _____. I'm _____ _____ _____.

G: 뭐 하고 있니?

B: 신문 읽고 있어. 이 신문 좀 봐.

G: 사진 속의 음식이 맛있어 보이네. 무엇에 관한 이야기야?

B: 요리에 관한 이야기야. 난 요리에 관심이 있어.

Everyday English 2. A Function Practice 2-(3)

G: _____ _____ _____ _____ to see a musical this Saturday?
I have some _____ _____.

B: Sure. I'm very _____ _____ musicals. What's the _____
_____?

G: It's *The Shower*. Hwang Sunwon _____ it.

B: Wow. I _____ _____ _____ _____ it.

G: 이번 주 토요일에 뮤지컬 보러 가는 게 어때? 무료입장권이 몇 장 있거든.
B: 물론이지. 나는 뮤지컬에 관심이 있어. 뮤지컬 제목이 뭐야?
G: 소나기야. 황순원이 썼어.
B: 와. 그것을 빨리 보고 싶어.

Everyday English 2 – B Listening Activity

Brian: Look! This is a chart about our _____ _____.

Sujin: _____ _____ _____ it more closely. The chart shows
that 30% of students _____ _____ _____ sports. The
school's Sports Day _____ _____ so much fun.

Brian: Right. The chart _____ _____ that 27% of students are
interested in actors. I know you are also _____ _____
_____ _____ them.

Sujin: Yes. I love them. _____ _____ you?

Brian: I'm _____ _____ _____ actors. I'm interested in
computer games. 20% of students are interested in them.

Sujin: Computer games are fun, but _____ them too much _____
_____ _____ _____ you.

Brian: I _____.

Brian: 봐! 이것은 우리 반 친구들의 관심에 대한 도표야.
Sujin: 자세히 보자. 학생들의 30%는 스포츠에 관심이 있구나. 운동회가 굉장히 재미있을 것 같아.
Brian: 맞아. 도표에 의하면 27%의 학생은 배우에 관심이 있어. 너도 배우들을 좋아한다고 알고 있어.
Sujin: 응. 배우를 좋아해. 너는?
Brian: 난 배우에는 관심이 없어. 난 컴퓨터 게임에 관심이 있어. 20%의 학생이 컴퓨터 게임에 관심이 있어.
Sujin: 컴퓨터 게임은 재밌지. 그러나 너무 많이 하는 것은 안 좋아.
Brian: 나도 동의해.

In Real Life

Junho: Adia, _____ _____ _____? We _____ _____
_____ our club next week.

Adia: I know. Which club do you _____ _____ _____, Junho?

Junho: I'm _____ _____ the photo club.

Adia: Sounds great. _____ _____ this chart. 80% of the photo
club's members _____ _____ they liked _____ _____
last year.

Junho: That's right. _____ _____ you, Adia? What's your
_____ _____?

Adia: I _____ _____ _____ the board game club. But _____
_____ its members said that they _____ _____ it much.

Junho: You're _____. 60% of its members said they didn't like it.

Adia: Yes. I'm _____ _____ _____ _____ it more.

Junho: Adia, 그것 아니? 우리는 다음 주에 동아리를 선택해야 해.
Adia: 알고 있어. 준호야, 어느 동아리를 마음에 두고 있니?
Junho: 나는 사진 동아리에 관심이 있어.
Adia: 좋아. 이 도표를 봐. 80퍼센트의 사진 동아리 회원들이 작년 활동을 좋아했다고 말했어.
Junho: 맞아, 너는 어떠니, Adia? 네가 가장 좋아하는 동아리는 무엇이니?
Adia: 나는 보드게임 동아리에 가입하고 싶어. 하지만 작년에 그 동아리의 회원들이 별로 좋아하지 않는다고 말했어.
Junho: 맞아. 60퍼센트의 회원들이 좋아하지 않는다고 말했어.
Adia: 그래. 나는 그것에 대해 좀 더 생각해 볼 거야.

Step2

※ 다음 우리말에 맞도록 대화를 영어로 쓰시오.

 해석

Everyday English 1. A Function Practice 2-(1)

B: _____

G: _____

B: _____

G: _____

B: 배가 고프네. 점심 먹었어?
G: 아니, 점심 같이 먹자. 좋아하는 음식이 뭐야?
B: 난 닭고기가 좋더라. 그것으로 주문하는 게 어때?
G: 좋은 생각이야.

Everyday English 1. B. Listening Activity

G: _____

_____

_____

_____

_____

G: 네가 좋아하는 취미는 뭐니? 우리는 학교 학생들에게 물어보았고 그들 모두가 질문에 대답을 했어. 대부분의 학생들이 영화 보는 것을 좋아한다고 했어. 남학생 20명과 여학생 42명이 영화가 좋대. 이것은 총 62명의 학생들이 영화 보는 것이 좋아하는 취미라고 말했음을 의미해. 많은 남학생들은 컴퓨터 게임을 좋아했어. 남학생 32명과 여학생 13명이 컴퓨터 게임하는 것을 좋아한대. 남학생 25명과 여학생 20명은 스포츠가 좋다고 했어. 그들이 좋아하는 스포츠는 축구, 야구, 그리고 농구였어.

Everyday English 2. A Function Practice 2-(1)

G: _____

B: _____

G: _____

B: _____

G: 너 피곤해 보인다. 무슨 일 있니?
B: TV 보느라 늦게까지 깨어 있었어.
G: 뭘 봤는데?
B: 여행 프로그램을 봤어. 나는 여행에 관심이 있거든.

Everyday English 2. A Function Practice 2-(2)

G: _____

B: _____

G: _____

B: _____

G: 뭐 하고 있니?
B: 신문 읽고 있어. 이 신문 좀 봐.
G: 사진 속의 음식이 맛있어 보이네. 무엇에 관한 이야기야?
B: 요리에 관한 이야기야. 난 요리에 관심이 있어.

Everyday English 2. A Function Practice 2-(3)

G: _____

B: _____

G: _____

B: _____

G: 이번 주 토요일에 뮤지컬 보러 가는 게 어때? 무료입장권이 몇 장 있거든.
B: 물론이지. 나는 뮤지컬에 관심이 있어. 뮤지컬 제목이 뭐야?
G: 소나기야. 황순원이 썼어.
B: 와. 그것을 빨리 보고 싶어.

Everyday English 2 – B Listening Activity

Brian: _____

Sujin: _____
_____

Brian: _____
_____

Sujin: _____

Brian: _____
_____

Sujin: _____

Brian: _____

Brian: 봐! 이것은 우리 반 친구들의 관심에 대한 도표야.
Sujin: 자세히 보자. 학생들의 30%는 스포츠에 관심이 있구나. 운동회가 굉장히 재미있을 것 같아.
Brian: 맞아. 도표에 의하면 27%의 학생은 배우에 관심이 있어. 너도 배우들을 좋아한다고 알고 있어.
Sujin: 응. 배우를 좋아해. 너는?
Brian: 난 배우에는 관심이 없어. 난 컴퓨터 게임에 관심이 있어. 20%의 학생이 컴퓨터 게임에 관심이 있어.
Sujin: 컴퓨터 게임은 재밌지. 그러나 너무 많이 하는 것은 안 좋아.
Brian: 나도 동의해.

In Real Life

Junho: _____

Adia: _____

Junho: _____

Adia: _____
_____

Junho: _____

Adia: _____
_____

Junho: _____

Adia: _____

Junho: Adia, 그것 아니? 우리는 다음 주에 동아리를 선택해야 해.
Adia: 알고 있어. 준호야, 어느 동아리를 마음에 두고 있니?
Junho: 나는 사진 동아리에 관심이 있어.
Adia: 좋아. 이 도표를 봐. 80퍼센트의 사진 동아리 회원들이 작년 활동을 좋아했다고 말했어.
Junho: 맞아, 너는 어떠니, Adia? 네가 가장 좋아하는 동아리는 무엇이니?
Adia: 나는 보드게임 동아리에 가입하고 싶어. 하지만 작년에 그 동아리의 회원들이 별로 좋아하지 않는다고 말했어.
Junho: 맞아. 60퍼센트의 회원들이 좋아하지 않는다고 말했어.
Adia: 그래. 나는 그것에 대해 좀 더 생각해 볼 거야.

※ 다음 우리말과 일치하도록 빈칸에 알맞은 것을 골라 쓰시오.

1 Hello, everyone! I'm Suji and I'm the _____ _____ the "_____ the _____" club.
A. Earth   B. leader   C. Save   D. of

2 _____ club is an _____ club.
A. environment   B. our

3 We do _____ work to _____ our _____.
A. protect   B. planet   C. volunteer

4 _____ our planet is _____, _____ it?
A. important   B. protecting   C. isn't

5 Last year, we _____ out a campaign to _____ food _____ in the school cafeteria.
A. carried   B. waste   C. reduce

6 The _____ was _____.
A. successful   B. campaign

7 This year, we are _____ some _____ activities _____.
A. abroad   B. preparing   C. special

8 So, if you are _____ in _____ the planet, please _____ us.
A. join   B. interested   C. saving

9 Hello, friends! I'm Diego _____ "Fly _____."
A. High   B. of

10 It is a _____ _____.
A. club   B. drone

11 We study _____ _____ of a drone and make some small drones _____ _____.
A. ourselves   B. part   C. every   D. by

12 When you have your _____ drone, you need to _____ _____.
A. own   B. hovering   C. practice

13 "_____" means _____ in the same _____ in the air.
A. place   B. staying   C. hovering

14 Once you are _____ at hovering, you _____ be _____ to fly your drone in different _____.
A. good   B. directions   C. ready   C. will

15 You're _____ excited, _____ you?
A. aren't   B. getting

1 모두들 안녕. 나는 수지이고 "Save the Earth" 동아리의 대표야.

2 우리 동아리는 환경 동아리야.

3 우리는 우리 행성(지구)을 지키기 위해 자원봉사 활동을 해.

4 지구를 지키는 것은 중요해. 그렇지 않니?

5 작년에 우리는 학교 식당에서 음식물 쓰레기 줄이기 캠페인을 했어.

6 캠페인은 성공적이었어.

7 올해 우리는 몇몇 특별한 해외 활동을 준비 중이야.

8 그러니, 지구를 구하는 데 관심이 있다면 우리와 함께하자.

9 안녕, 친구들! 나는 "Fly High"의 Diego야.

10 그건 드론 동아리야.

11 우리는 드론의 모든 부분을 공부하고 우리 스스로 작은 드론을 만들어.

12 네 드론이 있으면, 너는 공중 정지를 연습해야 해.

13 "공중 정지"란 공중에서 한자리에 머무는 것을 의미해.

14 공중 정지를 잘한다면, 너는 너의 드론을 다른 방향으로 날릴 준비가 될 거야.

15 점점 흥미가 생기지, 그렇지 않니?

16 Hello, I'm Junho. What do you _____ to do when you _____ beautiful _____?

A. want   B. scenery   C. see

17 You want to _____ a picture _____ it, _____ you?

A. don't   B. take   C. of

18 If you _____ our photo club, "Photo World," you can meet _____ photographers and learn their _____.

A. skills   B. join   C. famous

19 _____ December, you can _____ _____ in the school photo contest.

A. every   B. part   C. take

20 So, by _____ "Photo World" you can learn a new _____ and have a _____ of winning a prize!

A. chance   B. joining   C. hobby

21 _____ to my _____ club, "Story Singers"!

A. musical   B. welcome

22 My name is Olivia. In the musical club, _____ are two _____: actors and _____.

A. crew   B. groups   C. there

23 We first _____ the _____ of our musical and then write a story _____.

A. subject   B. choose   C. together

24 Then, the actors _____ singing and _____, while the crew make _____.

A. costumes   B. dancing   C. practice

25 We _____ our _____ in the school _____.

A. perform   B. festival   C. musical

26 You can _____ _____ _____ from me.

A. application   B. get   C. an

27 You will _____ _____ club, _____ you?

A. won't   B. join   C. our

---

16 안녕. 난 준호야. 너는 아름다운 풍경을 볼 때 무엇을 하고 싶니?

17 사진을 찍고 싶을 거야. 그렇지 않니?

18 우리 사진 동아리 "Photo World"에 가입한다면 너는 유명한 사진작가들을 만나고, 그들의 기술을 배울 수 있어.

19 매년 12월에 너는 학교 사진 대회에 참가할 수 있어.

20 그렇게 "Photo World"에 가입하는 것으로 너는 새로운 취미를 배우고 상을 받는 기회를 가질 수 있어!

21 나의 뮤지컬 동아리, "Story Singers"에 온 걸 환영해!

22 내 이름은 Olivia야. 뮤지컬 동아리에는 배우와 제작진이라는 두 그룹이 있어.

23 우리는 우선 뮤지컬의 주제를 고르고 함께 이야기를 써.

24 그리고는 제작진이 의상을 만드는 동안 배우들은 노래와 춤을 연습하지.

25 우리는 학교 축제에서 뮤지컬 공연을 해.

26 가입신청서는 나한테서 받을 수 있어.

27 너는 우리 동아리에 가입할 거야, 그렇지?

※ 다음 우리말과 일치하도록 빈칸에 알맞은 말을 쓰시오.

1 Hello, everyone! I'm Suji and I'm _____ _____ _____ the "_____ _____ _____" club.

2 Our club is _____ _____ _____.

3 We _____ _____ _____ _____ _____ _____ our planet.

4 _____ _____ _____ is important, _____ _____?

5 _____ _____, we _____ _____ a campaign _____ _____ _____ _____ in the school cafeteria.

6 The campaign _____ _____.

7 This year, we are _____ _____ _____ _____ _____ abroad.

8 So, if you _____ _____ _____ _____ _____ the planet, please _____ _____.

9 Hello, friends! I'm Diego _____ "Fly High."

10 _____ _____ a drone _____.

11 We study _____ _____ _____ _____ a drone and make some small drones _____ _____.

12 When you have _____ _____ _____, you _____ _____ _____.

13 "_____" means _____ _____ the same place in the air.

14 Once you _____ _____ _____ hovering, you will _____ _____ _____ your drone _____ _____.

15 You're _____ _____, _____ _____?

---

1 모두들 안녕. 나는 수지이고 "Save the Earth" 동아리의 대표야.

2 우리 동아리는 환경 동아리야.

3 우리는 우리 행성(지구)을 지키기 위해 자원봉사 활동을 해.

4 지구를 지키는 것은 중요해. 그렇지 않니?

5 작년에 우리는 학교 식당에서 음식물 쓰레기 줄이기 캠페인을 했어.

6 캠페인은 성공적이었어.

7 올해 우리는 몇몇 특별한 해외 활동을 준비 중이야.

8 그러니, 지구를 구하는 데 관심이 있다면 우리와 함께하자.

9 안녕, 친구들! 나는 "Fly High"의 Diego야.

10 그건 드론 동아리야.

11 우리는 드론의 모든 부분을 공부하고 우리 스스로 작은 드론을 만들어.

12 네 드론이 있으면, 너는 공중 정지를 연습해야 해.

13 "공중 정지"란 공중에서 한자리에 머무는 것을 의미해.

14 공중 정지를 잘한다면, 너는 너의 드론을 다른 방향으로 날릴 준비가 될 거야.

15 점점 흥미가 생기지, 그렇지 않니?

16 Hello, I'm Junho. What do you _____ _____ _____ when you _____ _____ _____ ?

17 You want _____ _____ _____ _____ _____ it, _____ _____ ?

18 If you _____ _____ _____ _____ , "Photo World," you can meet famous photographers and _____ _____ _____ .

19 _____ December, you _____ _____ _____ _____ _____ the school photo contest.

20 So, _____ _____ "Photo World" you can _____ _____ _____ _____ and have _____ _____ _____ _____ a prize!

21 _____ _____ my _____ club, "Story Singers"!

22 My name is Olivia. In the musical club, _____ _____ _____ : _____ and _____ .

23 We first _____ _____ _____ of our musical and then _____ _____ _____ _____ .

24 Then, the actors _____ _____ and _____ , _____ the crew _____ _____ .

25 We _____ our musical _____ _____ _____ _____ .

26 You _____ _____ _____ _____ from me.

27 You will _____ _____ _____ , _____ _____ ?

16 안녕. 난 준호야. 너는 아름다운 풍경을 볼 때 무엇을 하고 싶니?

17 사진을 찍고 싶을 거야, 그렇지 않니?

18 우리 사진 동아리 "Photo World"에 가입한다면 너는 유명한 사진작가들을 만나고, 그들의 기술을 배울 수 있어.

19 매년 12월에 너는 학교 사진 대회에 참가할 수 있어.

20 그렇게 "Photo World"에 가입하는 것으로 너는 새로운 취미를 배우고 상을 받는 기회를 가질 수 있어!

21 나의 뮤지컬 동아리, "Story Singers"에 온 걸 환영해!

22 내 이름은 Olivia야. 뮤지컬 동아리에는 배우와 제작진이라는 두 그룹이 있어.

23 우리는 우선 뮤지컬의 주제를 고르고 함께 이야기를 써.

24 그리고는 제작진이 의상을 만드는 동안 배우들은 노래와 춤을 연습하지.

25 우리는 학교 축제에서 뮤지컬 공연을 해.

26 가입신청서는 나한테서 받을 수 있어.

27 너는 우리 동아리에 가입할 거야, 그렇지?

※ 다음 문장을 우리말로 쓰시오.

1 ▸ Hello, everyone! I'm Suji and I'm the leader of the "Save the Earth" club.

➡ _____

2 ▸ Our club is an environmental club.

➡ _____

3 ▸ We do volunteer work to protect our planet.

➡ _____

4 ▸ Protecting our planet is important, isn't it?

➡ _____

5 ▸ Last year, we carried out a campaign to reduce food waste in the school cafeteria.

➡ _____

6 ▸ The campaign was successful.

➡ _____

7 ▸ This year, we are preparing some special activities abroad.

➡ _____

8 ▸ So, if you are interested in saving the planet, please join us.

➡ _____

9 ▸ Hello, friends! I'm Diego of "Fly High."

➡ _____

10 ▸ It is a drone club.

➡ _____

11 ▸ We study every part of a drone and make some small drones by ourselves.

➡ _____

12 ▸ When you have your own drone, you need to practice hovering.

➡ _____

13 ▸ "Hovering" means staying in the same place in the air.

➡ _____

14 ▸ Once you are good at hovering, you will be ready to fly your drone in different directions.

➡ _____

15 ▸ You're getting excited, aren't you?

➡ _____

16 ▶ Hello, I'm Junho. What do you want to do when you see beautiful scenery?

➡ _____

17 ▶ You want to take a picture of it, don't you?

➡ _____

18 ▶ If you join our photo club, "Photo World," you can meet famous photographers and learn their skills.

➡ _____

19 ▶ Every December, you can take part in the school photo contest.

➡ _____

20 ▶ So, by joining "Photo World" you can learn a new hobby and have a chance of winning a prize!

➡ _____

21 ▶ Welcome to my musical club, "Story Singers"!

➡ _____

22 ▶ My name is Olivia. In the musical club, there are two groups: actors and crew.

➡ _____

23 ▶ We first choose the subject of our musical and then write a story together.

➡ _____

24 ▶ Then, the actors practice singing and dancing, while the crew make costumes.

➡ _____

25 ▶ We perform our musical in the school festival.

➡ _____

26 ▶ You can get an application from me.

➡ _____

27 ▶ You will join our club, won't you?

➡ _____

Step4

※ 다음 괄호 안의 단어들을 우리말에 맞도록 바르게 배열하시오.

1 (everyone! / hello, // Suji / I'm / and / the / I'm / of / leader / the / club. / Earth" / the / "Save)
➡ _____

2 (club / is / our / environmental / an / club.)
➡ _____

3 (do / we / work / volunteer / protect / to / planet. / our)
➡ _____

4 (our / protecting / planet / important, / is / it? / isn't)
➡ _____

5 (year, / last / carried / we / a / out / campaign / reduce / to / waste / food / school / in / cafeteria. / the)
➡ _____

6 (campaign / the / successful. / was)
➡ _____

7 (year, / this / are / we / some / preparing / special / abroad. / activities)
➡ _____

8 (if / so, / are / you / in / interested / saving / planet, / the / us. / join / please)
➡ _____

9 (friends! / hello, / Diego / I'm / High." / "Fly / of)
➡ _____

10 (is / it / club. / drone / a)
➡ _____

11 (study / we / party / every / a / of / drone / and / make / small / some / ourselves. / by / drones)
➡ _____

12 (you / when / your / have / drone, / own / need / you / to / hovering. / practice)
➡ _____

13 (means / "Hovering" / staying / the / in / place / same / air. / the / in)
➡ _____

14 (are / you / once / good / hovering, / at / will / you / ready / be / fly / to / drone / your / different / directions. / in)
➡ _____

15 (getting / you're / you? / excited, / aren't)
➡ _____

1 모두들 안녕. 나는 수지이고 "Save the Earth" 동아리의 대표야.

2 우리 동아리는 환경 동아리야.

3 우리는 우리 행성(지구)을 지키기 위해 자원봉사 활동을 해.

4 지구를 지키는 것은 중요해, 그렇지 않니?

5 작년에 우리는 학교 식당에서 음식물 쓰레기 줄이기 캠페인을 했어.

6 캠페인은 성공적이었어.

7 올해 우리는 몇몇 특별한 해외 활동을 준비 중이야.

8 그러니, 지구를 구하는 데 관심이 있다면 우리와 함께하자.

9 안녕, 친구들! 나는 "Fly High" 의 Diego야.

10 그건 드론 동아리야.

11 우리는 드론의 모든 부분을 공부하고 우리 스스로 작은 드론을 만들어.

12 네 드론이 있으면, 너는 공중 정지를 연습해야 해.

13 "공중 정지"란 공중에서 한자리에 머무는 것을 의미해.

14 공중 정지를 잘한다면, 너는 너의 드론을 다른 방향으로 날릴 준비가 될 거야.

15 점점 흥미가 생기지, 그렇지 않니?

16 (I'm / hello, / Junho. // do / what / want / you / do / to / when / see / you / scenery? / beautiful)

➡ _____

17 (want / take / you / to / picture / a / it, / of / you? / don't)

➡ _____

18 (you / if / our / club, / photo / join / World," / "Photo / can / you / meet / photographers / famous / and / skills. / their / learn)

➡ _____

_____

19 (December, / every / can / you / take / in / part / school / contest. / the / photo)

➡ _____

20 (by / so, / joining / World" / "Photo / can / you / learn / new / a / hobby / and / a / chance / have / of / prize! / a / winning)

➡ _____

_____

21 (to / welcome / musical / my / club, / Singers"! / "Story)

➡ _____

22 (name / my / Olivia. / is / the / in / club, / musical / are / there / groups: / two / crew. / and / actors)

➡ _____

_____

23 (first / we / choose / subject / the / our / of / musical / then / and / write / together. / story / a)

➡ _____

24 (the / then, / actors / practice / and / singing / dancing, /. the / while / costumes. / make / crew)

➡ _____

_____

25 (perform / we / musical / our / the / in / festival. / school)

➡ _____

26 (can / you / get / application / me. / from / an)

➡ _____

27 (will / you / our / join / club, / you? / won't)

➡ _____

16 안녕, 난 준호야. 너는 아름다운 풍경을 볼 때 무엇을 하고 싶니?

17 사진을 찍고 싶을 거야, 그렇지 않니?

18 우리 사진 동아리 "Photo World"에 가입한다면 너는 유명한 사진작가들을 만나고, 그들의 기술을 배울 수 있어.

19 매년 **12**월에 너는 학교 사진 대회에 참가할 수 있어.

20 그렇게 "Photo World"에 가입하는 것으로 너는 새로운 취미를 배우고 상을 받는 기회를 가질 수 있어!

21 나의 뮤지컬 동아리, "Story Singers"에 온 걸 환영해!

22 내 이름은 Olivia야. 뮤지컬 동아리에는 배우와 제작진이라는 두 그룹이 있어.

23 우리는 우선 뮤지컬의 주제를 고르고 함께 이야기를 써.

24 그리고는 제작진이 의상을 만드는 동안 배우들은 노래와 춤을 연습하지.

25 우리는 학교 축제에서 뮤지컬 공연을 해.

26 가입신청서는 나한테서 받을 수 있어.

27 너는 우리 동아리에 가입할 거야, 그렇지?

※ 다음 우리말을 영어로 쓰시오.

1 모두들 안녕. 나는 수지이고 "Save the Earth" 동아리의 대표야.

➡ _____

2 우리 동아리는 환경 동아리야.

➡ _____

3 우리는 우리 행성(지구)을 지키기 위해 자원봉사 활동을 해.

➡ _____

4 지구를 지키는 것은 중요해, 그렇지 않니?

➡ _____

5 작년에 우리는 학교 식당에서 음식물 쓰레기 줄이기 캠페인을 했어.

➡ _____

6 캠페인은 성공적이었어.

➡ _____

7 올해 우리는 몇몇 특별한 해외 활동을 준비 중이야.

➡ _____

8 그러니, 지구를 구하는 데 관심이 있다면 우리와 함께하자.

➡ _____

9 안녕, 친구들! 나는 "Fly High"의 Diego야.

➡ _____

10 그건 드론 동아리야.

➡ _____

11 우리는 드론의 모든 부분을 공부하고 우리 스스로 작은 드론을 만들어.

➡ _____

12 네 드론이 있으면, 너는 공중 정지를 연습해야 해.

➡ _____

13 "공중 정지"란 공중에서 한자리에 머무는 것을 의미해.

➡ _____

14 공중 정지를 잘한다면, 너는 너의 드론을 다른 방향으로 날릴 준비가 될 거야.

➡ _____

15 점점 흥미가 생기지, 그렇지 않니?

➡ _____

16 안녕, 난 준호야. 너는 아름다운 풍경을 볼 때 무엇을 하고 싶니?

➡ _____

17 사진을 찍고 싶을 거야, 그렇지 않니?

➡ _____

18 우리 사진 동아리 "Photo World"에 가입한다면 너는 유명한 사진작가들을 만나고, 그들의 기술을 배울 수 있어.

➡ _____

19 매년 12월에 너는 학교 사진 대회에 참가할 수 있어.

➡ _____

20 그렇게 "Photo World"에 가입하는 것으로 너는 새로운 취미를 배우고 상을 받는 기회를 가질 수 있어!

➡ _____

21 나의 뮤지컬 동아리, "Story Singers"에 온 걸 환영해!

➡ _____

22 내 이름은 Olivia야. 뮤지컬 동아리에는 배우와 제작진이라는 두 그룹이 있어.

➡ _____

23 우리는 우선 뮤지컬의 주제를 고르고 함께 이야기를 써.

➡ _____

24 그리고는 제작진이 의상을 만드는 동안 배우들은 노래와 춤을 연습하지.

➡ _____

25 우리는 학교 축제에서 뮤지컬 공연을 해.

➡ _____

26 가입신청서는 나한테서 받을 수 있어.

➡ _____

27 너는 우리 동아리에 가입할 거야, 그렇지?

➡ _____

※ 다음 우리말과 일치하도록 빈칸에 알맞은 말을 쓰시오.

Project Work – Make your own club

1. A: What _____ we _____ our speaking club?

2. B: _____ _____ "Raise Your Voice?"

3. C: Good! Then, when and where _____ we _____?

4. D: _____ _____ in the music room.

5. B: _____ _____ on Mondays _____ _____?

6. A: _____ good.

1. A: 우리의 말하기 동아리를 뭐라 부를까?
2. B: "Raise Your Voice" 어때?
3. C: 좋아! 그럼, 우리 언제 어디서 만날까?
4. D: 음악실에서 만나자.
5. B: 방과 후 월요일이 어때?
6. A: 좋아.

Express Yourself

1. _____ "True Reporters"!

2. You want _____ _____ interesting _____ with your friends, _____ _____?

3. If you join our club, you will _____ _____ the school newspaper _____ _____.

4. We _____ and _____ in the library _____ _____ after school.

5. So, if you _____ _____ _____ _____ our club, come for an interview on Wednesday.

6. We _____ _____ _____ meet you!

1. "True Reporters'에 가입해!
2. 너는 흥미로운 소식을 친구들과 함께 공유하길 원하지, 그렇지 않니?
3. 만약 네가 우리 동아리에 가입한다면, 너는 매달 학교 신문을 만드는 것을 도울 거야.
4. 우리는 방과 후 매주 수요일마다 도서관에서 만나서 일해.
5. 그러니 만약 네가 우리 동아리에 가입하는 것에 관심이 있다면, 수요일에 면접을 보러 오렴.
6. 우리는 어서 너를 만나고 싶어!

Project Work

1. You _____ _____ speak well, _____ _____?

2. If you are _____ _____ _____ well, you _____ _____ the club, "Raise Your Voice"!

3. We _____ _____ in the music room every Monday after school.

4. If you learn to _____ _____, you may _____ _____ _____ change people's minds!

1. 너는 말을 잘하고 싶지, 그렇지 않니?
2. 만약 네가 말을 잘하는 것에 관심이 있다면, 너는 "Raise Your Voice" 동아리에 가입해야 해!
3. 우리는 매주 월요일 방과 후에 음악실에서 말하는 것을 연습해.
4. 만약 네가 말을 잘하는 것을 배운다면, 너는 사람들의 사고방식을 바꿀 수 있을 거야.

※ 다음 우리말을 영어로 쓰시오.

Project Work – Make your own club

1. A: 우리의 말하기 동아리를 뭐라 부를까?
➡ _____

2. B: "Raise Your Voice" 어때?
➡ _____

3. C: 좋아! 그럼, 우리 언제 어디서 만날까?
➡ _____

4. D: 음악실에서 만나자.
➡ _____

5. B: 방과 후 월요일이 어때?
➡ _____

6. A: 좋아.
➡ _____

Express Yourself

1. "True Reporters'에 가입해!
➡ _____

2. 너는 흥미로운 소식을 친구들과 함께 공유하길 원하지, 그렇지 않니?
➡ _____

3. 만약 네가 우리 동아리에 가입한다면, 너는 매달 학교 신문을 만드는 것을 도울 거야.
➡ _____

4. 우리는 방과 후 매주 수요일마다 도서관에서 만나서 일해.
➡ _____

5. 그러니 만약 네가 우리 동아리에 가입하는 것에 관심이 있다면, 수요일에 면접을 보러 오렴.
➡ _____

6. 우리는 어서 너를 만나고 싶어!
➡ _____

Project Work

1. 너는 말을 잘하고 싶지, 그렇지 않니?
➡ _____

2. 만약 네가 말을 잘하는 것에 관심이 있다면, 너는 "Raise Your Voice" 동아리에 가입해야 해!
➡ _____

3. 우리는 매주 월요일 방과 후에 음악실에서 말하는 것을 연습해.
➡ _____

4. 만약 네가 말을 잘하는 것을 배운다면, 너는 사람들의 사고방식을 바꿀 수 있을 거야.
➡ _____

※ 다음 영어를 우리말로 쓰시오.

01 throat

02 cause

03 match

04 desert

05 plant

06 festival

07 trash

08 forest

09 trip

10 brush

11 global

12 engineer

13 kick

14 fight

15 protect

16 terrible

17 volunteer

18 wash

19 wear

20 share

21 performance

22 map

23 solution

24 sneeze

25 guest

26 crybaby

27 togetherness

28 dust

29 seed

30 advice

31 past

32 future

33 hero

34 unwelcome

35 take a look at

36 keep on

37 can't wait to

38 throw away

39 not only A but also B

40 get rid of

41 look forward to -ing

42 come about

43 keep away from

※ 다음 우리말을 영어로 쓰시오.

01	차다	
02	축제	
03	경기	
04	숙제	
05	심다; 식물, 공장	
06	먼지	
07	쓰레기	
08	원인	
09	조언	
10	재채기하다	
11	울보	
12	영웅	
13	지도	
14	해결책	
15	씨앗	
16	환영 받지 못하는	
17	미래	
18	과거; 지나간	
19	친목, 연대감	
20	공연	
21	끔찍한	

22	숲	
23	기술자	
24	입다	
25	이를 닦다, 머리를 빗다	
26	보호하다	
27	싸우다	
28	자원봉사하다	
29	세계적인, 지구의	
30	씻다	
31	목(구멍)	
32	나누다	
33	여행	
34	사막	
35	~을 끄다	
36	~을 고대하다, 기대하다	
37	빨리 ~하고 싶어하다	
38	버리다	
39	A뿐만 아니라 B도	
40	~을 없애다	
41	~을 피하다	
42	발생하다	
43	계속하다	

※ 다음 영영풀이에 알맞은 단어를 <보기>에서 골라 쓴 후, 우리말 뜻을 쓰시오.

1 _____ : the person or thing that makes something happen: _____

2 _____ : the small hard part produced by a plant, from which a new plant can grow: _____

3 _____ : a large area of land that is thickly covered with trees: _____

4 _____ : a sports event where people or teams compete against each other: _____

5 _____ : a way of solving a problem or dealing with a difficult situation: _____

6 _____ : a person, especially a child, who cries too often or without good reason: _____

7 _____ : the natural world in which people, animals and plants live: _____

8 _____ : existing or happening over a large area or among many people: _____

9 _____ : to have or use something at the same time as somebody else: _____

10 _____ : to put plants, seeds, etc. in the ground to grow: _____

11 _____ : a large area of land that has very little water and very few plants growing on it: _____

12 _____ : the act of performing a play, concert or some other form of entertainment: _____

13 _____ : the happy feeling you have when you are with people you like, especially family and friends: _____

14 _____ : to offer to do something without being forced to do it or without getting paid for it: _____

15 _____ : an action or an opinion that is not correct, or that produces a result that you did not want: _____

16 _____ : a person, especially a man, who is admired by many people for doing something brave or good: _____

보기			
forest	widespread	seed	environment
performance	cause	togetherness	hero
volunteer	solution	plant	mistake
desert	crybaby	match	share

※ 다음 우리말과 일치하도록 빈칸에 알맞은 말을 쓰시오.

Everyday English 1 A. Function Practice 2-(1)

Lisa: Hey, Tom. _____ _____ _____ _____ to school today?

Tom: I _____ _____ _____. Did the teacher _____ _____ _____ _____?

Lisa: Yes. He _____ we _____ _____ lesson 3 in our English book.

Tom: Okay. _____ _____, Lisa.

Everyday English 1 A. Function Practice 2-(2)

B: The weather is so _____ today. _____ do you have an umbrella?

G: The _____ _____ _____ it _____ _____ this afternoon.

B: Oh, no. I _____ _____ that! I don't have an umbrella.

G: _____ _____. You can _____ my umbrella.

Everyday English 1 A. Function Practice 2-(3)

Jane: Do you want to _____ _____ _____, *The Big Zoo*?

Alex: No, I don't. My brother _____ the movie _____ _____. _____ _____ it was _____.

Jane: Then, what _____ we _____?

Alex: We _____ _____ _____ _____ in the park instead.

Everyday English 1 B. Listening Activity

Sujin: John, what _____ _____ your foot?

John: Last week, there was a soccer match. I _____ a rock _____ _____.

Sujin: Oh, your foot _____ _____ very much! Did you go to the hospital?

John: Yes, _____ _____ I _____ _____ soccer for a month.

Sujin: Oh, no. What _____ you _____ for the next game?

John: I'll _____ _____ find _____ soccer player.

Sujin: _____ _____ _____ _____ Kevin? He's _____ _____ soccer.

John: That's a good idea. I'll _____ _____ _____ now.

Everyday English 2 A Function practice 2-(1)

Brain: Susan, do you _____ _____ _____ a movie this Saturday?

Susan: Sure. _____ _____ do you want to watch?

Brain: The new superhero movie _____ _____ _____. I'm _____ _____ _____ _____ it.

Susan: Wow! I love superhero movies. _____ you _____!

Everyday English 2 B. Listening Activity

Chris: Do you _____ _____ _____ for this _____ Friday?

Emily: I do. I _____ at a lost pet center _____ _____.

Chris: _____ _____ you _____ at the lost pet center?

Emily: Well, I _____ the dogs _____ _____ _____ _____. Also, I help to wash them.

Chris: That _____ wonderful. Why do you go there _____ _____?

Emily: It's _____ I love animals. I want to become an animal doctor _____ _____ _____.

Chris: I love animals too. _____ I _____ you this Friday?

Emily: Sure. I _____ _____ _____ _____ you at the center.

In Real Life

Diego: Achoo! Achoo!

Suji: Did you _____ _____ _____, Diego?

Diego: No, I don't _____ _____, but I _____ _____ _____. Achoo!

Suji: Then, it must be _____ _____ the yellow dust. The _____ report _____ the yellow dust would be terrible today.

Diego: Oh, I _____ I'm _____ because of that. _____ we _____ the yellow dust?

Suji: Yes, we can. My club members are _____ _____ _____ some special activities _____.

Diego: What are they?

Suji: We're _____ _____ _____ trees in China because _____ _____ _____ the yellow dust comes from China.

Diego: That sounds good.

Suji: Yes. We are _____ _____ _____ _____ the yellow dust.

Brian: Susan, 이번 주 토요일에 영화 볼래?

Susan: 좋아. 넌 무슨 영화 보고 싶니?

Brian: 새로운 슈퍼 영웅 영화가 막 나왔어. 난 그 영화를 정말 보고 싶어.

Susan: 와! 나는 슈퍼 영웅 영화를 정말 좋아해. 그때 보자!

Chris: 다가오는 금요일에 계획 있니?

Emily: 있어. 난 금요일마다 유기동물 센터에서 자원봉사를 해.

Chris: 유기동물 센터에서 뭐해?

Emily: 음, 난 개를 산책시켜. 또한 씻기는 것도 도와.

Chris: 멋지구나. 왜 매주 거기에 가니?

Emily: 난 동물이 좋아. 장래에 수의사가 되고 싶어.

Chris: 나도 동물이 좋아. 이번 금요일에 같이 가도 될까?

Emily: 그래. 센터에서 보기를 기대해.

Diego: 에취! 에취!

Suji: 감기 걸렸니, Diego?

Diego: 아니, 아프진 않아. 하지만 재채기를 멈출 수가 없어. 에취!

Suji: 그럼 황사 때문일 거야. 일기 예보에서는 오늘 황사가 심각할 거라고 했어.

Diego: 아, 그것 때문에 재채기하나봐. 황사를 멈출 수 없을까?

Suji: 응, 우린 할 수 있어. 우리 동아리 회원들은 이국에서 특별한 활동을 할 준비를 하고 있어.

Diego: 그게 뭔데?

Suji: 우린 중국에 나무를 심을 계획을 하고 있어. 왜냐하면 황사의 대부분은 중국에서 오거든.

Diego: 멋지다.

Suji: 응. 우린 황사를 멈추길 기대하고 있어.

※ 다음 우리말에 맞도록 대화를 영어로 쓰시오.

Everyday English 1 A. Function Practice 2-(1)

Lisa: _____

Tom: _____

Lisa: _____

Tom: _____

Lisa: 안녕, Tom. 오늘 왜 학교에 오지 않았니?
Tom: 감기가 심했어. 선생님이 숙제를 내주셨니?
Lisa: 응. 그는 우리가 영어책에서 3과를 읽어야 한다고 말씀하셨어.
Tom: 알았어. 고마워, Lisa.

Everyday English 1 A. Function Practice 2-(2)

B: _____

G: _____

B: _____

G: _____

B: 오늘 날씨가 정말 좋다. 너는 왜 우산을 가져왔니?
G: 일기 예보에서 오늘 오후에 비가 온대.
B: 오, 이런. 나는 몰랐단 말야! 나는 우산이 없어.
G: 걱정 마. 나랑 우산 같이 쓰자.

Everyday English 1 A. Function Practice 2-(3)

Jane: _____

Alex: _____

Jane: _____

Alex: _____

Jane: 넌 Big Zoo라는 영화 보고 싶니?
Alex: 아니. 내 남동생이 지난주에 그 영화를 봤어. 끔찍하다고 말했어.
Jane: 그럼, 우리 뭐 할까?
Alex: 대신에 공원에서 산책을 할 수 있지.

Everyday English 1 B. Listening Activity

Sujin: _____

John: _____

Sujin: _____

John: _____

Sujin: _____

John: _____

Sujin: _____

John: _____

Sujin: John, 발이 어떻게 된 거야?
John: 지난주에, 축구 시합이 있었어. 난 실수로 돌을 찼어.
Sujin: 오, 발이 진짜 아팠겠다! 병원에는 갔었어?
John: 응, 의사가 난 한 달 동안 축구하면 안 된다고 했어.
Sujin: 아, 안됐다. 다음 시합은 어떻게 할 거니?
John: 난 다른 축구 선수를 찾아야 해.
Sujin: Kevin에게 물어보는 게 어때? 그는 축구를 잘해.
John: 좋은 생각이야. 지금 그에게 물어봐야겠다.

Everyday English 2 A Function practice 2-(1)

Brain: _____

Susan: _____

Brain: _____

Susan: _____

Everyday English 2 B. Listening Activity

Chris: _____

Emily: _____

Chris: _____

Emily: _____

Chris: _____

Emily: _____

Chris: _____

Emily: _____

In Real Life

Diego: _____

Suji: _____

Diego: _____

Suji: _____

_____

Diego: _____

Suji: _____

_____

Diego: _____

Suji: _____

_____

Diego: _____

Suji: _____

Brian: Susan, 이번 주 토요일에 영화 볼래?

Susan: 좋아. 넌 무슨 영화 보고 싶니?

Brian: 새로운 슈퍼 영웅 영화가 막 나왔어. 난 그 영화를 정말 보고 싶어.

Susan: 와! 나는 슈퍼 영웅 영화를 정말 좋아해. 그때 보자!

Chris: 다가오는 금요일에 계획 있니?

Emily: 있어. 난 금요일마다 유기동물 센터에서 자원봉사를 해.

Chris: 유기동물 센터에서 뭐해?

Emily: 음, 난 개를 산책시켜. 또한 씻기는 것도 도와.

Chris: 멋지구나. 왜 매주 거기에 가니?

Emily: 난 동물이 좋아. 장래에 수의사가 되고 싶어.

Chris: 나도 동물이 좋아. 이번 금요일에 같이 가도 될까?

Emily: 그래. 센터에서 보기를 기대해.

Diego: 에취! 에취!

Suji: 감기 걸렸니, Diego?

Diego: 아니, 아프진 않아. 하지만 재채기를 멈출 수가 없어. 에취!

Suji: 그럼 황사 때문일 거야. 일기 예보에서는 오늘 황사가 심각할 거라고 했어.

Diego: 아, 그것 때문에 재채기하나봐. 황사를 멈출 수 없을까?

Suji: 응, 우린 할 수 있어. 우리 동아리 회원들은 외국에서 특별한 활동을 할 준비를 하고 있어.

Diego: 그게 뭔데?

Suji: 우린 중국에 나무를 심을 계획을 하고 있어. 왜냐하면 황사의 대부분은 중국에서 오거든.

Diego: 멋지다.

Suji: 응. 우린 황사를 멈추길 기대하고 있어.

※ 다음 우리말과 일치하도록 빈칸에 알맞은 것을 골라 쓰시오.

The Green News

1 Many people are _____ masks so _____ they can keep _____ _____ an unwelcome guest in the spring: yellow dust.

   A. away   B. wearing   C. that   D. from

2 _____ year, _____ is _____ yellow dust in Korea.

   A. there   B. every   C. widespread

3 Many people _____ sick because the yellow dust _____ their eyes and _____.

   A. throats   B. hurts   C. become

4 _____ does the yellow dust _____ _____?

   A. about   B. come   C. why

5 Is there any _____ to _____ the yellow dust? Yes, _____ is!

   A. there   B. stop   C. way

6 Let's _____ a look at the causes of and the _____ to the problem of yellow dust _____ the work of some volunteers in Gansu Sheng, China.

   A. take   B. solutions   C. through

Li Na(16, a middle school student)

7 A _____ time ago, this _____ was a big _____.

   A. forest   B. place   C. long

8 But people began to cut _____ trees _____ that they could _____ cities.

   A. down   B. build   C. so

9 _____ time _____, the forest _____ many trees.

   A. passed   B. lost   C. as

10 _____, the forest became a desert and the desert _____ bigger and _____.

   A. became   B. bigger   C. finally

11 Now, when the spring _____ strong winds _____ the west, the yellow dust _____.

   A. spreads   B. brings   C. from

12 In the _____, most people did not know _____ to _____ the yellow dust problem.

   A. past   B. stop   C. how

녹색 뉴스

1 많은 사람이 봄에 찾아오는 반갑지 않은 손님인 황사 때문에 마스크를 끼고 있습니다.

2 매년 한국에는 황사가 널리 퍼집니다.

3 황사가 많은 사람들의 눈과 목을 아프게 해서 많은 사람들이 병에 걸립니다.

4 황사는 왜 일어나는 것일까요?

5 황사를 막을 수 있는 방법이 있을까요? 네, 있습니다!

6 중국의 간쑤성에 있는 자원봉사자들의 작업을 통해 황사의 원인과 해결책을 살펴봅시다.

리나(16, 중학생)

7 예전에 이곳은 큰 숲이었습니다.

8 그러나 사람들이 도시를 세우기 위해 나무를 베기 시작했습니다.

9 시간이 지나면서 숲은 많은 나무를 잃었습니다.

10 마침내, 숲은 사막이 되었고 사막은 점점 더 커졌습니다.

11 이제, 봄에 서쪽에서 세찬 바람이 불 때, 황사가 퍼집니다.

12 이전에는 대부분의 사람들이 황사 문제를 어떻게 막을 수 있는지 알지 못했습니다.

13 Now, many _____ _____ trees to _____ this problem.

    A. solve   B. plant   C. volunteers

Minsu(18, a high school student)

14 _____ trees in the desert _____ hard and _____ .

    A. expensive   B. is   C. planting

15 _____, many Chinese people know _____ they cannot live _____ they don't plant trees.

    A. if   B. that   C. however

16 They always _____ us, Korean volunteers, _____ we plant trees _____ them.

    A. because   B. with   C. thank

17 _____, we plant trees to _____ not only China but _____ Korea.

    A. also   B. help   C. however

Suji(15, a middle school student)

18 _____ first, I didn't know _____ to do to get _____ of the yellow dust.

    A. rid   B. what   C. at

19 Then, Minsu, my group _____ , told me that _____ trees can help to _____ the problem.

    A. solve   B. planting   C. leader

20 I also found out that _____ trees and _____ the environment _____ my family and me.

    A. planting   B. help   C. protecting

21 In China, many people are _____ trees in deserts so _____ they can _____ the spread of the yellow dust.

    A. stop   B. planting   C. that

22 The work is not _____ , but they are working _____ to _____ the world.

    A. easy   B. protect   C. hard

23 With this kind of global _____ , the seeds of hope will _____ on _____ .

    A. growing   B. togetherness   C. keep

---

13 이제는 많은 자원봉사자들이 이 문제를 해결하기 위해 나무를 심고 있습니다.

민수(**18**, 고등학생)

14 사막에 나무를 심는 것은 힘들고 비용이 많이 듭니다.

15 하지만 많은 중국인들은 자신들이 나무를 심지 않으면 살 수 없다는 것을 알고 있습니다.

16 그들은 우리가 그들과 나무를 심기 때문에 우리 한국인 봉사자들에게 늘 감사해 하고 있습니다.

17 그러나 우리가 나무를 심는 이유는 단지 중국만이 아니라 한국도 돕기 위해서입니다.

수지(**15**, 중학생)

18 처음에 저는 황사를 없애기 위해서 무엇을 해야 할지 몰랐습니다.

19 그 때, 우리 조장인 민수가 나무를 심는 것이 문제를 해결하는 데 도움이 된다고 얘기해 줬습니다.

20 저는 나무를 심고 환경을 보호하는 것이 우리 가족과 제 자신도 돕는 일이라는 것을 알게 되었습니다.

21 중국에서는 많은 사람들이 황사가 퍼지는 것을 막기 위해서 사막에 나무를 심고 있습니다.

22 이 작업은 쉽지 않지만 그들은 세계를 보호하기 위해서 열심히 일하고 있습니다.

23 이러한 세계적인 협업으로 희망의 씨앗은 계속해서 자랄 것입니다.

※ 다음 우리말과 일치하도록 빈칸에 알맞은 말을 쓰시오.

The Green News

1 Many people _____ _____ masks _____ _____ they
_____ _____ _____ _____ an _____ _____ in
the spring: yellow dust.

2 Every year, _____ _____ _____ yellow dust in Korea.

3 Many people _____ _____ _____ the yellow dust
_____ _____ _____ and _____.

4 Why _____ the yellow dust _____ _____?

5 Is there any _____ _____ _____ the yellow dust? Yes,
_____ _____!

6 Let's _____ _____ _____ _____ the causes _____
and the _____ _____ the problem of yellow dust _____
the work of some _____ in Gansu Sheng, China.

Li Na(16, a middle school student)

7 A long time _____, this place _____ _____ _____
_____.

8 But people began _____ _____ _____ _____ _____
_____ they _____ _____ cities.

9 _____ time _____, the forest _____ many trees.

10 _____, the forest _____ a desert and the desert _____
_____ _____ _____.

11 Now, when the spring _____ strong winds _____ the west,
the _____ _____ _____.

12 _____ _____ _____, most people did not know _____
_____ _____ the yellow dust problem.

녹색 뉴스

1 많은 사람이 봄에 찾아오는 반갑지 않은 손님인 황사 때문에 마스크를 끼고 있습니다.

2 매년 한국에는 황사가 널리 퍼집니다.

3 황사가 많은 사람들의 눈과 목을 아프게 해서 많은 사람들이 병에 걸립니다.

4 황사는 왜 일어나는 것일까요?

5 황사를 막을 수 있는 방법이 있을까요? 네, 있습니다!

6 중국의 간쑤성에 있는 자원봉사자들의 작업을 통해 황사의 원인과 해결책을 살펴봅시다.

리나(16, 중학생)

7 예전에 이곳은 큰 숲이었습니다.

8 그러나 사람들이 도시를 세우기 위해 나무를 베기 시작했습니다.

9 시간이 지나면서 숲은 많은 나무를 잃었습니다.

10 마침내, 숲은 사막이 되었고 사막은 점점 더 커졌습니다.

11 이제, 봄에 서쪽에서 세찬 바람이 불 때, 황사가 퍼집니다.

12 이전에는 대부분의 사람들이 황사 문제를 어떻게 막을 수 있는지 알지 못했습니다.

13 Now, many volunteers _____ trees _____ _____
_____ _____ .

Minsu(18, a high school student)

14 _____ _____ in the desert _____ hard and _____ .

15 _____ , many Chinese people know _____ they _____
_____ _____ _____ _____ _____ trees.

16 They _____ _____ us, Korean volunteers, _____ we
plant trees _____ _____ .

17 _____ , we plant trees _____ _____ _____ _____
China _____ _____ Korea.

Suji(15, a middle school student)

18 At first, I didn't know _____ _____ _____ to _____
_____ _____ the yellow dust.

19 Then, Minsu, my group leader, told me that _____ _____
_____ _____ _____ _____ _____ _____ _____ .

20 I also _____ _____ that _____ trees and _____ the
environment _____ my family and me.

21 In China, many people _____ _____ trees in deserts
_____ _____ they _____ _____ the spread of the
_____ _____ .

22 The work is not easy, but they _____ _____ _____
_____ _____ the world.

23 With this _____ _____ _____ _____ , the seeds of
hope will _____ _____ _____ .

---

13 이제는 많은 자원봉사자들이 이 문제를 해결하기 위해 나무를 심고 있습니다.

민수(**18**. 고등학생)

14 사막에 나무를 심는 것은 힘들고 비용이 많이 듭니다.

15 하지만 많은 중국인들은 자신들이 나무를 심지 않으면 살 수 없다는 것을 알고 있습니다.

16 그들은 우리가 그들과 나무를 심기 때문에 우리 한국인 봉사자들에게 늘 감사해 하고 있습니다.

17 그러나 우리가 나무를 심는 이유는 단지 중국만이 아니라 한국도 돕기 위해서입니다.

수지(**15**. 중학생)

18 처음에 저는 황사를 없애기 위해서 무엇을 해야 할지 몰랐습니다.

19 그 때. 우리 조장인 민수가 나무를 심는 것이 문제를 해결하는 데 도움이 된다고 얘기해 줬습니다.

20 저는 나무를 심고 환경을 보호하는 것이 우리 가족과 제 자신도 돕는 일이라는 것임을 알게 되었습니다.

21 중국에서는 많은 사람들이 황사가 퍼지는 것을 막기 위해서 사막에 나무를 심고 있습니다.

22 이 작업은 쉽지 않지만 그들은 세계를 보호하기 위해서 열심히 일하고 있습니다.

23 이러한 세계적인 협업으로 희망의 씨앗은 계속해서 자랄 것입니다.

※ 다음 문장을 우리말로 쓰시오.

The Green News

1 ▶ Many people are wearing masks so that they can keep away from an unwelcome guest in the spring: yellow dust.

➡ _____

2 ▶ Every year, there is widespread yellow dust in Korea.

➡ _____

3 ▶ Many people become sick because the yellow dust hurts their eyes and throats.

➡ _____

4 ▶ Why does the yellow dust come about?

➡ _____

5 ▶ Is there any way to stop the yellow dust? Yes, there is!

➡ _____

6 ▶ Let's take a look at the causes of and the solutions to the problem of yellow dust through the work of some volunteers in Gansu Sheng, China.

➡ _____

Li Na(16, a middle school student)

7 ▶ A long time ago, this place was a big forest.

➡ _____

8 ▶ But people began to cut down trees so that they could build cities.

➡ _____

9 ▶ As time passed, the forest lost many trees.

➡ _____

10 ▶ Finally, the forest became a desert and the desert became bigger and bigger.

➡ _____

11 ▶ Now, when the spring brings strong winds from the west, the yellow dust spreads.

➡ _____

12 ▶ In the past, most people did not know how to stop the yellow dust problem.

➡ _____

13 ▶ Now, many volunteers plant trees to solve this problem.

➡ _____

Minsu(18, a high school student)

14 Planting trees in the desert is hard and expensive.

➡ _____

15 However, many Chinese people know that they cannot live if they don't plant trees.

➡ _____

16 They always thank us, Korean volunteers, because we plant trees with them.

➡ _____

17 However, we plant trees to help not only China but also Korea.

➡ _____

Suji(15, a middle school student)

18 At first, I didn't know what to do to get rid of the yellow dust.

➡ _____

19 Then, Minsu, my group leader, told me that planting trees can help to solve the problem.

➡ _____

20 I also found out that planting trees and protecting the environment help my family and me.

➡ _____

21 In China, many people are planting trees in deserts so that they can stop the spread of the yellow dust.

➡ _____

22 The work is not easy, but they are working hard to protect the world.

➡ _____

23 With this kind of global togetherness, the seeds of hope will keep on growing.

➡ _____

※ 다음 괄호 안의 단어들을 우리말에 맞도록 바르게 배열하시오.

The Green News

1 (people / many / wearing / are / masks / that / so / can / they / away / keep / an / from / in / guest / spring: / the / unwelcome / dust. / yellow)

➡ _____

_____

2 (year, / every / is / there / yellow / widespread / Korea. / in / dust)

➡ _____

3 (people / many / sick / become / because / yellow / the / hurts / dust / their / throats. / and / eyes)

➡ _____

_____

4 (does / the / why / dust / yellow / about? / come)

➡ _____

5 (there / is / way / any / stop / to / yellow / the / dust? // is! / there / yes,)

➡ _____

_____

6 (take / let's / look / a / the / at / causes / and / of / solutions / the / problem / the / to / yellow / of / through / dust / work / the / some / volunteers / of / Gansu / China. / Sheng / in)

➡ _____

_____

_____

Li Na(16, a middle school student)

7 (time / a / ago, / long / place / this / a / was / forest. / big)

➡ _____

8 (people / but / to / began / down / cut / so / trees / that / could / they / cities. / build)

➡ _____

_____

9 (time / as / passed, / forest / the / trees. / many / lost)

➡ _____

10 (the / finally, / became / forest / desert / a / and / desert / the / bigger / and / became / bigger.)

➡ _____

_____

11 (now, / the / when / spring / strong / brings / from / winds / west, / the / yellow / the / spreads. / dust)

➡ _____

_____

12 (the / in / past, / did / people / most / not / how / know / stop / to / yellow / problem. / the / dust)

➡ _____

녹색 뉴스

1 많은 사람이 봄에 찾아오는 반갑지 않은 손님인 황사 때문에 마스크를 끼고 있습니다.

2 매년 한국에는 황사가 널리 퍼집니다.

3 황사가 많은 사람들의 눈과 목을 아프게 해서 많은 사람들이 병에 걸립니다.

4 황사는 왜 일어나는 것일까요?

5 황사를 막을 수 있는 방법이 있을까요? 네, 있습니다!

6 중국의 간쑤성에 있는 자원봉사자들의 작업을 통해 황사의 원인과 해결책을 살펴봅시다.

리나(16. 중학생)

7 예전에 이곳은 큰 숲이었습니다.

8 그러나 사람들이 도시를 세우기 위해 나무를 베기 시작했습니다.

9 시간이 지나면서 숲은 많은 나무를 잃었습니다.

10 마침내, 숲은 사막이 되었고 사막은 점점 더 커졌습니다.

11 이제, 봄에 서쪽에서 세찬 바람이 불 때, 황사가 퍼집니다.

12 이전에는 대부분의 사람들이 황사 문제를 어떻게 막을 수 있는지 알지 못했습니다.

13 (many / now, / plant / volunteers / trees / solve / to / problem. / this)

➡ _____

Minsu(18, a high school student)

14 (trees / planting / the / in / desert / hard / is / expensive. / and)

➡ _____

15 (many / however, / people / Chinese / that / know / cannot / they / if / live / don't / they / trees. / plant)

➡ _____

16 (always / they / us, / thank / volunteers, / Korean / we / because / with / trees / them. / plant)

➡ _____
_____

17 (we / however, / trees / plant / help / to / only / not / Korea. / also / but / China)

➡ _____

Suji(15, a middle school student)

18 (first, / at / didn't / I / what / know / to / do / get / to / of / rid / dust. / yellow / the)

➡ _____

19 (Minsu, / then / group / leader, / my / me / told / planting / that / can / trees / help / solve / to / problem. / the)

➡ _____
_____

20 (also / found / I / that / out / trees / planting / protecting / and / environment / the / my / help / me. / and / family)

➡ _____
_____

21 (China, / in / people / many / planting / are / in / trees / deserts / that / so / can / they / stop / spread / the / of / dust. / yellow / the)

➡ _____
_____

22 (work / the / not / is / easy, / they / but / working / are / to / hard / world. / the / protect)

➡ _____

23 (this / with / of / kind / togetherness, / global / seeds / the / hope / of / keep / will / growing. / on)

➡ _____
_____

13 이제는 많은 자원봉사자들이 이 문제를 해결하기 위해 나무를 심고 있습니다.

민수(**18**, 고등학생)

14 사막에 나무를 심는 것은 힘들고 비용이 많이 듭니다.

15 하지만 많은 중국인들은 자신들이 나무를 심지 않으면 살 수 없다는 것을 알고 있습니다.

16 그들은 우리가 그들과 나무를 심기 때문에 우리 한국인 봉사자들에게 늘 감사해 하고 있습니다.

17 그러나 우리가 나무를 심는 이유는 단지 중국만이 아니라 한국도 돕기 위해서입니다.

수지(**15**, 중학생)

18 처음에 저는 황사를 없애기 위해서 무엇을 해야 할지 몰랐습니다.

19 그 때, 우리 조장인 민수가 나무를 심는 것이 문제를 해결하는 데 도움이 된다고 얘기해 줬습니다.

20 저는 나무를 심고 환경을 보호하는 것이 우리 가족과 제 자신도 돕는 일이라는 것을 알게 되었습니다.

21 중국에서는 많은 사람들이 황사가 퍼지는 것을 막기 위해서 사막에 나무를 심고 있습니다.

22 이 작업은 쉽지 않지만 그들은 세계를 보호하기 위해서 열심히 일하고 있습니다.

23 이러한 세계적인 협업으로 희망의 씨앗은 계속해서 자랄 것입니다.

※ 다음 우리말을 영어로 쓰시오.

The Green News

1 많은 사람이 봄에 찾아오는 반갑지 않은 손님인 황사 때문에 마스크를 끼고 있습니다.

➡ _____

2 매년 한국에는 황사가 널리 퍼집니다.

➡ _____

3 황사가 많은 사람들의 눈과 목을 아프게 해서 많은 사람들이 병에 걸립니다.

➡ _____

4 황사는 왜 일어나는 것일까요?

➡ _____

5 황사를 막을 수 있는 방법이 있을까요? 네, 있습니다!

➡ _____

6 중국의 간쑤성에 있는 자원봉사자들의 작업을 통해 황사의 원인과 해결책을 살펴봅시다.

➡ _____

Li Na(16, a middle school student)

7 예전에 이곳은 큰 숲이었습니다.

➡ _____

8 그러나 사람들이 도시를 세우기 위해 나무를 베기 시작했습니다..

➡ _____

9 시간이 지나면서 숲은 많은 나무를 잃었습니다.

➡ _____

10 마침내, 숲은 사막이 되었고 사막은 점점 더 커졌습니다.

➡ _____

11 이제, 봄에 서쪽에서 세찬 바람이 불 때, 황사가 퍼집니다.

➡ _____

12 이전에는 대부분의 사람들이 황사 문제를 어떻게 막을 수 있는지 알지 못했습니다.

➡ _____

13 이제는 많은 자원봉사자들이 이 문제를 해결하기 위해 나무를 심고 있습니다.

➡ _____

Minsu(18, a high school student)

14 사막에 나무를 심는 것은 힘들고 비용이 많이 듭니다.

➡ _____

15 하지만 많은 중국인들은 자신들이 나무를 심지 않으면 살 수 없다는 것을 알고 있습니다.

➡ _____

16 그들은 우리가 그들과 나무를 심기 때문에 우리 한국인 봉사자들에게 늘 감사해 하고 있습니다.

➡ _____

17 그러나 우리가 나무를 심는 이유는 단지 중국만이 아니라 한국도 돕기 위해서입니다.

➡ _____

Suji(15, a middle school student)

18 처음에 저는 황사를 없애기 위해서 무엇을 해야 할지 몰랐습니다.

➡ _____

19 그 때, 우리 조장인 민수가 나무를 심는 것이 문제를 해결하는 데 도움이 된다고 얘기해 줬습니다.

➡ _____

20 저는 나무를 심고 환경을 보호하는 것이 우리 가족과 제 자신도 돕는 일이라는 것임을 알게 되었습니다.

➡ _____

21 중국에서는 많은 사람들이 황사가 퍼지는 것을 막기 위해서 사막에 나무를 심고 있습니다.

➡ _____

22 이 작업은 쉽지 않지만 그들은 세계를 보호하기 위해서 열심히 일하고 있습니다.

➡ _____

23 이러한 세계적인 협업으로 희망의 씨앗은 계속해서 자랄 것입니다.

➡ _____

※ 다음 우리말과 일치하도록 빈칸에 알맞은 말을 쓰시오.

Check Your Progress 1

1. G: I was _____ _____ yesterday.
2. B: Why, _____ _____?
3. G: Yesterday, I _____ _____ the park. Many people _____ _____.
4. B: _____ you _____ _____ that?
5. G: Of _____ _____. I was angry _____ I saw _____ _____ _____ the flowers and _____ the trees.
6. B: Oh, that _____ _____ _____.
7. G: Yes, I _____ them to _____, but they said they _____ _____ _____ the flowers or the trees.

1. G: 나 어제 무척 화가 났었어.
2. B: 왜, 무슨 일 있었어?
3. G: 어제, 나는 공원에 갔어. 많은 사람들이 그곳에 있었어.
4. B: 그것 때문에 화가 났어?
5. G: 당연히 아니지. 나는 그 사람들이 꽃을 뽑고 나무를 차는 것을 보고 화가 났어.
6. B: 오, 그건 좋지 않아.
7. G: 응, 나는 그들에게 멈추라고 말했지만, 그들은 꽃과 나무에 신경을 쓰지 않는다고 말했어.

After You Read

1. Diego: Yellow dust _____ _____ _____ in Korea.
2. Suji: Yes. Many people _____ _____ because of the _____ _____.
3. _____ _____, their throats hurt _____ _____ it.
4. Diego: That's right. Do you know _____ _____ _____ such problems?
5. Suji: In the past, many people _____ _____ trees _____ _____ cities.
6. This _____ the forests _____ _____ deserts of yellow dust.
7. Now, we _____ _____ trees together _____ _____ the yellow dust.
8. Diego: That's a good idea. _____ _____ trees, we can help the world.
9. Suji: Yes, _____ _____ _____, the world will become green again!

1. Diego: 한국에서 황사는 많은 문제를 유발해.
2. Suji: 응. 많은 사람들이 황사 때문에 아파.
3. 예를 들어, 황사 때문에 사람들 목이 아프지.
4. Diego: 맞아. 그러한 문제를 어떻게 해결해야 할지 아니?
5. Suji: 과거에는, 많은 사람들이 도시를 세우기 위해 나무를 베었어.
6. 이것이 숲을 황사의 사막으로 변하게 했지.
7. 이제, 우리는 황사를 멈추기 위해서 함께 나무를 심어야 해.
8. Diego: 그거 좋은 생각이네. 나무를 심음으로써, 우리는 세상을 도울 수 있어.
9. Suji: 응, 세계적 협업으로, 세상은 다시 푸르러 질 거야.이다.

Project Work

1. We _____ use cups when we _____ our teeth _____ _____ we can save water.
2. We _____ _____ _____ _____ water by using cups!

1. 우리는 물을 절약할 수 있도록 이를 닦을 때 컵을 사용해야 합니다.
2. 우리는 컵을 사용함으로써 물을 아끼는 것을 기대합니다.

Step2

※ 다음 우리말을 영어로 쓰시오.

Check Your Progress 1

1. G: 나 어제 무척 화가 났었어.
➡ _____

2. B: 왜, 무슨 일 있었어?
➡ _____

3. G: 어제, 나는 공원에 갔어. 많은 사람들이 그곳에 있었어.
➡ _____

4. B: 그것 때문에 화가 났어?
➡ _____

5. G: 당연히 아니지. 나는 그 사람들이 꽃을 뽑고 나무를 차는 것을 보고 화가 났어.
➡ _____

6. B: 오, 그건 좋지 않아.
➡ _____

7. G: 응, 나는 그들에게 멈추라고 말했지만, 그들은 꽃과 나무에 신경을 쓰지 않는다고 말했어.
➡ _____

After You Read

1. Diego: 한국에서 황사는 많은 문제를 유발해.
➡ _____

2. Suji: 응. 많은 사람들이 황사 때문에 아파.
➡ _____

3. 예를 들어, 황사 때문에 사람들 목이 아프지.
➡ _____

4. Diego: 맞아. 그러한 문제를 어떻게 해결해야 할지 아니?
➡ _____

5. Suji: 과거에는, 많은 사람들이 도시를 세우기 위해 나무를 베었어.
➡ _____

6. 이것이 숲을 황사의 사막으로 변하게 했지.
➡ _____

7. 이제, 우리는 황사를 멈추기 위해서 함께 나무를 심어야 해.
➡ _____

8. Diego: 그거 좋은 생각이네. 나무를 심음으로써, 우리는 세상을 도울 수 있어.
➡ _____

9. Suji: 응, 세계적 협업으로, 세상은 다시 푸르러 질 거야.
➡ _____

Project Work

1. 우리는 물을 절약할 수 있도록 이를 닦을 때 컵을 사용해야 합니다.
➡ _____

2. 우리는 컵을 사용함으로써 물을 아끼는 것을 기대합니다.
➡ _____

※ 다음 영어를 우리말로 쓰시오.

01 pond _____

02 bitter _____

03 scary _____

04 prepare _____

05 boring _____

06 chance _____

07 decide _____

08 famous _____

09 taste _____

10 blind _____

11 choose _____

12 opinion _____

13 accident _____

14 drummer _____

15 realize _____

16 terrible _____

17 scream _____

18 active _____

19 nurse _____

20 volunteer _____

21 appreciate _____

22 touching _____

23 social studies _____

24 librarian _____

25 overcome _____

26 experience _____

27 score _____

28 trouble _____

29 totally _____

30 thirsty _____

31 attack _____

32 miracle _____

33 composer _____

34 invite _____

35 give up _____

36 pass away _____

37 be able to _____

38 take care of _____

39 little by little _____

40 be proud of _____

41 put someone to bed _____

42 be afraid of _____

43 make a choice _____

※ 다음 우리말을 영어로 쓰시오.

01 수학 _____

02 고마워하다 _____

03 기적 _____

04 감동적인 _____

05 공격하다 _____

06 던지다 _____

07 경험 _____

08 사회 _____

09 사서 _____

10 인터뷰하다 _____

11 목마른 _____

12 완전히, 전적으로 _____

13 점수 _____

14 극복하다 _____

15 양 _____

16 어려운, 힘든 _____

17 경연 _____

18 초대하다 _____

19 곤경, 곤란 _____

20 작곡가 _____

21 준비하다 _____

22 비명을 지르다 _____

23 사고 _____

24 맛이 쓴, 씁쓸한 _____

25 끔찍한 _____

26 실현하다, 깨닫다 _____

27 무서운, 두려운 _____

28 유명한 _____

29 지루한, 재미없는 _____

30 의견 _____

31 선택하다 _____

32 눈이 먼, 맹인인 _____

33 간호사 _____

34 자원봉사하다 _____

35 ～을 두려워하다 _____

36 죽다 _____

37 ～을 돌보다 _____

38 ～을 자랑스러워하다 _____

39 조금씩, 천천히 _____

40 ～할 수 있다 _____

41 포기하다 _____

42 마침내 _____

43 누군가를 재우다 _____

※ 다음 영영풀이에 알맞은 단어를 <보기>에서 골라 쓴 후, 우리말 뜻을 쓰시오.

1 _____ : not able to see: _____

2 _____ : needing or wanting to drink: _____

3 _____ : a competition in which people try to win something: _____

4 _____ : known or recognized by very many people: _____

5 _____ : a person who is in charge of or works in a library: _____

6 _____ : a person who plays a drum or drums: _____

7 _____ : a situation that is difficult or has a lot of problems: _____

8 _____ : an act of using violence to try to hurt or kill somebody: _____

9 _____ : a person who writes music, especially classical music: _____

10 _____ : to be grateful for something that somebody has done: _____

11 _____ : to suddenly cry out in a loud and high voice because of pain, surprise, etc.:
_____

12 _____ : your feelings or thoughts about somebody/something, rather than a fact:
_____

13 _____ : causing feelings of pity or sympathy; making you feel emotional:
_____

14 _____ : an act or event that does not follow the laws of nature and is believed to
be caused by God: _____

15 _____ : to decide which thing or person you want out of the ones that are
available: _____

16 _____ : to succeed in dealing with or controlling a problem that has been preventing
you from achieving something: _____

보기			
touching	thirsty	miracle	trouble
appreciate	famous	scream	contest
choose	overcome	composer	opinion
librarian	attack	blind	drummer

※ 다음 우리말과 일치하도록 빈칸에 알맞은 말을 쓰시오.

Everyday English 1 A. Function Practice 2-(1)

G: We _____ _____ _____ a story for our school play.

B: _____ _____ _____ _____ one of Shakespeare's plays?

G: _____ _____ *Hamlet*? It's very _____.

B: _____ _____ _____, it's too sad for our school play. _____

_____ _____ _____.

G: 우리는 학교 연극을 위해 이야기를 골라야 해.
B: 세익스피어 희곡 중 하나를 고르는 것은 어때?
G: 햄릿은 어때? 그건 아주 유명하잖아.
B: 내 생각에는, 그건 학교 연극으로는 너무 슬픈 것 같아. 다른 이야기를 찾아보자.

Everyday English 1 A. Function Practice 2-(2)

G: What is _____ _____ _____?

B: _____ _____ _____ is *The Old Man and the Sea*.

G: Really? _____ _____ _____, it's a _____ _____.

B: _____ _____ _____ _____.

G: 가장 좋아하는 책이 뭐야?
B: 내가 가장 좋아하는 책은 '노인과 바다(The Old Man and the Sea,)'야.
G: 정말? 내 생각엔, 좀 지루하던데.
B: 모두가 다른 취향을 갖고 있지.

Everyday English 1 B. Listening Activity

Brian: What's the _____? You _____ _____.

Amy: _____ _____ _____ my history test. My history score is _____ _____ my math score.

Brian: _____ _____ _____ take Mr. Choi's afterschool class?

Amy: Well, I took his _____ _____ _____ last month, but it was a _____ _____ for me.

Brian: _____ _____ _____, his history class is _____ _____ his _____ _____ _____.

Amy: Really?

Brian: Yes. I also _____ _____ _____ _____ on my history test _____ _____ his class.

Amy: Maybe _____ _____ _____ _____ _____.
Thanks.

Brian: 무슨 일이야? 걱정하는 듯 보여.
Amy: 역사 시험이 걱정이야. 역사 성적이 수학 성적보다 낮거든.
Brian: 최 선생님의 방과 후 수업을 듣는 건 어때?
Amy: 글쎄. 지난달에 사회 수업을 들었는데 약간 지루하더라고.
Brian: 내 생각에는, 그의 역사 수업은 사회 수업보다는 더 재미 있어.
Amy: 진짜?
Brian: 응. 난 그 선생님 수업 듣고 나서 역사 성적도 올랐어.
Amy: 아마 나도 그 수업 들어야 할 것 같다. 고마워.

Everyday English2 A. Function Practice 2-(1)

G: _____ _____ _____ Lee Hee Ah, _____ _____?

B: _____ _____ _____. Who is she?

G: She plays the piano very well, _____ _____ she only has two fingers _____ _____ _____.

B: That's _____.

G: 너 이희아에 관해서 알지, 그렇지?
B: 아니, 몰라. 누구니?
G: 그녀는 각 손에 오직 두 개의 손가락만 가졌음에도 피아노를 굉장히 잘 쳐.
B: 정말 놀랍다.

Everyday English 2 A. Function Practice 2-(2)

Amy: I really love the drums, but I'm _____ _____ _____ playing. _____ I _____ _____ _____.

Bob: Hey, don't say that. You know about Rick Allen, _____ _____?

Amy: _____ _____ _____ _____. Isn't he the drummer with one arm?

Bob: Yes, he is. _____ _____ _____! _____ _____ _____ _____ _____!

Everyday English 2 B. Listening Activity

M: Hello. You all know me, _____ _____? As you can see, I don't have any arms or legs. When I was young, I was _____ and _____ about _____. Then one day, I read a story about a man _____ me. He said that _____ _____ _____ _____ in my life. I could be happy or _____ _____ _____. So, _____ _____ _____ _____ _____ _____. Now, I am a happy man. I give speeches around the world, and _____ _____ _____. Here is my message for you. In life, you have a choice: _____ or _____ ? _____ _____, _____ _____.

In Real Life

Olivia: What _____ you _____, Junho?

Junho: I'm _____ on my _____ _____. I _____ _____ _____ about a famous person. That person should have a story of _____ _____ in their life.

Olivia: Hmm. Who _____ you _____?

Junho: You _____ _____ Helen Keller, _____ _____? I _____ _____ write about her.

Olivia: _____ _____ _____, she is _____ _____. It may not be _____ .

Junho: Then, who _____ I _____?

Olivia: _____ _____ _____ the story about Little Annie?

Junho: Who is that?

Olivia: I will _____ _____ _____ _____ about her life. She'll be a _____ _____ for your project.

Amy: 난 진짜 드럼이 좋아. 그러나 난 연주를 잘하지 못해. 아마도 난 포기해야 하나봐.
Bob: 이봐, 그렇게 말하지 마. Rick Allen 알지, 그렇지?
Amy: 물론 알지. 그는 한쪽 팔만 있는 드러머 아냐?
Bob: 그래. 그 사람이야. 포기하지 마! 너 또한 할 수 있어.

M: 안녕하세요, 모두 저 아시죠, 그렇죠? 여러분이 보다시피, 저는 팔과 다리가 없습니다. 제가 어렸을 때 저 자신에 대해 슬프고 화가 났었습니다. 그런데 어느 날, 저와 같은 어떤 사람에 관한 이야기를 읽었습니다. 그는 내가 내 삶에 있어서 선택권이 있다고 말했습니다. 나는 나 자신에 대해 행복할 수도 화가 날 수도 있습니다. 그래서 난 내 삶을 사랑하기로 했습니다. 지금 저는 행복한 사람입니다. 저는 전 세계를 돌아다니며 강연을 하고 사람들에게 희망을 줍니다. 여기 제가 하고 싶은 말이 있습니다. 삶에 있어서, 당신은 선택권이 있습니다. 더 나아질 것이냐, 더 쓰라릴 것이냐? 나아지길 선택하세요. 쓰라린 것은 잊고요.

Olivia: 준호야, 뭐 하고 있니?
Junho: 역사 과제를 하고 있어. 유명한 사람에 관해 써야 해. 인생에 있어 어려움을 극복한 이야기가 있는 사람이어야 해.
Olivia: 음, 넌 누구를 골랐니?
Junho: Helen Keller에 관해 알지, 그렇지? 그녀에 관해 쓸 거야.
Olivia: 내 생각에는, 그녀는 너무 유명해. 재미없을지도 몰라.
Junho: 그럼, 누구를 골라야 할까?
Olivia: Little Annie에 관한 이야기를 아니?
Junho: 그게 누군데?
Olivia: 그녀의 삶에 관한 비디오를 보여줄게. 네 과제를 위한 좋은 주제가 될 거야.

※ 다음 우리말에 맞도록 대화를 영어로 쓰시오.

해석

Everyday English 1 A. Function Practice 2-(1)

G: _____

B: _____

G: _____

B: _____

G: 우리는 학교 연극을 위해 이야기를 골라야 해.
B: 셰익스피어 희곡 중 하나를 고르는 것은 어때?
G: 햄릿은 어때? 그건 아주 유명하잖아.
B: 내 생각에는, 그건 학교 연극으로는 너무 슬픈 것 같아. 다른 이야기를 찾아보자.

Everyday English 1 A. Function Practice 2-(2)

G: _____

B: _____

G: _____

B: _____

G: 가장 좋아하는 책이 뭐야?
B: 내가 가장 좋아하는 책은 '노인과 바다(The Old Man and the Sea,)'야.
G: 정말? 내 생각엔, 좀 지루하던데.
B: 모두가 다른 취향을 갖고 있지.

Everyday English 1 B. Listening Activity

Brian: _____

Amy: _____

Brian: _____

Amy: _____

Brian: _____

Amy: _____

Brian: _____

Amy: _____

Brian: 무슨 일이야? 걱정하는 듯 보여.
Amy: 역사 시험이 걱정이야. 역사 성적이 수학 성적보다 낮거든.
Brian: 최 선생님의 방과 후 수업을 듣는 건 어때?
Amy: 글쎄. 지난달에 사회 수업을 들었는데 약간 지루하더라고.
Brian: 내 생각에는, 그의 역사 수업은 사회 수업보다는 더 재미있어.
Amy: 진짜?
Brian: 응. 난 그 선생님 수업 듣고 나서 역사 성적도 올랐어.
Amy: 아마 나도 그 수업 들어야 할 것 같다. 고마워.

Everyday English2 A. Function Practice 2-(1)

G: _____

B: _____

G: _____

B: _____

G: 너 이희아에 관해서 알지, 그렇지?
B: 아니, 몰라. 누구니?
G: 그녀는 각 손에 오직 두 개의 손가락만 가졌음에도 피아노를 굉장히 잘 쳐.
B: 정말 놀랍다.

Everyday English 2 A. Function Practice 2-(2)

Amy: _____

Bob: _____

Amy: _____

Bob: _____

Everyday English 2 B. Listening Activity

M: _____

_____

_____

_____

_____

_____

_____

In Real Life

Olivia: _____

Junho: _____

_____

Olivia: _____

Junho: _____

Olivia: _____

Junho: _____

Olivia: _____

Junho: _____

Olivia: _____

Amy: 난 진짜 드럼이 좋아. 그러나 난 연주를 잘하지 못해. 아마도 난 포기해야 하나봐.

Bob: 이봐, 그렇게 말하지 마. Rick Allen 알지, 그렇지?

Amy: 물론 알지. 그는 한쪽 팔만 있는 드러머 아냐?

Bob: 그래. 그 사람이야. 포기하지 마! 너 또한 할 수 있어.

M: 안녕하세요, 모두 저 아시죠, 그렇죠? 여러분이 보다시피, 저는 팔과 다리가 없습니다. 제가 어렸을 때 저 자신에 대해 슬프고 화가 났었습니다. 그런데 어느 날, 저와 같은 어떤 사람에 관한 이야기를 읽었습니다. 그는 내가 내 삶에 있어서 선택권이 있다고 말했습니다. 나는 나 자신에 대해 행복할 수도 화가 날 수도 있습니다. 그래서 난 내 삶을 사랑하기로 했습니다. 지금 저는 행복한 사람입니다. 저는 전 세계를 돌아다니며 강연을 하고 사람들에게 희망을 줍니다. 여기 제가 하고 싶은 말이 있습니다. 삶에 있어서, 당신은 선택권이 있습니다. 더 나아질 것이냐, 더 쓰라릴 것이냐? 나아지길 선택하세요. 쓰라린 것은 잊고요.

Olivia: 준호야, 뭐 하고 있니?

Junho: 역사 과제를 하고 있어. 유명한 사람에 관해 써야 해. 인생에 있어 어려움을 극복한 이야기가 있는 사람이어야 해.

Olivia: 음, 넌 누구를 골랐니?

Junho: Helen Keller에 관해 알지, 그렇지? 그녀에 관해 쓸 거야.

Olivia: 내 생각에는, 그녀는 너무 유명해. 재미없을지도 몰라.

Junho: 그럼, 누구를 골라야 할까?

Olivia: Little Annie에 관한 이야기를 아니?

Junho: 그게 누군데?

Olivia: 그녀의 삶에 관한 비디오를 보여줄게. 네 과제를 위한 좋은 주제가 될 거야.

※ 다음 우리말과 일치하도록 빈칸에 알맞은 것을 골라 쓰시오.

1 There _____ a _____ _____ girl in a hospital.
A. blind   B. was   C. little

2 She was _____ _____.
A. angry   B. always

3 When people _____ to help her, she _____ and _____ them.
A. tried   B. attacked   C. screamed

4 People _____ her "Crazy Little Annie," and didn't _____ to help her _____.
A. anymore   B. try   C. called

5 The poor girl needed _____ to _____ _____ of her.
A. care   B. somebody   C. take

6 _____ day, an old nurse _____ _____ the hospital.
A. came   B. one   C. to

7 She _____ to _____ Annie.
A. help   B. volunteered

8 When Annie _____ her, she _____ _____ again.
A. throwing   B. met   C. started

9 _____, the nurse wasn't _____ _____ her.
A. of   B. however   C. afraid

10 The nurse said to Annie, "Hi, Annie. I'm Nurse Laura. I'm here to _____ your friend. I'll _____ be _____ for you."
A. there   B. always   C. be

11 Every night, Laura _____ to Annie's room and _____ her to _____.
A. went   B. bed   C. put

12 She said to Annie, "Annie, I _____ love you. I'll _____ be _____ for you."
A. there   B. always   C. do

13 Laura knew _____ Annie _____ love and _____.
A. understanding   B. needed   C. that

14 _____ Laura's _____, Annie got better little by _____.
A. with   B. little   C. help

15 Two years _____, Annie didn't _____ or _____ things.
A. later   B. throw   C. scream

16 She did _____ a _____ _____ person.
A. become   B. different   C. totally

1 한 병원에 어린 눈먼 소녀가 있었습니다.

2 그녀는 항상 화가 나 있었습니다.

3 사람들이 그녀를 도우려고 할 때, 그녀는 소리 지르고 공격했습니다.

4 사람들은 그녀를 "Crazy Little Annie"라고 불렀고 더 이상 그녀를 도우려 하지 않았습니다.

5 병원은 Annie를 돌봐줄 사람이 필요했습니다.

6 어느 날, 나이 든 간호사가 병원에 왔습니다.

7 그녀는 Annie를 도울 것을 자원했습니다.

8 Annie가 그녀를 만났을 때, 그녀는 다시 물건을 던지기 시작했습니다.

9 그러나 간호사는 그녀를 두려워하지 않았습니다.

10 간호사가 Annie에게 말했습니다. "안녕, 난 간호사 Laura야. 나는 너의 친구가 될 거야. 내가 항상 너의 곁에 있을게."

11 매일 밤, Laura는 Annie의 방으로 가서 그녀를 재웠습니다.

12 그녀는 Annie에게 말했습니다. "Annie, 나는 널 정말 사랑한단다. 나는 항상 너의 곁에 있을 거야."

13 Laura는 Annie에게 사랑과 이해가 필요하다는 것을 알았습니다.

14 Laura의 도움으로 Annie는 조금씩 좋아졌습니다.

15 2년 후, Annie는 비명을 지르거나 물건을 던지지 않았습니다.

16 그녀는 전혀 다른 사람이 되었습니다.

17 People _____ _____ her "Crazy Little Annie" _____.

A. call   B. anymore   C. didn't

18 Laura _____ to _____ the hospital _____ Annie.

A. with   B. leave   C. decided

19 She _____ Annie _____ a school _____ blind children.

A. to   B. for   C. took

20 Annie _____ her new school and _____ _____.

A. hard   B. studied   C. loved

21 She wanted to _____ a teacher and help _____ like Nurse Laura _____.

A. did   B. others   C. become

22 However, a _____ years _____, Laura passed _____.

A. away   B. few   C. later

23 Annie was very _____, but she did not _____ _____ on her dream.

A. up   B. sad   C. give

24 Then _____ _____, Annie _____ a nice doctor.

A. met   B. day   C. one

25 He _____ Annie to _____ _____.

A. see   B. well   C. helped

26 It was a _____ _____ Annie.

A. for   B. miracle

27 At _____, Annie _____ her dream and _____ a teacher.

A. became   B. realized   C. last

28 This _____ her a _____ to meet a _____ student.

A. special   B. gave   C. chance

29 The student wasn't _____ _____ hear or _____.

A. to   B. able   C. see

30 _____, she _____ and _____ things.

A. threw   B. instead   C. screamed

31 She was _____ _____ Crazy Little Annie.

A. like   B. just

32 Annie _____ to her, "Hi, Helen Keller. I'm your teacher, Anne Sullivan. I'll always _____ _____ for you."

A. there   B. said   C. be

17 사람들은 더 이상 그녀를 "Crazy Little Annie"라고 부르지 않았습니다.

18 Laura는 Annie와 병원을 떠나기로 결정했습니다.

19 그녀는 Annie를 시각장애인 학교에 데려갔습니다.

20 Annie는 새로운 학교를 좋아했으며 열심히 공부했습니다.

21 그녀는 선생님이 되어 간호사 Laura가 그랬듯 다른 사람들을 돕고 싶었습니다.

22 그러나 몇 년 후, Laura는 세상을 떠났습니다.

23 Annie는 매우 슬펐지만 그녀는 꿈을 포기하지 않았습니다.

24 그러던 어느 날, Annie는 좋은 의사를 만났습니다.

25 그는 Annie를 잘 볼 수 있게 도와주었습니다.

26 그것은 Annie에게 기적이었습니다.

27 마침내 Annie는 꿈을 실현하고자 교사가 되었습니다.

28 이것은 그녀에게 특별한 학생을 만날 기회를 주었습니다.

29 그 학생은 듣거나 볼 수 없었습니다.

30 대신에 그녀는 소리 지르고 물건을 던졌습니다.

31 그녀는 마치 "Crazy Little Annie" 같았습니다.

32 Annie는 그녀에게 말했습니다. "안녕, Helen Keller, 나는 너의 선생님 Anne Sullivan이야. 내가 항상 너의 곁에 있을게."

※ 다음 우리말과 일치하도록 빈칸에 알맞은 말을 쓰시오.

1 There _____ a _____ _____ _____ in a hospital.

2 She _____ _____ _____.

3 When people _____ _____ _____ her, she _____ and _____ them.

4 People _____ _____ "Crazy Little Annie," and didn't _____ _____ _____ _____ _____ .

5 The poor girl _____ _____ _____ _____ _____ _____ her.

6 _____ _____, an old nurse _____ _____ the hospital.

7 She _____ _____ _____ Annie.

8 When Annie _____ her, she _____ _____ again.

9 _____, the nurse _____ _____ _____ her.

10 The nurse said to Annie, "Hi, Annie. I'm Nurse Laura. I'm here _____ _____ _____ _____. I'll _____ _____ _____ for you."

11 _____ _____, Laura _____ _____ Annie's room and _____ _____ _____ _____.

12 She said to Annie, "Annie, I _____ _____ _____. I'll _____ _____ _____ for you."

13 Laura knew _____ Annie _____ love and _____.

14 _____ Laura's help, Annie _____ _____ _____ _____ _____.

15 Two years _____, Annie didn't _____ _____ _____ things.

16 She _____ a _____ _____ person.

1 한 병원에 어린 눈먼 소녀가 있었습니다.

2 그녀는 항상 화가 나 있었습니다.

3 사람들이 그녀를 도우려고 할 때, 그녀는 소리 지르고 공격했습니다.

4 사람들은 그녀를 "Crazy Little Annie"라고 불렀고 더 이상 그녀를 도우려 하지 않았습니다.

5 병원은 Annie를 돌봐줄 사람이 필요했습니다.

6 어느 날, 나이 든 간호사가 병원에 왔습니다.

7 그녀는 Annie를 도울 것을 자원했습니다.

8 Annie가 그녀를 만났을 때, 그녀는 다시 물건을 던지기 시작했습니다.

9 그러나 간호사는 그녀를 두려워하지 않았습니다.

10 간호사가 Annie에게 말했습니다. "안녕, 난 간호사 Laura야. 나는 너의 친구가 될 거야. 내가 항상 너의 곁에 있을게."

11 매일 밤, Laura는 Annie의 방으로 가서 그녀를 재웠습니다.

12 그녀는 Annie에게 말했습니다. "Annie, 나는 널 정말 사랑한단다. 나는 항상 너의 곁에 있을 거야."

13 Laura는 Annie에게 사랑과 이해가 필요하다는 것을 알았습니다.

14 Laura의 도움으로 Annie는 조금씩 좋아졌습니다.

15 2년 후, Annie는 비명을 지르거나 물건을 던지지 않았습니다.

16 그녀는 전혀 다른 사람이 되었습니다.

17 People didn't _____ _____ "Crazy Little Annie" _____ .

18 Laura _____ _____ the hospital _____ Annie.

19 She _____ Annie _____ a school _____ blind children.

20 Annie _____ her new school and _____ _____ .

21 She _____ _____ _____ a teacher and _____ _____ like Nurse Laura _____ .

22 However, _____ _____ _____ _____ , Laura _____ _____ .

23 Annie was very sad, but she _____ _____ _____ _____ on her dream.

24 Then _____ _____ , Annie _____ a nice doctor.

25 He _____ Annie _____ _____ _____ .

26 It was _____ _____ _____ Annie.

27 At last, Annie _____ her dream and _____ a teacher.

28 This gave her a _____ _____ _____ _____ _____ _____ .

29 The student _____ _____ _____ _____ or see.

30 _____ , she _____ and _____ things.

31 She was _____ _____ Crazy Little Annie.

32 Annie _____ _____ her, "Hi, Helen Keller. I'm your teacher, Anne Sullivan. I'll _____ _____ _____ for you."

17 사람들은 더 이상 그녀를 "Crazy Little Annie"라고 부르지 않았습니다.

18 Laura는 Annie와 병원을 떠나기로 결정했습니다.

19 그녀는 Annie를 시각장애인 학교에 데려갔습니다.

20 Annie는 새로운 학교를 좋아했으며 열심히 공부했습니다.

21 그녀는 선생님이 되어 간호사 Laura가 그랬듯 다른 사람들을 돕고 싶었습니다.

22 그러나 몇 년 후, Laura는 세상을 떠났습니다.

23 Annie는 매우 슬펐지만 그녀는 꿈을 포기하지 않았습니다.

24 그러던 어느 날, Annie는 좋은 의사를 만났습니다.

25 그는 Annie를 잘 볼 수 있게 도와주었습니다.

26 그것은 Annie에게 기적이었습니다.

27 마침내 Annie는 꿈을 실현하고자 교사가 되었습니다.

28 이것은 그녀에게 특별한 학생을 만날 기회를 주었습니다.

29 그 학생은 듣거나 볼 수 없었습니다.

30 대신에 그녀는 소리 지르고 물건을 던졌습니다.

31 그녀는 마치 "Crazy Little Annie" 같았습니다.

32 Annie는 그녀에게 말했습니다. "안녕, Helen Keller, 나는 너의 선생님 Anne Sullivan이야. 내가 항상 너의 곁에 있을게."

※ 다음 문장을 우리말로 쓰시오.

1 There was a little blind girl in a hospital.

➡ _____

2 She was always angry.

➡ _____

3 When people tried to help her, she screamed and attacked them.

➡ _____

4 People called her "Crazy Little Annie," and didn't try to help her anymore.

➡ _____

5 The poor girl needed somebody to take care of her.

➡ _____

6 One day, an old nurse came to the hospital.

➡ _____

7 She volunteered to help Annie.

➡ _____

8 When Annie met her, she started throwing things again.

➡ _____

9 However, the nurse wasn't afraid of her.

➡ _____

10 The nurse said to Annie, "Hi, Annie. I'm Nurse Laura. I'm here to be your friend. I'll always be there for you."

➡ _____

11 Every night, Laura went to Annie's room and put her to bed.

➡ _____

12 She said to Annie, "Annie, I do love you. I'll always be there for you."

➡ _____

13 Laura knew that Annie needed love and understanding.

➡ _____

14 With Laura's help, Annie got better little by little.

➡ _____

15 Two years later, Annie didn't scream or throw things.

➡ _____

16 She did become a totally different person.

➡ _____

17 People didn't call her "Crazy Little Annie" anymore.

➡ _____

18 Laura decided to leave the hospital with Annie.

➡ _____

19 She took Annie to a school for blind children.

➡ _____

20 Annie loved her new school and studied hard.

➡ _____

21 She wanted to become a teacher and help others like Nurse Laura did.

➡ _____

22 However, a few years later, Laura passed away.

➡ _____

23 Annie was very sad, but she did not give up on her dream.

➡ _____

24 Then one day, Annie met a nice doctor.

➡ _____

25 He helped Annie to see well.

➡ _____

26 It was a miracle for Annie.

➡ _____

27 At last, Annie realized her dream and became a teacher.

➡ _____

28 This gave her a chance to meet a special student.

➡ _____

29 The student wasn't able to hear or see.

➡ _____

30 Instead, she screamed and threw things.

➡ _____

31 She was just like Crazy Little Annie.

➡ _____

32 Annie said to her, "Hi, Helen Keller. I'm your teacher, Anne Sullivan. I'll always be there for you."

➡ _____

※ 다음 괄호 안의 단어들을 우리말에 맞도록 바르게 배열하시오.

1 (was / there / little / a / girl / blind / hospital. / a / in)
➡ _____

2 (was / she / angry. / always)
➡ _____

3 (people / when / to / tried / help / her, / screamed / she / them. / attacked / and)
➡ _____

4 (called / people / her / Little / "Crazy / Annie," / didn't / and / to / try / help / anymore. / her)
➡ _____

5 (poor / the / girl / needed / to / somebody / care / take / her. / of)
➡ _____

6 (day, / one / old / an / came / nurse / to / hospital. / the)
➡ _____

7 (volunteered / help / Annie. / she / to)
➡ _____

8 (Annie / when / her, / met / started / she / throwing / again. / things)
➡ _____

9 (the / however, / nurse / afraid / her / of / wasn't)
➡ _____

10 (nurse / the / to / said / Annie, / "Hi, / Annie. / I'm / Laura. / Nurse / I'm / to / here / your / be / friend. / I'll / for / be / you." / always / there)
➡ _____
_____

11 (night, / every / went / Laura / to / Annie's / and / room / put / bed. / to / her)
➡ _____

12 (said / she / to / Annie, / "Annie, / love / do / I / you. / I'll / be / for / there / you." / always)
➡ _____

13 (knew / Laura / that / needed / Annie / understanding. / and / love)
➡ _____

14 (Laura's / with / help, / got / Annie / little. / by / better / little)
➡ _____

15 (years / two / later, / didn't / Annie / or / scream / things. /. throw)
➡ _____

16 (did / she / become / totally / a / person. / different)
➡ _____

1 한 병원에 어린 눈먼 소녀가 있었습니다.

2 그녀는 항상 화가 나 있었습니다.

3 사람들이 그녀를 도우려고 할 때, 그녀는 소리 지르고 공격했습니다.

4 사람들은 그녀를 "Crazy Little Annie"라고 불렀고 더 이상 그녀를 도우려 하지 않았습니다.

5 병원은 Annie를 돌봐줄 사람이 필요했습니다.

6 어느 날, 나이 든 간호사가 병원에 왔습니다.

7 그녀는 Annie를 도울 것을 자원했습니다.

8 Annie가 그녀를 만났을 때, 그녀는 다시 물건을 던지기 시작했습니다.

9 그러나 간호사는 그녀를 두려워하지 않았습니다.

10 간호사가 Annie에게 말했습니다. "안녕, 난 간호사 Laura야. 나는 너의 친구가 될 거야. 내가 항상 너의 곁에 있을게."

11 매일 밤, Laura는 Annie의 방으로 가서 그녀를 재웠습니다.

12 그녀는 Annie에게 말했습니다. "Annie, 나는 널 정말 사랑한단다. 나는 항상 너의 곁에 있을 거야."

13 Laura는 Annie에게 사랑과 이해가 필요하다는 것을 알았습니다.

14 Laura의 도움으로 Annie는 조금씩 좋아졌습니다.

15 2년 후, Annie는 비명을 지르거나 물건을 던지지 않았습니다.

16 그녀는 전혀 다른 사람이 되었습니다.

17 (didn't / people / call / her / Little / "Crazy / anymore. / Annie")

➡ _____

18 (decided / Laura / leave / to / hospital / the / Annie. / with)

➡ _____

19 (took / she / to / Annie / school / a / children. / blind / for)

➡ _____

20 (loved / Annie / new / her / school / hard. / studied / and)

➡ _____

21 (wanted / she / become / to / teacher / a / and / others / help / Nurse / did. / like / Laura)

➡ _____

22 (a / however, / years / few / later, / passed / away. / Laura)

➡ _____

23 (was / Annie / sad, / very / she / but / not / did / up / give / dream. / her / on)

➡ _____

24 (one / then / day, / met / Annie / doctor. / nice / a)

➡ _____

25 (helped / he / to / Annie / well. / see)

➡ _____

26 (was / it / miracle / a / Annie. / for)

➡ _____

27 (last, / at / realized / Annie / dream / her / and / a / teacher. / became)

➡ _____

28 (gave / this / a / her / chance / meet / to / student. / special / a)

➡ _____

29 (student / the / wasn't / to / able / see. / or / hear)

➡ _____

30 (she / instead, / screamed / things. / threw / and)

➡ _____

31 (was / she / like / just / Annie. / Little / Crazy)

➡ _____

32 (said / Annie / her, / to / Helen / "Hi, / Keller. / I'm / teacher, / your / Sullivan. / Anne / I'll / be / always / you." / for / there)

➡ _____

---

17 사람들은 더 이상 그녀를 "Crazy Little Annie"라고 부르지 않았습니다.

18 Laura는 Annie와 병원을 떠나기로 결정했습니다.

19 그녀는 Annie를 시각장애인 학교에 데려갔습니다.

20 Annie는 새로운 학교를 좋아했으며 열심히 공부했습니다.

21 그녀는 선생님이 되어 간호사 Laura가 그랬듯 다른 사람들을 돕고 싶었습니다.

22 그러나 몇 년 후, Laura는 세상을 떠났습니다.

23 Annie는 매우 슬펐지만 그녀는 꿈을 포기하지 않았습니다.

24 그러던 어느 날, Annie는 좋은 의사를 만났습니다.

25 그는 Annie를 잘 볼 수 있게 도와주었습니다.

26 그것은 Annie에게 기적이었습니다.

27 마침내 Annie는 꿈을 실현하고자 교사가 되었습니다.

28 이것은 그녀에게 특별한 학생을 만날 기회를 주었습니다.

29 그 학생은 듣거나 볼 수 없었습니다.

30 대신에 그녀는 소리 지르고 물건을 던졌습니다.

31 그녀는 마치 "Crazy Little Annie" 같았습니다.

32 Annie는 그녀에게 말했습니다. "안녕, Helen Keller, 나는 너의 선생님 Anne Sullivan이야. 내가 항상 너의 곁에 있을게."

※ **다음 우리말을 영어로 쓰시오.**

1 한 병원에 어린 눈먼 소녀가 있었습니다.
➡ _____

2 그녀는 항상 화가 나 있었습니다.
➡ _____

3 사람들이 그녀를 도우려고 할 때, 그녀는 소리 지르고 공격했습니다.
➡ _____

4 사람들은 그녀를 "Crazy Little Annie"라고 불렀고 더 이상 그녀를 도우려 하지 않았습니다.
➡ _____

5 병원은 Annie를 돌봐줄 사람이 필요했습니다.
➡ _____

6 어느 날, 나이 든 간호사가 병원에 왔습니다.
➡ _____

7 그녀는 Annie를 도울 것을 자원했습니다.
➡ _____

8 Annie가 그녀를 만났을 때, 그녀는 다시 물건을 던지기 시작했습니다.
➡ _____

9 그러나 간호사는 그녀를 두려워하지 않았습니다.
➡ _____

10 간호사가 Annie에게 말했습니다. "안녕, 난 간호사 Laura야. 나는 너의 친구가 될 거야. 내가 항상 너의 곁에 있을게."
➡ _____

11 매일 밤, Laura는 Annie의 방으로 가서 그녀를 재웠습니다.
➡ _____

12 그녀는 Annie에게 말했습니다. "Annie, 나는 널 정말 사랑한단다. 나는 항상 너의 곁에 있을 거야."
➡ _____

13 Laura는 Annie에게 사랑과 이해가 필요하다는 깃을 알았습니다.
➡ _____

14 Laura의 도움으로 Annie는 조금씩 좋아졌습니다.
➡ _____

15 2년 후, Annie는 비명을 지르거나 물건을 던지지 않았습니다.
➡ _____

16 그녀는 전혀 다른 사람이 되었습니다.
➡ _____

17 사람들은 더 이상 그녀를 "Crazy Little Annie"라고 부르지 않았습니다.

➡ _____

18 Laura는 Annie와 병원을 떠나기로 결정했습니다.

➡ _____

19 그녀는 Annie를 시각장애인 학교에 데려갔습니다.

➡ _____

20 Annie는 새로운 학교를 좋아했으며 열심히 공부했습니다.

➡ _____

21 그녀는 선생님이 되어 간호사 Laura가 그랬듯 다른 사람들을 돕고 싶었습니다.

➡ _____

22 그러나 몇 년 후, Laura는 세상을 떠났습니다.

➡ _____

23 Annie는 매우 슬펐지만 그녀는 꿈을 포기하지 않았습니다.

➡ _____

24 그러던 어느 날, Annie는 좋은 의사를 만났습니다.

➡ _____

25 그는 Annie를 잘 볼 수 있게 도와주었습니다.

➡ _____

26 그것은 Annie에게 기적이었습니다.

➡ _____

27 마침내 Annie는 꿈을 실현하고자 교사가 되었습니다.

➡ _____

28 이것은 그녀에게 특별한 학생을 만날 기회를 주었습니다.

➡ _____

29 그 학생은 듣거나 볼 수 없었습니다.

➡ _____

30 대신에 그녀는 소리 지르고 물건을 던졌습니다.

➡ _____

31 그녀는 마치 "Crazy Little Annie" 같았습니다.

➡ _____

32 Annie는 그녀에게 말했습니다. "안녕, Helen Keller, 나는 너의 선생님 Anne Sullivan이야. 내가 항상 너의 곁에 있을게."

➡ _____

※ 다음 우리말과 일치하도록 빈칸에 알맞은 말을 쓰시오.

Check Your Progress

1. W: Hello, _____. I'm _____ music teacher, Ms. Song.

2. You know the _____ _____ contest is next Friday, _____ _____?

3. _____ _____ will _____ a song and _____ it.

4. You can _____ _____ _____ _____ _____.

5. Please _____ me _____ the names of your songs _____ _____ _____ _____ this week.

6. You _____ _____ _____ your homeroom teachers _____ _____ your performance.

7. I hope you _____ _____ _____ the singing contest. Thank you.

1. W: 안녕하세요, 학생 여러분. 저는 여러분의 음악 선생님인, 송 선생님이에요.
2. 여러분은 학급 노래 경연이 다음 주 금요일이란 걸 알죠, 그렇죠?
3. 각 학급은 노래를 준비해서 공연할 거예요.
4. 여러분은 어떠한 종류의 노래든 선택할 수 있어요.
5. 이번 주말까지 여러분의 곡의 제목을 알려주세요.
6. 여러분은 또한 여러분의 담임선생님과 공연을 함께 하도록 초대할 수도 있어요.
7. 저는 여러분이 노래 경연을 위한 준비를 즐기기를 희망해요. 감사합니다.

After You Read

1. _____ Annie,

2. _____ I first _____ you, you _____ _____ and _____ things.

3. _____, I _____ _____ _____ you.

4. You _____ _____ _____ see, so I knew that I needed _____ _____ _____ _____ you.

5. Every night, when I _____ _____ _____ _____, I could see that you _____ _____ _____ little by little.

6. _____ _____, you became a _____ _____ person.

7. I _____ _____ _____ you. I hope you _____ _____ _____ your new school.

8. _____ _____, Laura

1. Annie에게,
2. 내가 너를 처음 만났을 때, 너는 소리를 지르고 물건을 던지고 있었단다.
3. 하지만, 나는 네가 두렵지 않았어.
4. 너는 볼 수 없었고, 그래서 나는 내가 너를 돌볼 필요가 있다는 것을 알았지.
5. 매일 밤, 내가 너를 재울 때, 나는 네가 조금씩 나아지고 있다는 것을 알 수 있었단다.
6. 마침내, 너는 완전히 다른 사람이 되었지.
7. 나는 네가 매우 자랑스럽단다. 너의 새 학교에서 잘하기를 바란다.
8. 그럼 이만, Laura

※ 다음 우리말을 영어로 쓰시오.

Check Your Progress

1. W: 안녕하세요, 학생 여러분. 저는 여러분의 음악 선생님인, 송 선생님이에요.
➡ _____

2. 여러분은 학급 노래 경연이 다음 주 금요일이란 걸 알죠, 그렇죠?
➡ _____

3. 각 학급은 노래를 준비해서 공연할 거예요.
➡ _____

4. 여러분은 어떠한 종류의 노래든 선택할 수 있어요.
➡ _____

5. 이번 주말까지 여러분의 곡의 제목을 알려주세요.
➡ _____

6. 여러분은 또한 여러분의 담임선생님과 공연을 함께 하도록 초대할 수도 있어요.
➡ _____

7. 저는 여러분이 노래 경연을 위한 준비를 즐기기를 희망해요. 감사합니다.
➡ _____

After You Read

1. Annie에게,
➡ _____

2. 내가 너를 처음 만났을 때, 너는 소리를 지르고 물건을 던지고 있었단다.
➡ _____

3. 하지만, 나는 네가 두렵지 않았어.
➡ _____

4. 너는 볼 수 없었고, 그래서 나는 내가 너를 돌볼 필요가 있다는 것을 알았지.
➡ _____

5. 매일 밤, 내가 너를 재울 때, 나는 네가 조금씩 나아지고 있다는 것을 알 수 있었단다.
➡ _____

6. 마침내, 너는 완전히 다른 사람이 되었지.
➡ _____

7. 나는 네가 매우 자랑스럽단다. 너의 새 학교에서 잘하기를 바란다.
➡ _____

8. 그럼 이만, Laura
➡ _____

MEMO

영어 기출 문제집

적중100

정답 및 해설

금성 | 최인철

중 2

적중100

영어 문제집

1학기

정답 및 해설

금성 | 최인철

중 2

My Special Interests

Lesson 1

01 ③   02 ②   03 ①

04 leave[start] 05 (1) abroad   (2) order   (3) protect

    (4) Shall   06 ②

01 무대, 텔레비전 또는 영화에서 특히 직업으로 연기하는 사람을 나타내는 말은 actor(배우)이다.

02 protect: 보호하다

03 perform: 수행하다, 공연하다, 연주하다

04 주어진 단어의 관계는 반의어 관계이다. arrive: 도착하다, leave[start]: 떠나다[출발하다]

05 abroad: 해외로, order: 주문하다, protect: 보호하다, shall: ~할 것이다

06 주어진 문장에서 'waste'는 쓰레기를 의미하며 이와 같은 뜻을 나타내는 것은 ②번이다. 나머지는 모두 '낭비하다'를 뜻한다.

01 unable

02 (1) skill   (2) favorite   (3) scenery   (4) environmental

03 (1) Playing games too much is not good for your health.

    (2) What shall we call our English club?

    (3) You can have a chance of winning a prize.

04 (1) keep in shape

    (2) stayed up late

    (3) take part in

05 (1) The ball fell into the pond.

    (2) Why don't you take part in the school photo contest?

    (3) I don't have any interest in sports.

06 (A) interested   (B) able   (C) speech   (D) shall

01 주어진 단어의 관계는 반의어 관계이다. able: 할 수 있는, unable: 할 수 없는

02 skill: 기술, favorite: 가장 좋아하는, scenery: 풍경, environmental: 환경의

03 be good for: ~에 좋다, have a chance of -ing: ~할 기회가 있

04 keep in shape: 건강을 유지하다, stay up late: 늦게 까지 깨어 있다, take part in: ~에 참여하다

05 fall into: ~에 빠지다, take part in: ~에 참가하다, have an interest in: ~에 관심이 있다

06 be interested in: ~에 관심이 있다 be able to: ~할 수 있다

교과서
Conversation

1 (1) What's your favorite   (2) Which subject

    (3) Do you like playing

2 (1) I'm interested in

    (2) have in mind / an interest in

    (3) don't have any interest in

교과서 대화문 익히기

(1) T   (2) F   (3) T   (4) F

교과서 확인학습

Everyday English 1. A Function Practice 2 (1)

What's your favorite food / Why don't we order it

Everyday English 1. B. Listening Activity

What's your favorite hobby, they liked watching movies, a total of, watching movies was their favorite hobby, liked doing, favorite sports

Everyday English 2. A Function Practice 2 (1)

the matter / stayed up late to watch TV / I'm interested in traveling

Everyday English 2. A Function Practice 2 (2)

What, doing / Look at / What's the story about / I'm interested in cooking

Everyday English 2. A Function Practice 2 (3)

Why don't / I'm very interested in musicals / I can't wait to see it

Everyday English 2 – B Listening Activity

closely, 30% of students are interested in sports / you are also a big fan of them / I'm not interested in actors / playing them too much is not good for you

In Real Life

know what / Which club do you have in mind / I'm interested in the photo club / Sounds / this chart / What's your favorite club / I want to join the board game club. last year / right / think about

01 Because he stayed up late to watch TV.
02 He has an interest in traveling.
03 why the long face?
04 (in) choosing her friend's birthday present
05 I'm not interested in actors.
06 chart
07 9 students are interested in sports.

01 소년은 TV를 보느라 늦게까지 깨어 있었기 때문에 피곤해 보였다.

02 소년은 여행에 관심을 갖고 있다.

04 Jenny는 친구의 생일 선물을 고르는 데 어려움을 겪고 있다.

06 표, 목록 등의 형태로 정보를 나타내는 페이지나 쪽을 나타내는 말은 chart(도표)이다.

07 학급에 30명의 학생이 있는데 30%의 학생들이 스포츠에 관심이 있으므로 9명이 관심이 있다.

시험대비 기본평가

01 ④   02 (D) → (B) → (A) → (C)   03 ⑤
04 I'm interested in traveling.

01 ④번은 기대감을 표현한다.

02 (D) 무엇을 하고 있는지 질문 → (B) 대답 및 사진을 볼 것을 제안 → (A) 반응 및 무엇에 관한 이야기인지 질문 → (C) 내용 설명 및 관심 표현

03 What do you do?는 '직업'을 묻는 질문이다.

04 be interested in ~: ~에 관심이 있다

교과서

Grammar

핵심 Check   p.20~21

1 (1) are, will take care of   (2) if, will borrow
   (3) Unless,wil, do
2 (1) isn't she   (2) didn't you   (3) isn't he   (4) aren't you
   (5) aren't they   (6) didn't they   (7) does she

시험대비 실력평가   p.17~18

01 ⑤   02 ②, ④   03 ②
04 (A) 42 (B) 32 (C) 13 (D) 25
05 What color do you like best?
06 He is looking for a green baseball cap. 07 ②
08 I can't wait to see it.   09 ⑤   10 ⑤
11 80% of them were satisfied with its activities last year.
12 60% of them were not satisfied with its activities last year. 13 ⑤

01 ⑤번은 싫어함을 나타낸다.

02 밑줄 친 표현은 제안을 나타내는 표현으로 'How about ~?' 또는 'Let's ~'로 바꾸어 쓸 수 있다.

03 화자는 가장 좋아하는 취미에 대해 설명하였다.

06 남자는 초록색 야구 모자를 찾고 있다.

07 남자와 여자는 손님(customer)과 점원(clerk)의 관계이다.

08 can't wait to: ~가 기대된다

09 ⓐ는 '무료의'라는 의미로 이와 같은 의미로 쓰인 것은 ⑤번이다.

11 작년에 80퍼센트의 학생들이 사진 동아리 활동에 만족해 했다.

12 60퍼센트의 보드게임 동아리 회원들이 작년에 활동에 만족스러워하지 않았다.

13 야구에 관심이 있느냐고 묻고 있는데 축구를 잘 못한다는 대답은 어색하다.

시험대비 기본평가   p.22

01 (1) did → didn't   (2) will take → take
   (3) is → does   (4) make → will make
02 (1) will he   (2) do you   (3) isn't he   (4) isn't it
   (5) can she
03 (1) She is busy now, isn't she?
   (2) The man isn't ready to go, is he?
   (3) If she writes a letter, they will write back.
   (4) If my mom hears the news tomorrow, she will be surprised.

01 (1) 일반 동사 과거형에, 긍정문이므로 didn't you (2), (4) 조건의 부사절에서는 현재시제로 미래를 나타내며, 주절은 미래를 나타낼 경우 미래시제를 쓴다. (3) 일반동사 현재형에, 부정문이므로 does he

02 (1) 앞 문장에 조동사 will의 부정문이 쓰였으므로 부가의문문은 will you (2) 앞 문장에 일반동사 현재형 부정문이 쓰이고 있으므로 부가의문문은 do you (3), (4) be동사의 현재형이 앞 문장에 쓰이고 있으므로 isn't he와 isn't it (5) 앞 문장에 조동사 can이 부정문으로 쓰였으므로 can she

03 (1) be동사 현재형이 앞 문장에 있으므로 부가의문문은 isn't she (2) 앞 문장이 be동사 부정문이므로 부가의문문은 is he (3), (4) 조건의 부사절은 현재형으로 미래를 나타내며 주절의 시제는 내용에 맞게 쓴다.

시험대비 실력평가
p.23~25

01 ④ 02 ④ 03 ③ 04 ③

05 ⑤ 06 The sandwich was delicious, wasn't it? 07 ② 08 If you drink the water, you will get smaller. 09 ④ 10 ③

11 ④ 12 If it snows tomorrow, the mountain will be covered with snow.

13 ③ 14 ③ 15 is hot, I will eat[have]

16 ③ 17 ③ 18 ③ 19 You brushed your teeth three times a day, didn't you?

20 ⑤ 21 If I have some money, I will buy a bike[bicycle]. 22 ①, ④

23 You didn't wash your car, did you? 24 ④

01 앞 문장에 일반동사 긍정문이 쓰이고 있으므로 doesn't he

02 조건의 부사절에서 현재시제로 미래를 나타낼 수 있지만 주절의 시제는 의미와 일치시키는 것이 옳다.

03 앞 문장에 일반동사의 긍정문이 쓰였고, 주어가 3인칭 복수이므로 don't they

04 ⓐ, ⓓ는 조건의 부사절로 '~이라면'이라고 해석되고, ⓑ, ⓒ, ⓔ는 명사절 접속사로 '~인지 아닌지'로 해석된다.

05 ⑤ 주어는 3인칭 복수, 동사는 be동사 긍정문이 쓰이고 있으므로 aren't they가 옳다.

06 delicious 맛있는

07 앞 문장에 각각 be동사 과거형, 일반동사 과거형, 조동사 will의 긍정문이 쓰이고 있으므로 wasn't he, didn't she, won't he가 옳다.

08 조건의 부사절에서 현재시제로 미래를 나타낸다.

09 모두 일반동사의 과거형을 쓰고 있으므로 빈칸에 didn't he를 쓰는 것이 옳지만, ④번은 isn't he를 쓴다.

10 ③ 주절의 시제는 의미와 일치시켜야 한다. 따라서 will lend가 옳다.

11 부가의문문이 is he이므로 앞 문장에는 부정문이 쓰였음을 알 수 있다.

12 be covered with: ~으로 덮이다

13 파티에 초대되지 않았다는 것은 과거의 부정형으로 쓰므로 'wasn't invited to the party'라고 쓰며, 부가의문문은 was I를 쓴다.

14 앞 문장에 각각 조동사 can의 부정형, 일반동사 과거형의 긍정문, 조동사 will의 부정문이 쓰이고 있으므로 can he, didn't you, will she가 옳다.

15 조건의 부사절에서 현재시제로 미래를 나타내는 것에 유의한다.

16 앞 문장에 일반동사 과거형을 긍정문으로 쓰고 있으므로 부가의문문은 didn't he를 쓰는 것이 옳다.

17 ③ 앞 문장에서 be동사가 쓰였으므로 isn't it으로 쓰는 것이 옳다.

18 '이번 주에 방문할지를 말해 달라'는 의미로 쓰인 명사절 접속사 if이다. 따라서 의미와 시제를 일치시켜 will visit을 쓰고, '서두르지 않으면 버스를 놓칠 것이다'라는 의미가 자연스러우므로 Unless를 쓴다.

19 brush one's teeth: 이를 닦다

20 앞 문장에서 be동사 긍정형을 쓰고 있으므로 부가의문문은 aren't you를 쓴다.

21 조건의 부사절에서 현재시제로 미래를 나타낸다.

22 If ~ not은 Unless와 같다. 조건의 부사절에서는 현재시제로 미래를 나타내지만, 주절은 의미와 시제를 일치시키는 것에 유의한다.

23 wash a car: 세차하다

24 명사절 접속사와 조건의 부사절을 모두 이끌 수 있는 것은 if이다.

서술형 시험대비
p.26~27

01 You were late, weren't you

02 finish, will join

03 (1) didn't she
   (2) could he
   (3) do you
   (4) can she
   (5) didn't they
   (6) weren't they
   (7) didn't she

04 If I come to see you tomorrow, I will bring some DVDs.

05 If you don't reduce your speed, you will have an accident. / If you are smaller, you can go through the door. / If you join a club, you will make many friends.

06 If you don't walk quickly[fast], you will be late for

school. / Unless you walk quickly[fast], you will be late for school.

07 follow, will enter

08 It is your book, isn't it?

09 (1) helps, will help

   (2) closed, didn't you

   (3) are, will make

   (4) doesn't like, does she

   (5) exercise, will be

10 Unless she wants to talk with me, I will not talk with her.

11 if

12 The flowers are really beautiful, aren't they?

13 If you don't use soap, your clothes won't get clean. / If she wakes up early tomorrow, she will come here. / If you want to buy a car, what kind of car will you buy?

14 didn't she

15 aren't you, am late

16 (1) Don't be late, will you?

   (2) Stop playing computer games, won't[will] you?

01 '너는 오늘 아침에 늦었지, 그렇지 않니?' 묻는 상황이다.

02 함께 영화를 보러 가겠느냐는 물음에 조건의 부사절을 사용하여 일이 끝나면 함께 가겠다는 답변을 하고 있다.

03 앞 문장에 일반동사가 쓰인다면 do, does, did를 이용하여 긍정 혹은 부정의 부가의문문을 만든다. 조동사가 쓰인 경우 조동사의 긍정문이나 부정문으로 부가의문문을 만든다.

04 조건의 부사절에서는 현재시제로 미래를 나타낼 수 있지만 주절의 시제는 의미와 일치시켜야 한다.

05 reduce: ~을 줄이다 have an accident: 사고를 당하다 join: ~에 가입하다, 합류하다

06 If ~ not은 Unless와 같다.

07 조건의 부사절에서는 현재시제로 미래를 나타낼 수 있지만 주절의 시제는 의미와 일치시켜야 한다..

08 be동사는 '~이다'라는 의미이다.

09 조건의 부사절에서 현재시제로 미래를 나타낼 수 있으며, 부가의문문의 동사는 앞 문장에 쓰인 동사의 성질에 따르는 것에 유의한다.

10 'If ~ not'은 Unless와 같다.

11 내용상 조건의 부사절 접속사 if가 들어가는 것이 옳

12 앞 문장에 be동사의 긍정문이 쓰이고 있으며 주어가 3인칭 복수이므로 aren't they를 써서 부가의문문을 만든다.

13 get clean: 깨끗해지다

14 앞 문장에서 일반동사 과거형을 긍정문으로 쓰고 있으므로 부가의문문을 만들 때에는 didn't she를 쓰는 것이 옳다.

15 be동사 긍정문을 쓰고 있으므로 부가의문문은 aren't you를 쓴다.

16 (1) 명령문의 부가의문문은 will you를 쓴다. (2) 긍정 명령문의 부가의문문은 will you나 won't you를 쓴다.

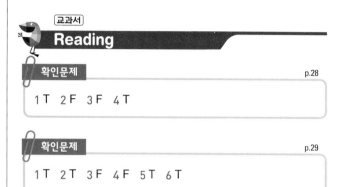

교과서 Reading

확인문제   p.28

1 T 2 F 3 F 4 T

확인문제   p.29

1 T 2 T 3 F 4 F 5 T 6 T

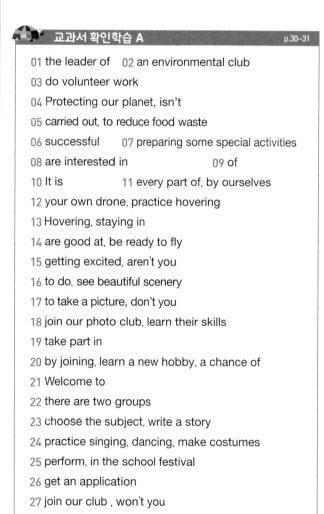

교과서 확인학습 A   p.30~31

01 the leader of   02 an environmental club

03 do volunteer work

04 Protecting our planet, isn't

05 carried out, to reduce food waste

06 successful   07 preparing some special activities

08 are interested in   09 of

10 It is   11 every part of, by ourselves

12 your own drone, practice hovering

13 Hovering, staying in

14 are good at, be ready to fly

15 getting excited, aren't you

16 to do, see beautiful scenery

17 to take a picture, don't you

18 join our photo club, learn their skills

19 take part in

20 by joining, learn a new hobby, a chance of

21 Welcome to

22 there are two groups

23 choose the subject, write a story

24 practice singing, dancing, make costumes

25 perform, in the school festival

26 get an application

27 join our club , won't you

교과서   p.32~33

1 Hello, everyone! I'm Suji and I'm the leader of the "Save the Earth" club.

2 Our club is an environmental club.

3 We do volunteer work to protect our planet.

4 Protecting our planet is important, isn't it?

5 Last year, we carried out a campaign to reduce food waste in the school cafeteria.

6 The campaign was successful.

7 This year, we are preparing some special activities abroad.

8 So, if you are interested in saving the planet, please join us.

9 Hello, friends! I'm Diego of "Fly High."

10 It is a drone club.

11 We study every part of a drone and make some small drones by ourselves.

12 When you have your own drone, you need to practice hovering.

13 "Hovering" means staying in the same place in the air.

14 Once you are good at hovering, you will be ready to fly your drone in different directions.

15 You're getting excited, aren't you?

16 Hello, I'm Junho. What do you want to do when you see beautiful scenery?

17 You want to take a picture of it, don't you?

18 If you join our photo club, "Photo World," you can meet famous photographers and learn their skills.

19 Every December, you can take part in the school photo contest.

20 So, by joining "Photo World" you can learn a new hobby and have a chance of winning a prize!

21 Welcome to my musical club, "Story Singers"!

22 My name is Olivia. In the musical club, there are two groups: actors and crew.

23 We first choose the subject of our musical and then write a story together.

24 Then, the actors practice singing and dancing, while the crew make costumes.

25 We perform our musical in the school festival.

26 You can get an application from me.

27 You will join our club, won't you?

시험대비 실력평가

p.34~37

01 (A)to protect (B)Protecting (또는 To protect)

02 ③   03 ③   04 abroad   05 ⑤

06 ③   07 It is a drone club.   08 It is

staying in the same place in the air.   09 ③

10 famous   11 ⑤   12 December   13 singing and dancing

14 You will join our club, won't you?   15 ②

16 ③   17 ⑤   18 isn't it   19 ⑤

20 ②   21 excited   22 ③

23 They study every part of a drone and make some small drones.   24 ④

25 beautiful scenery   26 ④

27 We can learn their skills.   28 ④   29 ③

30 The members choose the subject of their musical.

01 (A) '~하기 위해서'라는 의미의 to부정사를 쓰는 것이 자연스럽고, (B) 주어 역할을 하는 동명사 혹은 to부정사를 쓰는 것이 옳다.

02 '지구를 구하는 데 관심이 있다면'이 가장 자연스러우므로 if

03 글에 나와 있는 캠페인은 학교 식당에서 음식물 쓰레기를 줄이는 캠페인 하나이다.

04 abroad: 해외로

05 ① different ② same ③ high ④ small의 반의어이다.

06 (A) every+단수명사 (B) practice는 동명사를 목적어로 취하는 동사 (C) be ready to V: ~할 준비가 되다

07 Fly High는 드론 클럽이라고 하였다.

08 공중정지란 공중에서 한자리에 머무는 것이라고 하였다.

09 by Ving: V함으로써

10 '매우 잘 알려진'은 famous(유명한)이다.

11 지난 12월에 학교 사진대회에서 누가 상을 탔는지는 알 수 없다.

12 12월에 학교 사진대회가 있다.

13 practice는 동명사를 목적어로 취한다.

14 join: ~에 가입하다

15 위 글에서 subject는 '주제'라는 의미로 쓰였다.

16 ⓐ, ⓑ, ⓔ를 답할 수 있다.

17 ⓐ는 '~하기 위해서'라고 해석되는 부사적 용법의 to부정사 ① 명사적 용법 중 주어 ②, ④ want, try의 목적어 ③ 명사적 용법 중 목적어 ⑤ 부사적 용법 '~하기 위해서'

18 주어가 동명사구이므로 부가의문문에 인칭대명사 it을 사용한다.

19 동아리가 올해 하려는 특별한 활동이 무엇인지는 알 수 없다.

20 by oneself는 '혼자서, 도움 없이'라는 말이다. on one's own, without help와 같다.

21 사람이 흥미를 느낄 때는 excited를 쓴다.

22 드론을 한자리에 머물게 하는 공중정지를 연습해야 한다고 하였다.

23 동아리 회원들은 드론의 모든 부분을 공부하고 작은 드론을 만든다고 하였다.

24 빈칸에는 '사진을 찍다'는 의미를 완성하는 동사 take가 들어간

다. ① turn into: ~으로 변하다 ② fall into sleep: 잠들다 ③ have a good time: 재미있게 지내다 ④ take a walk: 산책하다 ⑤ put off: ~을 미루다

25 아름다운 풍경을 가리키는 대명사이다.

26 글의 내용상 사진 찍는 것을 의미한다.

27 우리는 유명한 사진작가들로부터 그들의 기술을 배울 수 있다.

28 (A) 절을 이끌고 있으므로 접속사 while (B) '나에게서'라는 의미이므로 출처를 나타내는 전치사 from (C) 앞 문장에서 조동사 will을 쓰고 있으므로 won't you

29 제작진과 배우가 함께 이야기를 쓴다고 하였다.

30 우선 뮤지컬의 주제를 고른다고 하였다.

07 get excited: 흥미를 느끼다

08 이때의 of는 동격을 나타낸다.

09 준호는 사진 동아리에 속해 있다.

10 답변으로 미루어 보아 사진 찍는 방법을 배우고 싶다고 말했음을 알 수 있다.

11 taking photos라고 써도 좋다.

12 가입신청서는 올리비아에게서 받을 수 있다고 하였다. 따라서 '올리비아가 너에게 가입신청서를 줄 것이다'라고 쓰면 된다.

13 동아리에는 배우와 제작진이라는 두 그룹이 있다고 하였다

14 조건의 부사절에서 현재시제로 미래를 나타낼 수 있으며, 주절은 의미에 맞게 미래시제를 쓰는 것에 유의한다.

15 제작진과 배우 두 그룹이 있다고 하였다.

서술형 시험대비　　p.38~39

01 you are interested in saving the planet[Earth] aren't you

02 They carried out a campaign to reduce food waste in the school cafeteria.

03 successful, wasn't it

04 Once you are good at hovering

05 I need to practice hovering.

06 are good at hoveringm, won't be ready

07 You are getting excited, aren't you?

08 a chance of winning a prize

09 He belongs to the photo club.

10 to take a picture

11 taking pictures , don't you

12 Olivia, will give, an application

13 actor, crew

14 If you are interested in dancing and singing in front of many people, you will like the musical club.

15 There are two groups.

01 위 글에서 지구를 구하는 데 관심이 있다면 함께 하자고 하였다. 따라서 '지구를 구하는 데 관심이 있지, 그렇지 않니?'라고 쓸 수 있다.

02 작년에 학교 식당에서 음식물 쓰레기 줄이기 캠페인을 했다.

03 캠페인이 성공적이라고 하였으므로 successful을 쓰고 부가의 문문을 넣는다.

04 공중정지를 잘한다면 드론을 다른 방향으로 날릴 준비가 될 것이라고 하였다.

05 드론이 있으면 공중정지를 연습해야 한다고 하였다.

06 Unless는 'if ~ not'이다. '공중정지를 잘하지 않으면, 드론을 다른 방향으로 날릴 준비가 되지 않을 것이다.'라고 말할 수 있다.

영역별 핵심문제　　p.41~45

01 careless　　02 ②　　03 ⑤　　04 ③

05 (1) stay up late　(2) keep in shape　(3) be good at
(4) take part in

06 (1) I'm interested in cooking.
(2) I'm ready to bake cookies.
(3) I'm a big fan of Queen.

07 (A) looking for (B) a few　08 cap　　09 ①

10 ⑤　　　　　11 Why don't we go to see a musical this Saturday?　　　12 ⑤

13 ⓐ actors, ⓑ computer games

14 How[What] about you? 15 ⑤

16 (C) → (B) → (A) → (D)　　17 ④　　18 ③

19 Keeping[To keep] a diary every day is not easy, is it?　　20 ④　　21 The cat is sitting on the bench, isn't it?　　22 ⑤　　23 can't ride bikes, can they　　24 ②　　25 ⑤

26 ②　　　　　27 If you don't turn down the radio, I will be annoyed.　　28 ②　　29 ③

30 ⑤　　　　31 ⑤번 → aren't you　　32 ④

33 ④　　　　34 They perform their musical in the school festival.

35 while I make costumes　36 costume

01 주어진 단어의 관계는 반의어 관계이다. careful: 주의 깊은, careless: 부주의한

02 무언가 또는 누군가를 사용되도록 또는 어떤 일을 하도록 준비되게 만드는 것을 나타내는 말은 prepare(준비하다)이다.

03 perform 수행하다, 공연하다

04 have an interest in: ~에 관심이 있다, take part in: ~에 참가하다, keep in shape: 건강을 유지하다

05 stay up late: 늦게 까지 깨어 있다, keep in shape: 건강을 유지하다, be good at: ~에 능숙하다, take part in: ~에 참여하

7

다

06 be interested in: ~에 관심이 있다, be ready to: ~할 준비가 되다, big fan: 열렬한 팬

07 look for: ~을 찾다, look after: ~을 돌보다, a few: 몇몇의, few: 거의 없는

08 위 대화에서 one이 가리키는 것은 모자(cap)이다.

09 동명사가 주어이므로 is가 알맞다.

10 3분의 1의 학생들이 사회를 공부하는 것에 관심이 있다는 것은 위의 설명과 일치하지 않는다.

12 (B)는 기대감을 표현하고 있으므로 'look forward to ~ing (~을 기대하다)'와 바꾸어 쓸 수 있다.

15 3분의 1 이상의 학생들이 배우에 관심이 있다는 설명은 일치하지 않는다.

16 (C) 무슨 일인지 질문 → (B) 피곤한 이유 설명 → (A) 무엇을 보았는지 질문 → (D) 대답 및 관심 표현

17 각 문장의 주어와 동사가 'Thomas Edison invented', 'The electric light bulb was'이므로 didn't he, wasn't it이 옳다.

18 조건의 부사절은 현재시제로 미래를 나타낼 수 있다. 단, 주절은 의미와 시제를 일치시킨다.

19 keep a diary: 일기를 쓰다

20 조건의 부사절에서 현재시제로 미래를 나타낼 수 있지만 주절은 의미와 시제를 일치시킨다.

21 sit은 자동사로 '~ 위에 앉다'는 표현은 sit on을 쓴다.

22 앞 문장에서 부정문이 쓰였으므로 부가의문문은 긍정문으로 쓴다.

23 글의 내용상 남동생들이 자전거를 못타지 않느냐는 질문에 탈 수 있다고 답하는 것이라고 볼 수 있다.

24 ②번은 '~인지 아닌지'로 해석되는 명사절을 이끄는 접속사 if이다.

25 ⑤번에는 did he가 들어가며 나머지는 모두 didn't he가 쓰인다.

26 Let me figure it out: 내가 확인해 볼게.

27 If ~ not은 Unless와 같다.

28 (A) '~하기 위해서'이므로 to protect, (B) 앞 문장의 동사가 be동사이고, 주어가 동명사이므로 isn't it, (C) join은 타동사이므로 전치사 없이 목적어를 취한다. 따라서 join이 맞다.

29 수지는 지구를 지키는 것은 중요하다고 하였다.

30 ⓐ be good at: ~을 잘하다 proud of: ~이 자랑스러운, be interested in: ~에 흥미를 느끼다, turn on/off: 불을 켜다/끄다, take off: 이륙하다, stay at: ~에 머무르다

31 앞 문장에서 be동사를 쓰고 있으므로 부가의문문을 만들 때 aren't you라고 써야 한다.

32 얼마나 많은 드론을 만들었는지는 알 수 없다.

33 동아리 가입을 위해서 가입신청서를 필요로 한다.

34 그들은 학교 축제에서 뮤지컬 공연을 한다고 하였다.

35 제작진이 의상을 만드는 동안 배우들은 노래와 춤을 연습한다고 하였다.

36 공연하는 동안에 배우들이 입는 옷은 costume(의상)이다.

01 ①   02 ⑤   03 (A) answered, (B) was, (C) were   04 ⑤

05 What's your favorite food?

06 They are going to order chicken.

07 ①   08 Which club do you have in mind?

09 ②   10 ④   11 ②   12 ③

13 will you do, have time tomorrow   14 ③

15 He always works hard, doesn't he?

16 If I don't see you tomorrow morning, I will call you tomorrow afternoon.   17 ②   18 ②

19 ⑤   20 ④   21 join our photo club, will teach

22 scenery   23 ⑤   24 ⑤

25 Olivia does. 또는 Olivia has applications.

01 이어지는 설명이 조사 결과를 나타내므로 ⓐ가 적절하다.

02 ⑤ 어느 과목이 가장 인기가 없는지는 알 수 없다

03 (A) 동사 answered가 적절하다, (B) 주어가 동명사 watching이므로 was가 적절하다, (C) 주어가 sports이므로 were가 적절하다.

04 여학생 사이에 가장 인기 없는 취미는 컴퓨터 게임하기이다.

06 그들은 치킨을 주문할 것이다.

07 ⓐ를 제외한 나머지는 모두 the board game club을 가리킨다.

09 (A) How about you?: 너는 어때? (B) 상반되는 내용을 연결하는 접속사는 but이다.

10 ④ Jenny의 친구는 스포츠에 관심이 없다.

11 가방을 또 잃어버리면 다시 사주지 않을 것이란 의미이다. 조건의 부사절로 현재가 미래를 대신하도록 하며 주절은 의미와 일치시킨다.

12 조건의 부사절에서는 현재시제로 미래를 나타내며, 주절의 시제는 의미와 일치시킨다.

13 내일 시간이 있으면 할 일에 대해 답하고 있으므로 '내일 시간이 있다면 무엇을 할 거야?'라고 묻는 것이 옳다.

14 ③ 주어가 3인칭 복수이므로 aren't they로 쓰는 것이 옳다.

15 빈도부사의 위치는 일반 동사 앞이다.

16 조건의 부사절은 현재 시제로, 주절은 의미에 맞게 미래 시제를 써서 문장을 만든다.

17 The news는 단수 주어이며 be동사의 과거형이 쓰이고 있으므로 wasn't it, 조건의 부사절은 현재시제로 미래를 나타낼 수 있으므로 uses가 옳다.

18 (B) 동아리 Fly High에 대한 설명 - (A) 만든 드론으로 공중 정지 연습 - (C) 공중정지를 잘하게 되면 다른 방향으로 드론을 날릴 수 있다

19 ⓐ에는 want의 목적어로 쓰이는 to부정사가 들어간다. What

are you going to do this weekend? 이번 주말에 뭐 할 거야?

20 ④ 학교 사진 대회는 겨울에 개최된다.

21 네가 우리 사진 동아리에 가입하면, 유명한 사진작가들이 너에게 그들의 기술을 가르쳐 줄 거야. will을 대신하여 can을 써도 좋다.

22 scenery(경치)를 풀이한 말이다.

23 배우들이 자신들의 할 일인 춤과 노래를 연습하는 동안 제작진들은 의상을 만든다.

24 부가의문문의 형태로 보아 will join으로 쓰는 것이 옳다.

25 가입신청서는 Olivia에게서 받을 수 있다고 하였다.

서술형 실전문제
p.50~51

01 Because 30% of students are interested in sports.

02 They are interested in computer games.

03 She thinks that it is not good for Brian.

04 If my mom teaches me English, I will study harder.

05 You were sick yesterday, weren't you

06 The boys want to play soccer, don't they?

07 didn't you, will you

08 If you are not[aren't] busy / Unless you are busy

09 ourselves

10 made my drone

11 some special activities , aren't you

12 Reducing food waste in the school cafeteria was your campaign, wasn't it?

13 if you are interested in saving the planet

01 Sujin은 30퍼센트의 학생들이 스포츠에 관심이 있기 때문에 학교 운동회가 매우 재미있을 것이라고 생각했다.

02 학생들의 5분의 1은 컴퓨터 게임에 관심이 있다.

03 Sujin은 컴퓨터 게임을 너무 많이 하는 것은 Brian에게 좋지 않다고 생각했다.

04 조건의 부사절은 현재시제로 미래를 표현한다.

05 대답으로 미루어 보아 어제 아프지 않았냐고 묻는 말을 쓰는 것이 옳다.

06 want는 to부정사를 목적어로 취한다. 소년들은 3인칭 복수이므로 don't they를 쓴다.

07 앞 문장에 일반동사 과거형이 쓰이고 있으므로 부가의문문은 didn't you, 조건의 부사절은 현재시제로 미래를 나타내지만 주절의 시제는 의미와 일치시키므로 will you를 써서 의문문을 완성한다.

08 'if ~ not'은 unless와 같다.

09 by oneself: 혼자서, 혼자 힘으로

---

10 드론 동아리에서 스스로 작은 드론을 만든다고 하였다. 드론을 날리고 있는 중이므로, 드론을 '만들었다'고 과거형으로 쓰는 것에 유의한다.

11 대답으로 미루어 보아 수지의 특별한 활동에 관한 질문임을 알 수 있다.

12 과거시제를 쓰는 것에 유의한다.

13 be interested in: ~에 관심이 있다

창의사고력 서술형 문제
p.52

|모범답안|

01 (A) sports, (B) 27%, (C) computer games

02 (1) If you drink milk, you will grow taller.

(2) If I meet my favorite movie star in person, I will be very happy.

(3) If I make many friends, I will become very busy.

(4) If I become a writer, I will write many exciting novels.

03 (1) Mary likes dolls, doesn't she?

(2) Joe doesn't hate to eat carrots, does he?

(3) You wanted to be a dentist, didn't you?

(4) Amelia will break the rule again, won't she?

(5) You spilled the water, didn't you?

(6) Your brother is good at swimming, isn't he?

01 (A) 도표에 따르면 30%의 학생들은 스포츠에 관심이 있다. (B) 배우들에게 관심이 많은 학생은 27%이다. (C) 20%의 학생들은 컴퓨터 게임에 관심이 있다.

단원별 모의고사
p.53~56

01 ①   02 ②   03 (1) by yourself

(2) carry out   (3) fall into

04 Watching movies is the most popular hobby among the students.

05 32 boy students like playing computer games.

06 Watching movies is the least popular hobby.

07 ⓐ: tired ⓑ: interested

08 I stayed up late to watch TV.

09 (1) By joining the club, you can keep in shape and reduce stress.

(2) I know (that) you are a big fan of *The Beatles*.

(3) Which activity do you have in mind?

10 (1) long face (2) carry out (3) by myself

11 It is a cap. 12 She is going to buy a cap. 13 ③

14 ③   15 He is not busy now, is he?

9

16 ⑤   17 If you are sick, I will take you to the
hospital.   18 ④   19 This year, they are
preparing some special activities abroad.
20 ⑤   21 ⑤   22 ③   23 ③
24 Sounds fun, doesn't it?   25 ⑤

01 더 이상 필요하지 않아서 내다버린 물질을 나타내는 말은
waste(쓰레기)이다.

02 주어진 문장을 비롯한 나머지 문장에서 application은 '신청서'
를 의미하지만 ②번은 '적용'을 뜻한다.

03 by oneself: 혼자서, carry out: 수행하다, fall into: ~에 빠
지다

04 학생들 사이에 가장 인기 있는 취미는 영화보기이다.

05 32명의 남학생들이 컴퓨터 게임하는 것을 좋아한다.

06 남학생들에게 가장 인기가 적은 취미는 영화 보는 것이다.

07 ⓐ tiring: 지치게 하는, tired: 지친, ⓑ be interested in: ~
에 관심이 있다

09 keep in shape: 건강을 유지하다, a big fan: 열렬한 팬, have
in mind: 마음에 두다

10 Why the long face?: 왜 우울하니? carry out: 수행하다, by
oneself: 스스로

11 여학생들에게 두 번째로 가장 인기 있는 선물은 모자이다.

12 Jenny는 친구의 생일 선물로 모자를 살 것이다.

13 앞 문장의 주어는 3인칭 복수, 동사는 일반 동사 과거형의 긍정
문이므로 didn't they라고 쓰는 것이 옳다.

14 Unless는 If ~ not이므로 부정문을 이끌지 않는다.

15 be busy: 바쁘다

16 앞 문장에 부정어가 있으므로 did he라고 쓰는 것이 옳다.

17 take: ~를 데리고 가다

18 지구를 구하는 캠페인이라고 하였으므로 음식물 쓰레기를 '줄이
기 위한' 캠페인이라고 쓰는 것이 자연스러우므로 reduce라고
쓰는 것이 옳다.

19 'This year, they are planning to do some special
activities abroad.'라고 써도 좋다.

20 얼마나 많은 양의 음식물 쓰레기를 줄였는지는 알 수 없다.

21 ① special ② protect ③ abroad ④ waste ⑤ attack: 공격
하다

22 공중정지를 잘하면 드론을 다른 방향으로 날릴 수 있다는 의미
가 가장 자연스러우므로 once가 가장 적절하다.

23 ③ by oneself(= on one's own): 스스로

24 Sounds fun: 재미있게 들리다

25 초보자를 위한 특별한 수업이 있다고 하였으므로 스스로 배워야
한다는 것은 글의 내용과 일치하지 않는다.

Planting Seeds of Hope

시험대비 실력평가   p.60

01 cause   02 ①   03 ⑤
04 (1) share (2) widespread (3) unwelcome
    (4) throat
05 ①   06 ②

01 주어진 단어의 관계는 반의어 관계이다. cause: 원인, result:
결과

02 주어진 문장에서 brush는 '~을 닦다'라는 의미로 이와 같은 의
미로 쓰인 것은 ①번이다. 나머지는 모두 '붓, 솔'을 의미한다.

03 togetherness: 친목, 연대감

04 unwelcome: 환영 받지 못하는, throat: 목, widespread: 널
리 퍼진, share: 나누다

05 그 부분에서 새로운 식물이 자랄 수 있는 식물에 의해 만들어지
는 작고 단단한 부분을 가리키는 말은 seed(씨앗)이다.

06 keep away from: 피하다, keep on: 계속하다, keep from
~ing: ~하는 것을 막다

서술형 시험대비   p.61

01 sick
02 (1) desert   (2) seed   (3) map   (4) trip
03 (1) My English teacher is not only kind but also
        popular.
    (2) Children are looking forward to receiving
        presents.
    (3) How can I find out the secret?
04 (1) wait to meeting   (2) come about
    (3) taking a look at
05 (1) masks   (2) plant   (3) spread   (4) volunteers
    (5) vet
06 (1) I'm looking forward to visiting Jejudo.
    (2) Let's take a look at the map.
    (3) My mother said I should keep away from bad
        friends.

01 주어진 단어의 관계는 반의어 관계이다. sick: 아픈, healthy:
건강한

02 desert: 사막, seed: 씨앗, map: 지도, trip: 여행

03 not only A but also B: A뿐만 아니라 B도

04 can't wait to: 빨리 ~하고 싶어하다, come about: 발생하다, take a look at: 살펴보다

05 boots: 장화, environment: 환경, rumor: 소문, vet: 수의사

Conversation

핵심 Check   p.62~63

1 (1) The weather report said (2) He told me that
  (3) He said we should read

2 (1) I'm looking forward to seeing animals
  (2) I'm so excited to be going camping
  (3) I can't wait to

교과서 대화문 익히기

Check(√) True or False   p.64

(1) T   (2) F   (3) F   (4) T

교과서 확인학습   p.66~67

Everyday English 1 A. Function Practice 2-(1)
I had a bad cold / He said

Everyday English 1 A. Function Practice 2-(2)
The weather report said it would rain this afternoon / You can share my umbrella

Everyday English 1 A. Function Practice 2-(3)
He said it was terrible / take a walk in the park

Everyday English 1 B. Listening Activity
by mistake / your foot must hurt very much / the doctor said / Why don't you ask Kevin, good at playing soccer

Everyday English 2 A Function practice 2-(1)
What movie do you want to watch / I'm looking forward to seeing it

Everyday English 2 B. Listening Activity
I volunteer at a lost pet center every Friday / I take the dogs out for a walk / I want to become an animal

doctor in the future / I look forward to seeing you at the center

In Real Life
I can't stop sneezing / because of the yellow dust. The weather report said, terrible / I'm sneezing because of that / We're planning to plant trees in China / We are looking forward to stopping the yellow dust

시험대비 기본평가   p.68

01 ①   02 (B) → (D) → (C) → (A)   03 오늘
오후에 비가 올 것이라는 것   04 ③

02 (B) 학교에 결석한 이유 질문 → (D) 결석한 이유 설명 → (C) 숙제 설명 → (A) 고마움 표현

04 share: 나누다, 공유하다

시험대비 실력평가   p.69~70

01 ②   02 They are going to see the new superhero movie.   03 ②   04 ①
05 ⑤   06 ④   07 ②
08 (A) terrible, (B) shall, (C) take   09 ⑤
10 They are going to see a movie this Saturday.
11 I'm looking forward to seeing it.

01 빈칸에 기대감을 나타내는 표현이 적절하다.

02 Brian과 Susan은 새로운 슈퍼 영웅 영화를 볼 것이다. 03 Yujin은 다친 다리를 걱정하고 있으므로 anxious(걱정스러운) 가 적절하다.

03 기대감을 나타내는 표현이 적절하다.

04 주어진 문장은 유기 동물 센터에서 무엇을 하는지에 대한 대답으로 적절하므로 (A)가 알맞다.

05 Chris는 매주 유기 동물 센터에 가지 않으므로 ⑤번에 답할 수 없다.

06 이어지는 대화에서 화기 난 이유를 정확히 설명하고 있으므로 (D)가 적절하다

07 Minji가 공원에서 많은 사람들 때문에 화가 났다는 설명은 대화의 내용과 일치하지 않는다.

08 (A) terrible: 지독한, 끔찍한, terrific: 빼어난, 뛰어난, (B) shell: 조개, shall: ~할 것이다, (C) take a walk: 산책하다

09 Jane과 Alex가 영화관에 갈 계획을 세웠다는 설명은 대화의 내용과 일치하지 않는다.

10 Brian and Susan은 이번 주 토요일에 영화를 볼 것이다.

11 look forward to ~: ~하기를 기대하다

01 (A) happy, (B) that, (C) can't

02 They are going to hear the school band performance.

03 ⓒ → kicking

04 꽃을 뽑고 나무를 발로 차는 사람들을 보고 화가 났다.

05 (A) sneezing, (B) because of, (C) comes

06 The yellow dust would be terrible today.

07 They're going to plant trees in China.

01 (A) 이어지는 대화에서 기대감을 나타내고 있으므로 happy가 적절하다. (B) 명사절을 이끄는 접속사 that이 알맞다. (C) can't wait to: 빨리 ~하고 싶다

02 소년과 소녀는 이번 주에 학교 밴드 공연을 들을 것이다.

03 picking과 병렬구조로 kicking이 알맞다.

05 (A) stop to ~: ~하기 위해 멈추다, stop ~ing: ~하는 것을 멈추다, (B) because of+명사(구), because+주어+동사, (C) dust는 셀 수 없는 명사

교과서
Grammar

1 (1) how to drive / how you[we] should

  (2) when to put / when I should put

  (3) whom to give / who(m) I should give

2 (1) so that / in order that

  (2) so that / in order that

  (3) so that / to serve

01 (1) how cook → how to cook

  (2) to do → should do

  (3) in that → so[in order] that

  (4) in order to → in order that

02 (1) should talk   (2) could come   (3) to thank

  (4) in order that   (5) to put

03 (1) Can you tell me where to write my name?

  (2) I don't know when to use this paper.

  (3) Speak clearly so that we can understand you.

  (4) Wear the glasses so that you can protect your eyes.

01 (1) '의문사+to부정사'는 '의문사+주어+should 동사원형'과 같다. (2) 두 번째 나오는 I를 생략하고 what to do로 쓸 수도 있다. (3) '내가 앉을 수 있도록'이라는 목적을 나타내야 하므로 so[in order] that을 쓴다. (4) 부사절을 이끌 수 있는 것은 that이다.

02 (1), (3) '의문사+to부정사'는 '의문사+주어+should 동사원형'과 같다. (2) 주절이 과거동사이므로 조동사는 could를 쓴다. (4) in order that은 so that과 같이 쓰일 수 있다.

03 (1) '어디에 써야 할지'이므로 의문사 where와 to부정사를 쓴다. (2) '언제 사용해야 할지'이므로 의문사 when과 to부정사를 쓴다. (3), (4) '~할 수 있도록'이므로 목적의 부사절을 이끄는 so that을 쓴다.

01 ②, ③   02 ②, ④   03 ③

04 I don't know when to go. / I don't know when I should go. 05 ③   06 ④   07 ②

08 what to wear   09 ⑤   10 ④

11 ④   12 what to drink   13 ③

14 ②   15 ④

16 Let me show you how to get there so that you won't get lost.   17 ③   18 ④

19 ④   20 I was so tired that I couldn't think what to do next.   21 ②

22 which pen to buy / which pen I should buy

23 so[in order] that it will be ready to eat by 6:30.

24 how

01 주변 모든 사람들이 행복을 느낄 수 있도록 좋은 말을 해준다는 의미이므로 목적의 부사절을 쓰는 것이 옳다.

02 목적의 부사절 so that은 in order that, in order to부정사로 바꿔 쓸 수 있다.

03 '의문사+to부정사', 목적을 나타내는 to부정사를 써야 한다.

04 when to go: 언제 갈지

05 what to say 혹은 what I should say라고 쓰는 것이 옳다. amuse: ~을 즐겁게 하다

06 목적의 부사절 so that은 in order that, 혹은 to부정사로 대신할 수 있다.

07 ⓑ what to do, ⓒ in order that, ⓓ to win이 옳다.

08 글의 내용상 무엇을 입어야 할지 모르겠다는 말이 들어가는 것이 옳다.

09 ⑤ for → to

10 '내일 일찍 일어날 수 있도록 일찍 잠자리에 들어라.'라는 의미이다.

11 ④번에는 '네가 나에 대해 걱정할 필요가 없도록 전화 하겠다.' 는 의미이다. 따라서 so that이 들어가며 나머지는 모두 원인을 나타내는 because가 쓰인다.

12 커피를 권하고 있으므로 무엇을 마실지 결정했느냐는 질문을 쓰는 것이 옳다.

13 '의문사+to부정사'는 '의문사+주어+should 동사원형'과 같다.

14 Mowgli가 배가 고파도 무엇을 할지 모르기에 친구 Baloo가 생선 잡는 법을 가르쳐 주었다고 쓰는 것이 가장 적절하다.

15 (A) 언제 교회로 가야 할지 (B) 은행으로 가는 방법 (C) 너무 당황해서 한 마디도 할 수 없었다.

16 get lost: 길을 잃다

17 'so ~ that ...'은 '너무 ~해서 …하다'이다.

18 수학을 잘 못한다고 말한 것으로 보아 문제를 푸는 방법을 묻는다고 볼 수 있다.

19 '어느 것'이라고 하였으므로 which를 쓰는 것이 옳다.

20 so tired that ~: 너무 피곤해서 ~한

21 '팔짝팔짝 뛰기 위해서 행복했다'라기 보다는 '너무 행복해서 팔짝팔짝 뛰었다'고 말하는 것이 자연스럽다. 따라서 so happy that ~으로 바꾸는 것이 어법상 바르다.

22 '어느 펜'이라고 하였으므로 which pen을 쓴다.

23 6시 30분까지는 먹을 준비가 되도록 5시에 오븐에 고기를 넣으라는 문장을 쓰면 된다.

24 말을 잘하는 사람이 아니기 때문에 대화를 시작하는 '방법'을 모른다는 문장이 자연스럽다.

🦉 서술형 시험대비
p.78~79

01 Tom studied hard so that he could pass the test. / Tom studied so hard that he could pass the test.

02 where to buy

03 Can you tell me how to play tennis well? / Can you tell me how I can play tennis well?

04 I won't get wet

05 (1) Please turn down the TV so that I can get to sleep.
(2) Can you give me a ride to the hospital so that I can see a doctor?
(3) The little girl pretended to be sick so that she could stay home from school.

06 Can you teach me how to swim so that I can swim well?

07 where to find a restroom

08 how to do kung fu / so that

09 You have been so kind that I don't know how to thank you.

10 reduce / could reduce food waste

11 so that they could go out with some friends.

12 (1) Amelia studied English hard so that she could become a tour guide.
(2) Amelia studied English hard in order that she could become a tour guide.
(3) Amelia studied English hard to become a tour guide.

13 (1) where to hand in the report
(2) what to do after graduating from college
(3) which dress to buy

14 I will take a taxi so that I won't be late.

01 위 문장은 목적을 나타내는 so that을 사용해서, 아래 문장은 원인과 결과를 나타내는 so ~ that을 사용해서 만들 수 있다.

02 답변으로 미루어 보아 어디에서 이 물건을 사는지 아느냐는 질문을 했다고 볼 수 있다.

03 '의문사+to부정사'는 '의문사+주어+should[can] 동사원형'과 같다.

04 '젖지 않도록'이라는 의미가 들어가는 것이 적절하다.

05 turn down: 소리를 낮추다 give somebody a ride: ~를 태워 주다 stay home from school: 학교에 안 가고 집에 있다

06 '수영하는 방법'이므로 how to swim을 쓴다.

07 Jason은 웨이터에게 어디에서 화장실을 찾을 수 있는지 묻고, 웨이터는 데려다주겠다고 하였다.

08 답변으로 보아 쿵푸를 가르쳐줄 수 있냐는 요청을 쓰는 것이 옳으며, '쿵푸를 잘할 수 있도록'이 자연스러우므로 목적의 부사절 so that을 쓴다.

09 how to thank you: 너에게 고마워할 방법

10 June은 음식물 쓰레기를 줄이는 방법을 알고 있기에 친구들이 음식물 쓰레기를 줄일 수 있도록 그 방법을 알려주었다고 할 수 있다.

11 친구들과 함께 놀기 위해서 베이비시터를 고용할 예정이라고 하였다.

12 목적의 부사절을 이끄는 so that, in order that을 활용하거나 to부정사의 부사적 용법 중 '목적'을 이용하여 문장을 만들 수 있다. (2) 'Amelia studied English hard in order[so as] to become a tour guide.'라고 써도 좋다.

13 (1) Jason은 그가 보고서를 어디에 제출해야 하는지 내게 물었다. (2) 대학 졸업 후에 무엇을 할지는 그녀가 결정할 문제다. (3) 어느 드레스를 사야 하는지 나는 결정하지 못했어.

14 take a taxi: 택시를 타다

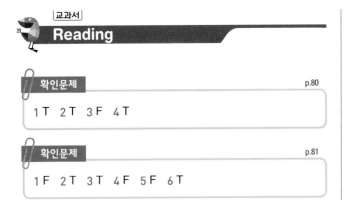

Reading

p.80

확인문제

1 T 2 T 3 F 4 T

확인문제   p.81

1 F 2 T 3 T 4 F 5 F 6 T

교과서 확인학습 A   p.82~83

01 are wearing, so that, can keep away from

02 there is widespread

03 become sick, hurts their eyes, throats

04 come about   05 to stop

06 take a look at, of, to, through

07 was a big forest

08 to cut down trees, could build   09 passed, lost

10 became, became bigger and bigger

11 brings, from, spreads   12 how to stop

13 plant, to solve this problem

14 Planting trees, is

15 However, that, live if they don't plant

16 thank, because, with them

17 However, to help, but also

18 what to do, get rid of

19 planting trees, to solve the problem

20 planting, protecting, help

21 are planting, so that, can stop

22 hard to protect

23 togetherness, keep on growing

교과서 확인학습 B   p.84~85

1 Many people are wearing masks so that they can keep away from an unwelcome guest in the spring: yellow dust.

2 Every year, there is widespread yellow dust in Korea.

3 Many people become sick because the yellow dust hurts their eyes and throats.

4 Why does the yellow dust come about?

5 Is there any way to stop the yellow dust? Yes, there is!

6 Let's take a look at the causes of and the solutions to the problem of yellow dust through the work of some volunteers in Gansu Sheng, China.

7 A long time ago, this place was a big forest.

8 But people began to cut down trees so that they could build cities.

9 As time passed, the forest lost many trees.

10 Finally, the forest became a desert and the desert became bigger and bigger.

11 Now, when the spring brings strong winds from the west, the yellow dust spreads.

12 In the past, most people did not know how to stop the yellow dust problem.

13 Now, many volunteers plant trees to solve this problem.

14 Planting trees in the desert is hard and expensive.

15 However, many Chinese people know that they cannot live if they don't plant trees.

16 They always thank us, Korean volunteers, because we plant trees with them.

17 However, we plant trees to help not only China but also Korea.

18 At first, I didn't know what to do to get rid of the yellow dust.

19 Then, Minsu, my group leader, told me that planting trees can help to solve the problem.

20 I also found out that planting trees and protecting the environment help my family and me.

21 In China, many people are planting trees in deserts so that they can stop the spread of the yellow dust.

22 The work is not easy, but they are working hard to protect the world.

23 With this kind of global togetherness, the seeds of hope will keep on growing.

시험대비 실력평가   p.86~89

01 ④   02 ②   03 ③   04 a big forest, a desert   05 ⑤

06 It was because they could build cities by cutting down trees.   07 ③   08 ⑤

09 Korea, China   10 ③

11 planting trees in deserts 12 the seeds of hope

13 ⑤   14 ②   15 ③

16 The yellow dust shows up in the spring.   17 ①, ⑤

01 목적을 나타내는 접속사가 들어가는 것이 옳다.

02 자원봉사자들의 작업을 통해 황사 문제의 원인과 해결책을 살펴보자고 하였으므로 ②번이 적절하다.

03 (A) widespread yellow dust가 주어이므로 there is (B) 종속절을 이끌고 있으므로 접속사 because (C) 의문문이므로 any

04 used to V는 '(과거에) ~이었다'는 의미이다.

05 황사가 얼마나 멀리까지 퍼지는지는 알 수 없다.

06 사람들이 나무를 베기 시작한 이유는 나무를 베어냄으로써 도시를 세울 수 있었기 때문이었다.

07 ⓐ는 완전한 문장을 이끄는 명사절 접속사 that이다. ③ 관계대명사 that은 불완전한 문장을 이끈다.

08 중국 사람들은 한국인 자원봉사자들에게 감사해 한다고 하였다.

09 not only A but also B = B as well as A: A 뿐만 아니라 B도

10 빈칸에는 목적의 부사절을 이끄는 so that이 들어간다. ① when ② Although[Though] ③ so that ④ so ⑤ although[though]

11 사막에 나무를 심는 일을 의미한다.

12 seed: 씨앗

13 hardly는 '거의 ~하지 않는'이라는 의미의 부정을 나타내는 부사이다. 글의 흐름상 hard를 쓰는 것이 옳다.

14 come about은 '발생하다'는 의미이므로 take place가 적절하다.

15 ③ once in two years: 2년에 한 번

16 글에 따르면 황사는 봄에 나타난다.

17 finally, in the end: 마침내

18 '의문사+to부정사'는 '의문사+주어+should+동사원형'과 같다.

19 (A) 사막이 되었다고 했으므로 lost many trees, (B) 서쪽에서 강한 바람을 몰고 와서 황사가 퍼지므로 brings (C) 문제를 해결하기 위해 나무를 심는 것이라고 할 수 있다.

20 물, 비, 나무 또는 식물이 거의 없는 넓은 면적의 땅이 '사막'이다.

21 in order that은 주어와 동사를 포함하는 절을 이끈다.

22 ⓒ는 '~하기 위해서'라고 해석되어 목적을 나타내는 부사적 용법의 to부정사이다. 따라서 ①번이 옳다.

23 나무를 심는 것이 황사 문제 해결을 도울 뿐만 아니라 나와 내 가족을 돕는 일이라고 하는 것이 가장 자연스럽다. 따라서 '게다가'

로 해석되는 in addition이 옳다.

24 민수: 황사가 한국에서 많은 문제를 초래하고 있다는 것을 아니? 수지: 정말? 난 몰랐어. 그 문제를 어떻게 해결해야 하는지 말해줄래?

25 수지가 오직 가족을 위해서 나무를 심는다는 것은 글의 내용과 일치하지 않는다.

26 나무를 심는 것은 힘들지만 → (C) 많은 중국 사람들이 나무를 심을 필요성을 알고 있고 → (A) 때문에 나무를 함께 심어주는 우리에게 고마워한다. → (B) 하지만 우리는 중국뿐만 아니라 한국을 위해서 나무를 심는다.

서술형 시험대비   p.90~91

01 사진 속에서 마스크를 쓰고 있는 이유를 묻고 있으므로 '반갑지 않은 손님을 피하기 위해서'라고 답하면 된다.

02 황사가 사람들을 병에 걸리게 한다고 하였다.

03 how to stop: 멈추는 방법

04 '황사 문제를 막을 방법'이 들어가는 것이 옳다.

05 봄바람이 서쪽에서부터 강한 바람을 몰고 와 황사가 퍼진다고 하였다. 따라서 황사는 서쪽에서 온다고 답할 수 있다.

06 목적의 부사절 so that은 절을 이끌기 때문에, in order to를 쓸 때에는 build cities만 쓴다.

07 자원봉사자들은 황사 문제를 해결하기 위해서 나무를 심는다고 하였다.

08 각각 한국 자원 봉사자들과 중국 사람들을 의미한다.

09 at first: 처음에

10 수지는 나무를 심고 환경을 보호하는 것이 자신과 가족을 보호

한다는 사실을 알았다고 하였다.

11 글에서 수지는 처음에 무엇을 해야 할지 몰랐다고 하였다. 빈칸에 맞게 '의문사+주어+should+동사원형'을 쓴다.

12 grew plants in a small garden at their house라고 써도 좋다.

13 많은 학생들이 나쁜 공기 때문에 아프게 되었다고 하였다. make를 사역동사로 쓰면 many students(목적어) become sick(목적보어)으로 문장을 완성할 수 있다.

14 '의문사+to부정사'는 '의문사+주어+should+동사원형'과 같다.

15 해석: 나무를 심음으로써, 그들은 환경을 보호하는 것을 도울 뿐만 아니라 희망의 씨앗을 심을 수 있다.

영역별 핵심문제

p.93~97

01 cause   02 ③

03 (1) I forgot to turn off the switch when leaving home.
  (2) Where does the yellow dust come from?
  (3) Do you enjoy taking a walk with your pet?

04 (1) keeps on
  (2) a long time ago
  (3) get rid of   05 ④

06 (1) Keep, away from (2) looking forward to
  (3) catch a cold (4) get rid of

07 ⑤   08 ①, ④   09 ④

10 The weather report said it would rain this afternoon.

11 She will share her umbrella.

12 (A) the yellow dust (B) some special activities

13 We are looking forward to stopping the yellow dust.   14 ③   15 ④

16 The wind was so strong that it blew my hat off my head. / Clara got a new job so that she could be closer to her house.   17 ④   18 ③

19 how to say sorry   20 ⑤   21 ②

22 Be quiet so[in order] that I can hear what Sharon is saying.   23 ④   24 ②

25 I turned off my cell phone so that I could enjoy watching the movie.   26 ⑤   27 ①

28 Because Korean volunteers plant trees with them.

29 growing plants   30 ③

31 to protect the environment   32 ④

33 ③

01 주어진 단어의 관계는 반의어 관계이다. cause: 원인, result: 결과

02 ③번 문장에서 past는 '과거'를 뜻한다.

04 keep on: 계속 ~하다, a long time ago: 오래 전에, get rid of: ~을 없애다

05 이곳에 자라는 식물이 거의 없거나 물이 거의 없는 넓은 지역의 땅을 가리키는 말은 desert(사막)이다.

06 keep away from: 피하다, look forward to: ~을 기대하다, get rid of: ~을 없애다, catch a cold: 감기에 걸리다

08 목적어로 that절을 취할 수 있는 것은 say와 explain이다. tell은 '간접목적어+that절'의 형식을 취한다.

09 이어지는 대화에서 Kevin에 대한 설명이 이어지므로 ⓓ가 적절하다.

11 비가 오면 소녀는 그녀의 우산을 소년과 같이 쓸 것이다.

14 황사를 멈추기 위해 할 수 있는 일이 아무것도 없다는 설명은 대화의 내용과 일치하지 않는다.

15 우유가 상하지 않도록 냉장고에 넣었다는 의미가 적절하다. so that을 이용하여 문장을 만든 ④번이 가장 적절하다.

16 '바람이 너무 강해서 내 머리에서 모자를 날려버렸다.' 'Clara는 집에 더 가까워지기 위해서 새로운 직장을 구했다.'가 자연스럽다.

17 '언제 마트에 갈지'라고 묻는 것이 옳다.

18 ⓐ how to behave 혹은 how I should behave ⓔ 주절이 과거시제이므로 시제 일치를 위하여 would understand를 쓰는 것이 옳다.

19 답변으로 보아 '그녀에게 미안하다고 말하는 방법을 모르겠어.'라고 말하는 것이 옳다.

20 'My heart beat so fast that I could hardly speak.'가 옳다.

21 그들이 그 일을 완벽하게 할 수 있도록 무엇을 할지 분명하게 말해주라는 의미이다.

22 Sharon이 말하고 있는 것을 들을 수 있도록 조용히 해달라는 문장을 쓰면 된다.

23 답변에서 가는 길을 설명해 주고 있으므로 '박물관에 가는 방법'을 묻는 말이 들어가는 것이 적절하다.

24 내가 책을 살 수 있도록 아빠가 내게 돈을 주셨다는 의미가 적절하다.

25 enjoy는 동명사를 목적어로 취하는 것에 유의한다.

26 나무를 심는 것이 비싸다고 했을 뿐 얼마인지는 나와 있지 않다.

27 (A) 동명사 주어이므로 단수 취급 (B) '나무를 심지 않으면'이라는 의미이므로 if (C) '돕기 위해서'라는 목적을 나타내므로 to부정사

28 한국인 자원봉사자들이 중국인들과 함께 나무를 심기 때문에 고마워한다고 하였다.

29 식물을 재배하는 것이 나쁜 공기 문제를 해결하는 데에 도움이 될 수 있다는 글이다.

30 친구의 조언으로 미루어 보아 '어디에 심어야 할지'를 쓰는 것이 가장 적절하다.

31 so that은 to부정사로 간단히 표현할 수 있다.

32 advice는 셀 수 없는 명사이다.

33 지민은 친구들과 함께 식물을 키울 것이라고 하였다.

단원별 예상문제   p.98~101

01 ⓑ → by   **02** ②   **03** ⑤   **04** ⑤

05 Because his brother said it was terrible.

06 ③   **07** ⑤

08 He hurt his foot during the soccer match last week.

09 Because he was good at playing soccer.

10 He shouldn't play soccer for a month.   **11** ③

12 ②   **13** ⑤   **14** what to eat and when to eat it.   **15** ①, ③

16 Helen studies English very hard so that she can get an A.

17 where to hang   **18** ③   **19** ②

20 ④   **21** planting trees   **22** ②

23 ③   **24** where I should grow, about growing, at our school   **25** seed

01 by mistake: 실수로

02 밑줄 친 (A)는 '~임에 틀림없다'는 확신을 나타내므로 이와 같은 의미로 쓰인 것은 ②번이다.

04 빈칸에 들어갈 말로 제안하는 표현이 적절하다.

05 Alex는 그의 남동생이 영화가 끔찍하다고 말했기 때문에 보고 싶어 하지 않았다.

06 (A)는 '심다'라는 의미로 이와 같이 쓰인 것은 ③번이다. ①, ④, ⑤: 식물, ②: 공장

07 대화를 통해 Suji의 동아리 회원들이 나무를 심기 위해 무엇을 준비하는지는 알 수 없다.

09 Sujin은 Kevin이 축구를 잘하기 때문에 John에게 추천하였다.

10 John은 한 달 동안 축구를 해서는 안 된다.

11 4월 1일에 시작해야 한다고 답하고 있으므로 '언제 시작할지 결정하자.'는 말이 들어가는 것이 적절하다.

12 '어디에 주차해야 할지'이므로 의문사 where를 써서 문장을 만든다.

13 where he should learn으로 쓰는 것이 옳다.

14 what to eat: 무엇을 먹을지 when to eat it: 그것을 언제 먹을지

15 '~하기 위하여'라는 목적을 나타내는 to부정사가 쓰였다. 따라서 in order that 혹은 so that을 사용하여 문장을 만들 수 있다.

16 Helen이 A를 받을 수 있도록 열심히 공부한다는 문장을 쓰면 된다.

17 where I should hang을 써도 좋다.

18 많은 나무를 잃고 마침내 사막이 되었다는 순서가 적절하다. whose가 쓰이며, 나머지는 모두 that이 들어갈 수 있다.

19 ⓐ는 to부정사의 부사적 용법 중 '목적'에 해당한다. 따라서 '~하기 위해서'라고 해석되는 ②번이 옳다.

20 사막이 숲이 되었다는 내용은 나와 있지 않다.

21 황사 문제 해결책은 나무를 심는 것이다. to plant trees라고 써도 좋다.

22 ⓐ 문제를 해결하고 싶지만 어디에 식물을 심어야 할지 몰랐고, ⓑ 행복한 이유를 설명하고 있으므로 각각 however, because가 옳다.

23 동아리 회원이 몇 명인지는 글에 나와 있지 않다.

24 식물을 어디에서 키워야 할지 몰라서 친구에게 조언을 구했다고 하였으므로 어법에 맞게 빈칸에 쓴다.

25 새로운 식물이 자라나는 작고 단단한 식물의 부분은 '씨앗'이다.

서술형 실전문제   p.102~103

01 I can't wait to see you at the center.

02 They are going to volunteer at a lost pet center this Friday.

03 Because he loves animals.

04 can you tell me what to do so that I can be smart?

05 can you borrow me some money so that I can pay my rent?

06 how to / I should think

07 I got a new job so that I could earn more money.

08 The man gave me some time in order that I could check my e-mail.

09 to keep away from an unwelcome guest in the spring: yellow dust

10 ⓐ what to do   ⓑ Wear a mask

11 they plant trees

12 The Chinese feel thankful to Korean volunteers.

13 They plant trees so that they can help not only China but also Korea.

02 Chris와 Emily는 이번 주 금요일에 유기동물센터에서 봉사활동을 할 것이다.

03 Chris는 동물들을 매우 좋아하기 때문에 Emily와 함께 하고 싶어 한다.

04 '내가 똑똑해지기 위해서'라고 했으므로 목적의 부사절 접속사 so that을 이용하여 문장을 만든다.

05 내가 임대료를 낼 수 있도록 돈을 빌려달라는 문장으로 쓸 수 있다.

06 '의문사+to부정사'는 '의문사+주어+should+동사원형'과 같다.

07 earn: ~을 벌다

08 check my e-mail: 나의 이메일을 확인하다

09 목적의 부사절 so that은 to부정사를 써서 나타낼 수 있다.

10 답변으로 보아 '무엇을 해야 할지 모르겠다.'는 말이 들어가는 것

이 옳으며 마스크를 쓰라고 답할 수 있다.

11 unless는 if~not과 같다.

12 중국 사람들은 한국인 자원봉사자들에게 늘 고마워한다고 하였다.

13 중국뿐만 아니라 한국을 돕기 위해서 나무를 심는다고 하였다. so that은 목적의 부사절이므로 주어와 동사를 포함하는 것에 유의한다.

창의사고력 서술형 문제
p.104

|모범답안|

01 (A) the soccer match last week

(B) play soccer for a month

(C) Kevin is good at playing soccer

02 (1) I don't know where to find my key.

(2) I would like to know where to go for the club meeting.

(3) Can you tell me when to go to the club meeting?

(4) I can't remember what to do for my homework. / Mom taught me how to bake cookies.

(5) Let me know when to ask the questions. / I wonder whom to ask the questions.

03 (1) Kevin went to England so that he could learn English.

(2) I bought the picture in order that I could give it to you.

(3) We need to exercise so that we can stay healthy.

(4) I study hard so that my mom can feel proud of me.

01 나는 오늘 John의 발을 보았을 때 놀랐다. 그는 지난주 축구 경기에서 그의 발을 다쳤다고 이야기했다. 나는 그의 발이 많이 다쳤음이 틀림없다고 생각했다. 그는 내게 그가 한 달 동안 축구를 해서는 안 된다고 이야기했다. 그는 다음 경기에 대해 걱정했다. 그래서 나는 Kevin을 그에게 추천했다. 왜냐하면 그는 축구를 잘하기 때문이다. John은 매우 기뻐 보였고 그가 다음 경기에 참여할 수 있는지 물어 보려고 그에게 갔다. 나는 그를 도와주어 기뻤다.

 단원별 모의고사
p.105~108

01 ②   02 (1) desert (2) volunteer activity

03 ④

04 (1) Mike speaks not only English but also French.

(2) We need to get rid of all this trash.

(3) Would you turn off the air conditioner?

05 He told me that it was terrible.

---

06 They are going to take a walk in the park.

07 (E) → (D) → (C) → (A) → (B) 08 ⓔ → seeing

09 volunteer 10 ①

11 I'm looking forward to the school festival this weekend. 12 ①   13 ④

14 Harry cleans his classroom so that it becomes very clean.   15 ①, ③   16 ③

17 He draws every day in order that he can become a painter.   18 ③   19 ②

20 to get rid of the yellow dust

21 planting trees   22 (C)–(A)–(D)–(B)

23 ④   24 ③   25 bad air

01 넓은 지역에 걸쳐서 또는 많은 사람들 사이에서 존재하거나 일어나는 것을 가리키는 말은 widespread(널리 퍼진)이다.

03 주어진 문장에서 match는 '시합, 경기'를 의미하며 이와 같은 뜻으로 쓰인 것은 ④번이다. ①, ③, ⑤번은 ~에 어울리다, ②번은 성냥을 의미한다.

06 Alex와 Jane은 함께 공원에서 산책을 할 것이다.

07 (E) 발을 다쳤음을 설명함 → (D) 병원에 갔었는지 질문 → (C) 대답 및 의사의 소견 설명 → (A) 다음 경기에 대해 질문 → (B) 대답

08 look forward to ~ing: ~하기를 기대하다

09 강요받거나 그것에 대해 돈을 받지 않고 무언가를 하기 위해 자청하는 것을 의미하는 것은 volunteer(자원봉사하다)이다.

12 긍정문에 대해 동의하는 표현으로 'So am I.'가 적절하다.

13 문장을 이끌고 있으므로 in order that이 옳다.

14 Harry의 교실이 깨끗해질 수 있도록 Harry가 청소를 한다는 문장으로 쓸 수 있다.

15 작가가 되기 위해서 많은 단편을 쓴다고 말할 수 있다. 목적의 부사절 접속사를 쓰는 것이 옳다.

16 내가 무슨 선물을 사야 할지 모르겠다는 의미이므로 what I should buy for her를 쓴다.

17 become: ~이 되다

18 나무를 심는 비용이 비싸지만 심어야 한다는 사실을 알고, 비단 중국을 위해서만이 아니라 한국을 위해서도 나무를 심는다는 내용이므로 however가 적절하다.

19 ② 해석: 사막에 나무를 심는 것이 비싸다고 말하기는 어렵다.

20 해결해야 할 문제는 황사를 없애는 것이다.

21 by Ving: V함으로써

22 아빠가 작은 정원에서 식물을 기르는 이유(C) → 나쁜 공기문제를 해결하기 위해 뭔가를 하고 싶은 지민에게 식물을 키우는 것이 문제 해결에 도움이 된다고 알려주지만 어디에 심어야 할지 지민은 모름(A) → 동아리 친구들에게 조언을 구하자 한 친구가 아이디어를 냄(D) → 동아리 회원들이 행복해 함(B)

23 ④ so as → so that

24 due to: ~ 때문에

25 나쁜 공기를 가리킨다.

I'll Always Be There for You.

시험대비 실력평가   p.112

01 attack   02 ⑤   03 ①

04 (1) His mother passed away when he was young.

(2) I'm getting better little by little.

(3) I have to take care of my younger sister.

05 ②   06 ①

07 (1) miracle   (2) taste   (3) touching   (4) thirsty

01 주어진 관계는 반의어 관계이다. attack: 공격하다, defend: 막다

02 be proud of: ~을 자랑스러워하다, take care of: ~을 돌보다, be afraid of: ~을 두려워하다

04 pass away: 죽다, little by little: 조금씩, 천천히

05 당신이 무언가를 성취하는 것을 막고 있는 문제를 다루거나 조절하는 데 성공하다를 가리키는 말은 overcome(극복하다)이다.

06 appreciate: 감사하다

07 miracle:기적, taste: 기호, 취향, touching: 감동적인, thirsty: 목마른

서술형 시험대비   p.113

01 receive

02 (1) In my opinion, it's a touching movie.

(2) What do you think of this picture?

(3) You know about Beethoven, don't you?

03 (1) nurse, blind   (2) be afraid of   (3) overcome

(4) passed away   (5) little by little (6) make a choice   04 blind

05 (1) In my opinion, she will be very happy if we visit her.

(2) When Annie started throwing things, the nurse wasn't afraid of her.

(3) I'll put the twins to bed.

06 (1) In my opinion, my English teacher is the kindest teacher in my school.

(2) Do you know about Mozart?

(3) Don't give up. You can do it too!

01 주어진 관계는 반의어 관계이다. send: 보내다, receive: 받다

03 pass away: 돌아가시다, little by little: 조금씩, make a choice: 선택하다

04 볼 수 없음을 나타내는 말은 blind이다.

교과서 Conversation

핵심 Check   p.114~115

1 (1) In my opinion

(2) What do you think about

(3) I believe you can make it

2 (1) don't you / Yes, I do   (2) I have no idea

(3) You know about

교과서 대화문 익히기

Check(√) True or False   p.116

(1) T   (2) F   (3) T   (4) F

교과서 확인학습   p.118~119

Everyday English 1 A. Function Practice 2-(1)

Why don't we choose / famous / In my opinion

Everyday English 1 A. Function Practice 2-(2)

In my opinion, boring / Everyone has different tastes

Everyday English 1 B. Listening Activity

worried / I'm worried about / social studies class / In my opinion, more interesting than / I should take his class too

Everyday English2 A. Function Practice 2-(1)

You know about / No, I don't / even though

Everyday English 2 A. Function Practice 2-(2)

not good at, give up / Of course I do / You can do it too

Everyday English 2 B. Listening Activity

sad, angry, myself / I had a choice / I decided to love my life / better, bitter, Choose better, forget bitter

In Real Life

history project, overcoming difficulties / don't you / too famous, interesting / Do you know

01 ①, ⑤　　02 ②, ④　　03 ②　　04 up

01 자신의 의견을 표현할 때, 'In my opinion' 또는 'I think ~' 등의 표현을 사용하여 나타낼 수 있다.

02 대화의 흐름상 상대방에게 Lee Hee Ah에 대해 알고 있는지 질문하는 표현이 적절하다.

03 대화의 흐름으로 보아 Amy는 Rick Allen을 알고 있으므로 ②번이 적절하다.

04 give up: 포기하다

01 Why　　　　02 ⑤　　　　03 ⓓ → interesting

04 ④　　　　05 She really loves the drums, but she's not good at playing.

06 Because he is the drummer with one arm.

07 ②　　　　08 ②　　　　09 ③　　　　10 ⑤

11 ④

01 Why don't we ~?: 우리 ~하는 게 어때?

02 소녀와 소년은 학교 연극으로 다른 이야기를 찾아볼 것이다.

03 interesting: 흥미로운, interested: 관심있는

05 Amy는 드럼을 매우 좋아하지만 연주를 잘하지는 못한다.

06 Rick Allen은 팔이 하나만 있는 드럼 연주가이다.

07 despair: 절망

08 화자는 '네 삶에 행복해라.'는 메시지를 전달하고 있다.

09 주어진 문장은 누구를 선택했느냐는 질문에 대한 대답으로 적절하므로 (C)가 적절하다.

10 대화를 통해 Little Annie가 Junho의 과제에 좋은 주제가 될 수 있는 이유는 알 수 없다.

11 너는 그에 대해 알고 있지, 그렇지?라는 질문에는 Yes, I do, 또는 No, I don't으로 대답한다.

01 She is worried about history.

02 It was a little boring for her.

03 His advice is to take Mr. Choi's afterschool class.

04 Because he got a high score on his history test after taking his class.

05 math → math score

06 (A)had a story of overcoming difficulties in life

(B)who I should choose

(C)Little Annie

(D)a video about her life

05 역사 점수와 수학을 비교할 수 없으므로 수학이 아니라 수학 점수로 고쳐야 한다.

06 오늘 Olivia를 만났을 때 나는 나의 역사 과제를 하고 있었다. 내 과제는 삶에서 어려움을 극복한 이야기를 갖고 있는 유명한 사람에 대해 쓰는 것이었다. 나는 Helen Keller를 생각하고 있었다. 하지만 Olivia는 그녀는 너무 유명해서 흥미롭지 않을 수 있다고 이야기 했다. 나는 그녀에게 프로젝트를 위해 누구를 선택해야하는지 물어보았다. 그녀는 Little Annie를 추천하였고 내게 그녀의 삶에 대한 비디오를 보여 주었다. 나는 내 주제를 선택할 수 있도록 도와준 그녀에게 고마웠다.

1 (1) to meet　(2) to tell me　(4) to write on

(5) to worry about

2 (1) The puppy does look cute.

(2) I did make the pizza by myself.

(3) Kelly does want to buy the car.

(4) The boy did understand what you said.

(5) We did have dinner together.

01 (1) believed → believe　(2) eat → to eat

(3) does → do　(4) to winning → to win

02 (1) to speak　(2) did　(3) to study　(4) to solve

(5) does

03 (1) Click the title of the message to read.

(2) There are many options to choose.

(3) I did win the first prize.

(4) You do have talent.

01 (1) 동사를 강조하는 do 뒤에는 동사 원형을 쓴다. (2) '먹을 어떤 것'이란 의미이므로 to eat으로 something을 수식하도록 만든다. (3) 복수 명사 주어이므로 do를 쓴다. (4) '이길 가능성'이므로 to win이 chance를 수식하도록 만든다.

02 (1), (3), (4) 번은 to부정사로 앞의 명사 the ability, no desire, another way를 수식하게 만든다. (2) 시점이 '어제'이므로 과거시제를 이용하여 동사를 강조한다. (5) 주어가 3인칭 단수이므로 does를 써서 동사를 강조하는 것에 유의한다.

03 (1) '읽을 메시지'이므로 to read가 the message를 수식하도

록 문장을 만든다. (2) '선택할 선택지'이므로 to부정사를 형용사 용법으로 써서 to choose가 options를 수식하게 만든다. (3), (4) 동사를 강조할 때 시제에 유의한다. 상을 탄 것은 과거이고 재능이 있다는 것은 현재로 표현한다.

시험대비 실력평가　　　　　　　p.127~129

01 ④　　　　02 ③　　　　03 ③
04 Molly did want to meet him soon.　　05 ③
06 ⑤　　　　07 The scissors do look dangerous.
08 ③　　　09 ②　　　10 ③　　　11 ⑤
12 I am looking for something to give to my mom.
13 ③　　　14 fighting → to fight / does need → do need　　15 ②
16 Junho does want to be a historian. 17 ⑤　18 ③
19 ②　　　　20 ④　　　　21 ③
22 I do need money to buy a car.
23 to go there

01 your feet은 복수명사이므로 do를 써서 동사를 강조한다. 나머지는 모두 does가 들어간다.

02 모두 to부정사의 형용사적 용법으로 쓰였으나 ③번은 부사적 용법 중 '목적'으로 쓰인 to부정사이다.

03 -thing으로 끝나는 대명사는 '형용사+to부정사' 어순으로 뒤에서 수식받는다.

04 wanted가 과거시제이므로 did를 써서 동사를 강조하고 want는 동사원형을 만들어 강조하는 문장을 쓸 수 있다.

05 Your pants는 복수 주어이므로 do를 써서 강조한다.

06 'The news does make me disappointed.'라고 쓰는 것이 옳다.

07 가위는 항상 복수 취급하는 명사이다. 따라서 강조하는 문장을 쓸 때 do를 쓰는 것이 옳다.

08 '사람을 들어올리는 능력'이란 의미이므로 to hold up을 써서 앞선 명사 the ability를 수식하도록 만드는 것이 옳다.

09 ⓑ와 ⓒ만 옳은 문장이다. ⓐ did keep, ⓓ My attempt to fix, ⓔ did steal로 고쳐야 한다.

10 '내려야 할 결정'이므로 to make가 an important decision을 수식하고, '정말로 심각하게 들린다'는 의미이므로 단수 주어에 맞추어 does를 써서 문장을 완성한다.

11 주어진 문장에서 쓰인 to부정사는 형용사적 용법이다. 따라서 '나를 저녁식사에 초대하는 친절함'으로 해석되는 ⑤번이 답이다.

12 '엄마께 드릴 어떤 것'이므로 to give to my mom이 something을 수식하도록 문장을 만든다.

13 과거에 만든 것이므로 did를 쓰고 뒤에 동사원형을 붙이는 것이

옳다.

14 '질병을 퇴치하는 능력'으로 to fight off illness가 the body's ability를 수식하도록 문장을 쓰는 것이 옳다. 또한 복수 주어 we이므로 do를 써서 강조한다.

15 복수 주어이므로 do를 써서 강조하는 것이 옳다.

16 3인칭 단수 주어에 현재시제이므로 does를 써서 문장을 만든다.

17 모두 복수 명사를 주어로 하고 있다.

18 강조하는 말이므로 주어와 시제에 맞추어 does play를 쓸 수 있다.

19 -one으로 끝나는 대명사이므로 '형용사+to부정사' 어순으로 뒤에서 수식한다

20 여기서 The Roberts는 Robert 부부를 의미하므로 do를 써서 동사를 강조하는 것이 옳다.

21 모두 '~하기 위해서'라고 해석되는 to부정사의 부사적 용법 중 '목적'이지만, ③번은 형용사로 쓰인 to부정사이다.

22 '자동차를 살 돈'이라고 하였으므로 to buy a car가 money를 수식하도록 문장을 만든다.

23 '그곳으로 가는'이 '방법'을 수식하는 구조이다. 따라서 the best way to go there를 쓸 수 있다.

서술형 시험대비　　　　　　　　p.130~131

01 There is no reason to accept her apology
02 Body language does vary from culture to culture.
03 A: do look busy, B: many things to do
04 (1) Parker does like to study math.
　　(2) Emily did go on winter vacation.
　　(3) Your mom did worry about you.
　　(4) They do know what to do next.
05 I have the right to protect my children.
06 do have, to say
07 did see a man standing over there
08 She does need some time to think about it.
09 did make
10 However, she did dance to music at the contest.
11 She had chances to talk about her life.
12 Her story did move many people.
13 I do want to eat something sweet.
14 to play or study with / 또는 to study or play with
15 I do appreciate your advice.
16 (1) does makes → does make
　　(2) do need → does need / to sleep → to sleep in
　　(3) does have → did have / talk → to talk

21

01 accept an apology: 사과를 받아들이다

02 vary: 다르다 from culture to culture: 문화마다

03 '정말로 바빠 보인다'고 하였으므로 동사를 강조하여 do look busy를 쓸 수 있다.

04 (1) 3인칭 단수 주어에 현재시제이므로 does를 써서 강조, (2), (3) 과거시제를 쓰고 있으므로 did를 써서 강조, (4) 복수 주어에 현재시제이므로 do를 써서 강조한다.

05 '보호할 권리'라고 하였으므로 to protect가 the right를 수식하게 문장을 만든다.

06 have many things to say: 할 말이 많이 있다

07 저쪽에 서 있는 남자를 정말로 봤다는 강조의 말을 쓸 수 있다.

08 '그것에 관하여 생각할 시간'이라고 하였으므로 'to think about it'이 some time을 수식하도록 문장을 만든다.

09 Susan이 이 인형을 정말로 만들었다는 강조의 말이 들어가는 것이 자연스럽다.

10 dance to music: 음악에 맞추어 춤을 추다

11 to talk about her life가 chances를 수식하는 구조이다.

12 과거동사이므로 did를 써서 강조문을 만든다. move: ~를 감동시키다

13 '달콤한 무언가'이므로 something sweet을 쓴다. -thing으로 끝나는 부정대명사는 형용사의 수식을 뒤에서 받는 것에 유의하여 답을 쓴다.

14 함께 공부하거나 놀 친구가 없다는 의미이다.

15 appreciate은 현재동사이며 주어가 I이므로 do를 써서 동사를 강조할 수 있다.

16 (1) 동사를 강조하는 does 뒤에는 동사원형이 온다. (2) Amelia는 3인칭 단수 주어이므로 does가 옳으며, 'sleep in a bed'이므로 to sleep in을 써야 한다. (3) yesterday이므로 did를 써서 동사를 강조해야 하며, '그와 대화할 시간'이란 의미이므로 to talk with him으로 time을 수식하는 것이 옳다.

Reading

확인문제   p.132

1 F   2 T   3 F   4 F   5 T

확인문제   p.133

1 T   2 T   3 F   4 F   5 T

교과서 확인학습 A   p.134~135

01 was, blind girl 02 always angry 03 tried to help, screamed, attacked   04 called her, try to help   05 somebody to take care of
06 came to   07 volunteered to help
08 started throwing   09 However, afraid of there   10 to be your friend, always be there   11 went to, put her to bed
12 do love you, always be there   13 that, needed
14 With, little by little
15 scream or throw different   16 did become, different   17 call her, anymore
18 to leave, with 19 took, to, for   20 loved, studied
21 to become, help others, did   22 a few years later, passed away   23 did not give up   24 one day, met
25 to see well   26 a miracle for   27 realized, became   28 to meet a special student
29 wasn't able to 30 Instead, screamed, threw
31 just like   32 said to, always be there

교과서 확인학습 B   p.136~137

1 There was a little blind girl in a hospital.

2 She was always angry.

3 When people tried to help her, she screamed and attacked them.

4 People called her "Crazy Little Annie," and didn't try to help her anymore.

5 The poor girl needed somebody to take care of her.

6 One day, an old nurse came to the hospital.

7 She volunteered to help Annie.

8 When Annie met her, she started throwing things again.

9 However, the nurse wasn't afraid of her.

10 The nurse said to Annie, "Hi, Annie. I'm Nurse Laura. I'm here to be your friend. I'll always be there for you."

11 Every night, Laura went to Annie's room and put her to bed.

12 She said to Annie, "Annie, I do love you. I'll always be there for you."

13 Laura knew that Annie needed love and understanding.

14 With Laura's help, Annie got better little by little.

15 Two years later, Annie didn't scream or throw things.

16 She did become a totally different person.

17 People didn't call her "Crazy Little Annie" anymore.

18 Laura decided to leave the hospital with Annie.

19 She took Annie to a school for blind children.

20 Annie loved her new school and studied hard.

21 She wanted to become a teacher and help others like Nurse Laura did.

22 However, a few years later, Laura passed away.

23 Annie was very sad, but she did not give up on her dream.

24 Then one day, Annie met a nice doctor.

25 He helped Annie to see well.

26 It was a miracle for Annie.

27 At last, Annie realized her dream and became a teacher.

28 This gave her a chance to meet a special student.

29 The student wasn't able to hear or see.

30 Instead, she screamed and threw things.

31 She was just like Crazy Little Annie.

32 Annie said to her, "Hi, Helen Keller. I'm your teacher, Anne Sullivan. I'll always be there for you."

시험대비 실력평가 p.138~141

01 ②　　　02 ④　　　03 She volunteered to help Annie.　04 blind　　05 ④　　06 ③
07 She did become a totally different person.
08 ④　　　09 She took Annie to a school for blind children.　10 ⓐto leave ⓑto become
11 ②　　　12 ②　　　13 꿈을 실현하고 교사가 된 것
14 ④　　　15 ④　　　16 ④　　　17 ④
18 ③　　　19 ③　　　20 ④　　　21 ④
22 She went to Annie's room and put her to bed.
23 ③　　　24 19개월이 되었을 때 매우 아팠던 것
25 ②
26 One day, Anne did make Helen feel water.
27 ④　　　28 see or hear, feel things　29 ④
30 The first thing that Helen felt was water.

01 모두 Annie를 가리키는 대명사이지만 ②번은 Laura이다.

02 Laura는 모두가 포기한 Annie를 돕겠다고 하였다.

03 Laura 간호사는 Annie를 돕겠다고 자원하였다.

04 '볼 수 없는' 것은 blind(눈 먼)이다.

05 빈칸 ⓐ에는 do를 써서 동사를 강조한다. 시점이 과거이므로 ④번에는 did가 들어간다.

06 get better: 좋아지다

07 과거동사이므로 did를 써서 강조한다.

08 Annie는 소리 지르거나 물건을 던지지 않는다고 하였다.

09 Laura는 병원을 떠나 Annie를 시각장애인 학교에 데려갔다고 하였다.

10 decide와 want는 모두 to부정사를 목적어로 취하는 동사이다.

11 ⓐ는 to부정사의 부사적 용법 중 '목적'에 해당한다. 따라서 '~하기 위해서'라고 해석되는 ②번이 옳다.

12 '마침내'라는 의미의 Finally가 대신 쓰일 수 있다.

13 교사가 되어 특별한 학생을 만날 기회를 얻은 것이다.

14 ④ Annie는 포기하지 않고 꿈을 실현하여 교사가 되었다.

15 특별한 학생은 Helen Keller이다.

16 눈 먼 소녀는 항상 화가 나 있어서 사람들을 공격했음 → 사람들은 소녀를 더 이상 도우려 하지 않음 → 어느 날 한 나이든 간호사가 Annie를 돕고자 하지만 Annie는 물건을 또 던짐 → 그러나 간호사는 두려워하지 않음

17 not ~ anymore는 '더 이상 ~하지 않은'이란 의미이다.

18 밑줄 친 ⓐ는 동사의 목적어로 쓰인 to부정사이다. ①, ④ 명사를 수식하는 형용사, ② 부사적 용법 중 목적, ③ plan의 목적어로 쓰인 to부정사, ⑤ 진주어로 쓰인 to부정사이다.

19 little by little: 조금씩

20 Laura가 Annie와 함께 병원을 떠나 Annie를 시각장애인 학교에 데려갔고, Annie는 새로운 학교를 좋아했다는 순서가 적절하므로 ④번에 들어가는 것이 옳다.

21 빈도부사의 위치는 조동사 뒤, 과거의 일이므로 did를 써서 동사를 강조하고, help others를 받아주는 말이므로 대동사로 did를 쓴다.

22 매일 밤 Annie의 방으로 가서 그녀를 재웠다고 하였다.

23 Annie가 왜 물건을 던지거나 소리 지르곤 했는지는 알 수 없다.

24 아팠던 이후로 듣거나 볼 수 없었다는 것이다.

25 결과를 이끄는 접속사 so가 적절하다.

26 일반동사의 과거형이므로 did를 써서 강조한다.

27 (A) ask+목적어+to부정사: 목적어가 V하도록 요청하다. (B) 부사절을 이끌고 있으므로 so that. (C) 둘 중 남은 하나는 the other이다. 정관사 the를 대신하여 Helen's가 있으므로 other만 쓸 수 있다.

28 Helen이 보거나 들을 수는 없었다 할지라도 사물을 느낄 수는 있었다.

29 ⓓ Helen은 오랫동안 Anne의 가르침을 이해하지 못했다.

30 Helen이 처음으로 느낀 것은 water(물)이었다..

01 I'll always be there for you.

02 People did call her "Crazy Little Annie."

03 She started to throw[throwing] things again.

04 I don't need anyone to help me.

05 Laura knew that Annie did need love and understanding.

06 helped others

07 People used to call Annie "Crazy Little Annie."

08 do love

09 ⓐpassed ⓑrealize ⓒto meet

10 (to) see

11 She met a nice doctor and was able to see well.

12 Anne made Helen feel water.

13 to teach our daughter

14 She began to write words into Helen's hand.

15 At this point, Helen did understand the lesson and wrote w–a–t–e–r on Anne's hand.

01 빈도부사의 위치에 유의하여 답을 쓴다.

02 과거동사이므로 did를 써서 동사를 강조하는 것에 유의한다.

03 Laura 간호사를 만났을 때 Annie는 다시 물건을 던지기 시작하였다.

04 부정문이므로 anyone을 쓰고, '나를 도와 줄 누군가'이므로 to help me가 anyone을 수식하도록 문장을 만들 수 있다.

05 과거동사이므로 did를 써서 강조하는 문장을 만든다.

06 Laura가 다른 사람들을 도왔던 것처럼 자신도 다른 사람들을 돕고 싶었다는 의미이다.

07 used to V: (과거에) ~하곤 했다

08 Annie는 새로운 학교를 좋아했다고 하였다.

09 ⓐ pass away: 세상을 떠나다 ⓑ 강조의 조동사 뒤에 동사원형, ⓒ a chance를 수식하는 형용사 용법의 to부정사

10 help는 준사역동사이다. to부정사나 원형부정사를 목적격 보어로 취한다.

11 Annie에게 기적은 좋은 의사를 만나 잘 볼 수 있게 된 것이었다.

12 make+목적어+원형부정사: 목적어가 V하게 하다

13 Helen을 가르쳐 달라고 부탁했다고 하였다.

14 Helen이 글자를 배울 수 있도록 Anne은 Helen의 손에 낱말을 쓰기 시작했다.

15 일반동사 과거형이므로 did를 써서 강조한다.

01 ①   02 ②   03 ④   04 ④

05 (1) At last (2) throw (3) decide (4) difficulties

06 ③   07 ⑤   08 They are going to find another story.   09 don't you?

10 two fingers 11 ⓔ → preparing   12 contest

13 ④   14 ①, ③   15 ⑤   16 ③

17 ⑤   18 Porter does enjoy watching movies on Saturday nights.   19 ③   20 ④

21 The Beatles did become a famous band.

22 ⑤   23 ④   24 I do need a chair to sit on.   25 ②

26 Tom does have something to show you.   27 ②

28 ④   29 ⑤

30 She screamed and attacked them.

31 She did not give up on her dream.

32 couldn't hear or see   33 ⑤   34 ③

01 사실보다는 누군가 또는 무언가에 대한 당신의 생각이나 느낌을 가리키는 말은 opinion(의견)이다.

02 composer: 작곡가

03 give up: 포기하다

04 throw: 던지다

06 주어진 문장에서 appreciate은 '감사하다, 고마워하다'를 나타내며 이와 같은 의미로 쓰인 것은 ③번이다. ①, ②번은 '감상하다' ④번은 '이해하다', ⑤번은 '인식하다'는 뜻을 나타낸다.

07 ⑤번을 제외한 나머지는 모두 제안을 나타낸다.

08 햄릿을 선택하는 대신 다른 이야기를 찾아볼 것이다.

10 Lee Hee Ah는 놀라운 피아니스트이다. 왜냐하면 그녀는 각 손에 오직 두 개의 손가락만 가졌음에도 피아노를 매우 잘 치기 때문이다.

11 enjoy는 동명사를 목적어로 취한다.

12 사람들이 무언가를 쟁취하려고 노력하는 경쟁을 가리키는 말은 contest(경연)이다.

13 학생들은 그들의 공연을 심사하기 위해 담임선생님을 초대할 수 있다는 진술은 위의 설명과 일치하지 않는다.

14 difficulty는 어려움을 뜻하며 이와 바꾸어 쓸 수 있는 것은 adversity(역경), hardship(고난, 어려움)이다.

16 ③ 시점이 last month이므로 did를 쓰는 것이 옳다.

17 흥미를 유발하는 사람이라는 의미이므로 interesting을 쓰고 –one으로 끝나는 부정대명사이므로 '형용사+to부정사' 어순으로 뒤에서 수식받는다.

18 현재시제에 주어가 3인칭 단수이므로 does를 써서 동사를 강조한다.

19 모두 명사적 용법의 to부정사이지만 ③번은 앞선 명사를 수식하는 형용사로 쓰인 to부정사이다.

20 현재 상황을 이야기하고 있으므로 do로 동사를 강조, -thing으

로 끝나는 대명사는 '형용사+to부정사' 어순으로 뒤에서 수식받으므로 ④번이 옳다.

21 시점이 과거이므로 did를 써서 동사를 강조한다.

22 ⑤ to talk to 혹은 to talk with를 쓰는 것이 옳다. ① found: 창립[설립]하다

23 과거의 일이므로 did를 쓰는 것이 옳다.

24 sit on[in] a chair이므로 to sit on[in]까지 쓰는 것에 유의한다.

25 주어진 문장의 to부정사는 형용사로 쓰였다. ② toys를 수식하는 to play with 역시 to부정사의 형용사적 용법이다.

26 '너에게 보여줄 것'이라고 하였으므로 something to show you라고 쓸 수 있다.

27 빈칸 ⓐ에는 take가 들어간다. ① look after: 돌보다 ② take off: 이륙하다 ③ look forward to: ~을 기대하다 ④ come up with: (생각을) 떠올리다 ⑤ make up one's mind: 결심하다

28 Annie가 물건을 집어던졌지만 간호사는 두려워하지 않았으므로 However가 가장 적절하다.

29 Laura는 Annie를 두려워하지 않았다고 하였다. threatened: 위협을 느끼다

30 사람들이 Annie를 도와주려 할 때 Annie는 소리 지르고 사람들을 공격하였다.

31 give up on: (~에 대해 기대 등을 갖기를) 포기[단념]하다

32 be able to 동사원형 = can 동사원형: ~할 수 있다

33 [D] 의사는 Annie가 잘 볼 수 있게 도와줌 - [A] 마침내 Annie는 꿈을 실현하여 교사가 됨 - [C] 이것은 그녀에게 특별한 학생을 만날 기회를 줌 - [B] 그 학생은 듣거나 볼 수 없었음

34 Annie는 Laura가 죽어서 슬펐던 것이다. walk away from: (힘든 상황이나 관계를 외면하고) 떠나다

단원별 예상문제
p.150~153

01 She recommends *Hamlet*.
02 He thinks that it's too sad for their school play.
03 ①, ③   04 ⑤   05 (D) → (B) → (C) → (A)
06 (A) boring, (B) has   07 ②
08 She thinks it is a little boring.   09 ④
10 ⑤   11 ③   12 ②
13 She does have something to discuss with you.
14 ①   15 ③   16 ⑤
17 I want to have the ability to speak English well.
18 ③   19 ④   20 She wanted to become a teacher and help others like Nurse Laura did.
21 scream   22 ④   23 ②   24 ③
25 did help Annie

01 소녀는 햄릿을 학교 연극으로 추천한다.

02 소년은 학교 연극으로 햄릿은 너무 슬프다고 생각한다.

03 pleased: 기쁜, confident: 자신감 있는, satisfied: 만족한

04 ⑤ Amy가 사회 시험에서 몇 점을 받았는지는 알 수 없다.

05 (D) 걱정을 이야기함 → (B) Rick Allen을 알고 있는지 질문 → (C) 대답 → (A) 격려

06 boring: 지루한, 따분한, bored: 지루해 하는, (B) everyone은 단수 취급하므로 단수 동사 has가 알맞다.

07 (C)는 기호 또는 취향을 나타내며 이와 같은 의미로 쓰인 것은 ②번이다.

08 소녀는 *The Old Man and the Sea*가 지루하다고 생각했다.

09 삶의 선택에 대한 이야기를 읽은 후 자신의 삶을 사랑하기로 결정했다는 내용이 자연스러우므로 (D)가 적절하다.

11 ⓑ, ⓓ, ⓔ가 옳은 문장이다. ⓐ does join, ⓒ something boring to see

12 모두 명사로 쓰인 to부정사이지만 ②번은 형용사로 쓰인 to부정사이다.

13 '너와 함께 논의할 무언가'이므로 to discuss with you가 something을 수식하도록 문장을 만든다.

14 mice는 mouse의 복수형임에 유의한다.

15 위 우리말을 영어로 쓰면 'I know that he does need my help.'이다.

16 동사를 강조하는 does 뒤에는 동사원형이 온다.

17 '영어를 잘 말할 수 있는 능력'이라고 하였으므로 to speak English well이 the ability를 수식하도록 문장을 만든다.

18 밑줄 친 ⓐ는 명사절 접속사로 완전한 문장을 이끈다. ③번은 불완전한 문장을 이끄는 관계대명사이다. beside the point: 핵심에서 벗어난

19 ④ Annie가 무엇을 공부했는지는 알 수 없다.

20 Annie는 선생님이 되어 간호사 Laura가 그랬듯 다른 사람들을 돕고 싶다고 하였다.

21 큰 목소리로 소리 지르는 것은 scream이다.

22 주어진 문장의 The student가 가리키는 것은 a special student이다.

23 ⓑ hardly → hard / hardly: 거의 ~하지 않는

24 ③ Laura는 간호사이다.

25 의사가 정말로 Annie가 잘 볼 수 있게 도왔다는 문장을 쓰는 문제이다. 동사를 강조하여 문장을 쓸 수 있다.

서술형 실전문제
p.154~155

01 They are talking about the topic for Junho's history project.

02 Because she is too famous and it may not be

interesting.

03 They are going to watch the video on Little Annie's life.

04 (C) → (B) → (D) → (A)

05 They were filled with the desire to see their homeland again.

06 (1) She does make me happy.

(2) I do have some time to help you.

07 something important to say

08 Mr. Jefferson does visit us very often.

09 to talk about

10 A[The] cameleon is famous for its ability to change colors.

11 With Laura's help, Annie did get better little by little.

12 does go to

13 Laura decided to leave the hospital with Annie.

14 ⓐ English book to read ⓑ English video to watch

15 English did become one of my favorite subject.

01 Olivia와 Junho는 Junho의 과제 주제에 대해 이야기하고 있다.

02 Olivia는 Junho의 프로젝트 주제로 Helen Keller는 너무 유명해서 흥미롭지 않을지도 모르기 때문에 좋아하지 않는다.

03 Olivia와 Junho는 Little Annie의 삶에 관한 비디오를 시청할 것이다.

04 (C) 알고 있는지 질문 → (B) 대답 및 구체적 설명 요청 → (D) 구체적 설명 → (A) 놀라움 표현

05 be filled with: ~으로 가득 차 있다 desire: 열망, 욕구

06 (1) make someone happy: ~를 행복하게 하다 (2) '너를 도와줄 시간'이므로 to부정사가 some time을 수식하도록 문장을 만든다.

07 -thing으로 끝나는 대명사의 수식은 '형용사+to부정사'의 어순으로 뒤에서 수식한다.

08 3인칭 단수 주어에 현재시제이므로 does를 써서 강조한다.

09 talk about something이므로 전치사 about을 쓰는 것이 옳다.

10 색깔을 바꾸는 능력'이므로 to change color가 its ability를 수식하도록 문장을 만들 수 있다.

11 일반동사 과거형을 쓰고 있으므로 did를 써서 동사를 강조한다.

12 그녀가 정말로 Annie의 방으로 매일 밤 간다는 말을 강조하는 문장이다.

13 Laura는 Annie와 함께 병원을 떠나기로 결정하였다.

14 to부정사의 형용사적 용법을 이용하여 쓸 수 있다.

15 문장 ⓓ는 동사를 강조하여 쓴 문장이다.

|모범답안|

01 (A) Mr. Choi's afterschool class

(B) it was a little boring for me

(C) he got a high score on his history test after taking Mr. Choi's class

(D) take his class

02 (1) William Hoy made up some signs to use.

(2) The government has a plan to create jobs.

(3) There are so many decisions to make.

(4) I want to have the ability to remember people's face well.

(5) We had a good opportunity to be friends with each other. / Is there a cheaper way to mail it?

03 (1) I do love your doll.

(2) She did ask me to help her.

(3) Thomas always does make me laugh.

(4) We did learn how to play the piano.

(5) Karen does call me every night.

01 내가 나의 역사 점수에 대해 걱정할 때 Brian이 내게 조언을 했다. 나는 내 역사 점수가 수학 점수보다 낮았을 때 충격을 받았다. 그때 Brian은 Choi 선생님의 방과 후 수업을 들을 것을 추천하였다. 처음에는 그의 수업을 또 다시 듣고 싶지 않았다. 왜냐하면 지난달 내가 그의 사회 수업을 들었을 때 내게는 좀 지루했기 때문이다. 하지만 그는 그의 역사 수업이 사회 수업 보다 더 흥미롭다고 말했다. 게다가 그는 Choi 선생님의 수업을 들은 후 역사 시험에서 높은 점수를 받았다고 말했다. 나는 내 역사 점수를 향상시키기 위해 그의 수업을 듣기로 결심했다.

01 ①, ③　　02 ⑤　　03 hope

04 He decided to love his life.

05 He gives speeches around the world, and gives people hope.

06 (A) the school radio's project, (B) a letter

07 ⑤

08 The class singing contest is supposed to be held.

09 They should hand in the title of their songs by the end of this week.

10 They can invite their homeroom teachers to join their performance.

11 (A) playing the drums, (B) give up, (C) the drummer with one arm

12 (1) I'll tell people that they should not give up

their dreams.

(2) My mother is proud of me.

(3) Mike is putting his baby to bed.   13 on[in]

14 ④   15 ④   16 ④

17 Ross did do his homework. 18 ①   19 ②, ④

20 (D)-(B)-(A)-(C)   21 ④   22 ⑤

23 ⑤

24 She lost her sight after she was very sick when she was 19 months old.

25 I think Helen does understand the lesson.

---

02 주어진 문장에서 touching은 '감동적인'이란 의미로 이와 같은 의미를 나타내는 것은 ⑤번이다. 나머지는 모두 '만지다'를 의미한다.

03 당신이 원하는 무언가가 일어날 것이라는 믿음을 가리키는 말은 hope(희망)이다.

04 화자는 그의 삶을 사랑하기로 결심했다.

05 화자는 전 세계의 사람들을 위해 강연을 하고 희망을 주고 있다.

08 다음 주 금요일에 학급 노래 경연이 열리기로 되어 있다.

09 학생들은 이번 주 내로 그들의 노래 제목을 제출해야 한다.

10 S학생들은 공연을 함께 하기 위해 담임선생님을 초대할 수 있다.

11 나는 내가 드럼을 매우 좋아하지만 잘하지 못해서 우울했다. 내가 Bob에게 이것에 대해 이야기했을 때 그는 내가 포기하지 않도록 많은 격려를 해주었다. 그는 팔 하나 뿐인 드러머 Rick Allen에 대해 이야기했다. 나는 Bob에게 매우 고마웠다. 왜냐하면 그는 내게 Rick Allen처럼 해낼 수 있다고 이야기해 주었기 때문이다.

13 They do need chairs to sit on[in].

14 '투표할 권리'이므로 the right to vote, teeth는 tooth의 복수형이므로 do를 써서 강조한다.

15 ④ a chance to hear로 쓰는 것이 옳다. ① come to ~: ~ 하게 되다

16 '나를 도와줄 사람'이므로 to help me를 써야 하고, 아무도 없었다고 하였으므로 긍정문에 no one을 쓴 문장이 가장 적절하다.

17 일반농사 과거시제이므로 did를 써서 강조한다.

18 (A) 글의 흐름상 Annie와 함께 병원을 떠난 것이다. (B) 동사를 강조하는 did 뒤에는 동사원형을 써야 하며, (C) to become과 병렬로 to help가 선생님이 되어 다른 사람들을 돕기를 원했다고 말하는 것이 내용상 올바르다.

19 Annie는 선생님이 되기를 원했고, 사랑한다고 말해준 것은 Laura이며, 사람들은 더 이상 Annie를 Crazy Little Annie라고 부르지 않았다.

20 Laura의 도움으로 조금씩 좋아진 Annie는 더 이상 사람들을

공격하지 않았고, 마침내 병원을 나와 시각장애인 학교에 다니며 선생님이 되기 위해 열심히 공부했다.

21 ⓓ는 Annie를 가리키는 소유격 대명사이다.

22 make는 사역동사로 쓰였다. 따라서 원형부정사 feel을 써야 한다.

23 ⑤ Helen의 부모님이 Anne Sullivan을 언제 만났는지는 알 수 없다.

24 Helen이 19개월이 되었을 때 매우 아팠고, 그 후 더 이상 보거나 들을 수 없었다고 하였다.

25 현재시제의 일반동사이므로 does를 써서 강조한다.

교과서 파헤치기

Lesson 1

단어 TEST Step 3   p.04

1 skill, 기술   2 abroad, 해외로   3 photographer, 사진사
4 waste, 쓰레기, 폐기물   5 favorite, 가장 좋아하는
6 chart, 도표, 표   7 prepare, 준비하다   8 protect, 보호하다
9 actor, 배우   10 environmental, 환경의   11 pond, 연못
12 classmate, 급우, 반 친구   13 application, 지원서
14 leader, 지도자   15 costume, 의상, 복장
16 planet, 행성

단어 TEST Step 1   p.02

01 구내식당	02 관심, 흥미	03 환경의
04 도움이 되는	05 가장 좋아하는	06 공중 정지
07 요리	08 보호하다	09 지원(신청)서, 적용
10 주문하다	11 의상, 복장	
12 유능한, ~할 수 있는		13 제작진 승무원 선원
14 해외에(서), 해외로	15 쓰레기, 폐기물	16 동아리
17 줄이다	18 급우, 반 친구	19 배우
20 전통적인	21 사진사	22 성공한, 성공적인
23 직원	24 경치, 풍경	25 합계, 총액
26 틀린, 잘못된	27 준비하다	28 수행하다, 공연하다
29 사회의	30 상, 상품	31 그릇, 접시
32 자원 봉사자; 자원하다		33 기술, 솜씨
34 지도자	35 ~할 준비가 되다	36 수행하다
37 건강을 유지하다	38 ~에 관심이 있다	39 혼자서
40 ~에 참가하다	41 늦게까지 깨어 있다	42 ~에 빠지다
43 ~에 능숙하다		

단어 TEST Step 2   p.03

01 chart	02 direction	03 staff
04 plate	05 skill	06 wrong
07 prize	08 leader	09 social
10 perform	11 planet	12 leave
13 scenery	14 prepare	15 drone
16 quite	17 order	18 pond
19 successful	20 volunteer	21 total
22 cafeteria	23 environmental	24 hovering
25 photographer	26 costume	27 traditional
28 abroad	29 waste	30 protect
31 application	32 interest	33 helpful
34 reduce	35 be interested in	36 stay up late
37 be ready to	38 take part in	39 carry out
40 by oneself	41 fall into	42 keep in shape
43 be good at		

대화문 TEST Step 1   p.05~06

Everyday English 1. A Function Practice 2-(1)
hungry, have lunch / Let's, favorite food / Why don't we / good idea

Everyday English 1. B. Listening Activity
favorite hobby, asked, all of them, Most, said, watching movies, a total of, watching movies, favorite hobby, playing computer games, liked doing, Their favorite sports

Everyday English 2. A Function Practice 2-(1)
look tired, the matter / stayed up late / did watch / watched, I'm interested in

Everyday English 2. A Function Practice 2-(2)
are, doing / reading, Look at / looks delicious, What's, about / is about cooking, interested in cooking

Everyday English 2. A Function Practice 2-(3)
Why don't we go / free tickets / interested in, musical's title / wrote / can't wait to see

Everyday English 2 – B Listening Activity
classmates' interests / Let's look at / are interested in / will be / also shows / a big fan of / How about / not interested in / playing, is not good for / agree

In Real Life
you know what, have to choose / have in mind / interested in / Look at / said that, its activities / How about, favorite club / want to join, last year, didn't like / right / going to think about

대화문 TEST Step 2   p.07~08

Everyday English 1. A Function Practice 2-(1)
B: I'm hungry. Did you have lunch?
G: No. Let's have lunch together. What's your favorite food?
B: I love chicken. Why don't we order it?
G: That's a good idea.

G: What's your favorite hobby? We asked the students at our school and all of them answered the question. Most of the students said they liked watching movies. 20 boys and 42 girls loved it. This means a total of 62 students said watching movies was their favorite hobby. Many boys liked playing computer games. 32 boys and 13 girls liked doing that. 25 boys and 20 girls liked sports. Their favorite sports were soccer, baseball, and basketball.

G: You look tired. What's the matter?

B: I stayed up late to watch TV.

G: What did you watch?

B: I watched a traveling program. I'm interested in traveling.

G: What are you doing?

B: I'm reading a newspaper. Look at this picture.

G: The food in the picture looks delicious. What's the story about?

B: The story is about cooking. I'm interested in cooking.

G: Why don't we go to see a musical this Saturday? I have some free tickets.

B: Sure. I'm very interested in musicals. What's the musical's title?

G: It's The Shower. Hwang Sunwon wrote it.

B: Wow. I can't wait to see it.

Brian: Look! This is a chart about our classmates' interests.

Sujin: Let's look at it more closely. The chart shows that 30% of students are interested in sports. The school's Sports Day will be so much fun.

Brian: Right. The chart also shows that 27% of students are interested in actors. I know you are also a big fan of them.

Sujin: Yes. I love them. How about you?

Brian: I'm not interested in actors. I'm interested in computer games. 20% of students are interested in them.

Sujin: Computer games are fun, but playing them too much is not good for you.

Brian: I agree.

Junho: Adia, you know what? We have to choose our club next week.

Adia: I know. Which club do you have in mind, Junho?

Junho: I'm interested in the photo club.

Adia: Sounds great. Look at this chart. 80% of the photo club's members said that they liked its activities last year.

Junho: That's right. How about you, Adia? What's your favorite club?

Adia: I want to join the board game club. But last year its members said that they didn't like it much.

Junho: You're right. 60% of its members said they didn't like it.

Adia: Yes. I'm going to think about it more.

본문 TEST Step 1   p.09~10

01 leader of, Save, Earth
02 Our, environmental
03 volunteer, protect, planet
04 Protecting, important, isn't
05 carried, reduce, waste
06 campaign, successful
07 preparing, special, abroad
08 interested, saving, join   09 of, High
10 drone club   11 every part, by ourselves
12 own, practice hovering
13 Hovering, staying, place
14 good, will, ready, directions   15 getting, aren't
16 want, see, scenery   17 take, of, don't
18 join, famous, skills
19 Every, take part
20 joining, hobby, chance
21 Welcome, musical
22 there, groups, crew
23 choose, subject, together
24 practice, dancing, costumes
25 perform, musical, festival
26 get an application   27 join our, won't

본문 TEST Step 2   p.11~12

01 the leader of, Save the Earth
02 an environmental club
03 do volunteer work to protect
04 Protecting our planet, isn't it
05 Last year, carried out, to reduce food waste

06 was successful

07 preparing some special activities

08 are interested in saving, join us 09 of

10 It is, club   11 every part of, by ourselves

12 your own drone, need to practice hovering

13 Hovering, staying in

14 are good at, be ready to fly, in different directions

15 getting excited, aren't you

16 want to do, see beautiful scenery

17 to take a picture of, don't you

18 join our photo club, learn their skills

19 Every, can take part in

20 by joining, learn a new hobby, a chance of winning

21 Welcome to, musical

22 there are two groups, actors, crew

23 choose the subject, write a story together

24 practice singing, dancing, while, make costumes

25 perform, in the school festival

26 can get an application

27 join our club, won't you

19 매년 12월에 너는 학교 사진 대회에 참가할 수 있어.

20 그렇게 "Photo World"에 가입하는 것으로 너는 새로운 취미를 배우고 상을 받는 기회를 가질 수 있어.

21 나의 뮤지컬 동아리, "Story Singers"에 온 걸 환영해!

22 내 이름은 Olivia야. 뮤지컬 동아리에는 배우와 제작진이라는 두 그룹이 있어.

23 우리는 우선 뮤지컬의 주제를 고르고 함께 이야기를 써.

24 그리고는 제작진이 의상을 만드는 동안 배우들은 노래와 춤을 연습하지.

25 우리는 학교 축제에서 뮤지컬 공연을 해.

26 가입신청서는 나한테서 받을 수 있어.

27 너는 우리 동아리에 가입할 거야, 그렇지?

본문 TEST Step 3   p.13~14

1 모두들 안녕. 나는 수지이고 "Save the Earth" 동아리의 대표야.

2 우리 동아리는 환경 동아리야.

3 우리는 우리 행성(지구)을 지키기 위해 자원봉사 활동을 해.

4 지구를 지키는 것은 중요해, 그렇지 않니?

5 작년에 우리는 학교 식당에서 음식물 쓰레기 줄이기 캠페인을 했어.

6 캠페인은 성공적이었어.

7 올해 우리는 몇몇 특별한 해외 활동을 준비 중이야.

8 그러니, 지구를 구하는 데 관심이 있다면 우리와 함께하자

9 안녕, 친구들! 나는 "Fly High"의 Diego야.

10 그건 드론 동아리야.

11 우리는 드론의 모든 부분을 공부하고 우리 스스로 작은 드론을 만들어.

12 네 드론이 있으면, 너는 공중 정지를 연습해야 해.

13 "공중 정지"란 공중에서 한자리에 머무는 것을 의미해.

14 공중 정지를 잘한다면, 너는 너의 드론을 다른 방향으로 날릴 준비가 될 거야.

15 점점 흥미가 생기지, 그렇지 않니?

16 안녕, 난 준호야. 너는 아름다운 풍경을 볼 때 무엇을 하고 싶니?

17 사진을 찍고 싶을 거야, 그렇지 않니?

18 우리 사진 동아리 "Photo World"에 가입한다면 너는 유명한 사진작가들을 만나고, 그들의 기술을 배울 수 있어.

본문 TEST Step 4 - Step 5   p.15~18

1 Hello, everyone! I'm Suji and I'm the leader of the "Save the Earth" club.

2 Our club is an environmental club.

3 We do volunteer work to protect our planet.

4 Protecting our planet is important, isn't it?

5 Last year, we carried out a campaign to reduce food waste in the school cafeteria.

6 The campaign was successful.

7 This year, we are preparing some special activities abroad.

8 So, if you are interested in saving the planet, please join us.

9 Hello, friends! I'm Diego of "Fly High."

10 It is a drone club.

11 We study every part of a drone and make some small drones by ourselves.

12 When you have your own drone, you need to practice hovering.

13 "Hovering" means staying in the same place in the air.

14 Once you are good at hovering, you will be ready to fly your drone in different directions.

15 You're getting excited, aren't you?

16 Hello, I'm Junho. What do you want to do when you see beautiful scenery?

17 You want to take a picture of it, don't you?

18 If you join our photo club, "Photo World," you can meet famous photographers and learn their skills.

19 Every December, you can take part in the school photo contest.

20 So, by joining "Photo World" you can learn a new

a chance of winning a prize!

21 Welcome to my musical club, "Story Singers"!

22 My name is Olivia. In the musical club, there are two groups: actors and crew.

23 We first choose the subject of our musical and then write a story together.

24 Then, the actors practice singing and dancing, while the crew make costumes.

25 We perform our musical in the school festival.

26 You can get an application from me.

27 You will join our club, won't you?

구석구석지문 TEST Step 1　　　　　　p.19

Project Work – Make your own club

1. shall, call
2. How about
3. should, meet
4. Let's meet
5. How about, after school
6. Sounds

Express Yourself

1. Join
2. to share, news, don't you
3. help make, every month
4. meet, work, every Wednesday
5. are interested in joining
6. can't wait to

Project Work

1. wanto to, don't you
2. interested in speaking, should join
3. parctice speaking
4. speak well, be able to

구석구석지문 TEST Step 2　　　　　　p.20

Work Together Step 3

1. A: What shall we call our speaking club?
2. B: How about "Raise Your Voice?"
3. C: Good! Then, when and where should we meet?
4. D: Let's meet in the music room.
5. B: How about on Mondays after school?
6. A: Sounds good.

Express Yourself

1. Join "True Reporters"!
2. You want to share interesting news with your

---

friends, don't you?

3. If you join our club, you will help make the school newspaper every month.

4. We meet and work in the library every Wednesday after school.

5. So, if you are interested in joining our club, come for an interview on Wednesday.

6. We can't wait to meet you!

Project Work

1. You want to speak well, don't you?

2. If you are interested in speaking well, you should join the club, "Raise Your Voice"!

3. We practice speaking in the music room every Monday after school.

4. If you learn to speak well, you may be able to change people's minds!

9 share, 공유하다   10 plant, 심다   11 desert, 사막
12 performance, 공연   13 togetherness, 친목, 연대감
14 volunteer, 자원봉사하다   15 mistake, 실수
16 hero, 영웅

단어 TEST Step 1 — p.21

01 목(구멍)	02 원인	03 경기
04 사막	05 심다; 식물, 공장	06 축제
07 쓰레기	08 숲	09 여행
10 이를 닦다, 머리를 빗다		11 세계적인, 지구의
12 기술자	13 차다	14 싸우다
15 보호하다	16 끔찍한	17 자원봉사하다
18 씻다	19 입다	20 나누다
21 공연	22 지도	23 해결책
24 재채기하다	25 손님	26 울보
27 친목, 연대감	28 먼지	29 씨앗
30 조언	31 과거, 지나간	32 미래
33 영웅	34 환영 받지 못하는	35 ~을 살펴보다
36 계속하다	37 빨리 ~하고 싶어하다	
38 버리다	39 A뿐만 아니라 B도	40 ~을 없애다
41 ~을 고대하다, 기대하다		42 발생하다
43 ~을 피하다		

단어 TEST Step 2 — p.22

01 kick	02 festival	03 match
04 homework	05 plant	06 dust
07 trash	08 cause	09 advice
10 sneeze	11 crybaby	12 hero
13 map	14 solution	15 seed
16 unwelcome	17 future	18 past
19 togetherness	20 performance	21 terrible
22 forest	23 engineer	24 wear
25 brush	26 protect	27 fight
28 volunteer	29 global	30 wash
31 throat	32 share	33 trip
34 desert	35 turn off	
36 look forward to -ing		37 can't wait to
38 throw away	39 not only A but also B	
40 get rid of	41 keep away from	
42 come about	43 keep on	

단어 TEST Step 3 — p.23

1 cause, 원인   2 seed, 씨앗   3 forest, 숲
4 match, 경기   5 solution, 해결책   6 crybaby, 울보
7 environment, 환경   8 widespread, 널리 퍼진

대화문 TEST Step 1 — p.24~25

Everyday English 1. A Function Practice 2-(1)
Why didn't you come / had a bad cold, give us any homework / said, should read / Thank you

Everyday English 2. A Function Practice 2-(2)
nice, Why / weather report said, would rain / didn't know / Don't worry, share

Everyday English 2. A Function Practice 2-(3)
watch the movie / watched, last week, He said, terrible / shall, do / can take a walk

Everyday English 1 B. Listening Activity
happened to / kicked, by mistake / must hurt / the doctor said, shouldn't play / will, do / need to, another / Why don't you ask, good at playing / go ask him

Everyday English 2 A Function practice 2-(1)
want to watch / What movie / just came out, looking forward to seeing / See, than

Everyday English 2 B. Listening Activity
have any plans, coming / volunteer, every Friday / What do, do / take, out for a walk / sounds, every week / because, in the future / Can, join / look forward to seeing

In Real Life
catch a cold / feel sick, can't stop sneezing / because of, weather, said / guess, sneezing, Can't, stop / preparing to do, abroad / planning to plant, a lot of / looking forward to stopping

대화문 TEST Step 2 — p.26~27

Everyday English 1. A Function Practice 2-(1)
Lisa: Hey, Tom. Why didn't you come to school today?
Tom: I had a bad cold. Did the teacher give us any homework?
Lisa: Yes. He said we should read lesson 3 in our English book.
Tom: Okay. Thank you, Lisa.

B: The weather is so nice today. Why do you have an umbrella?

G: The weather report said it would rain this afternoon.

B: Oh, no. I didn't know that! I don't have an umbrella.

G: Don't worry. You can share my umbrella.

Jane: Do you want to watch the movie, The Big Zoo?

Alex: No, I don't. My brother watched the movie last week. He said it was terrible.

Jane: Then, what shall we do?

Alex: We can take a walk in the park instead.

Sujin: John, what happened to your foot?

John: Last week, there was a soccer match. I kicked a rock by mistake.

Sujin: Oh, your foot must hurt very much! Did you go to the hospital?

John: Yes, the doctor said I shouldn't play soccer for a month.

Sujin: Oh, no. What will you do for the next game?

John: I'll need to find another soccer player.

Sujin: Why don't you ask Kevin? He's good at playing soccer.

John: That's a good idea. I'll go ask him now.

Brain: Susan, do you want to watch a movie this Saturday?

Susan: Sure. What movie do you want to watch?

Brain: The new superhero movie just came out. I'm looking forward to seeing it.

Susan: Wow! I love superhero movies. See you then!

Chris: Do you have any plans for this coming Friday?

Emily: I do. I volunteer at a lost pet center every Friday.

Chris: What do you do at the lost pet center?

Emily: Well, I take the dogs out for a walk. Also, I help to wash them.

Chrls: That sounds wonderful. Why do you go there every week?

Emily: It's because I love animals. I want to become an animal doctor in the future.

Chris: I love animals too. Can I join you this Friday?

Emily: Sure. I look forward to seeing you at the center.

Diego: Achoo! Achoo!

Suji: Did you catch a cold, Diego? looking forward to stopping

Diego: No, I don't feel sick, but I can't stop sneezing. Achoo!

Suji: Then, it must be because of the yellow dust. The weather report said the yellow dust would be terrible today.

Diego: Oh, I guess I'm sneezing because of that. Can't we stop the yellow dust?

Suji: Yes, we can. My club members are preparing to do some special activities abroad.

Diego: What are they?

Suji: We're planning to plant trees in China because a lot of the yellow dust comes from China.

Diego: That sounds good.

Suji: Yes. We are looking forward to stopping the yellow dust.

p.28~29

01 wearing, that, away from

02 Every, there, widespread

03 become, hurts, throats

04 Why, come about   05 way, stop, there

06 take, solutions, through

07 long, place, forest

08 down, so, build

09 As, passed, lost

10 Finally, became, bigger

11 brings, from, spreads

12 past, how, stop

13 volunteers plant, solve

14 Planting, is, expensive

15 However, that, if

16 thank, because, with

17 However, help, also   18 At, what, rid

19 leader, planting, solve

20 planting, protecting, help

21 planting, that, stop

22 easy, hard, protect

23 togetherness, keep, growing

p.30~31

01 are wearing, so that, can keep away from, unwelcome guest   02 there is widespread

03 become sick because, hurts their eyes, throats

04 does, come about

05 way to stop, there is
06 take a look at, of, solutions to, through, volunteers
07 ago, was a big forest
08 to cut down trees so that, could build
09 As, passed, lost
10 Finally, became, became bigger and bigger
11 brings, from, yellow dust spreads
12 In the past, how to stop
13 plant, to solve this problem
14 Planting trees, is, expensive
15 However, that, cannot live if they don't plant
16 always thank, because, with them
17 However, to help not only, but also
18 what to do, get rid of
19 planting trees can help to solve the problem
20 found out planting, protecting, help
21 are planting, so that, can stop, yellow dust
22 are working hard, to protect
23 kind of global togetherness, keep on growing

본문 TEST Step 3   p.32~33

1 많은 사람이 봄에 찾아오는 반갑지 않은 손님인 황사 때문에 마스크를 끼고 있습니다.

2 매년 한국에는 황사가 널리 퍼집니다.

3 황사가 많은 사람들의 눈과 목을 아프게 해서 많은 사람들이 병에 걸립니다.

4 황사는 왜 일어나는 것일까요?

5 황사를 막을 수 있는 방법이 있을까요? 네, 있습니다!

6 중국의 간쑤성에 있는 자원봉사자들의 작업을 통해 황사의 원인과 해결책을 살펴봅시다.

7 예전에 이곳은 큰 숲이었습니다.

8 그러나 사람들이 도시를 세우기 위해 나무를 베기 시작했습니다.

9 시간이 지나면서 숲은 많은 나무를 잃었습니다.

10 마침내, 숲은 사막이 되었고 사막은 점점 더 커졌습니다.

11 이제, 봄에 서쪽에서 세찬 바람이 불 때, 황사가 퍼집니다.

12 이전에는 대부분의 사람들이 황사 문제를 어떻게 막을 수 있는지 알지 못했습니다.

13 이제는 많은 자원봉사자들이 이 문제를 해결하기 위해 나무를 심고 있습니다.

14 사막에 나무를 심는 것은 힘들고 비용이 많이 듭니다.

15 하지만 많은 중국인들은 자신들이 나무를 심지 않으면 살 수 없다는 것을 알고 있습니다.

16 그들은 우리가 그들과 나무를 심기 때문에 우리 한국인 봉사자들에게 늘 감사해 하고 있습니다.

17 그러나 우리가 나무를 심는 이유는 단지 중국만이 아니라 한국도 돕기 위해서입니다.

---

18 처음에 저는 황사를 없애기 위해서 무엇을 해야 할지 몰랐습니다.

19 그 때, 우리 조장인 민수가 나무를 심는 것이 문제를 해결하는 데 도움이 된다고 얘기해 줬습니다.

20 저는 나무를 심고 환경을 보호하는 것이 우리 가족과 제 자신도 돕는 일이라는 것임을 알게 되었습니다.

21 중국에서는 많은 사람들이 황사가 퍼지는 것을 막기 위해서 사막에 나무를 심고 있습니다.

22 이 작업은 쉽지 않지만 그들은 세계를 보호하기 위해서 열심히 일하고 있습니다.

23 이러한 세계적인 협업으로 희망의 씨앗은 계속해서 자랄 것입니다.

본문 TEST Step 4 - Step 5   p.34~37

1 Many people are wearing masks so that they can keep away from an unwelcome guest in the spring: yellow dust.

2 Every year, there is widespread yellow dust in Korea.

3 Many people become sick because the yellow dust hurts their eyes and throats.

4 Why does the yellow dust come about?

5 Is there any way to stop the yellow dust? Yes, there is!

6 Let's take a look at the causes of and the solutions to the problem of yellow dust through the work of some volunteers in Gansu Sheng, China.

7 A long time ago, this place was a big forest.

8 But people began to cut down trees so that they could build cities.

9 As time passed, the forest lost many trees.

10 Finally, the forest became a desert and the desert became bigger and bigger.

11 Now, when the spring brings strong winds from the west, the yellow dust spreads.

12 In the past, most people did not know how to stop the yellow dust problem.

13 Now, many volunteers plant trees to solve this problem.

14 Planting trees in the desert is hard and expensive.

15 However, many Chinese people know that they cannot live if they don't plant trees.

16 They always thank us, Korean volunteers, because we plant trees with them.

17 However, we plant trees to help not only China but also Korea.

18 At first, I didn't know what to do to get rid of the yellow dust.

19 Then, Minsu, my group leader, told me that planting trees can help to solve the problem.

20 I also found out that planting trees and protecting the environment help my family and me.

21 In China, many people are planting trees in deserts so that they can stop the spread of the yellow dust.

22 The work is not easy, but they are working hard to protect the world.

23 With this kind of global togetherness, the seeds of hope will keep on growing.

구석구석지문 TEST Step 1   p.38

Check Your Progress 1

1. so angry
2. what happened
3. went to, were there
4. Were, angry about
5. course not, because, those people picking
6. is not good
7. told, stop, didn't care about

After You Read

1. causes many problems
2. become sick, yellow dust
3. For example, because of
4. how to solve
5. cut down, to build
6. made, turn into
7. must plant, to stop
8. By planting
9. with global togetherness

Project Work

1. should, brush, so that
2. look forward to saving

구석구석지문 TEST Step 2   p.39

Check Your Progress 1

1. G: I was so angry yesterday.
2. B: Why, what happened?
3. G: Yesterday, I went to the park. Many people were there.
4. B: Were you angry about that?
5. G: Of course not. I was angry because I saw those people picking the flowers and kicking the trees.
6. B: Oh, that is not good.
7. G: Yes, I told them to stop, but they said they didn't care about the flowers or the trees.

After You Read

1. Diego: Yellow dust causes many problems in Korea.
2. Suji: Yes. Many people become sick because of the yellow dust.
3. For example , their throats hurt because of it.
4. Diego: That's right. Do you know how to solve such problems?
5. Suji: In the past, many people cut down trees to build cities.
6. This made the forests turn into deserts of yellow dust.
7. Now, we must plant trees together to stop the yellow dust.
8. Diego: That's a good idea. By planting trees, we can help the world.
9. Suji: Yes, with global togetherness, the world will become green again!

Project Work

1. We should use cups when we brush our teeth so that we can save water.
2. We look forward to saving water by using cups!

단어 TEST Step 1　　　　　p.40

01 연못	02 맛이 쓴, 씁쓸한	03 무서운, 두려운
04 준비하다	05 지루한, 재미없는	06 기회
07 결정하다	08 유명한	09 기호, 취향
10 눈이 먼, 맹인인	11 선택하다	12 의견
13 사고	14 드럼 연주자	15 실현하다, 깨닫다
16 끔찍한	17 비명을 지르다	18 활발한
19 간호사	20 자원봉사하다	21 고마워하다
22 감동적인	23 사회	24 사서
25 극복하다	26 경험	27 점수
28 곤경, 곤란	29 완전히, 전적으로	30 목마른
31 공격하다	32 기적	33 작곡가
34 초대하다	35 포기하다	36 죽다
37 ~할 수 있다	38 ~을 돌보다	39 조금씩, 천천히
40 ~을 자랑스러워하다		41 누군가를 재우다
42 ~을 두려워하다	43 선택하다	

단어 TEST Step 2　　　　　p.41

01 math	02 appreciate	03 miracle
04 touching	05 attack	06 throw
07 experience	08 social studies	09 librarian
10 interview	11 thirsty	12 totally
13 score	14 overcome	15 sheep
16 difficult	17 contest	18 invite
19 trouble	20 composer	21 prepare
22 scream	23 accident	24 bitter
25 terrible	26 realize	27 scary
28 famous	29 boring	30 opinion
31 choose	32 blind	33 nurse
34 volunteer	35 be afraid of	36 pass away
37 take care of	38 be proud of	39 little by little
40 be able to	41 give up	42 at last
43 put someone to bed		

단어 TEST Step 3　　　　　p.42

1 blind, 눈이 먼　　2 thirsty, 목마른　　3 contest, 경연

4 famous, 유명한　　5 librarian, 사서

6 drummer, 드럼 연주자　　7 trouble, 곤경

8 attack, 공격　　9 composer, 작곡가

10 appreciate, 고마워하다　　11 scream, 비명을 지르다

12 opinion, 의견　　13 touching, 감동적인

14 miracle, 기적　　15 choose, 선택하다

16 overcome, 극복하다

대화문 TEST Step 1　　　　　p.43~44

Everyday English 1. A Function Practice 2-(1)

have to choose / Why don't we choose / How about, famous / In my opinion, Let's find another story

Everyday English 2. A Function Practice 2-(2)

your favorite book / My favorite book / In my opinion, little boring / Everyone has different tastes

Everyday English 1 B. Listening Activity

matter, look around / I'm worried about, lower than / Why don't you / social studies class, little boring / In my opinion, more interesting than, social studies class / got a high score, after taking / I should take his class too

Everyday English2 A. Function Practice 2-(1)

You know about, don't you / No, I don't / even though / on each hand / amazing

Everyday English 2 A. Function Practice 2-(2)

not good at / Maybe, should give up / don't you / Of course I do / Don't give up, You can do it too

Everyday English 2 B. Listening Activity

don't you, sad, angry, myself, like / I had a choice, angry about myself, I decide to love my life, give people hope, better, bitter, Choose better, forget bitter

In Real Life

are, doing / working, history project, need to write / overcoming difficulties / did, choose / know about, don't you / chose to / In my opinion, too famous, interesting / should, choose / Do you know / show you a video / great topic

대화문 TEST Step 2　　　　　p.45~46

Everyday English 1. A Function Practice 2-(1)

G: We have to choose a story for our school play.

B: Why don't we choose one of Shakespeare's plays?

G: How about Hamlet? It's very famous.

B: In my opinion, it's too sad for our school play. Let's find another story.

Everyday English 2. A Function Practice 2-(2)

G: What is your favorite book?

B: My favorite book is The Old Man and the Sea.

G: Really? In my opinion, it's a little boring.

B: Everyone has different tastes.

Everyday English 1 B. Listening Activity

Brian: What's the matter? You look worried.

Amy: I'm worried about my history test. My history score is lower than my math score.

Brian: Why don't you take Mr. Choi's afterschool class?

Amy: Well, I took his social studies class last month, but it was a little boring for me.

Brian: In my opinion, his history class is more interesting than his social studies class.

Amy: Really?

Brian: Yes. I also got a high score on my history test after taking his class.

Amy: Maybe I should take his class too. Thanks.

Everyday English2 A. Function Practice 2-(1)

G: You know about Lee Hee Ah, don't you?

B: No, I don't. Who is she?

G: She plays the piano very well, even though she only has two fingers on each hand.

B: That's amazing.

Everyday English 2 A. Function Practice 2-(2)

Amy: I really love the drums, but I'm not good at playing. Maybe I should give up.

Bob: Hey, don't say that. You know about Rick Allen, don't you?

Amy: Of course I do. Isn't he the drummer with one arm?

Bob: Yes, he is. Don't give up! You can do it too!

Everyday English 2 B. Listening Activity

M: Hello. You all know me, don't you? As you can see, I don't have any arms or legs. When I was young, I was sad and angry about myself. Then one day, I read a story about a man like me. He said that I had a choice in my life. I could be happy or angry about myself. So, I decided to love my life. Now, I am a happy man. I give speeches around the world, and give people hope. Here is my message for you. In life, you have a choice: better or bitter? Choose better, forget bitter.

In Real Life

Olivia: What are you doing, Junho?

Junho: I'm working on my history project. I need to write about a famous person. That person should have a story of overcoming difficulties in their life.

Olivia: Hmm. Who did you choose?

Junho: You know about Helen Keller, don't you? I chose to write about her.

Olivia: In my opinion, she is too famous. It may not be interesting.

Junho: Then, who should I choose?

Olivia: Do you know the story about Little Annie?

Junho: Who is that?

Olivia: I will show you a video about her life. She'll be a great topic for your project.

본문 TEST Step 1   p.47~48

01 was, little blind
02 always angry
03 tried, screamed, attacked
04 called, try, anymore
05 somebody, take care
06 One, came to
07 volunteered, help
08 met, started throwing
09 However, afraid of
10 be, always, there
11 went, put, bed
12 do, always, there
13 that, needed, understanding
14 with, help, little
15 later, scream, throw
16 become, totally different
17 didn't call, anymore
18 decided, leave, with
19 took, to, for
20 loved, studied hard
21 become, others, did
22 few, later, away
23 sad, give up
24 one day, met
25 helped, see well
26 miracle for
27 last, realized, became
28 gave, chance, special
29 able to, see
30 Instead, screamed, threw
31 just like
32 said, be there

본문 TEST Step 2   p.49~50

01 was, little blind girl
02 was always angry
03 tried to help, screamed, attacked
04 called her, try to help her anymore
05 needed somebody to take care of
06 One day, came to
07 volunteered to help
08 met, started throwing
09 However, wasn't afraid of
10 to be your friend, always be there

11 Every night, went to, put her to bed

12 do love you, always be there

13 that, needed, understanding

14 With, got better little by little

15 later, scream or throw

16 did become, totally different

17 call her, anymore

18 decided to leave, with   19 took, to, for

20 loved, studied hard

21 wanted to become, help others, did

22 a few years later, passed away

23 did not give up   24 one day, met

25 helped, to see well   26 a miracle for

27 realized, became

28 chance to meet a special student

29 wasn't able to hear

30 Instead, screamed, threw   31 just like

32 said to, always be there

1 한 병원에 어린 눈먼 소녀가 있었습니다.

2 그녀는 항상 화가 나 있었습니다.

3 사람들이 그녀를 도우려고 할 때, 그녀는 소리 지르고 공격했습니다.

4 사람들은 그녀를 "Crazy Little Annie"라고 불렀고 더 이상 그녀를 도우려 하지 않았습니다

5 병원은 Annie를 돌봐줄 사람이 필요했습니다.

6 어느 날, 나이 든 간호사가 병원에 왔습니다.

7 그녀는 Annie를 도울 것을 자원했습니다.

8 Annie가 그녀를 만났을 때, 그녀는 다시 물건을 던지기 시작했습니다.

9 그러나 간호사는 그녀를 두려워하지 않았습니다

10 간호사가 Annie에게 말했습니다. "안녕, 난 간호사 Laura야. 나는 너의 친구가 될 거야. 내가 항상 너의 곁에 있을게."

11 매일 밤, Laura는 Annie의 방으로 가서 그녀를 재웠습니다.

12 그녀는 Annie에게 말했습니다. "Annie, 나는 널 정말 사랑한단다. 나는 항상 너의 곁에 있을 거야."

13 Laura는 Annie에게 사랑과 이해가 필요하다는 것을 알았습니다.

14 Laura의 도움으로 Annie는 조금씩 좋아졌습니다.

15 2년 후, Annie는 비명을 지르거나 물건을 던지지 않았습니다.

16 그녀는 전혀 다른 사람이 되었습니다.

17 사람들은 더 이상 그녀를 "Crazy Little Annie"라고 부르지 않았습니다.

18 Laura는 Annie와 병원을 떠나기로 결정했습니다.

19 그녀는 Annie를 시각장애인 학교에 데려갔습니다.

20 Annie는 새로운 학교를 좋아했으며 열심히 공부했습니다.

21 그녀는 선생님이 되어 간호사 Laura가 그랬듯 다른 사람들을 돕고 싶었습니다.

22 그러나 몇 년 후, Laura는 세상을 떠났습니다.

23 Annie는 매우 슬펐지만 그녀는 꿈을 포기하지 않았습니다.

24 그러던 어느 날, Annie는 좋은 의사를 만났습니다.

25 그는 Annie를 잘 볼 수 있게 도와주었습니다.

26 그것은 Annie에게 기적이었습니다.

27 마침내 Annie는 꿈을 실현하고자 교사가 되었습니다.

28 이것은 그녀에게 특별한 학생을 만날 기회를 주었습니다.

29 그 학생은 듣거나 볼 수 없었습니다.

30 대신에 그녀는 소리 지르고 물건을 던졌습니다.

31 그녀는 마치 "Crazy Little Annie" 같았습니다.

32 Annie는 그녀에게 말했습니다. "안녕, Helen Keller, 나는 너의 선생님 Anne Sullivan이야. 내가 항상 너의 곁에 있을게."

1 There was a little blind girl in a hospital.

2 She was always angry.

3 When people tried to help her, she screamed and attacked them.

4 People called her "Crazy Little Annie," and didn't try to help her anymore.

5 The poor girl needed somebody to take care of her.

6 One day, an old nurse came to the hospital.

7 She volunteered to help Annie.

8 When Annie met her, she started throwing things again.

9 However, the nurse wasn't afraid of her.

10 The nurse said to Annie, "Hi, Annie. I'm Nurse Laura. I'm here to be your friend. I'll always be there for you."

11 Every night, Laura went to Annie's room and put her to bed.

12 She said to Annie, "Annie, I do love you. I'll always be there for you."

13 Laura knew that Annie needed love and understanding.

14 With Laura's help, Annie got better little by little.

15 Two years later, Annie didn't scream or throw things.

16 She did become a totally different person.

17 People didn't call her "Crazy Little Annie" anymore.

18 Laura decided to leave the hospital with Annie.

19 She took Annie to a school for blind children.

20 Annie loved her new school and studied hard.

21 She wanted to become a teacher and help others like Nurse Laura did.

22 However, a few years later, Laura passed away.

23 Annie was very sad, but she did not give up on her dream.

24 Then one day, Annie met a nice doctor.

25 He helped Annie to see well.

26 It was a miracle for Annie.

27 At last, Annie realized her dream and became a teacher.

28 This gave her a chance to meet a special student.

29 The student wasn't able to hear or see.

30 Instead, she screamed and threw things.

31 She was just like Crazy Little Annie.

32 Annie said to her, "Hi, Helen Keller. I'm your teacher, Anne Sullivan. I'll always be there for you."

3. Each class will prepare a song and perform it.

4. You can choose any kind of song.

5. Please let me know the names of your songs by the end of this week.

6. You can also invite your homeroom teachers to join your performance.

7. I hope you enjoy preparing fot the singing contest. Thank you.

After You Read

1. Dear Annie,

2. When I first met you, you were screaming and throwing things.

3. However, I wasn't afraid of you.

4. You weren't able to see, so I knew that I needed to take care of you.

5. Every night, when I put you to bed , I could see that you were getting better little by little.

6. At last , you became a totally different person.

7. I am so proud of you. I hope you do well in your new school.

8. Yours truly, Laura

구석구석지문 TEST Step 1   p.57

Check Your Progress

1. students, your

2. class singing, don't you

3. Each class, prepare, perform

4. choose any kind of song

5. let, know, by the end of

6. can also invite, to join

7. enjoy preparing for

After You Read

1. Dear

2. When, met, were screaming, throwing

3. However, wasn't afraid of

4. weren't able to, to take care of

5. put you to bed, were getting better

6. At last, totally different

7. am so proud of, do well in

8. Yours truly

구석구석지문 TEST Step 2   p.58

Check Your Progress

1. W: Hello, students. I'm your music teacher, Ms. Song.

2. You know the class singing contest is next Friday, don't you?

MEMO

적중 100

영어 기출 문제집

정답 및 해설

금성 | 최인철